In Their Own Words

A Documentary History of Western Civilization from the Middle Ages to the End of World War II

Jamie H. Eves
University of Connecticut
Eastern Connecticut State University
Three Rivers Community College

KENDALL/HUNT PUBLISHING COMPANY
4050 Westmark Drive   Dubuque, Iowa 52002

Cover image provided by Corbis.

Copyright © 2005 by Jamie H. Eves

ISBN 978-0-7575-1792-1

Kendall/Hunt Publishing Company has the exclusive rights to reproduce this work,
to prepare derivative works from this work, to publicly distribute this work,
to publicly perform this work and to publicly display this work.

All rights reserved. No part of this publication may be reproduced,
stored in a retrieval system, or transmitted, in any form or by any
means, electronic, mechanical, photocopying, recording, or otherwise,
without the prior written permission of Kendall/Hunt Publishing Company.

Printed in the United States of America
10 9 8 7 6 5

Dedication:

For my students at the University of Connecticut, Eastern Connecticut State University, Saint Joseph College, Albertus Magnus College, Three Rivers Community College, and Central Connecticut State University, who taught me as much as I taught them;

and

for adjunct faculty everywhere, dedicated professionals without whom higher education in the United States could not function, especially Margaret Robinson, Nancy Steenberg, Calvin Saxton, Theodore Piecyk, W. Guthrie Sayen, Jeffrey De Luca, Hope Ball, Michael Donahue, Janet Rider, and Brad Hale, with whom I have shared both work space and fellowship;

and

for Dr. Ronald Koons, Dr. James McKelvey, and Dr. Edmund Wehrle, who taught me how to teach.

All royalties from the sale of this book are donated to the Windham Textile and History Museum in Willimantic, Connecticut.

-TABLE OF CONTENTS-

I: The People of the Plow: Life in the High Middle Ages, c. 900 – c. 1310	[1]
The Background	[1]
The Documents	[9]
1. Medieval People: William Langland	[11]
from *Piers the Plowman*	[12]
2. Medieval Religion: Dante Alighieri	[13]
from *Divine Comedy*	[13]
II: When Whirl Was King: Modernization and the Renaissance, c. 1310 – c. 1550	[18]
The Background	[18]
The Documents	[28]
1. The Black Death: Giovanni Boccaccio	[28]
from *The Decameron*	[29]
2. The Hundred Years War: Christine de Pisan	[31]
from *Ditie de Jehanne d'Arc* [*Hymn of Jeanne d'Arc*]	[32]
3. Progress: Thomas More	[35]
from *Utopia*	[36]
III: God, Gold, Glory…and Grub: The Expansion of the West, c. 1450 – c. 1750	[39]
The Background	[39]
The Documents	[50]
1. The Expansion of the West as a Heroic Epic: Luis Vaz de Camoes	[51]
from *The Lusiads*	[52]
2. The Expansion of West as the Oppression of Innocents: Bartolome de Las Casas	[60]
from *The Devastation of the Indies*	[61]
IV: This World with Devils Filled: The Reformation and the Sundering of Religious Unity in the West, 1571 – 1648	[65]
The Background	[65]
The Documents	[74]
1. The Reformation as Good versus Evil: Martin Luther	[75]
"Ein Feste Burg"	[75]
2. The Reformation as a War of Words: The Council of Trent	[75]
from *Index of Prohibited Books*	[76]
3. Establishing an Ideologically "Pure" Community in America: Anne Bradstreet	[77]
from "A Dialogue Between Old England and New; Concerning Their Present Troubles, Anno 1642"	[78]
4. The Decline of a Superpower: Miguel de Cervantes	[80]
from *Don Quixote*	[81]
V: And All Was Light: Science, Constitutionalism, and the Age of Reason, 1543 – 1789	[83]
The Background	[83]
The Documents	[92]
1. Constitutionalism and Human Rights: John Locke	[92]
from *Treatise on Government*	[93]
2. Slavery and Human Rights: Olaudah Equiano	[94]
from *The Interesting Narrative of the Life of Olaudah Equiano, or Gustavus Vasa, the African*	[95]

VI: Liberty! Equality! Fraternity!: Liberal Democracy, Capitalism, and the West's
    Age of Revolution, c. 1750 – c. 1850 [100]
        The Background [100]
        The Documents [108]
            1. The French Revolution: The National Assembly [108]
                Declaration of the Rights of Man and Citizen [108]
            2. The Haitian Revolution: Toussaint L'Ouverture [109]
                from Toussaint L'Ouverture's Letter to the Directory [109]
            3. The Industrial Revolution: Harriet Hanson Robinson [110]
                from *Loom and Spindle* [111]
        Declaration of Man and Citizen Role-Playing Exercise [114]

VII: Lives of Quiet Desperation: Western Ideology in the Age of "Isms," c. 1790 – c. 1870 [117]
        The Documents [117]
            1. Classical Liberalism: Thomas Paine [118]
                from *The Rights of Man* [119]
            2. Classical Conservatism: Edmund Burke [122]
                from *Reflections on the Revolution in France* [124]
            3. Early Feminism: Mary Wollstonecraft [127]
                from *A Vindication of the Rights of Women* [128]
            4. Early Environmentalism: Henry David Thoreau [131]
                from *The Maine Woods* [134]
                from *Walden* [137]
            5. Early Socialism: Karl Marx [138]
                from *The Communist Manifesto* [139]
            6. Early Nationalism: Giuseppe Mazzini [141]
                from *The Duties of Man* [141]
        Modern Isms Role-Playing Exercise [143]

VIII: The Golden Age of the West?: Prosperity, Power, and Disappointment in the
    Nineteenth Century, 1815 – 1914 [145]
        The Background [145]
        The Documents [159]
            1. Abolition: Mary Prince and Susanna Strickland Moodie [159]
                from *The History of Mary Prince, A West Indian Slave* [160]
            2. Woman Suffrage: Elizabeth Cady Stanton [162]
                from The Declaration of Sentiments [163]
            3. Temperance: Frances Willard [164]
                from *My Happy Half-Century: The Autobiography of an American Woman* [164]
            4. Imperialism: Rudyard Kipling, Mark Twain, and Pauline Johnson [165]
                "The White Man's Burden" [166]
                "The Battle Hymn of the Republic (Brought Down to Date)" [167]
                "The Corn Husker" [167]

IX: The Sound of Things Breaking: The Crisis of the West, 1914 – 1945 [168]
        The Background [168]
        The Documents [187]
            1. Laissez-Faire: Andrew Carnegie [187]
                from "Wealth" [187]
            2. Social Democracy: Theodore Roosevelt [189]
                from "The New Nationalism" [190]
            3. The Forces of Reaction: Sergyei A. Nilhus [191]
                from *The Protocols of the Learned Elders of Zion* [193]
        Reichstag Role-Playing Exercise [195]

Epilogue [197]

-CHAPTER I-
THE PEOPLE OF THE PLOW:
LIFE IN THE HIGH MIDDLE AGES
c. 900 - c. 1310

Seven hundred years ago Western Civilization was overwhelmingly traditional, not modern; rural, not urban; agricultural, not industrial. The economy was manorial, the politics feudal, the society based on something that historians call trifunctionalism, and the majority ideology firmly rooted in Roman Catholic dogma. Everyday life was communal. The vast majority of the people were peasants, men, women, and children who dwelt not in sprawling cities or suburbs, but in small, tightly knit villages of only 200 to 500 inhabitants, separated from other, similar villages by wide, sweeping, open grain fields and semi-roadless stretches of forest and swamp. These villagers were farmers – most of them anyway – who worked their common fields together, communally, with heavy, massive plows that could only be drawn by teams of six or eight brawny oxen. Most of them lived without much privacy, in flimsy wattle-and-daub cottages, surrounded by their curious neighbors, their livestock, and (although they would have been astonished to know it) clouds of deadly bacteria. Few of them had much in the way of formal education – indeed, most of them were illiterate – but they knew each other intimately.

The West is no longer like that. Today, life is modern, not traditional. Our lives are shaped by capitalism rather than manorialism, by liberal democracy rather than feudalism, by socio-economic class rather than trifunctionalism, and by science as much as by religion. We are fiercely individualistic rather than communal, and we cherish our privacy and independence. Most of us live in cities or suburbs instead of rural villages and in sturdy, scrubbed houses with thick, soundproof walls that keep nosy neighbors, wandering livestock, and most germs safely at bay. Nature is more distant. Artifice is more widespread. The majority have high school educations. Many have been to college. But frequently we wonder if we truly know each other.

Something happened that caused the West to change. The purpose of this book is to find out what.

-The Background-

What Is Western Civilization?

We begin with a few definitions.

The word "civilization" has three meanings. First, in its original sense, it combines the Latin root *cives* (meaning, roughly, "city-state") with the Anglo-French suffix "-ization" (meaning "process") to indicate a historical process in which urban and civic life developed out of an earlier, more natural existence. For the West, the process of civilization began in the Middle East c. (for *circa*, a Latin word meaning "approximately") 4,000 BCE (which stands for "Before the Common Era," a religiously neutral way of saying "BC") and ended c. 600 BCE, when literacy became firmly established among the upper classes in southern Europe. The process was the result of another, earlier historical transition that occurred between c. 8,000 and c. 4,000 BCE, known as the Neolithic or Agricultural Revolution, which was a switch from a prehistoric gathering and hunting way of life to an economy based on fixed-site farming.

Second, the word "civilization" can also be used to refer to any culture that has undergone the process of civilization. In this sense of the word, a civilization can be defined as any culture that has advanced beyond the gatherer-hunter way of life and embraced agriculture, cities, writing, science, and other "civilized" attributes.

Accordingly, William Duiker and Jackson Spielvogel, the authors of a best-selling college-level history textbook, describe the advent of civilization in the Middle East:

> For hundreds of thousands of years, human beings lived in small communities, seeking to survive by hunting, fishing, and foraging in an often hostile environment. Then, in the space of a few thousand years, there was an abrupt change of direction as humans in a few widely scattered areas of the globe began to master the art of cultivating food crops. As food production increased, the population in such areas grew, and people began to congregate in larger communities. Cities appeared and became centers of cultural and religious development. Historians call this process the beginnings of civilization.

Duiker and Spielvogel then go on to list what they consider to be the key characteristics of civilization, some of which are admirable, but some of which are not. These include: more intensive forms of agriculture (often featuring irrigation), permanent towns and cities (often with walls), large populations (at least, larger than the ten or twenty people that were characteristic of prehistoric gatherer-hunter bands), forms of government more complex than simple tribes, bureaucracy, mass armies, mass warfare, rigid and hierarchical social classes (usually consisting of five main groups: priests, warriors, businesspeople, peasants, and slaves), slavery (rare among gatherer-hunters, but unfortunately commonplace among civilized peoples), centrally organized religions (known as "churches"), temples, prostitution, commerce, money, sophisticated crafts and technologies, metal-working, architecture, writing, mathematics, and science.[1]

Unfortunately, these first two definitions of civilization, while quite valuable for scholars and students of Ancient History, are not terribly useful for those of us who study Modern History. The reason for this is that, by 1300, when the Modern epoch began, the vast majority of all the people throughout the entire world were already civilized. Fortunately, as Thomas H. Greer and Gavin Lewis, the authors of *A Brief History of the Western World*, point out, there exists a third, more useful, definition of civilization. They write:

> The word "civilization," as it is used in the study of history, can mean either of two different things. First of all, it refers to an advanced form of culture – that is, of the sum total of social habits, beliefs, arts, and institutions of a group of people. Any human group, no matter how simple its way of life, possesses a culture; civilization, on the other hand, is a developed and complex type of culture, based on such features as city life, language and law, division of labor, and advanced arts and sciences. But such developed forms of culture vary greatly over time and place – in their beliefs and values, their styles of art, their writing systems, their government structures, and countless other features. Consequently, we speak not only of "civilization" in general, but also of different individual civilizations.[2]

According to this third definition, a civilization can also be a cluster (or system) of culturally related peoples, linked by common history, beliefs, ways of life, and/or environments, in the way that Americans, Britons, and Germans (or Chinese, Japanese, and Koreans; or Arabs, Iranians, and Turks; or Gujaratis, Bengalis, and Sinhalese) are connected to each other by their similar cultures and beliefs. Today, Americans, Britons, and Germans share a common alphabet (the Latin alphabet), the same root language (Old Germanic), a core of common religious beliefs (Judeo-Christianity), similar political systems (liberal democracy), and a common economic system (state capitalism). Even where they differ, they are alike: Americans, Britons, and Germans can debate issues like universal health care, abortion, women's rights, and the separation of church and state, but they do so within a common framework of political discourse – they can easily understand each other's points of view, even if they disagree on the particulars. Shared cultural attributes like alphabets, language families, religions, political systems, economies, literatures, lifestyles, myths, histories, technologies, philosophies, art styles, music, and foodways are the building blocks of civilizations, the ether through which cultural literacy and civil communication flow. As the economic historian Immanuel Wallerstein writes, whether people realize it or not civilization in this sense of the word provides the "cultural and even legal coherence" and "set of parameters within which social action [takes] place."[3]

All of humanity thus can be divided into several different civilizations or culture-systems, each of which developed historically out of its own discrete historical and environmental circumstances, none of which is any more or less "civilized" than the others, but each of which is unique and distinct. Civilizations in this sense of the word are usually named for the parts of the world where they originated.[4] They include Eastern Civilization (Eastern Europe), East Asian Civilization (China, Korea, Japan, and Vietnam), South Asian Civilization (India, Pakistan, Bangladesh, Nepal, and Sri Lanka), Southeast Asian Civilization (Malaysia, Indonesia, Thailand, Cambodia, and Burma), Islamic Civilization (the Muslim Middle East), Sub-Saharan African Civilization (Africa south of the Sahara Desert), and Western Civilization.

"Western Civilization" (or "the West") can thus be defined as a system of similar cultures that arose sometime in the fifth and sixth centuries CE ("Common Era") in the western (hence its name) part of Europe. Today, it includes all of the European countries that use the Latin alphabet and where Roman Catholicism and Protestantism historically have been – and remain -- the prevailing religions. It includes the United Kingdom and Ireland; France and Monaco; Spain, Portugal, and Andorra; Italy, San Marino, and the Vatican; Belgium, the Netherlands, and Luxembourg; Germany, Austria, Switzerland, and Lichtenstein; Denmark, Norway, Sweden, Iceland, and Finland; Estonia, Latvia, and Lithuania; Poland; the Czech Republic and Slovakia; Hungary; Romania; Slovenia; and Croatia. It also includes the United States, Canada, Australia, New Zealand, most of the countries of Latin America, and other places that in recent times have been colonized by peoples who came from Western Europe. It is, in short, our civilization, the one to which we belong.

What Existed Before Western Civilization?

Western Civilization is not terribly old. Unlike the much older East Asian and South Asian civilizations, it did not come into being until the 400s-500s CE, when the western portion of the old Roman Empire crumbled and fell to so-called "barbarian" invaders from the cold reaches of northern Europe. It was only then that the highly urbanized Latin culture of Rome merged with the generally rural Germanic and Celtic cultures of the

---

[1] William J. Duiker and Jackson J. Spielvogel, *The Essential World History* (2002), 1: 1.
[2] Thomas H. Greer and Gavin Lewis, *A Brief History of the Western World* (2002), 1: 6.
[3] Immanuel Wallerstein, *The Modern World System I: Capitalist Agriculture and the Origins of the European World-Economy in the Sixteenth Century* (1974), 18.
[4] Greer, *Brief History of the Western World*, 1: 6-7.

invaders. Together, the two groups – Romans and barbarians – combined to create a new, syncretic culture: Western Civilization.

Because it is syncretic, Western Civilization has roots that thrust further back in time, deep into the Classical world of Greece and Rome, its parent civilization, for before there was Western Civilization, there was its forerunner: Classical Civilization. Classical Civilization was a itself a congeries of cultures, the urbanized, commercial, and agricultural peoples who, from the 800s BCE until the fall of Rome in 476 CE, fought and flourished, labored and lived, in the sandy shores and sun-drenched slopes of the Mediterranean Sea. Like all civilizations, Classical Civilization had been literate, with poets, dramatists, philosophers, historians, merchants, and lawyers. It had had sophisticated art, science, and mathematics. Its principal languages had been Greek and Latin, the learned tongues of Socrates, Plato, Pythagoras, Aristotle, Livy, Cicero, Horace, Virgil, and Augustine. Its chief religions had been the polytheistic paganism of Zeus, Hera, Jupiter, and Juno and the monotheistic Judaism and Christianity of Abraham, Moses, Jesus, and Paul.

Although Classical Civilization had collapsed in 476 CE, several of its features remained, to become tightly woven into the fabric of its successor and supplanter, Western Civilization. Christianity and Judaism persisted, of course, although in altered forms. Together, the two religions provided a philosophical core for the West. The Latin language and alphabet also survived, giving the West a linguistic unity – at least, for the intelligentsia, who for the next millennium wrote and read in Latin rather the vernacular. Greek science and mathematics also persisted, at least partially, providing another base. Some Greek and Roman literature remained, too, enough to provide Western writers with ideal forms to be imitated, although frequently they were glossed over by a new veneer of religious literature. The imperial legacy of Alexander and Caesar continued to tantalize Western kings, and if none succeeded in rebuilding the Roman Empire, it was not for want of trying. Other surviving Classical ideas included the Roman legal system, Greek medicine, and Greek and Roman history, geography, and cosmography. The idea (if not always the reality) of market-oriented commerce also survived, as did the concepts of money, paved roads (although not the knowledge of how to repair them), the arch, the scratch plow, the wheel, and the square sail, along with the knowledge of smelting iron and making chariots, swords, and armor. The idea of slavery survived, too, as did the knowledge of raising wheat and grapes as cultivated crops and cows and horses as livestock. Still-usable remnants of Rome's once-great walled cities, paved roads, and arched aqueducts remained in use for centuries, visible reminders of a glorious but partially departed past.

Significantly, Classical Civilization had been a forerunner not only of the West, but also of two other civilizations, Eastern Civilization and Islamic Civilization. Together, the three civilizations were like jealous sisters that across the centuries battled one another over their Classical inheritance in countless bitter wars. Eastern Civilization was the eldest sister, the most urbane and centralized, largely Greek and Slavic in language, characterized by the Greek alphabet and the Eastern Orthodox Church. Islamic Civilization was the youngest of the three, but also the fastest growing and most ambitious, mostly Arab and Iranian in language, characterized by the graceful Arabic alphabet and the new religion of Islam. Western Civilization was the middle sister, comparatively backward and shy, sometimes given to jealous rages. It was a synthesis of Roman, Germanic, Basque, Celtic, North Slavic, and Magyar (Hungarian) cultures. It was characterized by the Latin alphabet and the primacy of the Roman Catholic Church.

The High Middle Ages

After the fall of Rome, the West entered into its first era, 476 to c. 1500, a thousand-year epoch known to historians as the Middle Ages (or the Medieval Period), so-called because it came between the earlier Classical Period and the later Early Modern Period. Because the West initially was the least prosperous, commercial, literate, scientific, and urbanized of the three sisters, the first half of the Middle Ages (from 476 until c. 900) is sometimes known by the rather foreboding appellation of the "Dark Ages." Recently, historians have decided that the name "Dark Ages," while dramatic and easy to remember, is too pejorative – that is to say, too laden with negative bias – and have renamed the period the Early Middle Ages, a less interesting but more neutral-sounding term. Whatever we choose to call it, it was a time when population decreased, government weakened and became less stable, commerce declined, literacy fell, and art and science regressed and became more primitive.

Around 900 conditions began to change, and a new era, the High (or Central) Middle Ages, began. The most important change was that the climate improved. It was the time of the so-called climatic optimum, a relatively warm, dry period that lasted from c. 900 until c. 1310. The wheat-, grape- and hay-based agriculture of the West, which required warm, rainy springs and hot, dry, sunny summers, was now able to spread northward and eastward throughout most of Europe. The heartland of Western agriculture shifted north, away from the drought-prone Mediterranean to the so-called "champion lands" of northern Europe (the English word "champion," like the French word *champagne*, comes from the Latin *campus*, which means, simply, a field or cleared area), a broad, fertile plain of wet, heavy, dark, clayey soil, which stretched for thousands of miles along the low, well-watered coast of northern Europe, from France and England in the west, on through the Low Countries and Germany, and into Poland, southern Scandinavia, and the Baltic States. The core of the champion lands was the rich French duchy of Champagne, with its rolling hills, green fields, full rivers, and dark, fertile soil. With plenty of food from the new farms, the West's population began to rise, from just 25 million in 900 (about what it had been in 476) to 75 million in 1310.[5]

Population growth meant more mouths to feed, a fact that stimulated the expansion of agriculture even further. Pioneer farmers moved ever east and north, pushing the frontiers of Western Civilization outward, into the waterlogged marshes and bogs, into the high rugged hills and mountains, into the far eastern fringes of the champion lands, and into the cold forests and rocky islets of the icy north. More food also meant more trade, and the old market-based economy of Classical times, mostly moribund in the Early Middle Ages, now returned and grew. Medieval people were good practical engineers, skilled in working in iron and wood, and understood the principles of levers, pulleys, and gears. Several new technologies stimulated even greater productivity, including the three-field system of agriculture (which permitted crop rotation and fallowing), the massive moldboard plow (which provided for faster and deeper plowing, and which was necessary in order to farm the heavy, clayey soils of the champion lands), and the windmill and water wheel (which made grinding grain into meal and flour more efficient).

More than anything else, it was the new moldboard plow that symbolized and shaped High Medieval culture. Big and powerful, it was capable of ripping through the heavy soils of the champion lands with a speed and efficiency that the scratch plows of Classical times could never have hoped to match. Without the big plows, the expansion of the High Medieval frontier would have taken centuries longer, and the growth of the West would have slowed to a crawl. Without them, large stretches of the champion lands – the parts with the heaviest, thickest soils – would have remained forested and unproductive for centuries. Without them, the High Medieval economy would not have functioned as efficiently and productively it did. But the big plows were heavy and cumbersome. They required six or more brawny oxen to pull them. Few individual families could afford plows that big and teams that large. Consequently, farmers were forced to work together, pooling their resources and labor in order to plow their land and tend their crops. The big plows meant that High Medieval culture was of necessity communal, rather than individual, with the small agricultural settlement or village the nexus of economic life. And although the big plows speeded the rapid clearing of the once-vast European oak forest, they also meant that much of the cleared land had to be devoted to pasture, for the mighty oxen that pulled them ate a great deal. The big plows thus shaped Western Civilization in vital and intrinsic ways. Truly, the men and women who farmed the champion lands were the People of the Plow.[6]

Because of the People of the Plow were successful farmers, Western Civilization functioned well during the High Middle Ages. Most people had enough to eat. Violence was kept to a minimum. People were reasonably content. The success of high Medieval culture rested on four bases or pillars: manorialism (the economic system), feudalism (the political system), Roman Catholicism (the majority belief system), and trifunctionalism (the social system).

Manorialism

For all its improvements over the Early Middle Ages, the West in the High Middle Ages was still fundamentally a peasant culture. Peasants (the word means, literally, "country people") were small, semi-subsistence farmers who, on the village level, produced most of their own food, clothing, tools, furniture, and other goods. Ninety percent of the People of the Plow were peasants, so agriculture was the era's chief "industry." It was important that they be good at it.

Because agriculture had spread so widely across the continent during the High Middle Ages, by 1300 most of Western Europe – once thickly wooded – had been largely deforested, an open countryside of fields and farms rather than a land of trees and woods as it had once been. Charles Bowlus, an environmental historian, describes the changes that occurred:

> *In the year 1050, Europe was a sylvan sea with only isolated islands of human habitation. Although the populations around the hamlets could be quite dense, the forests were seen as the enemy of man, the abode of hobgoblins and demons, unsuitable for human habitation. In contrast, by 1300 there were villages almost everywhere and forests almost nowhere.[7]*

Most of early-fourteenth-century Europe's nearly 70 million peasants did not live separately on individual farmsteads, as most agriculturalists do today, but instead clustered into compact rural villages of between 200 and 500 inhabitants. Numbering in the tens of thousands, these simple settlements served as the basis of the Medieval economy. They were organized communally, according to what historians today call the manorial system. A manor (*seigneurie* in French) was a middle-sized agricultural estate that usually measured somewhere between 20 and 30 square miles. It was worked by the peasants but managed (at least in theory) by a lord (*seigneur* in French), who was either an individual knight or lady, or an arm of the Roman Catholic Church such as a monastery or convent. A manor typically included a single village, along with all of the attendant fields,

---

[5] Emmanuel Le Roy Ladurie, *Times of Feast, Times of Famine: A History of Climate Since the Year 1000* (1971), 312-313; Charles R. Bowlus, "Ecological Crisis in Fourteenth-Century Europe," in *Historical Ecology: Essays in Environmental and Social Change*, ed. Lester J. Bilsky (1980), 88-91.
[6] Jean Gimpel, *The Medieval Machine: The Industrial Revolution of the Middle Ages* (1976), 1-28.
[7] Bowlus, "Ecological Crisis," 88.

pastures, and woodlands surrounding it. Occasionally, two manors shared a village, although that was the exception, not the rule.[8]

Only a few peasants were yeomen (YOH-men), free men and women who owned their own small plots, came and went as they wished, and owed nothing to the local lord. The overwhelming majority were instead villeins (vill-AINS) (from the same Latin root as "villager") or serfs (a synonymous term), who were bound by law to work on the manors and prohibited from moving without their lords' permission. Villeins were not slaves. They were not any man's property, they could not be bought or sold, and they enjoyed important legal rights and privileges. But neither were they free. They were bound to the manor, owing their lords certain boons (*droits* in French) in the form of work, produce, or (occasionally) cash. In return, the lords were supposed to protect them from robbers, bandits, and marauding knights, provide them with the land they farmed, and enforce customary law and order.[9]

Three different types of villeins existed. Most were husbandmen (literally, "house-bondsmen"), who had the right to erect a house in the village, cultivate the land around their house (about an acre in size, these areas were known as crofts and typically contained the family's vegetable garden), farm several strips of land in the manor's three great fields, and use the manor's commons to graze their livestock. Other villeins were poor cotters (literally, "cottagers"), also known as crofters, who had the right to their cottages and crofts, but not to use the great fields or the commons. Finally, there were a few *famuli* (fam-EW-lee) (Latin for "dependants"), who had no houses or land at all, but lived instead in the lord's large manor house and worked as laborers or servants. (Although most famuli were villeins, a few were slaves, despite the fact that slavery didn't really fit into the manorial economy, which used villeins rather than slaves as the chief source of labor.)[10]

Legally, the land in the manor was divided into two parts. The *demesne* (deh-MAIN) (another French term) belonged directly to the lord, although the manor's villeins worked it for him as one of their boons. The rest was held by the villeins, but by custom was administered by the lords or their agents (known as reeves or bailiffs), who collected a kind of rent from the villeins in the form of boons. No fences separated the strips in the great fields, which were large and open to accommodate the big moldboard plows. Husbandmen had the exclusive and hereditary right to farm their scattered strips, and were entitled to keep the produce they harvested from them.[11]

Few of the lords actually administered their manors themselves – most, after all, were warrior knights, too busy jousting, wooing fair damsels, going on pilgrimages, administering provinces, or fighting wars and Crusades to be bothered with such mundane tasks as business. Instead, they appointed one of their villeins as reeve (or one of the village yeomen as bailiff) to actually manage the manor on a day-to-day basis. Although usually illiterate, most reeves and bailiffs were highly qualified, competent men with good business sense, much respected by their fellow villagers.[12]

Whether they were villeins or yeomen, the villagers as a group produced most of their own food, clothing, tools, and housing. They dined principally on a monotonous diet of porridge (gruel), pottage (poh-TAHJ) (soup), bread, ale, beer, and wine. They raised grain, legumes, or grapes in the three great fields (collectively known as the outfield), and vegetables in their crofts (collectively called the infield). They collected fuel from the surrounding woodland. In most years they managed to produce small surpluses, which they sold at regional fairs (like the famous Champagne Fairs in France) or in local market towns. Most villages contained a small gristmill that belonged to the lord, who charged a fee for its use. Hunting was reserved for the lords, under the theory that, as knights, they needed the opportunity to practice their warrior killing skills.

The lords lived either in big, sturdy, roomy manor houses (which sometimes were great stone castles or *chateaux*, but usually were just big houses) or, more likely, in greater comfort in a nearby city or town. The peasants lived in ramshackle wattle-and-daub cottages, so flimsy that they rebuilt them every few years. Cottages lacked permanent enclosed fireplaces, so babies and infants were swaddled to keep them from crawling unwittingly into the open hearths or pulling pots of boiling pottage onto themselves. Wells lacked raised sidewalls, and a not uncommon cause of death was falling into them and drowning. Schools were non-existent and few peasants were literate.[13]

The newly invented moldboard plows were efficient at turning over the thick, clayey soil of the champion lands, but also expensive. Big and heavy, they required several brawny horses or oxen to pull them. Most peasant families could afford neither plows of their own, nor the teams to pull them. Rather, they owned them communally, with each family supplying a horse or ox for the team. Each plow was equipped with a curved wood-and-iron coulter, a new invention that turned over and aerated the soil. The peasants used dung from their livestock as fertilizer, although without barns to collect it most of the manure was lost in the fields to rain and snow.[14]

In any given year, the villagers left one of the three great fields fallow. They planted a second with grains (normally wheat, but sometimes oats, barley, or rye, especially in the cold country north of the champion

---

[8] Frances Gies and Joseph Gies, *Life in a Medieval Village* (1990), 1-7.
[9] Marc Bloch, *Feudal Society* (1961), 241-280.
[10] Gies and Gies, *Life in a Medieval Village*, 67-87.
[11] Ibid, 44-66.
[12] George C. Homans, *English Villagers of the Thirteenth Century* (1941), 285-308.
[13] Gies and Gies, *Life in a Medieval Village*, 88-105.
[14] William H. TeBrake, *Medieval Frontier: Culture and Ecology in Rjinland* (1985), 23-41.

lands), demanding crops that drained most of the nutrients from the soil. They planted the third field with peas, beans, or clover, which as "nitrogen-fixers" restored some of the nutrients drained by the grain. Grapes grew in separate vineyards.

As the population grew, most of Europe's old wild forestland was cleared for agriculture, a process called assarting. Many of the assarts (new lands) were on the frontier (regions known in German as *marks* and in English as marches), most of which were in Poland, Bohemia, Austria (*Ostermark*, or "Eastern March"), Hungary, Scandinavia (*Danmark*, or "Danish March"), Iceland, Greenland, and Iberia, and on islands, mountains, and marshes. Much of the Medieval frontier had been opened by military aggression – the German *drang nach osten* (DRAHNG NAHK AHSTEN) ("drive to the east") against the Poles, Czechs, and other Slavs; the Viking conquests of northern Scandinavia, the Baltic States, and other areas; the Spanish and Portuguese Reconquista in Iberia; and the Crusades in the Middle East.[15]

Most villagers led decent, if unexciting lives. Disease was minimal. Food was sufficient. The family was the basis of peasant life, with age- and gender-specific tasks and chores that kept most people busy for about six hours each day. Men plowed, planted, and harvested the outfield, and looked after the horses, sheep, and oxen. Women gleaned (collected the stubble and loose grain from the outfield after harvest), tended the gardens in the infield, cared for the cows, goats, chickens, and geese, made butter and cheese, and cooked. Women spun thread (hence the term "spinster") using a small hand-held tool known as a distaff, but men wove cloth.[16]

Most villagers were relatively content and thus reluctant to move to the frontier – they generally refused to go unless pushed out by overpopulation or enticed by generous offers from the marcher lords, who sometimes promised to make them yeomen if they agreed to move. Still, enough peasants moved to the frontier so that villeinage (serfdom) declined steadily throughout the High Middle Ages. The myth of the *village immobile* (the unchanging village) was just that – a myth. Village life did change, although slowly. As the population grew, a steady stream of villagers either made their way to the frontier, became journeymen (landless traveling laborers), or found their way into the growing *bourgs* (French for "burghs" or "cities"). Any villein who succeeded in living in a bourg undetected for a year and a day was automatically declared free – hence the phrase, "city air makes you free." Yet most of the villeins chose to remain in their villages, where they were guaranteed enough land to work and a family to help them do it.

Compared to modern cities, Medieval bourgs were small, dirty, and unhealthy. City air might make one free, but it could just as easily make one dead. Venice and Paris – the largest bourgs in the Medieval West – had fewer than 200,000 inhabitants. Most bourgs had less than 10,000. Bourgs lacked sewers (other than the streets, ditches, and rivers) and lights, but had plenty of thieves and robbers. Ringed by ponderous stonewalls for defense, Medieval bourgs were "walking cities," meaning that a person could walk from the central market square to the outer wall in less than an hour. Streets were narrow and dirty, animals roamed loose, rats and fleas abounded (as they also did in the villages), drinking water was often polluted with human and animal waste and with offal from the slaughterhouses, water was regarded as unhealthy and people seldom bathed, and most houses were dark and gloomy, lit only by the dim glow of fire.

Feudalism

If manorialism was the economic system of the Medieval West, feudalism was the political system. Based both on the principles of monarchy (one-person rule) and dynasticism (succession by the previous monarch's closest blood relative), feudalism had emerged at the beginning of the High Middle Ages to provide political stability and relative peace after the turmoil and bloodshed of the Early Middle Ages. In the Early Middle Ages warrior lords like the Frankish king Charlemagne had fought incessant wars, ravaged each other's manors, forged short-lived empires that lasted only until the monarchs themselves died, and were unable to control the bandits and rowdies that roamed the countryside. To be sure, in the High Middle Ages the lords still fought among themselves – as warrior knights, it was, after all, the only thing they really knew how to do – but feudalism imposed strict limits on their warfare. Feudalism did not produce peace, but rather a kind of controlled aggression that managed to leave the valuable manors mostly intact and the peasants largely alive.

According to the late, great French social historian Marc Bloch, the basic premise of feudalism was that, except for the very highest-ranking lords, every lord was some other lord's "man." In theory the lowest-ranking lords (the ordinary knights) swore allegiance to the middle-rank lords (the earls, counts, barons, dukes, viscounts, margraves, landgraves, princes, etc), who in turn swore allegiance to the highest-ranking lords (the kings and emperors). This system of allegiance – where almost every lord was, in Bloch's words, "another man's man" – was known as "vassalage," a power relationship that existed only among the lords and did not involve the peasants, clergy, or burghers. A lord who swore allegiance to another lord was called his vassal; the lord to whom the allegiance was sworn was called the liege. Most lords were both vassals and lieges at the same time – vassals to greater lords and lieges to lesser ones.

Under feudalism, the lieges promised to protect their vassals from attack by other lords. In return, the vassals promised to serve in their lieges' armies in time of war. Medieval armies thus consisted of relatively small

---

[15] Ibid, 41-52.
[16] Gies and Gies, *Life in a Medieval Village*, 106-128.

squads of mounted, armored knights. Because only lords could be knights, and because each knight had to supply his own horse, chain mail, shield, sword, lance, and squire, which could be quite expensive, armies were small in size, rarely exceeding more than a few hundred fighters. This limited the amount of damage they could do. As part of the feudal arrangement, the vassals turned legal ownership of their manors over to their lieges, who then returned them to the vassals as something called "fiefs," which meant that when the vassals died, their lands could be assumed only by a single heir, to be determined by customary law - usually it was the eldest surviving son - and whose inheritance was supposedly protected by the liege. Thus manors, counties, earldoms, baronies, margravates, duchies, kingdoms, etc., were left intact over many generations, rather than being subdivided among a multitude of children and other kin. If a disgruntled second son or distant cousin showed up with a gang of knights to try to take over (and sometimes they did), the legitimate heir could call upon the liege for assistance, who was honor-bound to render it. Dynasties thus developed. The arrangement between liege and vassal was sealed with a blood oath, supposedly sanctifying it in God's eyes.

Under feudalism, governments remained small and local, with the vassals left in almost complete control of the day-to-day operations of their fiefs. Almost all taxes were paid to the local lord. With few exceptions (Paris and London were two), capital cities did not exist - nor did large, centralized government bureaucracies. Kings lived rather simply on their own manors, in their own castles. They did appoint a few royal officers, such as sheriffs (literally, "shire reeves") and coroners (literally, "crowners") who investigated blood crimes, but these were exceptions to the rule.[17]

Roman Catholicism

Medieval Western people believed in religious universalism, which is to say that, with but a few exceptions, they expected that everyone would belong to the same church. The Middle Ages was an Age of Faith, in the West as well as elsewhere. Religion stood at the center of intellectual life, which by definition made the West a theocentric society. Medieval scholars - most of whom were monks, nuns, or priests - looked to religion, not science, to explain the mysteries of the universe.

As a consequence, there was a very real unity, or catholicism, to Western religious and intellectual life. (Today, the very word "catholic" is sometimes used to mean "universal," although originally it derived from the Latin *cathedra*, meaning "seat" or "headquarters.") Religious minorities existed in the West, to be sure - there were Jews, Muslims, Eastern Orthodox Christians, and probably a few old pagans who still worshipped Zeus or Odin or kept to the traditions of the druids - but in most areas they numbered less than a tenth of the population. The vast majority of the Western people were Roman Catholics, lifelong members of what they reverently called "Holy Mother Church." It is important to note that Roman Catholics were not the only Christians in the world at the time. The Orthodox Christian Church held sway in Eastern Europe, the Coptic Christian Church predominated in Ethiopia, and several smaller Christian churches existed in the Middle East and India, although the dominate Muslims and Hindus vastly outnumbered them. But in the West, the Roman Catholic Church was supreme. Most Western people could not imagine it being any other way. Unity was vital. A religiously divided society, they were sure, would soon fall apart.

The peoples of the high Medieval West organized their Church the same way they organized everything else: hierarchically. In fact, the literal translation of the Greek word hierarchy is "holy rule". The Church was headed by a pope (literally, "father") who resided either in the large, old bourg of Rome or (during the years of the Great Schism) in Avignon (Ah-vig-NAHN), a small, sleepy bourg in southern France on the banks of the Rhone River. A hierarchy of red-robed cardinals, archbishops, bishops, abbots, and abbesses completed the religious elite. These men (for other than the abbesses who managed the convents, all of them were male) were normally the sons of lords.

The Church divided Western Europe into several dozen administrative districts, called dioceses, each administered by a bishop or archbishop who was based in a central bourg called a "see." Most sees boasted large, elegant stone cathedrals with beautiful stained-glass windows, high, vaulted ceilings, and elegant flying buttresses. These stunning structures inspired awe and served as diocesan headquarters, which was why they were called cathedrals.

Unlike bishops, most priests, monks, and nuns were of peasant stock. Priests tended to the Church's thousands of parishes, most of which were coterminous with a particular village or manor. Each parish had a chapel, usually a small, plain structure made of wood or stone and situated near the village center. It might - or might not - have a stained-glass window, hand-carved altar, or a wall adorned with poorly painted icons, the loving if crude labor of a local peasant artist. Like the bishops, the priests, too, were all males.

In addition to the cathedrals and chapels, there were also a few thousand isolated monasteries and convents - cloistered communities of male monks and female nuns, devout men and women who had withdrawn from the distractions of the workaday world in order to focus more intensely on God - located in isolated places and headed by learned abbots and abbesses. Monks and nuns were cloistered, which is to say that they were permitted only limited contact with the outside world. Monasteries and convents hired peasants to be their

---

[17] Bloch, *Feudal Society*, 145-175, 219-230.

reeves or bailiffs. However, by the end of the Middle Ages, this isolation was breaking down, and some of the monks and nuns were venturing out into the wider world.

Medieval Christians believed as a matter of faith that, in Classical times, Jesus of Nazareth (c. 5 BCE – 29 CE) had walked the earth as the prophesied messiah (or Christ, from the Greek *kristos*, meaning "the anointed one") of the Old Testament of the Bible – the son of God come to earth to deliver divine grace and redeem His followers from the consequences of original sin. Christians accepted the four official Gospels of the Bible – Matthew, Mark, Luke, and John – as true accounts of Jesus's life, teachings, message, miracles, and resurrection. They believed in His promise of personal salvation: that if they unreservedly accepted Him as their savior, their souls might, upon death, and after a period of cleansing punishment in purgatory, ascend to heaven ("paradise"), there to dwell for eternity with God, Jesus, the various saints (extremely pious individuals who had been blessed by God, the most important of whom was Jesus's human mother, the Virgin Mary), and other worthy departed Christians. Christians viewed Jesus's suffering on the cross as the ultimate expression of His divine love, and considered it tangible evidence that God still loved them and would care for them, despite their own sinfulness. They considered Jesus's resurrection as sufficient proof of His divinity. Because many of Jesus's teachings were in the form of parables (stories) that were sometimes difficult to understand, Catholics accepted the need for religious leaders – bishops and priests – to interpret the Gospels for them. They believed that if they prayed to the saints, then miracles might be performed for them. And they believed that if they prayed for the dead, their prayers would shorten the deceased one's stay in purgatory and speed him or her towards heaven.

Catholics also believed that they must follow the various rules set forth by the Church, as well as participate in it's official sacraments of communion, confession, baptism, matrimony, and last rites. Priests were deemed necessary for the proper function of these rituals. Catholics believed that they must have their children baptized by a priest or their souls might be lost to Satan, that they must confess their sins to a priest at least once a year, that only a priest could absolve them of their sins, and that they could obtain God's grace only through the ceremony of Holy Communion, during which a priest ritually transformed ordinary bread and wine into the body and blood of Christ

For nonbelievers (and erring Christians), entry into heaven was not possible; the souls of such persons were damned, destined to spend eternity in the grim pits of hell, writhing in everlasting torment under the lash of demons. Since this was obviously a horrid fate not to be wished on anyone, good Catholics were enjoined to "save" those in danger of damnation, by converting nonbelievers and admonishing errant believers to mend their ways.

Since, aside from the saints, everyone – no matter how well intentioned – was bound to sin (sin was only human, after all) most Catholics did not expect to enter heaven immediately upon death; rather, they anticipated (usually with much dread) having to spend a prolonged period of time in purgatory, doing penance for their sins. Only after having suffered in purgatory might their souls be sufficiently cleansed to enable them to ascend to heaven. Consequently, most Catholics anticipated their deaths with considerable apprehension about the state of their souls. They also viewed suffering as redemptive, that only through suffering could anyone attain his true potential as a worthy being. Thus criminals were sentenced to suffer. Such a viewpoint doubtless made suffering easier to bear.

Many Medieval Christians viewed the fact that minority populations of Jews, Muslims, pagans, and heretics (nonconforming Christians) living among them as a potential threat to the ideal of one church of all believers. If the nonbelievers performed a useful function, as the Jews did in trade and commerce, they were barely tolerated and frequently were made the victims of cruel persecutions. Otherwise they were not tolerated at all.

Trifunctionalism

Trifunctionalism is the rather unwieldy term that social historians have invented to describe the Medieval social system. As previously noted, Medieval Western society was hierarchical, with each person having his or her "place" in the hierarchy. Generally, society was divided into three broad estates: the First Estate (clergy), Second Estate (lords), and Third Estate (commoners). The Third Estate was a broad category, comprising 95% of the population. It consisted of the peasants (yeomen and villeins), *bourgeoisie* (bor-zhwah-ZEE) (a French term for merchants, lawyers, teachers, engineers, and master craftsmen), journeymen, apprentices, and "men without masters" (mostly urban or migrant laborers). One's estate was not a determined by wealth – some bourgeois were as rich as lords, and priests, monks, and nuns took vows of poverty – but of function. It was a Medieval cliché to term the First Estate "those who pray," the Second Estate "those who fight," and the Third Estate "those who work." To the Medieval mind, that was the natural order of things.

As the bourgs grew in the High Middle Ages, the number of *bourgeois* (bor-ZHWAH) (members of the bourgeoisie), journeymen, apprentices, and men without masters grew as well. By 1300 some bourgeois had achieved considerable wealth. Often, they leased manors from down-on-their-luck lords, becoming *rentiers* (rahnt-ee-AYS) (a French term for landlords). Unlike the peasants, journeymen, and men without masters, most bourgeois were literate.

As commerce grew throughout the High Middle Ages, the bourgeoisie became more active. Trade routes, over the Alps, through the champion lands, and by sea, connected Italy, the most urbanized part of Western

Europe, with the Low Countries, a rich cloth-producing region in the delta of the Rhine River, as well as with the Champagne Fairs and the North Sea and Baltic Sea fisheries. North Sea bourgeois organized the Hansa, a great commercial league of northern maritime bourgs that dominated the fish trade.

Yet for all their wealth, the bourgeoisie had less status in the Medieval West than the clerics or lords. They could not become officers in the army or high-ranking bureaucrats. They were not permitted to wear furs, symbols of noble status. They became resentful of their status and talked about change.

Conclusion

From these beginnings until approximately the 1300s, Western Civilization was what historians and other social scientists sometimes call a traditional or pre-modern culture. Typically, traditional cultures are rural, local, communalistic, theocentric, and agrarian. They have limited technologies but exceedingly complex and hierarchical social systems. They have age and gender divisions of labor, and usually focus on the family and the village as the primary units of production. They are usually patriarchal and tend to be somewhat suspicious of outsiders. Most of all, they prefer well-known, time-honored practices to untested innovations, the safety of group solidarity to the risks of individualism, and the warm embrace of revealed religion to the cold uncertainty of discovered science. Such values did not make the People of the Plow primitive or backwards or even wrong. But they were not modern.

-The Documents-

Reading Documents in Translation

Historians, reporters, sociologists, anthropologists, historical geographers, historical pathologists, lawyers, demographers, archivists, political scientists, philosophers, literary critics, historical ecologists, genealogists, and other people concerned about what happened in the past rely heavily on documents (written eyewitness accounts) for evidence. For historians, documents are the chief (although not exclusive) source of information about the past. However, reading and analyzing documents correctly is neither straightforward nor easy. In fact, a big part of historians' training – probably the biggest part – is learning how to correctly interpret documents.

One problem with interpreting documents is that most of them are written in languages other than Modern English. Consequently, they need to be translated. But no translation – no matter how skilled the translator – can possibly capture the complete and exact meaning of the original text. Something is always "lost in the translation." For example, in the fourteenth century, near the end of the Middle Ages, the witty English courtier Geoffrey Chaucer wrote a series of earthy, humorous, and keenly perceptive story-poems known as *The Canterbury Tales*. In these stories, a group of English pilgrims, who represented a wide range of Medieval occupations – knight, miller, reeve, cook, lawyer, shipman, prioress, monk, nun, priest, physician, pardoner, wife, friar, clerk, merchant, squire, franklin, and others – traveled to the English town of Canterbury to pray at the shrine of Saint Thomas a Becket, a famous Christian martyr whose remains were thought to bring miracles. Chaucer's stories are well crafted and detailed, and contain a wealth of information about everyday life in Medieval England. Consequently, historians consider them important historical documents. And since Chaucer wrote in English rather than Latin, translating them should not be necessary, right? Wrong. Chaucer wrote in English, all right, but it was Middle English, the language of the High Middle Ages, not Modern English, which did not come into existence until later, in the sixteenth century. For example, in the original Middle English, the opening stanza of *Canterbury Tales* reads as follows:

> Whan that Aprille with his shoures soote
> The droghte of Marche hath perced to the roote,
> And bathed every veyne in swich licour,
> Of which vertu engendred is the flour;
> Whan Zephirus eek with his swete breeth
> Inspired hath in every holt and heeth
> The tendre croppes, and the yonge sonne
> Hath in the Ram his halfe cours y-ronne,
> And smale fowles maken melodye,
> That slepen al the night with open ye,
> (So priketh hem nature in hir corages):
> Than longen folk to goon on pilgrimages,
> And palmers for to seken straunge strondes,
> To ferne halwes, couthe in sundry londes;
> And specially, from every shires ende
> Of Engelond, to Caunterbury they wende,

>The holy blissful martir for to seke,
>That hem hath holpen, whan that they were seke.[18]

Obviously, this passage needs to be translated. One authority on Middle English translates it as follows:

>When the sweet showers of April fall and shoot
>Down through the drought of March to pierce the root,
>Bathing every vein in liquid power
>From which there springs the engendering of the flower,
>When also Zephyrus with his sweet breath
>Exhales an air in every grove and heath
>Upon the tender shoots, and the young sun
>His half-course in the sign of the Ram has run,
>And the small fowl are making melody
>That sleep away the night with open eye
>(So nature pricks them and their heart engages)
>Then people long to go on pilgrimages
>And palmers long to seek the stranger strands
>Of far-off saints, hallowed in sundry lands,
>And specially, from every shire's end
>In England, down to Canterbury they wend
>To seek the holy blissful martyr, quick
>In giving help to them when they were sick.[19]

This is a good translation. But it is not an exact one. For example, notice that in the translation, the second-to-last last line ends with the word "quick." Yet in the original, no such word exists. Why, then, did the translator include it? Because he wanted to preserve Chaucer's original A-A-B-B rhyme scheme and needed a Modern English word that rhymed with "sick." In Chaucer's day, "seke" (sick) rhymed with "seke" (seek), but when the poem is translated into Modern English, the original rhyme is lost. So the translator added a new word, in order to restore the rhyme. Was the change significant? Maybe. The new, modern translation implies that Chaucer believed that people who visited shrines and prayed to saints generally expected quick cures for whatever maladies plagued them. However, the original document was actually silent about whether saints acted quickly or slowly, about whether miracles occurred immediately or later. Maybe pilgrims did expect quick cures. Maybe they didn't. But the original document does not provide us with that information, and it is wrong to presume that it does.

Another problem with translations is that different translators come up with different translations. This is because documents like *Canterbury Tales* really have four different aspects to them, all of which need be translated: the broader meaning embedded in the whole document as the author intended the readers to understand it; the narrower meanings contained in the words the author chose to use; the formats in which the author chose to arrange and present the words; and the various clichés, asides, parables, oblique references, and other "hidden meanings" the author inserted as background and which frequently tell us a lot about the times and places in which the author lived. It is virtually impossible for a single translation, even a good one, to capture all four of these aspects. The problem can be amply illustrated by referring to another fourteenth-century story-poem, *Divine Comedy* by the great Italian poet Dante Alighieri, parts of which you will soon read. In the original poem, written in Florentine (a Medieval version of Italian), the first stanza of Canto III – Dante's famous rendition of the words inscribed above the gateway leading into hell – reads as follows:

>*Per me si va ne citta dolente,*
>*Per me si va ne l'etterno dolore,*
>*Per me si va tra la perduta gente.*
>*Giustizia mosse il mio alto fattore:*
>*Fecemi la divina podestate,*
>*La soma sapienza e 'l primo amore.*
>*Dinanzi a me non fuor cose create*
>*Se non etterne, e io etterno duro.*
>*Lasciate ogne speranza, voi ch'intrate.*

One scholar translates these lines like this:

>Through me you pass into the city of wo:
>Through me you pass into eternal pain:
>Through me among the people lost for aye.
>Justice the founder of my fabric moved:
>To rear me was the task of power divine,
>Supremest wisdom, and primeval love.
>Before me things create were none, save things
>Eternal, and eternal I endure.

---

[18] Geoffrey Chaucer, in R. Morris, ed., *The Prologue, the Knightes Tale, the Nonne Preestes Tale, from the Canterbury Tales by Geoffrey Chaucer* (1893), 1-2.

[19] Geoffrey Chaucer, *The Canterbury Tales*, trans. N. Coghill (1952), 25.

All hope abandon, ye who enter here.[20]

But a second scholar translates them somewhat differently (and in capital letters):

    I AM THE WAY INTO THE CITY OF WOE.
    I AM THE WAY TO A FORSAKEN PEOPLE.
    I AM THE WAY INTO ETERNAL SORROW.
    SACRED JUSTICE MOVED MY ARCHITECT.
    I WAS RAISED HERE BY DIVINE OMNIPOTENCE,
    PRIMORDIAL LOVE AND ULTIMATE INTELLECT.
    ONLY THOSE ELEMENTS TIME CANNOT WEAR
    WERE MADE BEFORE ME, AND BEYOND TIME I STAND.
    ABANDON ALL HOPE, YE WHO ENTER HERE.[21]

Which translation is correct? The answer depends on how you look at it. The first translation is more literal, more of a word-by-word translation, but the second retains Dante's original A-B-A rhyme scheme and is easier to read. Which translation is best? Once again, it depends on which aspect of the document – the broad meaning, the narrow meaning, the structural meaning, or the hidden meaning – that a historian most wishes to examine.

Faced with such widely differing translations, some historians prefer prose translations – those that translate Medieval poetry into Modern English prose, and thus permit both the translator and the reader to focus on broad meaning, narrow meaning, and hidden meaning, and ignore the structural meaning. Yet artistry and format have great historical significance, and should not be ignored. Chaucer and Dante, for example, deliberately chose to write in poetry rather than prose. In fact, most Medieval writers chose to tell their stories in the form of poems, and most Medieval readers preferred poetry to prose. Why? In an age of limited literacy, poems were easier to read, recite aloud, and memorize. Rhyme, alliteration, meter, metaphor, simile, brevity, and repetition – all found in poetry – were common and familiar mnemonic devices, important literary traditions that permitted the majority of Medieval people – those who were either illiterate (could not read), non-literate (chose not to read), or semi-literate (read only a little) – to remember and repeat the stories. Poetical translations thus retain the flavor of Medieval times and the social power of Medieval stories in ways that prose translations cannot.

Consequently, students should keep in mind that no translation is – or can be – perfect. Reading a document in translation can give the reader the gist of it, but not every aspect or nuance. Something will always be missing, "lost in the translation." In the final analysis, fully understanding and appreciating historical documents requires learning the languages and the historical contexts in which they were written. Absent that, careful historians know not to attempt to exegete (construct literal, detailed, word-by-word, minute interpretations of) translated documents.

Medieval People: William Langland

William Langland (born c. 1332) was a fourteenth-century English monk of peasant stock. Angry at the corruption he saw in his society, he wrote a long, satirical poem called *Piers the Plowman*. Langland himself is the narrator of the story, whom you will meet in the excerpt below, which is from Chapter One. Piers (Middle English for "Peter") the Plowman, the central character, is introduced later on in the story, in Chapter Two, and so does not appear in the excerpt. The poem is very traditional, in the sense that Langland hoped to persuade his fellow Europeans to return to what he considered time-honored values. His gripe was not with traditional society per se, but with what he saw as the abandonment of traditional values by his fellow Englishmen and Englishwomen. He railed against clergy who were corrupt and not doing their jobs, lords who neglected to protect the people, and bourgeois who put on airs and acted like lords. However, people who did follow traditional lifestyles – peasants who worked their fields, monks and nuns who kept their vows of poverty, priests who devoted parish resources to helping the poor, workers who did their jobs, people who put faith before material well-being – were good and deserved respect. The excerpt gives a good description of the various different sorts of people, good and bad, who made up Medieval society. How many types can you find? The excerpt is a prose translation that synthesizes several different poetical translations from Middle English. It retains most of Langland's meaning, most of his vocabulary, a lot of the background, and a good deal of the alliteration that he used as his chief mnemonic device. It sacrifices his meter and word order, and some of his vocabulary. In its original form, the first paragraph looked like this:

    In a somer sesun, whon softe was the sonne,
    I schop me into a shroud, as I a schep were;
    In habite as an hermite unholy of werkes
    Wente I wyde in this world wondres to here;

---

[20] Dante Alighieri, in H. F. Cary, ed. and trans., *The Vision; or Hell, Purgatory, and Paradise of Dante Alighieri* (1875), 62.
[21] Dante Alighieri, in J. Ciardi, ed. and trans., *The Inferno: A Verse Rendering for the Modern Reader* (1954), 42.

> Bote in a Mayes morwnynge on Malverne hulls
> Me bifel a ferly, of fairie, me-thoughte.

Material that is enclosed in brackets is not part of the original text, but rather commentary that I have added for purposes of clarification.

from PIERS THE PLOWMAN [22]

In a summer season, when the sun was soft, I dressed myself in old clothes, as if I were a shepherd; and thus garbed as an unemployed monk, I wandered far and wide into the world, hoping to hear of wonderful things. But one May morning, in the Malvern Hills, a mysterious thing befell me, as if by fairy magic.

Weary from my wanderings, I stopped to rest under a broad bank by the side of a stream; and as I lay down and leaned out and looked into the water, it sounded so merry that I soon fell asleep. Then I had a marvelous dream: I was in a wilderness, I could not tell where. I looked to the east and saw a fine tower on top of a hill, set high against the sun. Beneath the tower yawned a deep abyss, with a dungeon in it, surrounded by a deep, dark ditch, dreadful to see. Between the tower and the dungeon I saw a fair field, filled with folk, all manner of men, both poor and rich, working and wandering in their worldly affairs.

Some of the people put themselves to work plowing. Seldom knowing pleasure, they set and sowed, sweating with their labor, producing the food that the wasters and gluttons consumed. Other people in the field thought only of their vanity, always dressing in comely clothes. But many others lived strict lives, full of prayer and penance for the love of God and the hope of someday attaining Heaven-rich bliss; for these were the anchorites [apprentice monks] and monks, who remained in their cells [rooms] rather than roaming about the countryside seeking sensual pleasures. Others chose to live by trade, and they were much better off, for it appears that such men always thrive. Some were clever minstrels, earning their sustenance with their singing. But others were japers and jesters, Judas's children, inventing fantastic tales about themselves and posing as fools, yet having wits enough to work if they wanted to. What St. Paul preached about them, I dare not say here, but it is sufficient to say, "He that speaks filth is Lucifer's servant." Bums and beggars bustled about, until their bags and their bellies were crammed with bread. These robbers and knaves lived by their wits and fought for their ale, for God knows that in gluttony they go to bed, and the next day arise with ribaldry. Sleep and sloth surround them forever.

Pilgrims and palmers banded together to visit the shrines at Composetella and Rome. They went forth on their way with many wise tales, and took leave to lie about it all their lives thereafter. Groups of monks with hooked staves were on their way to Walsingham, with their wenches following after. These were great, long lubbers who loathed work, clothing themselves in robes so everyone would know they were monks, and strutting about as monks so as to have an easy life.

I found friars there – all four orders of them – preaching to the people for what profit they could get. [Friars were a new kind of monk, ones who went out into the world rather than living in isolated or cloistered monasteries.] In their greed for fine robes they misconstrued the Gospels, glossing over the details to suit their listeners. Many of these Doctors of Divinity could dress as well as they liked, for their money and their merchandise met together. Now that charity had become a business, and religious orders had become the chief shriveners to the lords, many mysterious things have befallen us in the last few years. Unless these friars can better hold together to the ideals of Mother Church, the worst mischief in the world will mount up fast.

Over there was a pardoner, who preached as if he was a priest. He brought forth from his robes a bull [official Church document], stamped with bishops' seals, and said that he had the power to absolve sinners who had been false, or not fasted, or had otherwise broken their vows. Ignorant men believed him and liked his words well, and came up to him and knelt to kiss the bull. He held the bull before them, blurring their eyes, and with his roll of parchment raked in their rings and brooches. Thus the people gave their gold to help these gluttons, and gave their trust to such lecherous scoundrels! Was the bishop worthy, and kept his ears open, his seals would not have been sent to deceive the people. But it was not entirely the bishop's doing that this boy preached; for the pardoner divided the silver with the parish priest – money that otherwise would go to the poor people of the parish. Other

---

[22] Translation by the author.

parish priests complained to their bishops that their parishes had been poor since the time of the Plague; so they asked his license and leave to live in London, to sing masses for simony, as silver is sweet.

Over there a hundred men in silk gowns stood swaying from side to side and making speeches. They were lawyers who served at the bar, pleading the law to get their pence and pounds. It was not for the love of our Lord that they unloosed their lips, for you might better measure the mist on the Malvern Hills than get even a mumble out of their mouths until the money was shown!

And over there I saw bold bishops and Doctors of Divinity. Clerks of account came by to serve the king....

I also saw in the field barons and bourgeois and bondsmen, as you shall soon hear; bakers, butchers, and brewers many; workers of wool and weavers of linen; tailors, tanners, and tinkers aplenty; masons, miners, and many other craftspeople; dikers and diggers that drive forth the long day with bawdy songs like, "Dieu vous save, Dame Emme!"; cooks and their helpers crying, "Hot pies, hot! Good geese and pigs! Go we to dine, go we!"; and tavern keepers bawling, "Wine of Spain! Wine of Gascony! Wash down your roast with wine from the Rhineland and La Rochelle!" All this I saw while sleeping, and a great deal more besides.

Medieval Religion: Dante Alighieri

Unquestionably, he was the greatest of all the poets to write in Italian (some would say in any language), and Dante Alighieri (DAHN-tay Al-eh-GAYR-ee) (1265-1321) was Medieval, not modern. Like Langland, Dante wrote poetry, not prose, although he used rhyme rather than alliteration as his chief mnemonic device, and his skill as a poet far surpassed Langland's. His great epic poem, *Divine Comedy* (in the Middle Ages a "comedy" was any story with a happy ending), dealt not with modern themes, but with traditional religion; it was a dizzying, terrifying, and ultimately joyful journey through hell, purgatory, and heaven, and a powerful reaffirmation of Medieval Christian theology. For Dante, hell ("inferno") was no mere theological construct, but a real place, located somewhere below the surface of the earth. Mount Etna, an active volcano in Italy, was not just a natural phenomenon, but also the entryway to hell. Heaven was equally real, located in outer space. Purgatory was a mountain somewhere on the far side of the earth. (Compare Dante's "inferno" to Langland's "deep abyss, with a dungeon in it, surrounded by a deep, dark ditch, dreadful to see.") Typical of Medieval Christians, Dante depicted hell as consisting of nine descending levels, a series of gloomy pits that led ever deeper into the bowels of the earth, and which culminated in a vast ice sheet at the planet's frozen core in which a snarling Satan stood imprisoned. Heaven, too, had nine levels (for Medieval people believed in the necessity of divine balance), represented by the sun, the moon, the six known planets (Mercury, Venus, Mars, Jupiter, Saturn, and Neptune), the stars, and the "plenum mobile," an unknowable place that supposedly lay somewhere beyond the stars. In *Divine Comedy* the spirit of the old pagan Roman poet Virgil (representing human reason) took Dante on a tour of hell and purgatory. An angel (representing faith and having the appearance of Dante's dead lover, Beatrice) guided the final ascent into heaven, for as a non-Christian, Virgil was unable to make the trip – and thus in the poem faith triumphed over reason. The following excerpt is a prose revision of a poetical translation (Cary, 62, 188-193, 218-222, 522-523, and 544-545). Material that appears in brackets was not part of the original document; it was added for the sole purpose of clarifying some of the more difficult passages. Ellipses (either three dots or four asterisks) mean that part of the original document was omitted. In the first scene, Dante and Virgil pass through the gates of hell.

from *DIVINE COMEDY*[23]

PART I: INFERNO [HELL]

CANTO III

[The Gateway to Hell]

"Through me you pass into the city of woe. Through me you pass into eternal pain. Through me pass the people lost forever. My founder was moved by justice. To build me was the task of divine power, supreme wisdom, and primeval love. Nothing was created before me, except for those things that are eternal, and through eternity will I endure. Abandon all hope, ye who enter here."

I saw these words, in dim colors, inscribed over the lofty arch of a gateway. I said to Virgil, "Master, these words convey hard meaning."

---

[23] Based on Dante, *Vision*, 62, 188-193, 218-222, 522-523, 544-545.

As if prepared for my remark, Virgil replied, "At this point you must leave all distrust behind you; at this point vile fear must be extinguished. We have come to the place I have told you about. Here, we will see souls doomed to every conceivable misery, who intellectual good have lost." And he stretched his hand to mine and gave me a pleasant look, at which I was cheered. And into that secret place he led me on....

CANTO XXXVIII

[The Sowers of Discord]

[Dante depicted each of the various pits of hell as offering a particular kind of punishment for a different kind of sinner – an idea that Medieval Christianity ironically had borrowed from Islam. The ninth pit of the eighth level was reserved for "sowers of discord," a group that – according to Dante – included the Muslim prophet Mohammad, Mohammad's son-in-law Ali, the old Roman Tribune Curio, and others. In this way Dante reinforced the Medieval ideals of social unity and religious universalism, or one church of all believers. Because Islam was Christianity's chief rival, its very existence seemed to Dante – as it did to most Medieval Christians – to seriously undermine those ideals. For that reason Dante viewed Islam and Mohammad as evil. Obviously, religious toleration was not a chief characteristic of Medieval Western culture. God punished Mohammad and the other sowers of discord by forcing them to march in a circle while a demon cut them into pieces with his sword. Each spirit repeatedly endured the intense pain of being torn apart, healed, and then was cut again – and again, and again, and again, over and over, throughout all eternity. As they had divided society, now they, too, were rent asunder by the demon's bloody sword. Mohammad was cloven from his chin to his buttocks and Ali from the top of his head to his chin. Another spirit carried his own severed head as if it were a lantern, and Curio had his tongue cut out for having spoken the words that had led to a horrific civil war. Dante's imagery is vivid – and terrifying.]

W̲ho, even in words unfettered by rhyme and meter, would be fully able to tell of the wounds and blood that now I saw, no matter how often he repeated the tale? No tongue could equal so vast a theme; speech and thought alike were both impotent. If, collected in one hand, stood all the people who ever poured their blood upon Apulia's [Apulia is a large region of Italy] happy soil – or all the people who were slain by the Trojans – or all the people who were killed in that long war when, as writes Rome's historian, Livy, who errs not, the measured booty of captured rings made so high a pile, [this is a reference to the deadly Punic Wars, fought in Classical times between Rome and Carthage] – or all the multitude that felt the grating force of Guiscard's Norman steel [this is a reference to Robert Guiscard, a Norman warrior-knight, whose forces conquered the Italian city-state of Naples in the High Middle Ages] – or all of Duke Manfredi's dead soldiers, whose bones are still gathered at Ceperano, where treachery branded the Apulian name [this is a reference to the troops of Duke Manfredi of Naples, who were defeated and killed by Guiscard's forces after their Apulian allies treacherously switched sides and turned the vital mountain pass at Ceperano over to the Normans] – or all the dead that lie beyond thy walls, oh city of Tagliacozzo that was conquered by old Alardo, one with his limbs pierced, another with them lopped clean away – all of these tragedies were but things of naught, when compared to the hideous sights of the ninth chasm of the eight level of Hell.

A wine barrel that has lost its middle or side stave gapes not so wide as one of the souls I saw here, his body torn from his chin down to his rectum. His entrails dangled between his legs. His midriff lay open to view, along with that wretched ventricle that turns englutted food into shit [i.e., his colon].

While I tremulously fixed my gaze on him, he also eyed me. Pulling open his breast with his hands, he cried, "See now how I rip myself open. See how Mohammad is mangled. And in front of me walks Ali, weeping, his face cleft from his forelock to his chin. And the others, too, whom you see here with us – while they lived they also sowed scandal and schism, and therefore thus are themselves now rent in Hell. A fiend [i.e., a demon] stands here behind us, and with his sword hacks us cruelly, slivering us again and again as we march 'round and 'round along this dismal path. Our gashes heal before we pass him [so that he can cut us open anew each time we go by]. But say, who are you, who stand musing on that ledge? Are you lingering up there in order to delay the pain that was sentenced upon you for your own crimes?"

"Death has not yet overtaken him," my guide [i.e., Virgil] replied, "nor does any sin lead him here for torment. Rather, that he may conduct a full appraisal of your state, I who am dead must conduct him through the depths of hell, from orb to orb. Trust my words, for they are true."

More than a hundred spirits, when they heard this, stood in the pit to look at me, through their amazement momentarily forgetful of their pain. [Then Mohammad said to me,] "Thou, who perhaps will soon see the sun again, take this warning to Dolcino. [Dolcino was a renegade Christian monk and would-be religious reformer who was condemned by the pope as a heretic because he advocated communal property and communal sex, and eventually was burned at the stake along with his lover, Margaret.] Bid him, if he wishes not to soon follow me here, that he supply himself with good stores of food, lest imprisoning snows make him a victim of Novara's power." [Novara was a mountainous region in Italy where Dolcino and his followers holed up before they were captured. Dante here shows that spirits in hell are able to foretell future events.] Thus spoke Mohammad, with his foot upraised for stepping, as he prepared to move on.

Another wraith, pierced in the throat, his nostrils mutilated beneath his eyebrows and with one ear lopped off, who like the rest stood gazing at me with wonder, before the others could advance, bared his windpipe, which was all oversmeared with crimson stain. "O thou," said he, "whom sin condemns not, and whom once (unless I am mistaken) I have seen above on Latian ground [this spirit is telling Dante that he recognizes him, having seen him once before, in the Italian region of Latium, when both of them were alive], recall to mind Piero of Medicina [this is a reference to a man who stirred up dissention in the Italian city of Medicina, near Bologna] if, when you return again to the surface, you should behold the pleasant land that slopes from Vercelli to Mercabo [this is a reference to the Italian region of Lombardy, where the city of Fano was located]. And when you are there, warn those two men whom the city of Fano boasts as her worthiest sons – Guido del Cassero and Angelo da Cagnano – that if it is given to us spirits here in Hell to predict the future, that they will be cast out overboard and drowned under the waves near the city of Cattolica, through the perfidy of an evil, one-eyed tyrant. Nowhere between Cyprus and the Balearic Islands [by this reference, Dante meant the length and breadth of the entire Mediterranean Sea] has Neptune seen a murder so foul as this one, not even those committed by pirates or the Argive crew of old. That one-eyed traitor (whose realm one spirit here wishes that his own eye had never caught sight of) shall bring Guido and Angelo for a conference with him, then so shape his end that they shall need not be able to offer up vow or prayer against Mount Focara's wind."

I answered, "If you wish me to carry tidings of you to those above, tell me, who is the spirit for whom the sight of Lombardy would wake such sad memories?"

Immediately, he laid his hand on the cheek of one of his fellow spirits, and opened his jaws and cried, "Here! This is he that I spoke of. He cannot speak for himself, this outcast. He is the one who eased the doubt in Julius Caesar's mind by telling him, 'To men who are prepared, delay is harmful.'" [Dante is referring to Curio, a renegade Roman tribune who urged Caesar to take his armies across the Rubicon River in northern Italy, invade Rome, overthrow the republic, make himself dictator, and begin the deadly Roman Civil War, which left Caesar dead, the republic in ruins, and the empire in its stead.] Oh, how terrified I thought the spirit of Curio seemed, who spoke those foolhardy words, whose tongue was now cut from his throat.

PART III: PARADISO [HEAVEN]

[Like hell, heaven, too, had nine levels, a mirror image that signified cosmic balance. On the first level, the moon, Dante met spirits who made vows of chastity and religious life, but had been forced by circumstances to abandon those vows. On the second level, Mercury, he met the Roman Emperor Justinian, the great lawgiver from Classical times, along with many other spirits. On the third level, Venus, he met deceased friends. On the fourth level, the sun, he met Saint Thomas Aquinas, other saints, and the Biblical King Solomon. On the fifth level, Mars, he encountered the souls of great warriors and crusaders. On the sixth level, Jupiter, he met the souls of those who had administered justice in the world. On the seventh level, Saturn, he found the souls of good monks and nuns. On the eighth level, the stars, he saw Christ ascend to the ninth level in Mary's arms, and conversed with Saint Peter, Saint John, Saint James, and Saint Benedict. On the ninth and final level, beyond the stars, he saw God.]

CANTO XXIII

[Jesus and Mary]

[Christians believed that Jesus, who had lived at the beginning of the Common Era, was the Christ (which means "the anointed one"), the prophesied Messiah of the Bible. They also considered Him the Son of God, although born of Mary, a human woman. And they believed that He was the Savior, whose agonizing death of the cross had absolved humankind of original sin and permitted His followers' spirits to attain heaven after their deaths – provided, of course, that they had faith, did good works, and followed the sacraments of Holy Mother Church. God, they believed, existed in three parts, known collectively as the Holy Trinity: the Father (Creator), Holy Spirit (essence of goodness and unity in the universe), and Son (Jesus, who was both God and the Son of God). Medieval Christians sometimes viewed the Father and Holy Spirit as remote and unknowable, but considered the Son close, human-like, approachable, and compassionate. They also venerated the spirit of Mary, who existed in heaven along with other Christian spirits, but was especially pure and compassionate. They frequently prayed for her assistance, believing that her maternal personality made her especially tender and merciful. In the following scene, Mary and Jesus, accompanied by angels, ascend from the eighth heaven to the ninth, to join with God.]

Of that fair flower [i.e., Mary], whose name I invoke in prayer both morning and evening, my soul with all its might collected, on the goodliest ardor fixed and, as the bright dimensions of the star [i.e., Mary] in heaven excelling, as once here on earth, were, in my eyes livelily portrayed. Lo! From within the sky a lamp [i.e., the angel Gabriel] fell, circling in the fashion of a diadem, and girt the star [i.e., Mary], and – hovering round it – wheeled. [Dante has just compared Mary to bright star, with the angel Gabriel a smaller light orbiting around it.]

The sweetest melody, the one that most touches the spirit, would seem as crass as a torn cloud when it grates with thunder, when compared to the sound of that lyre [i.e., Gabriel's harp] wherewith the goodliest sapphire [i.e., Mary] that inlays the floor of heaven was crowned. "I am Angelic Love, who with hovering flight enwheels [i.e., orbits] the lofty rapture from that inspired womb, where our desire [i.e., Jesus] did once dwell. And around thee so, Lady of Heaven [i.e., Mary], I will hover; as long as your Son shall follow you, and I shall gather joy from your presence when you gild the highest sphere."

Such the circling melody seemed to say. And, as it ended, all the other lights [i.e., the other angels] took up the same song, and echoed Mary's name.

The robe [the "robe" Dante is referring to is the plenum mobile, or the ninth level of heaven where God dwelled, the outer reaches of space that Medieval thinkers believed surrounded and moved the eight lower levels, and which enfolded the rest of the universe like a robe], that with its regal folds enwraps the world, and burns and quivers with the nearby breath of God, had so far retired its inner hem and skirting over us, that yet no glimmer of its majesty had streamed unto me: therefore were my eyes were unable to pursue the crowned flame [i.e., Mary], that towering rose, and sought the seed [i.e., Jesus] it bore. And like the babe that stretches forth its arms with eagerness toward the breast after milk is taken, so the fervent band of angels outstretched their wavy summits, through zealous love to Mary. Then, now in view, they halted and sang "Regina Coeli" ["Regina Coeli" was an anthem Christians sang in honor of Mary, usually at Easter] so sweetly, the delight of hearing it has never left me.

Oh! What overflowing plenty is piled up in those rich-laden coffers. [Here Dante is speaking metaphorically of the chests full of heavenly rewards achieved by those souls who, in life, had been pious and good.] Those who sowed good seed below, now get to keep the harvest. Here are treasures tasted, that with tears were won in the Babylonian exile, when gold had failed them. Here, in synod high of ancient council with the new convened, under the Son of Mary and of God, victorious he [i.e., Saint Peter] his mighty triumph holds, to whom the keys of glory were assigned.

CANTO XXVIII

[God]

As I turned, I saw what no one in the ninth level of heaven could miss: a point, from which darted light so sharp that no unclosed eye could bear to see its keenness. The point was so small that the least star we know from earth seemed like the moon when set by its side, as star by side of star. And it was as far away, perhaps, as is the halo from the light that paints it, when most dense the vapor spreads. There wheeled around the point a circle of fire, more rapid than the speediest motion that surrounds the world. And another circle of fire enringed the first, and a third the second, and a fourth the third, and a fifth encompassed the fourth, which a sixth next bound, and over this a seventh reached a circumference so ample that its bow could have scarcely been entirely held within the span of Juno's messenger. Beyond the seventh ring ensued yet another two. And every one, as more in number distant from the first, was tardier in motion, and glowed with the purest flame the nearer it was to the point, as if partaking more, I thought, of the point's reality.

My beloved guide [i.e., Beatrice] saw me in anxious, suspenseful thought, and spoke: "Heaven, and all nature, hangs upon that point you see at the center of the conjoined circles. You should know that the more intense the love, the swifter, more winged, the orbit of the circle."

[The point of light was God. The rings of fire were the nine choirs of angels that surrounded Him.]

-CHAPTER II-
WHEN WHIRL WAS KING:
MODERNIZATION AND THE RENAISSANCE
c. 1310 - c. 1550

Centuries before the Renaissance, the fourth-century BCE Greek playwright Aristophanes (448-388 BCE), trying to explain the rapid social and cultural changes that occurred in his own tumultuous times, wrote, "Whirl is king, having deposed Zeus." [24] Although he didn't know it (for the term had not yet been invented), he was describing what historians today call "modernization," the process in which a culture becomes less traditional and more modern. (The opposite process, in which a culture becomes less modern and more traditional, is called "traditionalization.") By "whirl," Aristophanes meant "rapid change," and by "having deposed Zeus," he meant that new, more modern ideas had risen to supplant the old, traditional viewpoints that had once dominated Greek culture and thought, that modern humanism and science had "deposed" traditional pagan religion and taken over Classical Greek culture. Aristophanes exaggerated - he was a dramatist, after all - for humanism never did depose religion, not completely, not in Classical times. But he was right when he observed that rapid changes had occurred. Today, most historians view Aristophanes's era as one of several periods of history that was characterized by intense bursts of modernization. Another such period was the Renaissance, which began in Italy in the fourteenth century CE. This chapter examines the process of modernization as it occurred in the fourteenth and fifteenth-century West. We will see that modernization was closely linked to the value system of a rising social class, the bourgeoisie or urban middle class. We will also see that a series of calamities paved the way for modernization by weakening the four pillars that supported Western Civilization during the High Middle Ages.

-The Background-

The Late Middle Ages

During the High Middle Ages (c. 900-1310), Western Civilization functioned reasonably well. Most people had enough to eat. War was limited mostly to members of the second estate. Most people found comfort in the teachings of the Church. But in the Late Middle Ages (c. 1310-1500) a series of debilitating disasters struck the West and cracked the four pillars of Medieval society (manorialism, feudalism, Roman Catholicism, and trifunctionalism). The historian Jan Huizinga refers to this time of change as "the waning of the Middle Ages."[25] The key events of the period - global cooling, an ecological crisis, the Black Death, the Hundred Years War, the Wars of the Roses, two peasant revolts, a revolt of the Italian city-states against the Holy Roman Empire, and the temporary split in the Roman Catholic Church known as the Great Schism - combined to fundamentally alter the traditional Western way of life. Truly, it was an age when "whirl was king."

The Climatic Minimum

In the early 1300s, writes the environmental historian Charles Bowlus, the balmy climatic optimum of 900-1310 came to an abrupt end. A new era began, characterized by cooler, wetter weather. During the warm years of the High Middle Ages, the average annual temperature in Europe had been quite mild, with conditions even warmer than today. Late summers were hot and dry, ideal for ripening crops of wheat or grapes. As a result, Medieval Europeans successfully farmed areas that today are too cold or wet for agriculture. For example, according to another environmental historian, Emmanuel Le Roy Ladurie, in Iceland and Greenland Viking settlers produced lush fields of hay, which served as feed for their livestock. Peasants in Scotland, Norway, and northern Sweden successfully grew wheat. In England, farmers routinely harvested grapes for wine. Europeans pastured cattle and sheep in the high meadows of the Alps and other mountains. To be sure, cautions Le Roy Ladurie, the warm climate was not the *only* reason that agriculture expanded during the High Middle Ages, but it was an important factor.[26]

---

[24] Aristophanes's quote - "Whirl is king, having deposed Zeus" - is from Carl L. Becker, *The Heavenly City of the Eighteenth-Century Philosophers* (1932), 15.
[25] Jan Huitzinga, *The Waning of the Middle Ages* (1954), passim.
[26] Charles R. Bowlus, "Ecological Crisis in Fourteenth-Century Europe," in Lester J. Bilsky, ed., *Historical Ecology: Essays on Environment and Social Change* (1980), 89; Emmanuel Le Roy Ladurie, *Times of Feast, Times of Famine: A History of Climate Since the Year 1000* (1971), 254-264; Clive Ponting, *A Green History of the World: The Environment and the Collapse of Great Civilizations* (1991), 121-123.

But after 1310, Bowlus writes, the weather began to deteriorate. A climatic minimum began. Temperatures dropped. Late summers became overcast and rainy, making it difficult for certain crops to ripen. By the 1500s the average annual temperature had declined by about two degrees from what it had been in the High Middle Ages, and remained low until the mid-1800s. It was a period that some historians – with admitted melodrama – have since dubbed "the Little Ice Age".[27]

Le Roy Ladurie writes that mountaintop glaciers groaned down the valleys of the Alps, obliterating villages and destroying farmland and high pastures. In Iceland and Greenland the hay crops failed, and most of the livestock starved. Desperate and hungry, Icelanders took to the sea and became fisherfolk. Pack ice spilled out of the Arctic and flooded the North Atlantic Ocean, blocking ship travel between Europe and Greenland, isolating the colony. By 1500 Greenland had perished, cut off from European supplies and overrun by the more ecologically fit Inuit (In-EW-it) peoples (Eskimos), who were advancing rapidly from the west.[28]

No longer able to rely on wheat, which requires relatively warm, dry weather in order to ripen, Scottish and Norwegian farmers switched to oats, a hardier grain. They soon discovered that most Europeans considered oats a fit food for livestock only, not people. The market for Scottish farm produce consequently declined. Desperate, Scottish farmers fled the cold, harsh Highlands for the milder Lowlands. In England and Germany the change in the weather forced farmers to substitute beer and ale (made from grain) for wine (made from grapes, a more climate-sensitive crop), a serious problem in an Age of Faith when wine played a vital role in the Roman Catholic liturgy. Norwegians and Swedes moved south, crowding the warmer areas around the seaside bourgs of Oslo, Stockholm, and Malmo. The Baltic Sea froze in the winter, altering the migratory patterns of herring and forcing Scandinavian and German fishermen to head out into the dangerous waters of the North Sea to look for fish. England's Thames (TEMS) River froze in the wintertime, and poor people built temporary shanties on the ice.

With insufficient fodder for their livestock, farmers in many northern countries were forced to slaughter the majority of their animals in the fall, leaving scant meat, butter, and cheese for winter. The Church, seeking to alleviate the resulting shortages, declared that, in addition to the traditional "meatless" Fridays, there would be two additional "meatless" days each week. The demand for fish consequently soared. Farm prices increased. Famines occurred.[29]

According to Bowlus, the colder, wetter weather weakened manorialism, which had been based on the ability of the lords to bind the villeins to the manors. Because the weather now made agriculture in certain places more difficult, the lords who owned the manors in those now-cold countries could no longer force their villeins to stay and work, because to stay and work meant to starve. In such areas both the lords and the villeins slowly began to leave the traditional villages, seeking new, warmer land elsewhere.

Many villeins moved either to the growing bourgs and became landless laborers, migrated to the burgeoning seaports and became landless fishermen, or (especially in England and Scotland) took to the highways as unemployed, landless vagabonds. In each case they became "men without masters," which made them all the harder for the authorities to control. Crime increased. These villeins had become free, although in their case, "Freedom [was often] just another word for nothing left to lose." While the climatic minimum was not severe enough to destroy manorialism completely, it weakened it badly.

An Ecological Crisis

The climatic minimum served to exacerbate an already fast-brewing ecological crisis, the consequence of generations of population growth, deforestation, fuel shortages, erosion, soil exhaustion, and food shortages. According to Bowlus:

> Shortly after 1300 things went wrong. Two centuries of uncontrolled expansion had been purchased on credit using as collateral Europe's natural resources, which were rapidly being depleted. The resource base simply was not sufficient to sustain growth given the technology available at that time. In the thirteenth century man had seemed triumphant over nature, [but] in the fourteenth century nature turned the tables, and Europeans experienced a series of [ecological] crises that undermined not only the economy but the ability of states to govern, the power of the church to provide leadership, and the possibility for theologians to explain the world as a rationally ordered whole."[30]

The rapid population growth and territorial expansion of 900-1310 finally caught up with the West. Not only had the population of Europe as a whole nearly tripled in that time, but the number and size of the bourgs had grown at an even faster pace. Although Western cities in 1310 were still smaller than their counterparts in the Middle East, India, and China, they were nevertheless much larger than at the beginning of the High Middle

---

[27] Bowlus, "Ecological Crisis," 94; Le Roy Ladurie, *Times of Feast, Times of Famine*, 264-270; Ponting, *Green History*, 123.
[28] Le Roy Ladurie, *Times of Feast, Times of Famine*, 264-270; Alfred W. Crosby, *Ecological Imperialism: The Biological Expansion of Europe, 900-1900* (1986), 45-57.
[29] Bowlus, "Ecological Crisis," 95.
[30] Ibid, 94-95.

Ages. In 900 the largest bourgs in the West had contained only about 10,000 inhabitants, and most had been considerably smaller. But by 1310, following four centuries of sustained growth, writes Bowlus, "some of the larger Italian towns had populations that surpassed the 100,000 mark, while some northern ones had around 40-60,000 inhabitants." Bourgs that big had little choice but to import large quantities of food – not just from the surrounding countryside as they had always done, but from regions hundreds of miles away. The hungry city folk created an unprecedented demand for food, which in turn put a severe strain on village agriculture. To meet the growing demand, in the High Middle Ages the lords and villeins had cleared vast new tracts of land for agriculture. The result had been a serious, continent-wide deforestation that by the Late Middle Ages had reached crisis proportions. The loss of woodland meant that there was less wood for fuel, and so an acute energy shortage struck. And because the roots of the trees had stabilized the soil, deforestation meant that erosion, floods, and soil loss now occurred. Moreover, generations of overfarming had led to soil exhaustion, especially with the two chief sources of fertilizer – ashes and manure – now both in short supply (Bowlus, 91-95).[31]

By 1310 these problems had combined to create serious shortages. Bowlus writes:

> The most spectacular example of ecological disaster in the fourteenth century is evidence of general and recurring famine. There had been famines in the twelfth and thirteenth centuries, but those had largely occurred in regions where local crops had failed and cereals could not be imported from elsewhere because of lack of port facilities or financial strength in the region affected. There are no recorded examples of general famines in Europe between 1100 and 1300. In the fourteenth century general famine became common, however, the most serious coming between the years 1315 and 1317. The summer of 1314 had been an unusually wet year [it was the beginning of the climatic minimum], and yields were low all over Europe. When abnormal rainfall continued in 1315, crisis loomed on the horizon. By the spring of 1316 stored reserves had been exhausted and mass starvation stalked the land. In those parts of Europe from which we possess good statistical data, it is known that the price of grain increased from three to five times. Moreover, the data suggests that after 1300 general famine became a specter that Europeans had to face once each decade. In some Flemish towns, one person in ten died during the years 1315-17. There were frequent grain riots in the towns and even some reports of cannibalism.[32]

The Black Death

In 1347 – three decades into the cold and rain of the climatic minimum and food and fuel shortages of the ecological crisis – another great calamity struck the West. A fleet of Italian cargo ships set sail from the Ukraine, carrying a load of much-needed grain. But when the ships reached the southern Italian city of Messina a few weeks later, the entire crew was dead or dying, felled by a mysterious disease. Although alert authorities attempted to halt the spread of the disease by quarantining all ships arriving from the Black Sea, the pestilence nevertheless got ashore. Quickly, it spread throughout Europe. People who became infected developed large, foul-smelling, dark-colored blood blisters called "buboes" in their armpits and groins. They became feverish and incoherent. Most died within twenty-four hours of the first symptoms.[33]

Europeans called the malady the Black Death, a fearful reference to the dreaded dark-colored buboes that meant almost certain doom. It was the bubonic plague, an especially virulent species of bacteria that had appeared several times before in European history, each time causing widespread misery and death. This time it had arrived via Ukraine from China over the Great Silk Road, a trans-Asiatic trade route reopened by the Mongol Empire in the 1200s.[34]

The plague, writes the environmental historian Robert Gottfried, spread in at least three ways. First, the bacteria were carried in the saliva of rat fleas, and rats had gotten into the Ukrainian grain. Once arrived in Europe, the infected fleas (themselves immune to the bacteria) spread to European rats. As the rats died, the fleas jumped onto other mammals, including humans, infecting them as well. Second, the breath of infected people also transmitted the bacteria. Third, the disease could be spread by sexual contact.[35]

But nobody knew any of this at the time. Because microscopes had not been invented yet, no one in the West knew that germs existed, much less caused disease. Educated people (bishops, abbots, abbesses, some of the lords, the bourgeoisie) believed instead in the prevailing theory of the four humors (that a person's health or "humor" was determined by a proper balance of four essential bodily fluids: blood, phlegm, bile, and "black bile") and the theory of miasmas (that disease was spread by breathing damp, bad-smelling air). Yet bleeding, purging, blistering, covering up foul odors with the pleasing scents of cut flowers and perfumes – none of these

---

[31] Ibid, 91-95.
[32] Ibid, 95-97.
[33] Robert S. Gottfried, *The Black Death: Natural and Human Disaster in Medieval Europe* (1983), xiii-xiv, 42-53; Norman F. Cantor, *In the Wake of the Plague: The Black Death and the World It Made* (2001), 7-9, 21-25.
[34] Gottfried, *Black Death*, 33-37.
[35] Ibid, xiii.

traditional remedies did any good against the plague. For some baffled and anxious Europeans, it seemed as if the disease might be some sort of terrible punishment sent by God. But why, they wondered, was God angry with them? What terrible thing had they done to merit His divine wrath?[36]

The Black Death struck first in Europe's teeming bourgs, where people and rats crowded closely together, and where the unsuspecting merchants and grain dealers carried it from other locales. But soon it spread to the rural areas as well, where it ravaged the villages and manors that were so vital to the Medieval economy. It affected all three estates, clergy, lords, and commoners, writes the historian Norman Cantor. No group was spared. Priests giving last rites and nuns and monks tending to the sick caught the disease and died. The young English princess Joan, on her way to wed the equally young Castilian prince Pedro, caught the disease as she traveled south, and she died, too, quarantined in the French bourg of Bordeaux (Bor-DOH). In England the Archbishop of Canterbury, the country's most esteemed clergyman, died. When the plague reached the headquarters of the Roman Catholic Church in Avignon, France, it breached the papal palace itself. The pope, the leader of all Western Christendom, also became infected and died. There seemed, Cantor says, no way of stopping its horrific advance.[37]

Church officials attempted to reassure people that the plague was simply a disease, something that could be explained scientifically. But some of the more independent-minded priests (and there have always been independent-minded priests) proclaimed that it was instead a scourge from God, a righteous punishment for the sinful behavior of mankind. Such priests began to dole out harsher penances at confession, an action that understandably angered many of their parishioners. Elsewhere, groups of pious monks, seeking to purify their own souls with excessive pain and suffering, wandered the countryside, praying, doing penance, and flagellating each other with whips.[38]

Before the epidemic ran its course, about one-third of the population of Europe lay dead. The Black Death wiped out whole villages. In the bourgs, where the officials were better organized than in the countryside, successfully stemmed the disease by burning the infected bodies of the victims, cleaning up bad-smelling heaps of garbage, and removing the foul-smelling slaughterhouses that attracted the rats. City employees, mournfully crying, "Bring out your dead," roamed the streets, pulling creaking carts stacked high with reeking cadavers. Although no one understood why, Gottfried points out that these things usually helped. Burning the clothing of the dead killed the fleas that infested the clothing. Quickly disposing of the dead, cleaning up the garbage, and closing the slaughterhouses reduced the number of rats. Slowly, the death rate in the cities abated.[39]

According to Cantor, children attempted to relieve the stress by inventing a new nursery rhyme, "Ring around the rosies, a pocket full of posies," which chillingly concluded, "Atchoo, atchoo, we all fall down." "Ring around the rosies" referred to red circles that appeared around the flea bites (as with today's Lyme disease); "a pocket full of posies" referred to the practice of carrying fresh-cut flowers to cover the miasmas; "atchoo, atchoo" referred to the spread of the disease by breath; and "we all fall down" referred to the seemingly inevitable death of everyone.[40]

The impact of the Black Death on Western Civilization, writes Gottfried, was enormous. For one thing, it weakened manorialism. In many areas, such as France, England, Scotland, the Netherlands, Italy, and northern Germany, villeinage almost ceased. The plague was awful for those villeins who became infected and died, but ironically benefited those who survived. With one-third of the villeins dead, by the late 1300s Europe faced an acute labor shortage. Many lords sought to solve the situation by enticing other lords' villeins to leave their manors and come and work for them, an illegal but inevitable expedient.[41]

Shrewd villeins took advantage of the situation to negotiate for better conditions. Many of the old droits were eliminated, and those that remained were frequently converted to less onerous cash payments. Moreover, villeins sometimes succeeded in winning the right to move from manor to manor as they pleased. In fact, in many parts of Europe the peasants became yeomen – *meteyers* (met-ay-YAYS) (French for "sharecroppers") rather than serfs.[42]

In another change, some manors switched from planting grain to raising livestock, which required less labor. The increasing reliance on meat stimulated the spice trade with Asia (for nutmeg, cloves, pepper, curry, sugar, and cinnamon) and Africa (for pepper and salt). Moreover, many doctors falsely believed that nutmeg was a cure for the plague, a circumstance that greatly increased the demand for the spice.[43]

Further, with the population reduced by one-third, there was now plenty of land for all, and – for awhile – assarting ceased. The German drang nach osten ended, much to the relief of the Poles and Czechs who had been its victims. Suddenly freed from foreign attack, Poland revived under King Ladislas II (1386-1434). The Crusades against the Middle East also came to a close.[44]

---

[36] Ibid, 1-15, 106-113.
[37] Gottfried, *Black Death*, 54-76; Cantor, *In the Wake of the Plague*, 29-62.
[38] Gottfried, *Black Death*, 77-103.
[39] Ibid, 104-128.
[40] Cantor, *In the Wake of the Plague*, 5.
[41] Gottfried, *Black Death*, 135-140.
[42] Ibid, 135-140.
[43] Ibid, 138.
[44] Ibid, 136.

Ironically, in the long run the Black Death resulted in an increase in the population. Peasants responded to the labor shortage by having more children. And with more food to go around, more children survived infancy. The result was a sharp increase in the birthrate, and by 1500 Europe's population had recovered. The birthrate continued to be high, however, so that after 1500 overpopulation once again became a problem.

In the bourgs, officials responded to the plague by forming the West's first public health departments, which stimulated the development of modern medicine and hygiene. Innovative burgomasters implemented new pest control programs, hiring experts like the fabled Pied Piper of Hamlin (the Pied Piper himself was a myth, but Hamlin was a real, rat-infested bourg in northern Germany) to exterminate the rats that they suspected of somehow being linked to the plague.[45]

When lords died without heirs, rich bourgeois sometimes purchased their manors and became rentiers, thus undermining trifunctionalism by contributing to the rise of the bourgeoisie.[46]

Finally, the inability of the Church to halt the plague through prayer (along with public dislike of the harsher penances some of the priests were handing out) undermined confidence in Holy Mother Church herself.

The four pillars of the traditional West were beginning to crumble.[47]

The Hundred Years War

War as well as disease contributed to the decline of traditional culture in the West, according to Barbara Tuchman. When the king of France died in 1328 without a direct heir, his distant cousin Edward III of England laid claim to the throne. The French lords, however, disliked the idea of having an English king. They backed another claimant instead, installing him as Philippe VI. Furious, Edward invaded France, plunging the two countries into a devastating war that would last for more than a century and in the process fundamentally transform both of them.

During the first phase of the war (1328-64), the English generally won. Their knights routed the French at Crecy (Kray-SEE) (1346) and Poitiers (Pwah-tee-AY) (1356). But after that the war bogged down. During the second phase (1364-1415) the fighting was indecisive. A stalemate occurred, and many knights died on both sides. The stalemate was particularly bad for England, which had a much smaller population than France, and hence fewer knights.

The third, decisive phase (1415-29) began with a great English victory at the Battle of Agincourt (Ah-zhin-COR) (1415). Running desperately low on knights, the English king reorganized his army, replacing his knights with yeomen armed with longbows. When the mounted French knights charged, the English yeomen opened fire. Arrows, propelled by the powerful bows, ripped through the knights' armor and the French were defeated. It was the beginning of the end for Medieval knights as a fighting force. The English also began using total war, destroying French manors as well as French armies in a desperate attempt to ruin the French economy and end the stalemate.

But the French quickly adapted to the new warfare and adopted the English tactics themselves. Led by a mysterious teenage girl, Jeanne d'Arc (Joan of Arc), who claimed to have been guided by visions from God, they won the pivotal Battle of Orleans in 1429. Although English troops later captured Jeanne and burned her at the stake as a witch, French forces – benefiting from a larger population base, fighting on home soil, and the inspiring memory of the martyred Sainte Jeanne – turned the tide. The war was over. But it had brought about profound change.

The Hundred Years War undermined feudalism. It replaced mounted knights with yeoman archers. It showed that dynastic succession did not always lead to a peaceful transfer of power. By finding a place in the army for commoners, it undermined trifunctionalism. Finally, kings realized that the key to winning wars was not to accumulate knights as vassals, but instead to raise taxes and hire large numbers of mercenary archers and pikemen – a very modern idea, indeed.[48]

The Wars of the Roses

No sooner was the Hundred Years War over than England plunged into a dynastic crisis of its own. It began when several of the great lords who were allied with the self-important Duke Richard of York (and who were backed by the increasingly vocal London bourgeoisie) demanded that hapless King Henry VI (the loser in the Hundred Years War) dismiss several of his advisors who were allied with Richard's enemy, the cranky, haughty, much-disliked Duke of Lancaster.

Behind the demand lay a more serious problem. Rootless veterans of the Hundred Years War – yeoman mercenaries – wandered the countryside, causing trouble. Henry was an indecisive king, unable to enforce the

---

[45] Ibid, 104-128.
[46] Ibid, 146-147.
[47] Gottfried, *Black Death*, 129-160; Cantor, *In the Wake of the Plague*, 27-146.
[48] Barbara W. Tuchman, *A Distant Mirror: The Calamitous Fourteenth Century* (1978), passim; Edward Peters, *Europe and the Middle Ages* (1989), 293-302.

law and bring order to the realm. The strong-willed Richard thought he could do better. And the order-loving bourgeoisie were quite willing to let him try.

The Yorkists (whose symbol was a white rose) defeated the Lancastrians (whose symbol was a red rose) in battle in 1455 and captured Henry. Imprisoning the old king, Duke Richard ruled as regent until 1460, when he was killed in another battle with a Lancastrian force, which recaptured Henry. At that point Richard's son, the rage-filled, ambitious young Edward of York, took command of the Yorkist forces and counterattacked, pillaged the Lancastrian manors, and killed any peasants who accidentally got in his way. Total war had come to stay. Edward re-recaptured Henry, who finally died in 1464. The old king out of the way at last, Edward of York proclaimed himself King Edward IV.

Supported by the bourgeoisie, who as always, sought law and order above all else, Edward IV ruled England ruthlessly, by fair means and foul. He deliberately weakened the power of the great lords, even those who had once supported him. He executed most of the Lancastrians. Only sporadic fighting continued. The Yorkists had won.

However, in 1470 Edward IV himself died, under mysterious circumstances. By law, the crown passed to his son, the boy-king Edward V. But the real power behind the throne was the boy's sinister uncle, Richard of York. Falsely accusing his opponents of witchcraft, Richard succeeded first in having young Edward V declared illegitimate (which meant that he was not legally entitled to be king), then murdered him, and finally in 1483 crowned himself King Richard III. He was one of the most despised monarchs in English history.

By now pretty much everyone in England was disgusted with the whole struggle. There had been much more bloodshed, destruction of property, and political turmoil than the bourgeoisie had bargained for. But people were also afraid of Richard III, and most of the older Lancastrian lords, who ordinarily would have been the ones to lead the opposition, were dead, the victims of years of Yorkist persecutions. It thus fell to a young Lancastrian lord, Henry Tudor, the Earl of Richmond, the well-liked, levelheaded lover of Richard's comely niece Elizabeth of York (Edward IV's daughter and Edward V's older sister), to organize the opposition. Henry needed to act quickly, for the rapacious Richard, anxious to cement his power, wanted the fair Elizabeth for himself! Henry, who was also the half-nephew of old King Henry VI, succeeded in uniting both the majority of the Yorkists (who, as it turned out, were more loyal to the fair Elizabeth than to the sinister Richard) and the remaining Lancastrians into a single force. His army defeated and slew Richard in 1485 at Bosworth Field. Henry married Elizabeth and became King Henry VII. The war was over at last.

But the years of fighting had undermined feudalism even further, at least in England. Most of the soldiers who fought in the war were mercenaries, not knights, and much of the action had been financed not by the lords but by the London bourgeoisie. And once again, the weaknesses of dynastic succession had been revealed. Trifunctionalism also declined, for the war had weakened the lords and built up the bourgeoisie.[49]

The Italian Revolts

Just as the Hundred Years War and the Wars of the Roses undermined feudalism and trifunctionalism in France and England, so the Italian Revolts weakened the old order in Italy and Germany.

In the High Middle Ages most of northern Italy had been part of the vast Holy Roman Empire, or German Reich ("Reich" is the German word for "Empire"), the largest and most important Western state in the High Middle Ages. The Reich had been declining for about a century, but it was still strong and much respected by the other, smaller Western states. Although a little more than half of the inhabitants of the Reich were Germans, substantial numbers of Italians, Rhenish, French, Provencals, Dutch, Flemings, Czechs, Poles, and Danes lived there as well. The Reich was large, ramshackle, and decentralized. It had no permanent capital city, and its government was located wherever the kaiser (emperor) happened to be at the moment.

Between 1250 and 1350 the various city-states in northern Italy revolted against the Reich and became independent. (A city-state is a country composed of a central bourg, along with the surrounding countryside. Most city-states were geographically about the size of Rhode Island.) The revolts were led not by the Italian lords, but by the bourgeoisie, who used their growing wealth to hire mercenary troops. Independence achieved, they organized their city-states into miniature oligarchic republics, where they held most of the power. The most important of the Italian city-states were Florence (a major cultural center), Pisa (the site of a great university), Milan (a cloth-producing bourg in the heart of Italy's best farm country), and Venice and Genoa (seaports and commercial centers).

The Italian revolts also brought change in Germany. Discouraged by the inability of the kaiser and his knights to defeat the upstart Italian bourgeoisie and their mercenary armies, the German lords reorganized the Reich, stripping the kaiser of much of his power. They even eliminated dynastic succession, declaring that henceforth all kaisers would be elected by seven of Germany's greatest lords, collectively known as the Electors. Bereft of strong leadership, the Holy Roman Empire continued to decline.[50]

---

[49] A. R. Meyeres, *England in the Late Middle Ages* (1978), 115-131, 199-210; Peters, *Europe and the Middle Ages*, 299; John A. Merriman, *A History of Modern Europe from the Renaissance to the Present* (1996), 197; J. H. Hexter, Richard Pipes, and Anthony Molho, *Europe Since 1500* (1971), 208.

[50] Hexter, *Europe Since 1500*, 26-30.

Peasant Revolts

Two major peasant revolts also occurred during the Late Middle Ages. In neither case did the peasants seek to overthrow the old Medieval system of manorialism, feudalism, Roman Catholicism, and trifunctionalism. Rather, they revolted because – like William Langland – they believed that the lords were not doing their proper duty under the system. In other words, the rebels were traditionalists who sought to preserve Medieval society in its ideal form, not destroy it.

For precedent, recall the famous legend of Robin Hood, which is based loosely on events in the 1200s, during the High Middle Ages. In the story, the Merry Men were a band of outlaw English rebels. They were comprised mainly of peasants like Little John, Alan a Dale, and Will Scarlet, but were actually led by a renegade priest, Friar Tuck, and a minor knight, Sir Robin of Locksley. And they fought not to overthrow the English monarchy, but to preserve it – to halt the plans of the regent, Prince John, and his henchman, the Sheriff of Nottingham, from usurping the throne while good King Richard I Lionheart was away on Crusade.

Two similar – although far larger – peasant revolts occurred in the Late Middle Ages: the Jacquerie (Zhahk-ah-REE) in France (1358) and Wat Tyler's Peasant Revolt in England (1381). In each case, the peasants revolted because they believed the lords were abusing them, contrary to the ideal of manorialism. In each case the rebels turned to the king for help. And in each case the king sided with the lords, put down the rebellion, and executed the bewildered leaders.

The peasants were shocked. The king, after all, was supposed to protect them from oppressive lords, not side with them. A few peasants – the English priest John Ball, for example – wondered on their way to the scaffold if the old traditional Medieval system might not be all it was cracked up to be. Recalling that there had been neither lords nor peasants in the biblical Garden of Eden, Ball bitterly rhymed, "When Adam delft and Eve spann / Who was then the gentleman?" But most of the peasant rebels simply shrugged and returned to their labors. They were not yet ready to challenge the old order.

Still, in both cases the revolts subtly undermined the old system, by shifting power from the lords (who were unable to suppress the revolts by themselves) to the kings (who, thanks to their mercenary bowmen, were).[51]

The Great Schism

By the end of the High Middle Ages the papacy had become even more highly politicized than usual. The pope and most of the ranking bishops had become less and less pious churchmen than venal Italian politicians using Rome (the Church's headquarters throughout most of the Middle Ages) as their base of operations. Northern kings, lords, and others in France, Germany, England, and elsewhere in the Champion Lands resented this Italian domination of the Church. In 1309 the crafty King Philippe IV of France openly challenged the status quo by engineering the election of a French pope, who promptly moved the Church's headquarters north of the Alps to the sleepy French bourg of Avignon. This event, too, would contribute to the decline of Medieval civilization.

Italians were outraged. They were sure that it was a dastardly French scheme to undermine the independence of Holy Mother Church. The Italian writer Petrarch, recalling the biblical story of how the ancient Hebrews had been held captive in Babylon, acidly referred to the move to Avignon as the "Babylonian Captivity" of the papacy. For the most part, the Avignon popes were good popes, but because they were based in France many Europeans didn't trust them. Finally, in 1377 the Italians elected their own pope, based once again in Rome.

Now there were two popes, one in Rome and one in Avignon, which meant that the Church was hardly universal. Each pope appointed his own bishops, who argued with each other about who were the "true" bishops. Each bishop invested his own priests, who argued about who were "true" priests. Under Roman Catholic doctrine, only officially invested priests could preside over the Church's seven holy sacraments – communion, baptism, confirmation, penance, matrimony, holy orders, and last rites. What happens, people wondered, if my priest is not a "real" priest? Am I not really baptized? Have I not really received absolution for my sins? Is my marriage legitimate? Are my children bastards? Can I get into heaven? In an Age of Faith, these were serious questions. Without one truly universal church, how would people know which church was the "real" Church, which interpretations of scripture were correct and which were heresies? At mass, believers continued to recite the Church's time-honored Nicene (NYE-seen) Creed, which contained the key phrase, "I believe in one Church, holy, catholic, and apostolic." But in the days of the Great Schism those words seemed a mockery.

Eventually the Great Schism ended. In 1418 the Council of Constance – a great meeting of Church leaders from all over Europe held in the German bourg of Constance – agreed to move the papacy from Avignon back to Rome. But faith in Holy Mother Church had been shaken, and people were now asking questions.[52]

---

[51] Tuchman, *Distant Mirror*, 171-182; 372-378.
[52] Peters, *Europe and the Middle Ages*, 282-286; Hexter, *Europe Since 1500*, 39-43; Merriman, *History of Modern Europe*, 94-96; Tuchman, *Distant Mirror*, 328-339.

Modernization Theory

Historians refer to the fourteenth and fifteenth centuries not only as the Late Middle Ages (the era when traditional medieval culture began to wane) but also as the Renaissance (the age when modern culture began its rise). "Renaissance" is a French word that means "rebirth," and historians originally applied it to the period 1310-1550 because they viewed it as a time when western Europeans rediscovered many of the "lost" aspects of the old Classical Civilization. But in truth, the era was more of a "naissance" ("birth") than a "renaissance" ("rebirth"), for it was a time when new, modern ideals were being born.

Many historians explain the changes that occurred during the Renaissance by invoking something known as "modernization theory." Modernization theorists claim that, while traditional people were rural, agrarian, and theocentric, modern people are urban, industrial, and scientific. While traditional people stressed membership in a community and preferred small, local governments, modern people emphasize individual rights and believe in strong centralized governments. While traditional people valued stability, modern people believe that change is not only possible, but desirable. While traditional people clung to the values of the peasantry, modern people reflect the value system of the bourgeoisie.

According to modernization theory, traditional cultures and modern cultures are total opposites. The historian Richard D. Brown writes:

> In large part the model of a modern society may be seen as the polar opposite of the traditional model. While stability rules one, dynamism pervades the other. Change, in all spheres of life, is a characteristic feature of the modern society, and from this reality flow many of its distinctive elements. The desire to manipulate the environment through the use of technology becomes a prevalent goal, since change (for the better) is viewed as a real possibility. The passage of time is no longer an endless repetition; instead time is a scarce commodity proceeding rapidly into the future. To a significant degree life becomes a race against death for achievement.[53]

According to modernization theory, modern cultures are not only more dynamic and technology-oriented than traditional cultures, but also more cosmopolitan, commercial, and diverse, with a greater toleration for minorities. Writes Brown:

> Where localism was dominant in the traditional model, cosmopolitanism rules modern society. Extensive commerce and communications widen physical as well as psychological experience. The economy itself is so specialized that social diversity grows out of the structure of production and distribution in addition to regional variation. The social structure and the roles it creates no longer follow the prescriptions of the past, and instead conform to the shifting character of the economic and political structure.[54]

Modernization theory also claims that modern cultures are more rationalistic than traditional cultures. "To say that rationalism is dominant [in modern cultures] is not to suggest that modern society is any more rational in objective terms than traditional society," writes Brown, but "the difference is in the deliberate, self-conscious belief in rational analysis as a way of understanding reality rather than turning to supernatural means."[55] This emphasis on rationalism rather than faith makes modern cultures more scientific than traditional cultures. It also makes modern politics more theoretical. Brown explains:

> The political order of the modern model is distinguished by its origins, its self-conscious theoretical justification, its levels of popular participation, and its bureaucracy. Modern polities never presume to possess an ageless, distant past. Instead, they claim a specific, historic beginning, and with this beginning goes an explanation seeking to justify the polity to its constituents. The form may be authoritarian or parliamentary, it may be highly centralized or not, but whatever its particular character, it always possesses a starting point and a rationale. Its origins are human and known rather than divine or mysterious.[56]

Finally, modernization theory holds that modern culture is more individualistic than traditional culture, which was more community-oriented. Brown writes, "Whereas the traditional personality shows passive and localist proclivities, the modern personality exhibits a significant drive for individual autonomy and initiative."[57]

World-System Theory

Not all historians accept modernization theory, however. A vocal minority strongly disagrees with it. The bone of contention is that modernization theory is based on the assumption that in every historical epoch there

---

[53] Richard M. Brown, *Modernization: The Transformation of American Life, 1600-1865* (1976), 12.
[54] Ibid, 13.
[55] Ibid, 14.
[56] Ibid, 15.
[57] Ibid, 15.

exists a consensus or general agreement among most people about what constitutes a good and just society. Thus, according to modernization theory, in traditional cultures most people accept traditional values, while in modern cultures most people subscribe to modern beliefs.

But advocates of world-system theory (the chief alternative to modernization theory) challenge this assumption. They believe that societies are characterized not by consensus, but by conflict – conflict among ethnic and religious subcultures, states, and various social classes; conflict between men and women; and conflict between people and their environment. In other words, rather than one traditional value system (and thus one traditional culture), world-system theorists argue that many different, competing value systems existed in the Middle Ages and later: separate value systems for the peasants, lords, and clergy; for men and women; for Christians, Jews, pagans, and heretics; for farmers and city people; and for Poles, Italians, and other ethnic groups – not to mention all of the value systems of the world's other civilizations with which the West frequently came into conflict. Historical change occurred when those different systems came into conflict with each other – conflicts that world-systems theorists view as inevitable – and in process were forced to transform themselves.

World-system theorists believe that concepts like "traditional" and "modern" are in reality culture-biased generalizations; that what modernization theorists think of as "modern" is in fact nothing more than their own personal value system, the value system of the Western white male bourgeoisie, and it only seems modern because the modernization theorists mistakenly think of themselves as typical of the modern age. But that, say the world-system theorists, is not true. The working class, women, ethnic and religious minorities, and people outside of the West have different values.

World-system theorists thus reject the idea that there are only two cultural archetypes, traditional and modern. They believe instead that numerous such types exist. Thomas Shannon, a proponent of world-system theory, writes:

> World-system theorists reject the structuralist-fundamentalist theory of modernization, which considered societies relatively stable systems of interrelated parts. Each part, such as the kinship system, did something necessary (had a "function" or social consequence) for the other parts and for the system as a whole. Each part was related to and dependent upon the others. Social change was therefore the process by which the social system gradually adapted to a changing environment. Because of the system's interrelatedness, if once one element of the system changed, the others had to change.[58]

Shannon cites what he considers to be five major problems with modernization theory. First, he does not agree that societies are as stable as modernization theorists believe; rather, he thinks that all societies have fierce internal conflicts and rivalries (based on class, gender, religion, ethnicity, etc.), and it is these conflicts, not consensus, that precipitate major historical change. Second, he does not agree that the various parts of societies are as interrelated as modernization theorists think they are; it is possible, he believes, to change one part without fundamentally affecting the others (in other words, a culture might exhibit a combination of "modern" and "traditional" characteristics without being schizophrenic). Third, he believes that modernization theory is based primarily on the experience of Western Civilization and does not sufficiently take into account changes that have occurred in other parts of the world. Fourth, he thinks that modernization theory errs in presupposing that historical change is normally gradual or "evolutionary" and argues instead that abrupt or "revolutionary" changes like conquest or colonization are actually more common. Fifth, he believes that modernization theory does not sufficiently "take into account the role of power, exploitation, and conflict in the relationships both within and among societies."[59]

In this book, I will usually take the perspective of modernization theory. However, I hold open the possibility that the criticisms of world-system theorists like Shannon might be valid. In the end you, as mature students of history, will have to make up your own minds about which theory, modernization theory or world-system theory, in your opinion sufficiently explains the history of the West from the 1300s to the present.

The Renaissance

There were two phases to the Renaissance. During the first phase, c. 1310-1400, modernization was confined mostly to the newly independent city-states of northern Italy – Florence, Venice, Milan, Pisa, Genoa, and others – and so is often called the Italian Renaissance. After 1400 it spread to the rest of Western Europe (aided by a new invention, the printing press, which first appeared in the West in c. 1450), and hence is known as the Northern Renaissance. (According to some scholars, the Northern Renaissance did not end with the Late Middle Ages in 1500, but continued on into the 1500s the early 1600s – thus incorporating the Reformation and the era of Shakespeare and Cervantes.)

As the power and prestige of the Western lords declined, the fortunes of the bourgeoisie rose. It was they who had organized and financed the Italian Revolts and who governed the newly independent Italian city-states. It was they who organized and maintained the vital trade networks that transported food and fuel from the far-

---

[58] Thomas R. Shannon, *An Introduction to the World-System Perspective* (1996), 2.
[59] Ibid, 8.

flung rural regions to the hungry bourgs. It was they who implemented the new public health systems that had emerged in the wake of the Black Death. It was they who had lurked behind the Wars of the Roses, urging the order-loving Duke Richard of York to usurp the power of the befuddled and ineffective King Henry VI, and who at the war's end stood as new King Henry VII's chief political and economic advisors. It was they who increasingly had come to dominate politics in the West's growing bourgs. And it was they who had used their commercial fortunes to acquire many of Europe's manors in the years following the Black Death. First in Italy, and then in the rest of the West, they had by the mid-1300s become prosperous and powerful enough to imprint their values and ideals onto the rest of Western Civilization. In many ways, the modern Western mind-set was their invention.

There were three principal aspects of Renaissance thought: the switch from theology to humanism, the recovery of Classical learning, and rise of the bourgeois ideal.

Humanism

The term humanism refers to the bourgeoisie's growing preoccupation with matters of the material world, as opposed to the divine world of the afterlife. Traditional writers like Dante and Langland had described Christian theology and cosmography in intricate detail. But Renaissance writers, while remaining deeply religious, began more and more to write about the material world as well. Traditional people had accepted the world the way it was, with all its misery and trouble. They were not happy when bad things occurred, but were nevertheless resigned to them. After all, famines, plagues, and wars were simply God's will. But the humanists of the Renaissance rejected this view. Instead, they came to believe in progress, that with effort, human beings could make the world a better place. They just had to figure out how to do it.

The Florentine author Giovanni Boccaccio (Boh-CAHTCH-ee-oh) (1313-1375) described the impact of the Black Death on Italian society. Baldassare Castiglione (Cah-STIG-lee-ohn) (1478-1529) – the "Miss Manners" of the Renaissance – wrote a how-to book for courtiers, those rich, young bourgeois who hung about the courts of the rulers of the newly independent Italian city-states. The businessman and amateur historian Leonardo Bruni (BREW-nee) (1370-1444) examined the Florentine political system and declared that it depended on the active and virtuous participation of the Florentine bourgeoisie. The sly politician Niccolo Machiavelli (1469-1527), in his famous book *The Prince*, looked at Italian politics in general and gave practical advice – not all of it virtuous – to rulers. Christine de Pisan (Pee-SAHN) (c. 1364-1431), a transplanted Venetian bourgeoise (bor-ZHWAHZ) living in France, wrote about history, virtuous women, and the Hundred Years War. A young English bureaucrat named Thomas More (1478-1535) created a mythical nation he called Utopia as a model for Western leaders to follow.

None of these writers focused primarily on religion, although all of them were devout Roman Catholics and Christian principles permeated their works and provided the vital background for many of their ideas. Rather, they examined most closely the ins and outs of politics and society in *this* world. They did not ignore religion, but they did focus more on everyday life than the afterlife, and on the natural rather than the supernatural.[60]

Renaissance art, like literature, also reflected the new humanism. Italian painters like Leonardo da Vinci (1452-1519), Donata di Donatello (1386-1466), Raffaello da Urbino ("Raphael," 1483-1520), and Michelagnolo Buonarroti ("Michelangelo," 1475-1564) strove for realism rather than iconography in their art. And although they continued to make many religious paintings and sculptures – da Vinci's "The Last Supper" and Michelangelo's "Pieta" and "David" are excellent examples – they also produced scenes of everyday life. The most famous painting of the Renaissance, da Vinci's "Mona Lisa," was, after all, a portrait of an Italian bourgeoise.[61]

Humanism was not a rejection of religion; as has been stated, most of the leading humanists were deeply religious, and religious themes were well represented in Renaissance literature and art. But traditionalists like William Langland feared that old-time religion was under assault, nevertheless. They especially complained about what they considered the new worldliness of the Church itself, and the seeming preoccupation of many of the younger Church leaders with constructing magnificent cathedrals, involving themselves in politics, patronizing Renaissance artists, and encouraging physicians and scientists in their research. A backlash was brewing.

A Classical Revival

Renaissance Europeans also sought to recover Classical learning, much of which had been "lost" (or, more accurately, "misplaced") after the fall of Rome. The advent of the Black Death sparked European physicians to pore over countless Classical medical texts – copied and preserved by generations of Christian, Jewish, and Muslim scholars – searching for cures and treatments. Increased trade, especially across the Mediterranean Sea

---

[60] Renaissance writers are discussed in Merriman, *History of Modern Europe*, 61-65; and Hexter, et al., *Europe Since 1500*, 84-99.
[61] Renaissance artists are discussed in Hexter, et al., *Europe Since 1500*, 99-113.

between Italy and the Middle East, exposed the rising European merchants to Islamic scholarship. European traders discovered that Arab scholars had preserved and translated many Classical texts. As practical businesspeople, the merchants who comprised the core of the bourgeoisie were attracted to the logic and reason of Classical thought.

Petrarch (PEE-trark) (1304-74), a Florentine writer and teacher, was especially enamored of the elegant logic, language, and argumentation that had been used by the first-century BCE Classical Roman statesman, writer, and lawyer Cicero. Petrarch impressed upon his students – who included Boccaccio – the practical value of emulating Cicero's methods of reasoning and seeking workable solutions to life's problems. The way to recognize educated people, Petrarch insisted, was by their clear, persuasive, and grammatical writing. Bruni, too, admired Cicero, and held him out to his fellow Florentines as a prime example of the efficacy of civic duty – the motivating force of all true statesmen, who strove to improve their communities rather than their pocketbooks. No matter that Cicero, like most Classical writers, had been a pre-Christian pagan. No matter that he had been a privileged aristocrat. No matter that he had been a cranky old fusspot. To the Renaissance mind, a good idea was a good idea, and pagan, Muslim, Jewish, or any other kind of learning was every bit as valuable as Christian theology.

The result of all this was a kind of Classical revival. Classical philosophies like Stoicism and Epicureanism were reexamined and tried on again, like old clothes found in the back of a closet that have unexpectedly come back into style. Classical historians, geographers, scientists, and mathematicians were reread with renewed interest. Classical poets like Virgil suddenly found new popularity. Pagan mythology reappeared in art, as in Alessandro di Botticello's ("Sandro Botticelli") "The Birth of Venus," a depiction of the pagan goddess Venus standing splendidly nude on a giant oyster shell – hardly a traditional Christian scene![62]

The Bourgeois Ideal

Also evident in Renaissance thought was the growing influence of what historians call the bourgeois ideal, the value system of the rising bourgeoisie. To be sure, like the humanist poets and artists, the bourgeoisie remained committed to the Christian religion and Christian theology. Most Renaissance bourgeois tried to follow Christ's teachings in their everyday lives. But as men and women of business, they also valued the stuff of trade and commerce, things that shaped their own way of life. The chief elements of the bourgeois ideal were materialism (valuing material goods), formal education (valuing reading, writing, and math, which were key to successful business transactions), civic duty (wealthy bourgeois believed that they had a duty to improve their communities by voting and holding office, especially in the oligarchic republics of north Italy), the bourgeois work ethic (most bourgeois believed that promotions and office-holding should be based on ability, not birth), the rule of law (they believed that the law enforced contracts and kept the highways free of robbers), and – perhaps most important – a belief in progress, that idea that people did not have to accept the misery of the world, but – if they tried – they could make it a better place. For better or worse, these values still remain at the center of modern Western life.[63]

-The Documents-

The Black Death: Giovanni Boccaccio

Giovanni Boccaccio (1313-1375) was the son of an Italian merchant father and French mother. He was born in Paris while his father was there on business, but grew up in the Italian city-state of Florence. As a young man he moved to Naples, another Italian city-state, where he was one of several writers who received the patronage (financial support) of Naples's King Roberto. There, he studied under the great Italian Renaissance humanist scholar, Petrarch. Boccaccio wrote *The Decameron* in 1349-51, while still a student. The book begins with ten young people fleeing from Florence in 1348 to escape the bubonic plague. They reach a peaceful, prosperous countryside, where over a two-week period each takes his or her turn as "king" or "queen" over the others. Each of the "kings" and "queens" tells ten stories – 100 stories in all – and thus the book is really a collection of short stories. The underlying theme of all the stories, however, is the lives and values of the Italian bourgeoisie. Reflecting the growing literacy of the Italian bourgeoisie, Boccaccio intended *The Decameron* to be read, not recited, and for that reason he wrote it in prose, not poetry. The following excerpt, taken from the beginning of the book, describes the impact of the plague on Florence and its people.

---

[62] Merriman, *History of Modern Europe*, 60-61; Hexter, et al., *Europe Since 1500*, 65-69.
[63] Hexter, et al., *Europe Since 1500*, 80-82.

from *THE DECAMERON* [64]

INTRODUCTION

Whenever I reflect how disposed you ladies [Boccaccio directed The Decameron primarily at female readers] are by nature to compassion, I cannot help being apprehensive that the book I now offer for your acceptance should have such a melancholy beginning. For it calls to mind the remembrance of that most fatal plague, so terrible still in the memories of us all, an account of which is in the front of this book. But be not frightened too soon, as if you expected to meet with nothing else. This beginning, disagreeable as it is, is like a rugged and steep mountain placed before a delightful valley, which appears more beautiful and pleasant because the way to it was more difficult, for as joy usually ends with sorrow, so again the end of sorrow is joy. To this short fatigue (I call it short, because it is contained in few words), immediately succeed the mirth and pleasure I had before promised you, and which, but for that promise, you would scarcely expect to find. And in truth, could I have brought you by any other way than this, I would gladly have done it. But, as the occasion of the occurrences about which I am going to treat could not be made without such a relation, I am forced to use this Introduction.

In the year then of our Lord 1348, there happened in Florence, the finest city in all Italy, a most terrible plague that, whether owing to the influence of the planets or that it was sent from God as a just punishment for our sins, had broken out some years before in the East. After passing from place to place and making incredible havoc all the way, it had now reached westward to the above-mentioned city, where in spite of all the means that art and human foresight could suggest, such as keeping the city clear from filth and excluding all suspected persons – and notwithstanding frequent consultations with other peoples in other lands about what else could be done, nor omitting prayers to God in frequent processions – in the spring of the foregoing year it began to show itself in a sad and strange manner.

Different from what it had been in the East, where bleeding from the nose was the fatal prognostic, here there appeared certain tumors in the groin or under the armpits, some as big as a small apple, others as an egg; and afterwards purple spots in most parts of the body, in some cases large and but few in number, in others less and more numerous, both sorts the usual harbingers of death. To the cure of this malady, neither medical knowledge nor the power of drugs had any effect; whether because the disease was in its own nature mortal, or that the physicians (the number of whom, taking quacks and women pretenders into account, was grown very great) could form no just idea of the cause, nor consequently ground a true method of cure – whichever was the reason, few or none escaped, but generally died the third day from the first appearance of the symptoms, without a fever or other bad circumstance attending. And the disease, by being communicated from the sick to the well, seemed daily to get ahead, and to rage the more, as fire will do, by laying on fresh combustibles. Nor was it caught only by conversing with or coming near the sick, but even by touching their clothes, or anything that they had before touched. It is strange, what I am going to mention, for had I not seen it with my own eyes, and were there not many witnesses to attest to it besides myself, I should never venture to relate, however credibly I might have been informed about it – such, I say, was the quality of the pestilential matter as to pass not only from man to man, but what is more strange, and has been often known, that anything belonging to the infected, if touched by any other creature, would certainly infect and even kill that creature in a short space of time. And one instance of this kind I took particular notice of; namely, that the rags of a poor man just dead, being thrown into the street, and two hogs coming by at the same time, and rooting amongst them, and shaking them about in their mouths, in less than an hour turned round, and died on the spot.

These accidents, and others of a like sort, occasioned various fears and devices amongst those people that survived, all tending to the same uncharitable and cruel end, which was to avoid the sick and everything that had been near them, expecting by that means to save themselves. Some, holding it best to live temperately, and to avoid excesses of all kinds, formed into groups and shut themselves up from the rest of the world; eating and drinking moderately of the best, and diverting themselves with music and such other entertainments as they might have within doors, never listening to anything from without, to make them uneasy. Others maintained free living to be a better preservative, and would balk no passion or appetite they wished to gratify, drinking and reveling incessantly from tavern to tavern, or in private houses, which were frequently found deserted by the owners, and

---

[64] Giovanni Boccaccio, *The Decameron by Giovanni Boccaccio*, trans. W. K. Kelly (1895), 1: 7-19.

therefore common to everyone, but avoiding, with all this irregularity, to come near the infected. And such, at that time, was the public distress, that the laws, human and divine, were not regarded; for the officers who should have put them in force being either dead, sick, or in want of persons to assist them, everyone did just as he pleased. A third sort of people chose a method between these two. Not confining themselves to rules of diet like the former and yet avoiding the excesses of the latter, they ate and drank what their appetites required. And instead of shutting themselves up, they walked everywhere, with perfumes and nosegays [i.e., bouquets of flowers] to smell, as holding it best to corroborate the brain, for they supposed the whole atmosphere to be poisoned with the stink of dead bodies, arising partly from the distemper disease itself and partly from the fermenting of the medicines within them. Others of a more cruel disposition, as perhaps the more to keep themselves safe, declared that the only remedy was to avoid it. Persuaded, therefore, of this, and taking care for themselves only, man and women in great numbers left the city, their houses, relatives, and effects [i.e., personal property], and fled into the country; as if the wrath of God had been restrained to visit those only within the walls of the city, or else concluding that none ought to stay in a place thus doomed to destruction.

Divided as they were, neither did all die nor all escape; but falling sick indifferently, as well those of one as of another opinion, they who first set the example by forsaking others now languished themselves without mercy. I pass over the little regard that citizens and relations showed to each other; for their terror was such that a brother even fled from his brother, a wife from her husband, and, what is more uncommon, a mother from her own child. On which account members that fell sick could have no help but what was supplied by the charity of friends, who were very few, or the avarice of servants. And even these were scarce, and at extravagant wages, and so little used to the business that they were fit only to reach what was called for, and observe when their employers died. And their desire of getting money often cost them their lives. From this desertion of friends and scarcity of servants, an unheard-of custom prevailed: no lady, however young or handsome, would disdain being attended by a man-servant, whether young or old it mattered not, and to expose herself naked to him, the necessity of the disease requiring it, as though it were to a woman, which might make those who recovered less modest for the time to come. And many lost their lives, who might have escaped, had they been looked after at all. So that, between the scarcity of servants and violence of the distemper, such numbers were continually dying as made it terrible to hear as well as to behold.

Whence, from mere necessity, many customs were introduced, different from what had been before known in the city. It had been usual, as it now is, for the women who were friends and neighbors to the deceased to meet together at his house, and to lament with his relations. At the same time, the men would get together at the door with a number of clergy, according to the person's status and wealth. And the corpse was carried by people of his own rank, with the solemnity of candles and singing, to that church where the person had desired to be buried. But such custom was now laid aside, and so far from having a crowd of women to lament over them, great numbers of people passed out of the world without a single person present. And few had the tears of their friends at their departure, for now those friends would laugh and make themselves merry, for even the women had learned to postpone every other concern to that of their own lives. Nor was a corpse attended by more than ten or a dozen people, nor were any of those people citizens of high status, but rather fellows hired for the purpose, who would put themselves under the bier [i.e., a platform for transporting dead bodies], and carry it with all possible haste to the nearest church. And the corpse was interred without any great ceremony, and wherever they could find room.

With regard to the lower sort, and many of a middling rank, the scene was still more affecting. [Notice that Boccaccio was not referring to the three traditional Medieval estates of clergy, lords, and commoners, but to something more akin to the urban upper class, middle class, and working class of modern times.] For they staying at home, either through poverty or hopes of succor in distress, fell sick daily by thousands, and, having nobody to attend them, generally died. Some breathed their last in the streets and others shut in their own houses, in which case the stench that came from them made the first discovery of their deaths to the neighborhood. And, indeed, every place was filled with the dead. A method now was taken, as well out of regard to the living as pity for the dead, for the neighbors, assisted by what porters they could meet with, to clear all the houses, and lay the bodies at the doors. Every morning great numbers might be seen brought out in this manner, from whence they were carried away on biers or tables, two or three at a time. Sometimes it has happened that a wife and her husband, two or three brothers, and a father and son, have been laid on together. It has been observed also, whilst two or three priests have walked before a corpse with their crucifix, that two or three sets of porters have fallen in with them, and where they knew but of one, they have buried six, eight, or more. Nor was there any to follow and shed a few tears over them, for things were come to pass that men's lives were no more regarded than the lives of so many beasts. Hence it plainly appeared that the wisest, in the ordinary course of things, and by a common train of calamities, could never be taught – namely, to bear them patiently – this, by the excess of those calamities, was now grown a familiar lesson to the most simple and unthinking. The consecrated ground no longer containing the numbers which were continually brought thither, especially as they were desirous of laying everyone in the parts allotted to their families, they were forced to dig trenches, and to put them in by hundreds, piling them up in rows, as goods are stowed in a ship, and throwing in a little earth till they were filled to the top.

Not to rake any farther into the particulars of our misery, I shall observe that it fared no better with the adjacent countryside. The various manors about us presented the same view in miniature with the city, and you might see the poor distressed peasants with their families, without either the help of physicians or care of servants, languishing on the roads, in the fields, and in their own cottages, and dying rather like cattle than human creatures, and growing dissolute in their manners like the city people, and careless of everything. Supposing every day to be their last, their thoughts were not so much employed in how to improve, as in how to make use of their substance for their present support. It happened that the flocks and herds, and the dogs themselves, ever faithful to their masters, being driven from their own homes, would wander, no regard being had to them, among the forsaken harvest. And many times, after they had filled themselves in the day, they would return of their own accord like rational creatures at night.

What can I say more, if I return to the city? – Unless that such was the cruelty of Heaven, and perhaps of men, that between March and July following, it is supposed, and made pretty certain, that upwards of a hundred thousand souls perished in the city, whereas before that calamity Florence was not supposed to have contained so many inhabitants. What magnificent dwellings, what noble palaces, were then depopulated to the last person! What families extinct! What riches and vast possessions left, and no known heir to inherit! What numbers of both sexes in the prime and vigor of youth – whom in the morning neither Galen, Hippocrates, nor Aesculapius himself [three famous physicians of Classical times], but would have declared in perfect health – after dining [eating their midday meal] heartily with their friends here, have supped [eaten their evening meal] with their departed friends in the other world!

But I am weary of recounting our late miseries. Therefore, passing by everything that I can well omit, I shall only observe that, the city being almost without inhabitants, it happened one Tuesday in the morning, as I was informed by persons of good status, that seven ladies all in deep mourning, as most proper for that time, had been attending divine services (they being now the whole surviving congregation) in the Church of Santa Maria Novella....

The Hundred Years War: Christine de Pisan

Christine de Pisan (c. 1363-1429) helped carry the Renaissance from Italy north to France. Born in the Italian city-state of Venice, she accompanied her parents to Paris in 1369, when she was five or six years old. Her father, Tomasso de Pizzano (the family originally came from the small Italian city of Pizzano, near Venice), joined the court of King Charles (SHARL) V ("the Wise") of France as a royal physician and astrologer. Unlike most Medieval kings, Charles was a scholar, not a warrior, and devoted much of his time and energy to promoting science, literature, and art. Tomasso educated his sons, but as a girl Christine had no formal education, although she did learn to read and write. Christine would always view him as the ideal monarch. When she was fifteen, Christine married Etienne du Castel, a royal secretary. She was deeply in love and would always remember Etienne (Eh-TYEN) as kind, sensitive, and loving. Hungry for knowledge, Christine read widely in history, religion, and other topics, becoming a truly self-educated scholar.

But in her twenties, Christine's life began to unravel. King Charles died in 1380 and his successor, the boy-king Charles VI, reorganized the royal court and reduced Tomasso's salary. Broken, Tomasso died soon after. In 1390 Etienne, too, died suddenly. Only twenty-six, Christine was left a widow, with three children, a niece, two younger brothers, and a mother to support. Worse, Etienne had not told her anything about his financial affairs. As a woman, she was not expected to play a role in business. Numerous unscrupulous creditors appeared, seeking to take advantage of the naive young widow, and it took Christine several years to straighten out Etienne's accounts.

Desperate for income, Christine became a professional writer, the first woman in the West to do so. She penned short poems, long ballads, histories, biographies, and other works of poetry and prose. By her own account, she authored fifteen book-length works and many shorter pieces. There were not yet printing presses in Christine's day (the printing press first appeared in Europe in c. 1450, two decades after her death), so all of her works had to be hand copied and illuminated (illustrated) by scribes and illuminators. Under these circumstances, it was not possible for authors like Christine to sell their books to a mass market – there simply were not enough copies to go around. Consequently, she and other professional writers derived their incomes not from sales, but from the patronage (financial support) of wealthy lords and bourgeois who, influenced by the ideal of civic duty, as a public service paid them to write. Christine's patrons included the king's brother Louis (Loo-EE), the Duke of Orleans, and uncle Philippe, the Duke of Burgundy; Queen Isabeau; and Jean Gerson, the Chancellor of the University of Paris, among others. Written in late Medieval French, her works were also translated into several other languages and were among the first Western books printed after the invention of the printing press in c. 1450. For about a century after her death she remained one of the West's most popular writers.[65]

Artistically, Christine's best works were her short poems. For example, upon Etienne's death she wrote the following haunting poem:

> Anguished grief, immoderate fury,
> Grievous despair, full of madness,
> Endless languor and a life of misfortune,
> Full of tears, anguish and torment,
> Doleful heart, living in darkness,
> Wraithlike body on the point of death,
> Are mine continually without cease;
> And thus I can neither be cured nor die.

But her most historically significant works were those that dealt with the important social and political issues of the day. She wrote political allegories highly critical of the French lords for being too interested in power struggles and warfare, and not paying enough attention to the arts, justice, and the economy. She correctly predicted that, unless the lords put aside their petty squabbles, England would gain advantage in the Hundred Years War, as it did at the Battle of Agincourt. Taking umbrage at the way male writers conventionally portrayed women as weak, conniving, insipid, or unreliable, she responded with a spirited book-length poem, *Cupid's Letter*, in which she resolutely defended women's virtues, vowing, "Between Mother Nature and myself / As long as the world lasts, we won't let / Women be so uncherished and unloved." In a later prose work, *The Book of the City of Ladies*, she presented biographies and stories of great women from history and legend, a riposte to those who thought that women had never done anything important. And in 1429, shortly before her death, she wrote a thundering epic-length poem, *Hymn of Jeanne d'Arc*, which lauded the accomplishments of the young French heroine.

Hymn of Jeanne d'Arc was written in late Medieval French and featured a traditional A-B-A-B rhyme scheme. But it also featured several modern ideas. First of all, it was a paean to a great woman who had accomplished daring deeds far beyond anything that men were capable of doing, and thus can be viewed as proto-feminist. Second, it was a patriotic call to the French people to unite and defend their cherished country against the English invaders, and thus can also be seen as proto-nationalist. Christine viewed the Hundred Years War as a disaster, far more than just another Medieval power struggle. For Christine, far more was at stake than who got to sit on the throne of the France. For her, the war was an epochal death-struggle between two mighty nations, the French and the English, two mortal enemies locked in combat, representing good and evil. Christine loved France with all the fervid intensity of an immigrant, and dearly wanted it to win. Jeanne's decisive role in repelling the invaders seemed to Christine to be … well, miraculous. The poem does not completely break with traditional Medieval values, for it accepts that Jeanne was divinely inspired and exhorts the French knights to fight on for God and king, traditional values. But it goes beyond the traditional and touches the modern when Christine begs her adopted countrymen to battle, too, for their nation, for France itself – a modern viewpoint that embodies the developing bourgeois ideal of civic duty. The language of the poem indicates that Christine herself knew that something new, something unprecedented, something modern, was occurring. The emergence of a woman leader and the rise of a new, powerful, and energetic French patriotism was, she wrote, "*chose est nouvelle!*" – "something that is new!" Change was in the air, and she welcomed it.

from *DITIE DE JEHANNE D'ARC [HYMN OF JEANNE D'ARC]*

> *Je, Christine, qui ay ploure*
> *XI ans en abbaye close,*
> *Ou j'ay tousjours puis demoure*
> *Que Charles (c'est estrange chose!),*
> *Le filz du roy, se dire l'ose,*
> *S'en fouy de Paris de tire,*
> *Par la traison la enclose,*

---

[65] Andrea Hopkins, *Most Wise and Valiant Ladies* (1997), 108-131; Tuchman, *Distant Mirror*, 209-219.

Ore a prime me prens a rire. [66]

I, Christine, who have wept
For eleven years in a cloistered abbey,[67]
Where I have stayed every day
Since Charles (this is a strange thing!),
The son of the king, I dare to say,
Fled from Paris in haste,[68]
Was cloistered by treason,[69]
But now, for the first time, begin to laugh.

I laugh openly for joy,
Because the wintry season
Departs, when I was forced
To confine myself sadly in a cage.[70]
But now I will change my language[71]
From weeping to singing, because I have recovered
The good season.
Well have I endured my part.

In the year one thousand and 429
The sun begins to shine again.
It brings back the good, new season
That no one has seen
For a long time, during which in grief
Most people lived; I myself am one of them.
But I no longer grieve about anything,
Now that I see that which I desire.

* * * *

And you, Charles, king of the French,
Seventh of that noble name,
Who had been crushed by such a great war
Before things turned out all well for you,
Now, by God's grace, see your renown
Lifted on high by the Maiden[72]
Who has made submit beneath your flag
Your enemies (something that is new!)

* * * *

And you, blessed Maiden,[73]

---

[66] The first stanza is from Christine's original late medieval French. The following verse translation is mine. For the original late medieval French version, see Angus J. Kennedy and Kenneth Varty, *Ditie de Jehanne D'Arc* (1977), posted at www.smu.edu/ijas/cdepisan/text.html (retrieved 5/28/2004).
[67] In 1418 Christine moved to a convent in Poissy, northwest of Paris, where her daughter was a nun. The language of her language suggests that she may have moved there as a safe refuge during the turmoil of the war.
[68] Prince Charles, the future King Charles VII of France, son of Charles VI. Charles had fled the capital to escape both English troops and his political enemies among the French lords.
[69] This is probably a reference to the machinations of Jean the Fearless, Duke of Burgundy (the son of Christine's former patron, Philippe the Bold), who was scheming to overthrow the king and gain the throne for himself.
[70] By "wintry season," Christine meant the dark years between the terrible French defeat at Agincourt in 1415 and Jeanne d'Arc's great victory at Orleans in 1429. Christine spent most of those years cloistered at Poissy, neither writing nor publishing.
[71] With the victory at Orleans, Christine had quite literally recovered her voice – her "language" – and once more began to write.
[72] "La Pucelle," literally, "the Virgin," a reference to Jeanne d'Arc, "La Pucelle d'Orleans" ("the Maid of Orleans").
[73] Hopkins points out that Christine began this poem with the phrase "Je, Christine" ("I, Christine"), and now switches to "tu, [Jehanne]" ("you, Jeanne"), giving the work a touching "woman-to-woman" character. Hopkins writes: "There is a most moving resonance about the way in which France's first woman of letters opens her poem; speaking in her own voice and conscious of the fame she has

Are you to be forgotten,
Given that God honored you so much
That you untied the rope
That held France so tightly bound?
Could one ever praise you enough,
When to this land, humiliated
By war, you have bestowed peace?

* * * *

Of what others can more be said,
Or about other great feats of times past?
Moses, upon whom God in His bounty
Many blessings and virtues bestowed,
He delivered, without being wearied,
The people of God out of Egypt,
Miraculously. In the same way, you have redeemed
Us from evil, noble Maiden! [74]

Considering your person,
That you are a young maiden,
To whom God gives the strength and power
To be the champion, and she
Who gives to France the breast
Of peace and sweet nourishment,
And to overthrow the rebels,
Truly you see an extraordinary thing! [75]

For if God performed through Joshua
Such a great number of miracles,
Conquering places, and thrashing enemies,
Holding them with fury, well, Joshua was a man,
Strong and powerful. But you, after all,
Are a woman – a simple shepherdess –
But braver than any man ever was in Rome!
As far as God is concerned, your coming was easily accomplished.

* * * *

Much is made of Gideon,
Who was a simple workman,
And it was God, so the story tells,
Who made him fight. Nobody could stand
Against him, and he conquered everything.
But that miracle is not as striking
As the one God has performed
This time, it is apparent.

* * * *

Ha! What an honor for the feminine
Sex! It is apparent that God loves it,
When all these wretched people

---

achieved for herself after her years of work, she says 'Je, Christine' greets and congratulates 'Tu, Jehanne' – woman speaking to woman – self-taught scholar and author speaking to visionary warrior saint and heroine – an event unprecedented in the whole of European history up to that day" (Hopkins, *Most Wise and Valiant Ladies*, 131).

[74] In this stanza Christine compared the female Jeanne to the male Moses, pointing out that both were saviors of their people.

[75] In this stanza – arguably the heart of the poem – Christine maintains that Jeanne's success came not because she had "masculine" traits, but rather because she was female. Hopkins writes: "Here Christine manages in one stunning metaphor to put her finger succinctly on the enigma and the marvel of Joan of Arc, and also to sum up her own lifelong arguments in favour of recognizing the true value of the female sex. She recognizes that Joan is not merely a pseudo man, a soldier, bullying and swaggering and growing rich on the sufferings of others; Joan is actually motivated by a deep desire to put an end to the conflict, throw the English out of France, restore order and peace, make life tranquil and prosperous again. And this was a role she specifically claimed for women" (Ibid, 131).

Who destroyed the whole kingdom –
Now recovered and made safe by a woman,
Something that five thousand men could not have done –
Along with the traitors have been exterminated.
Before the event no one would scarcely have believed this possible.

A little girl of sixteen years
(Isn't this something quite supernatural?),
Who does not even notice the weight of the arms she bears –
Indeed, it seems that her upbringing
Prepared her for this, so strong and durable is she!
And before her go fleeing
The enemy. Not one of them can stand up to her.
She does this for all to see.

And she drives the enemy out of France,
Recapturing castles and towns.
Never did anyone see greater strength,
Even in hundreds or thousands!
Of our brave and able men,
She is the supreme captain.
Such strength had neither Hector nor Achilles!
This is God's doing. It is He who leads her.

Progress: Thomas More

Thomas More (1478-1535) was an English bureaucrat, statesman, political philosopher, and author who lived during the time of the Northern Renaissance. As a young man, More had joined the small but growing bureaucracy of King Henry VII, the victor in the Wars of the Roses. (More was only eight years old when Henry had triumphed over Richard III at Bosworth Field). Eager and capable, More was soon knighted and rose to become one of the most trusted advisors to Henry's son and successor, Henry VIII. But when Henry VIII broke with the Roman Catholic Church in 1534 and founded the Church of England (an event described in Chapter IV), More refused to support him. For that affront, Henry had him executed. Considering More a martyr to the Catholic cause, the Roman Catholic Church beatified him as Saint Thomas.

More wrote the fictional work *Utopia* in 1515 when he was still a bright-eyed young bureaucrat, full of the hopes and ideals of the Renaissance. In Part I of the novel, he had his several characters meet in France to discuss the ins and outs of European politics; this section of the book is pretty technical, rather dull, and not terribly relevant to today's society. But Part II is much more interesting. In this section one of the characters, a "renowned traveler," described to the others the fictional island nation of Utopia, recently "discovered" in the Americas. The name was a pun: "utopia" is Greek for "nowhere."

More was a sharp critic of traditional Western politics and wanted to reorganize society, to make it more functional, rational, urbane, and humane. In short, he sought progress. Utopia was More's idea of the ideal society, of the way life would be if everything was perfect. In Utopia, duty to the community took precedence over individual liberties. For that reason, it is tempting to conclude that More was a modern socialist or communist. Don't do it! Communism would not be invented for another 300 years. Rather, More's emphasis on the community over the individual reflects traditional Medieval values. It is based on More's vision of Holy Mother Church as (ideally) a community of all believers. In many ways, the nation of Utopia is organized rather like a monastery or convent. This is the great irony of the book: More wanted to modernize Western society, but he based his program on traditional values.

As a Renaissance book, *Utopia* reflects a blend of traditional and modern ideas. On the one hand, Utopian society is communalistic as opposed to individualistic, and Utopians do not value gold, but they do value religion. But on the other hand, Utopian society reflects certain aspects of the bourgeois ideal, such as civic duty and education.

Utopia is also a Renaissance book in the sense that it was part of the era's rediscovery of Classical learning. The idea for the book itself and for many of its particulars came from *The Republic* by Plato (427-347 BCE), a renowned Classical Greek political philosopher who also sought to create a fictional ideal commonwealth.

More wrote *Utopia* in Latin, with elegant and proper grammar, for he was a very learned scholar. But it was soon translated into English and, with the aid of a new invention, the printing press, distributed widely throughout England and the West. (Although first invented centuries earlier in China, the printing press with movable type did not appear in the West until c. 1450, in the Holy Roman Empire. It reached England in c. 1500, shortly before More wrote *Utopia*.) Printed English-language editions of *Utopia* were widely read by the fast-rising English bourgeoisie, who liked of some of More's ideas but disapproved of others. The excerpt below is from a 1904 reprint of Ralph Robynson's 1556 English translation of *Utopia*, which was an improved version of

Robynson's earlier 1551 edition. Robynson's sixteenth-century English differs markedly from our own twenty-first-century language, but it is still readable as "modern" English. It is therefore a good starting point for students who are just beginning to grapple with the intricacies of reading old documents. Try translating it. Notice that Robynson's spelling varies; it is readily apparent that dictionaries did not yet exist in the 1500s. Also notice that numbers were still being rendered in Roman numerals.[76]

from *UTOPIA* [77]

CHAPTER I

The Ilande of Vtopia conteyneth in bredthe in the myddell part of it (for there it is brodest) CC. miles. Whiche bredthe continueth through the moste parte of the lande, sauing that by lytle and lytle it commeth in and waxeth narrower towards both the ends.

* * * *

There be in the Ilande .liiii. large and faire cities or shiere townes, agreyng all together in one tonge, in lyke maners, institucions, and lawes. They be all set and situate a lyke, and in all poyntes fashioned a lyke, as farfurth as the place or plotte suffereth. Of thies cities they that be nighest together be xxiiii. myles a sonder. Again there is none of them distaunt from the next aboue one dayes iorneye a fote.

There cum yearly to Amaurote out of euery cytie .iii. olde men, wyse and well experienced, there to entreate and debate of the common matters of the lande. For thys cytie (because it standeth iust in the muddes of the Ilande, and is therefore moste mete for the embassadours of all partes of the realme) is taken for the chiefe and head cytie. The precincts and boundes of the shieres be so commodiously appointed out, and set furth for the cities, that neuer a one of them all hath of anye side lesse then xx. myles of grounde, and of som side also muche more, as of that part where the cities be of farther distaunce a sonder. None of the cities desire to enlarge the boundes and lymites of their shieres. For they count them selfes rather the good husbandes, then the owners of their landes.

They haue in the countrey in all partes of the shiere howses or fermes buylded, wel appointed and furnished with all sortes of instruments and tooles belonging to husbandrie. Thies houses be inhabited of the cytezens, whiche cum thither to dwel by course. No howsholde or ferme in the countrey hath fewer then .xl. persones, men and women, besides two bonden men, whiche be all vnder the rule and order of the good man and the good wife of the house, beynge bothe very sage and discrete persones. And euery .xxx. fermes or famelies haue one heade ruler, whiche is called a Phylarche, being as it were a hed baylyffe. Out of euery one of thies famelies or fermes cummeth euery yeare into the cytie .xx. persones whiche haue contynewed .ii. yeres before in the countrey. In their place so manye freshe be sent thither out of the citie, whiche of them that haue bene there a yeare all ready, and be therefore expert and conninge in husbandry, shalbe instructed and taught; and they the next yeare shall teache other. This order is vsed, for feare that other skarsenes of victualles or some other like incommoditie shuld chaunce through lake of knowledge, yf they should be al together newe and fresh and vnexperte in husbandrie.

* * * *

CHAPTER III

Euerye thirty families or fermes chewse them yearlye an officer, whyche in their olde language is called the Syphograunte, and by a newer name the Phylarche. Euery tenne Syphoagrauntes, with all their 300 families, bee vnder an officer whyche was ones called the Tranibore, now the chiefe Phylarche.

Moreouer, as concerninge the electyon of the Prynce, all the Syphoagrauntes, which be in number 200, first be sworne to chewse him whome they thynke moste mete and expedyente. Then by a secrete electyon they name prynce one of those .iiii. whome the people before

---

[76] J. Churton Collins, "Introduction," in Thomas More, *Sir Thomas More's Utopia*, ed. J. Churton Collins (1904), vii-lii.
[77] Thomas More, *Sir Thomas More's Utopia*, ed. J. Churton Collins (1904), 48, 50-51, 57-65.

named vnto them. For owte of the .iiii. quarters of the citie there be .iiii. chosen, owte of euerye quarter one, to stande for the election, whiche be put vp to the counsell. The princes office contineweth all his liffe time, onles he be deposed or put downe for suspition of tirannye. They chewse the tranibores yearlye, but lightlye they chaunge them not. All the other offices be but for one yeare. The Tranibores euerye daye, and sumtymes, if neade be, aftener, come into the councell howse with the prynce. Theire councell is concernynge the common wealth. Yf there be annye controuersyes amonge the commoners, whyche be very fewe, they dyspatche and ende them by and by. They take euer ii. Siphograntes to them in cowncell, and euerye daye a newe coupel. And that ys prouydede that no thynge towchyng the common wealthe shalbe confyrmed and ratified, on les yt haue bene reasonede of and debatede iii, dayes in the cowncell, before yt be decreed. It is deathe to haue annye consultatyon for the common wealthe owte of the cownsell, or the place of the common electyon. Thys statute, they saye, was made to thentente, that the prynce and Tranibores myghte not easely conspire together to oppresse the people by tyrannye, and to chaunge the state of the weale publique. Therefore matters of greate weyghte and importaunce be brought to the electyon house of the syphograuntes, whyche open the matter to their familyes; and afterwarde, when they haue consulted among them selfes, they shewe their deuyse to the cowncell. Sumtyme the matter is brought before the cowncell of the hole Ilande.

CHAPTER IV

Husbandrye is a scyence common to them all in-generall, both men and women, wherin they be all experte and cunnynge. In thys they be all instructe euen from their youth; partely in scholes with traditions ans precepts, and partely in the contrey nighe the cytye, brought vp as it wer in playing, not onlye beholdynge the vse of it, but by occasion of exercisinge their bodies practisinge it also.

Besides husbandry, which (as I sayde) is common to them all, euery one of them learneth one or other seuerall and particuler science, as hys owne proper crafte. That is most commonly other clothe-workinge in wolle or flaxe, or masonrie, or the smythes crafte, or the carpentes scyence. For there is none other occupacyon that anye numbre to speke of doth vse there. For their garments, whyche through owte all the Ilande be of one fassion, (sauynge that there is a difference betwene the mans garmente and the womans, betwene the married and the unmaryed), and this one continueth for euer more unchaunged, seemly and comely to the eye, no let to the mouynge and weldynge of the bodie, also fitte bothe for winter and summer; as for thies garments (I saye), euery familye maketh theire owne. But of the other foreseyde craftes euerye man learneth one; and not only the men, but also the women. But the women, as the weaker sorte, be put to the easere craftes. They worke wull and flaxe. The other more laborsome sciences be committed to the men. For the moste parte euerye man is brought vp in his fathers craft. For moste commonly they be naturally therto bente and inclined. But yf a mans minde stonde to anny other, he is by adoption put into a famelye of that occupation which he doth most fantasy. Whome not only his father, but also the magistrates do diligently looke to, that he be putt to a siscrete and an honest householder. Yea and if anny person, when he hath lerned one crafte, be desierous to lerne another, he ys lykewyse suffrede and permytted. When he hathe learned bothe, he occupyeth whether he wyll; onles the cytye haue more neade of the one then of the other.

The chyefe and almoste the onlye office of the Syphograuntes ys to see and take hede that no man sytte ydle, but that euerye one applye hys owne crafte wyth earneste delygence; and yet for all that not to be weryed from earlye in the mornynge to late in the euenynge wyth contynuall woke, lyke laborynge and toylynge beastes. For thys ys worse then the myserable and wretced condytyon of bondemen; whyche neuer the lesse is almoste euery where the lyffe of woorkemen and artyfycers, sauynge in vtopia. For they, dyuydinge the daye and the nyghte into xxiiii. iust houres, appoynte and assygne only vi. of those houres to woorke; iii. before none, vpon the whyche they goo streyghte to dyner; and after dyner, when they haue rested ii houres, then they woorke iii; and vpon that they goo to supper. Aboute viii. of the clocke in the euenynge (cowntynge one of the clocke at the fyrste houre after none) they go to bedde. viii. houres they giue to sleape. All the voide time, that is betweene the houres of woorke, slepe, and meate, that they be suffered to bestowe, euerye man as he lyketh beste hym selfe: not to thyntente they shoulde myspende thys tyme in ryote, or sloughfullenes; but, beynge then licensed from the laboure of theyr owne occupacyons, to bestowe the time wel and thriftily vpon some other good science, as shall please them. For yt ys a solempne custome there, to haue lectures daylye earle in the morning; wher to be present they onlye be constreined that be namelye chosen and appointed to learnynge. How be yt a greate multytude of euerye sorte of people, bothe men and women, goo to heare lectures; some one and some an other, as euerye mans nature is inclyned. Yet, this notwithstonding, yf any man had rathere bestowe thys tyme vpon hys owne occupation (as yt chaunceth in manye, whose myndes ryse not in the contemplatyon of annye scyence liberal) he is not letted nor prohibited, but is also praysed and commended, as profitable to the common wealthe.

****

Now, Syre, in theire apparel marke, I praye yow, howe few woorkemen they neade. Fyrste of all, whyles they be at woorke, they be couered homely with leather or skinnes that will last .vii. yeares. When they go further a brode, they caste vpon them a cloke, whyche hydeth the other homelye apparel. Thyes clookes thoroughe owte the hole Ilande be all of one coloure, and that is the naturall colour of the wul. They therfor do not only spende muche lesse wullen clothe than is spente in othere contreys, but also the same standeth them in muche lesse coste. But lynen clothe ys made wyth lesse laboure, and ys therefore hadde more in vse. But in lynen clothe onlye whytenesse, in wullen onlye clenlynes, ys regardede. As for the smalnese or finesse of the threde, that ys no thynge passed for. And thys ys the cause wherfore in other places .iiii. or v. clothe gownes of dyuers colours, and as manye sylke cootes, be not enoughe for one man. Yea, and yf he be of the delicate and nyse sorte, x. be to fewe; where as there one garmente wyll serue a man mooste commenlye .ii. yeares. For whie shoulde he desire moo? Seeing if he had them, he should not be the better hapt or couered from colde, nother in his apparel any whyt the cumlyer.

-CHAPTER III-
GOD, GOLD, GLORY...AND GRUB:
THE EXPANSION OF THE WEST
c. 1450 – c. 1750

Beginning in the 1400s, Western Europeans in ever-increasing numbers left their troubled, changing homeland and sailed forth to encounter other civilizations. In the process they explored, traded, stole, conquered, enslaved, killed, raped, warred, colonized, farmed, fished, taught, and converted other peoples to Christianity. Historians often sum up the European's motives with the hackneyed phrase, "God, gold, and glory." But the West had another goal, too: grub, or food, for in the Age of Expansion Europe was wracked with food shortages that had been brought by the climatic minimum and ecological crisis. By the time the Age was over, Western Civilization had expanded to include not only its original homeland in Western Europe, but also vast new territories in North and South America, Australia, New Zealand, and other parts of the world. This chapter examines why and how this expansion occurred, focusing first on the role played by the Portuguese Prince Henrique (known in English as Henry the Navigator), second on the role played by the Genoese explorer Cristoforo Columbo (known in English as Christopher Columbus), and third on the experiences of two other key participants, the lyric Portuguese poet Luis Vaz de Camoes and the fiery Spanish friar Bartolome de Las Casas. Like most Westerners, Camoes considered the expansion of the West a great and heroic achievement, and in his poetry he boasted of the bravery and prowess of the explorers. Las Casas, however, took a different view. Deeply ashamed of the ways that Western colonists had abused and exploited the native peoples of the Americas, he pleaded for better treatment. This chapter also explores some of the major consequences of the Age of Expansion: the European conquest of the Americas, the advent of racism and race-based slavery, the creation of the triangular trade and corporations, the emergence of the West and the world's economic and military powerhouse, and the historical process of Westernization.

-The Background-

Prince Henry the Navigator

The story of the expansion of the West begins in the small, impoverished country Portugal. In the early 1400s Christian Portuguese knights banded together to drive the Muslims from the western portion of the rugged Iberian Peninsula and founded the modern state of Portugal, named for the small seaside bourg of Oporto in the northern part of the country that was its original capital. Not stopping there, in 1415 they crossed the narrow Strait of Gibraltar and attacked the Muslims in their North African stronghold of Morocco. One of the younger sons of the Portuguese King Joao (Hoe-OW) I, a twenty-one-year-old warrior knight named Prince Henrique (Hen-REE-kay), planned and executed the attack and captured the thriving commercial city of Ceuta (Say-EWTA). In Ceuta Henrique learned from the Moroccans (whom he and the other Europeans called Moors) that vast reservoirs of valuable gold, salt, and pepper lay to the south, somewhere across the searing sands of the Sahara Desert. Henrique also heard rumors of a mysterious Christian kingdom, the so-called Kingdom of Prester John (it was in fact Ethiopia) located somewhere in the heart of Africa, a potential ally against the Muslims. He may have heard, too, that even farther to the south lay a water route around Africa to the fabled Spice Islands of Asia.

Henrique knew that his father ruled over a poor and troubled kingdom. Small, dry, and mountainous, Portugal produced little in the way of valuable trade goods. Its merchants exported mostly cheap goods (salt, wine, fruit, oil, honey, cork, and dried shellfish) to northern Europe, but imported expensive staples (grain, flour, salted fish, dairy products, and wood for fuel and shipbuilding) and manufactured products (cloth and metal goods). Moreover, Portugal was at the extreme western edge of Europe, on the edge of the sea, where the high cost of transportation drove up prices, and everything from luxuries to manufactured products to vital Asian spices cost more than elsewhere. Nor could Portugal acquire additional farmland by expanding its territory within Europe, for Joao had just recently (in 1411) concluded a 101-year peace treaty with the larger, stronger Christian kingdom of Castile, Portugal's only land neighbor. Portugal's only options were to expand overseas or stay poor.

However, the conquest of Ceuta turned out to be an expensive mistake - a pointless drain on the kingdom's meager treasury. Portugal had to keep several thousand troops stationed in Ceuta, in order to defend the city against a seemingly endless series of Moroccan counter-attacks. Moreover, Henrique's knights had been unable to capture any of the farmland surrounding the city, which meant that the Portuguese had to provision Ceuta themselves, another expense. Worst of all, after the conquest Ceuta's once-flourishing trade with Sub-Saharan Africa - something the Portuguese had been counting on to provide needed income - quickly dried up, diverted by the Moroccans to their own port city of Tangier (Tan-JEER). Portugal attempted to capture Tangier in addition to Ceuta, but failed miserably, repulsed by the superior forces of the mighty Moroccan monarch,

Sala-ben-Sala. These failed attempts at forming an African empire cost Portugal not only money, but also the lives of several thousand of its best troops, including Henrique's own younger brother, Prince Fernando.

Yet the Portuguese could not simply pull out. If they failed to find some way to achieve a victory, they would lose face in Europe. But even worse, without some sort of ongoing holy war against the Muslims to keep them occupied, the bored Portuguese knights might decide to fight among themselves, overthrow the king, terrorize the peasants, invade Castile, or something else equally foolish and destructive. Something had to be done.

Faced with all of these problems, Henrique came up with a plan. It was risky and fraught with difficulties, but if he could pull it off, it would make Portugal rich, mighty, and great. If he could persuade the Portuguese knights to put up their lances and horses and shields and become sea captains instead, he might be able to channel their restless warrior energy towards less destructive ends, sending them forth on glorious overseas quests. If his captains could link up with Ethiopia, the two Christian peoples might join forces and launch a holy war to drive the Muslims out of Africa. If the captains could reach Sub-Saharan Africa by sea, they could trade directly for African gold and pepper, bypassing the avaricious Moroccan middlemen who had hitherto controlled the trade. And best of all, if his captains could circumnavigate Africa and reach Asia by sea, they could bring home valuable cargoes of Asian spices, avoid the powerful Turkish and Italian middlemen who controlled the spice trade, and make a fortune. Here in Africa, Henrique believed, lay Portugal's destiny: a sea empire for God, Gold, and Glory.

Henrique thus turned his castle (manor house) in the sleepy southern Portuguese town of Sagres (Sah-GRESS) into a busy headquarters for exploration. Workmen constructed new docks at the nearby port town of Lagos (LAY-gohs). It was like a fifteenth-century version of NASA, with Sagres as Mission Control and Lagos as Cape Canaveral. Knowing that Portugal was technologically backward, Henrique brought in experienced Jewish and Italian mariners and cartographers to teach his knights how to build and pilot the new ships he intended to build – much as in the 1960s NASA used experienced German rocket scientists. These advisors assembled the new technologies necessary for exploration, imported from the Middle East as part of the Renaissance: astrolabes, magnetic compasses, lateen sails, Hindu-Arabic numerals, and gunpowder. They redesigned the cog, a traditional European ship, adding triangular Arab-style lateen sails, sternpost rudders, and (for defense) high forecastles and aftcastles armed with cannon. The result was an entirely new kind of ship, the sleek, maneuverable, fortress-like caravel, larger, sturdier, and better armed than the Arab dhow, and faster and more maneuverable than the Chinese junk.

Then Henrique sent forth his captains to explore the nearby waters of the eastern Atlantic Ocean and the northwestern coast of Africa. Although he himself never again left Portugal (the expedition to Ceuta was the only time Henrique ever left his homeland), and although he never became king (his father Joao I was succeeded by his older brother, Duarte), he nevertheless became known to history as Prince Henry the Navigator, the greatest of the Portuguese.[78]

The Portuguese Explore Africa

Between 1434 and 1498 one Portuguese caravel after another took its turn beating down the west coast of Africa. As with the exploration of space in the twentieth century, their progress was painfully slow. For the first fifteen years, Henrique's nervous, untested captains refused to sail beyond the safety of Africa's Cabo Bojador (Boh-hah-DOOR), fearful that the water was too shallow for their caravels (it was only about two meters deep along the shore), the currents too strong for their sails, and the sun so hot that it would set their ships on fire. Then in 1435 Captain Gil Eanes (Ee-AH-ness) swallowed hard, crossed himself, and sailed out to sea beyond the sight of the land. He skirted the shallow inshore waters and strong longshore currents and passed Cabo Bojador. It was the fifteenth-century equivalent of putting the first person in space, and Eanes became as famous back home as Yuri Gagarin or John Glenn would five hundred years later. The next year another expedition, led by Captain Afonso de Baldaya, took the same route past Cabo Bojador and continued on to scout the arid region of Rio de Oro, where the golden sands of the Sahara swept right to the edge of the Atlantic. In 1441 Captain Nuno Tristao (TREEST-ow) sailed even further, reaching the sere, white cliffs of Cabo Branco (White Cape). Here, inexplicably (for no plants grew in this desert region that he could see), he found people – probably Tuareg (TEW-ah-reg) nomads who had come by camel from an inland oasis in order to fish or hunt seabirds – and brought home two of them as captives. Three years later Eanes, on another voyage, purchased 200 African slaves from another group of Tuaregs near Cabo Branco, and the Atlantic slave trade began. (When Tristao attempted to capture more slaves at Cabo Branco a few years later, the outraged natives killed him and most of his crew.)

The next year Captain Dinis Dias (Dee-ASS) finally completed the first stage of the exploration of Africa, sailing past the Sahara and coming upon a long, green cape that swept serenely into the turquoise waters of the South Atlantic. He found thousands of people living there. They were Senegalese, black Africans. Dias had passed the Sahara. He named the cape Cabo Verde (VER-day) (Green Cape). Nearby, he saw a mighty river, the Senegal, whose cool, brown waters reached deep into the African interior. The Senegalese told him that millions

---

[78] University of Calgary Applied History Group, www.acs.ucalgary.ca/applied_history, n. p., retrieved 6/2/2003; J. H. Parry, *The Age of Reconnaissance* (1963), 146.

of people lived upriver. The Portuguese had at long last reached Sub-Saharan Africa. It was like reaching the moon.

While Eanes, Dias, and the others mapped the west coast of Africa as far south as Cabo Verde, other Portuguese captains made further out to sea, where they charted the winds and ocean currents. They discovered numerous islands – first the Madeira (Mah-DARE-ah) Archipelago, then the Canaries, the Azores, and finally the Cabo Verde Islands. Except for the Canaries, these islands were all uninhabited, so Portugal "claimed" them by "right of discovery." Taking advantage of the islands' rich volcanic soils and warm semi-tropical climates, the Portuguese cleared trees and built plantations, where they grew sugar cane, grapes, and other valuable crops, using the labor of slaves acquired from the African mainland.

The Portuguese did not establish colonies on the mainland. Tropical diseases like malaria and yellow fever proved to be especially deadly, and the African kingdoms they encountered were far too strong and populous for them to conquer. They did, however, establish trading posts, known as "factories," because the chief merchant in charge was called a "factor." (The captains, as former knights, refused to sully their hands with mundane commerce, and left the business of trade to the professional merchants who sailed with them. Frequently these merchants were Italians, like the tall, prematurely gray Genoese Cristoforo Columbo [1451-1506].)

Whether Portuguese or Italian, the factors swapped European guns, gunpowder, and metal goods for African gold, spices, food, and slaves. At one factory the Portuguese were able to trade for so much gold that they jokingly named the place "El Mina" – "the Mine." They named the various stretches of African coast for the goods they acquired there: the Gold Coast, Grain Coast, Ivory Coast, and ominously, Slave Coast. Henrique himself came to oppose the slave trade as a mistake, but by then it was too late, and he was unable to stop it before his death in 1460.

Yet it was Henrique who established most of the procedures that, in the decades to come, would become the hallmarks of Western expansion. Writes one historian:

> By systematically exploring the African coast, Prince Henry inaugurated a policy of exploration that built upon the knowledge of previous voyages. Instead of remaining content with the extent of existing knowledge, Prince Henry used the end of one voyage as the beginning for the next. Other aspects of Prince Henry's system were equally as remarkable. The Portuguese practice of recruiting [or capturing] members of the indigenous population who became interpreters helped to lay both the intellectual and financial groundwork for future voyages. By using interpreters in this manner, Prince Henry was able to build an effective and reliable source of information about the areas to be explored by Europeans. Interpreters also significantly contributed to the European voyages of exploration by allowing Europeans to communicate with indigenous populations in a peaceful manner. Such relations were important to establishing friendly trade and gathering information.[79]

Other practices that can be traced to Henrique include: the use of Italian navigators, cartographers, and merchants to supplement the work done by his own captains and sailors, the claiming of new territories by "right of discovery," the establishment of large tropical plantations using slave labor, the resulting Atlantic slave trade, the construction of trading factories, the fighting with the Muslims, the conversion of other peoples to Christianity, and the judging of non-Western peoples by Western cultural standards.

After Henrique's death the Portuguese government took over the project – it was by then far too big for private enterprise to handle – and more expeditions were sent forth. The government also dispatched a covert agent – the wily spy Pedro da Covilha (Co-VEEL-ah) – to the Middle East, where he secretly copied Arab maps of the northeast coast of Africa. Then in 1488 Captain Bartolomeo Dias rounded the southern tip of Africa (he named it the Cape of Storms, but the Portuguese king changed it to the Cape of Good Hope) and at long last glimpsed the Indian Ocean. Running low on supplies, however, he returned home without going any further.[80]

The Portuguese Reach Asia

In 1497-98 the captain-knight Vasco da Gama (GAH-mah) sailed from Portugal to India and back again, the first to do so. Impatient, vain, hard-driving, hungry for glory, and prone to violence, Gama was a typical fifteenth-century explorer. He made more enemies than friends. Following a minor disagreement, he bombarded the Muslim city of Mozambique (mo-zam-BEEK) on the east coast of Africa. In city after city, he received a chilly reception from the Africans, most of whom were Muslims and not at all pleased to see a fleet of well-armed caravels warping into their harbors, dun-colored sails emblazoned with the bright red crosses of Christendom. In all likelihood, Gama would not have made it from Africa across the Indian Ocean to India (the last leg of his journey) had he not succeeded in acquiring an experienced navigator, the Omani mariner Ibn Majid, along the way. But with Majid's help, the little fleet managed to cross the Indian Ocean in only twenty-eight days. Gama received an even colder reception in India than he had in Africa. "May the devil take thee!"

---

[79] University of Calgary Applied History Group.
[80] Ibid.; Parry, *Age of Reconnaissance*, 146-153.

one Indian told him after his sailors desecrated a Hindu shrine. "What brought you hither?" asked another. He could not have been pleased when Gama replied ominously that he had come in search of spices – and Christians. Gama further alienated the Indians when he kidnapped locals to act as "interpreters." They were glad to see him go.

Three things surprised Gama about the Indian Ocean spice trade, and he was shrewd enough to take advantage of them. The first was that, rather than two or three vast oriental empires as he had expected, most of the land along the coast was divided into small, weak city-states, ripe for plunder. The second was that African and Asian merchants had been trading with each other for centuries, and across vast distances; in India he found goods that had come from Europe, North Africa, Malaya, China, Japan, the Middle East, and East Africa. Over the years the Indian Ocean merchants had developed their own set of rules for commerce, a system that worked so well that their ships – mostly sleek but small Arab dhows – were only lightly armed. The third was that European trade goods were greatly inferior to those of Asia and Africa, and as a result most of the Indian Ocean merchants didn't really want them. Europe's major export was heavy woolen cloth, which was not exactly in great demand in the steamy tropics where most people preferred cotton or silk. To make money in the spice trade, the West was going to have to come up with new products that the Asians wanted.[81]

The next year Gama returned to India at the head of a large fleet of caravels, bristling with cannon, and defeated a combined Indian-Ottoman fleet sent to stop him. The key element operating in da Gama's favor was the fact that the Indian Ocean merchants did not heavily arm their ships, and neither the Ottoman Empire nor the various Indian city-states had sufficient well-armed warships to repulse the invaders. But the caravels were also better warship than the smaller, slighter, dhows. Following his victory, Gama established a lucrative "sea empire" in the Indian Ocean. Gama and his successor, Duke Afonso da Albuquerque, constructed a string of fortified factories at strategic locations along the coast, including Mozambique (on the coast of Africa), Hormuz (Hor-MOOZ) (at the entrance to the Persian Gulf), Goa (on the coast of India), and Malacca (Mah-LAH-kah) (at the entrance to the China Sea), ensuring that Portugal would control the Indian Ocean and the spice trade well into the 1600s. So important was Malacca to global commerce that its name gave rise to the Arabic word *malakat*, meaning "market." [82]

The Spanish Conquer America

Meanwhile, the two old Medieval Christian kingdoms of Castile and Aragon had joined forces to drive the Muslims out of the rest of the Iberian Peninsula. To seal their alliance, Castile's shrewd, hard-driving, Muslim-hating Queen Ysabel I (r. 1475-1504) married Aragon's thoughtful young bachelor King Fernando II (r. 1479-1516). In 1492 the two monarchs conquered the Muslim Kingdom of Granada (Grah-NAH-dah), the last Muslim stronghold in Iberia. They then merged the three old kingdoms – Castile, Aragon, and Grenada – to form the mighty new super-state of Spain.

Eager to have Spain join in Portugal's overseas successes, Ysabel hired the eccentric Genoese-Portuguese navigator and factor Cristoforo Columbo ("Cristobal Colon" in Spanish, "Christopher Columbus" in Latinized English) – who had previously sailed to Africa with the Portuguese, worked as a factor at El Mina, married a minor Portuguese noblewoman, and lived for a time on the Portuguese island of Madeira – to reach Asia by sailing west, an undertaking that most sober scholars knew was impossible in a small sailing ship like a caravel (no caravel was big enough to carry the supplies necessary to last the entire trip).

Instead of Asia, Columbo found America. (Indeed, if America had not been there, Columbo and his crew would certainly have starved long before their three little caravels could have reached Asia.) Did he, therefore, "discover" America? Hardly. First of all, millions of people already lived there, the Native Americans, the descendants of at least three waves of immigrants who had trekked from Siberia to Alaska thousands of years earlier. The earliest wave, the so-called Paleo-Indians, had arrived perhaps as early as 30,000 BCE, although the date is little better than a guess; the most recent wave, the Inuit (In-OO-it) (Eskimos), had made their journey around 5,000 BCE. Second, other Westerners had been to America before Columbo. Viking sea rovers had rowed their dragon-prowed longships across the North Atlantic some time near the beginning of the High Middle Ages, founding colonies on Greenland and Newfoundland. However, cut off from the rest of the West by sea ice during the climatic minimum, prevented by the deteriorating climate from raising enough hay for their livestock, and outfought by the better-adapted Inuit, the Viking colonies had disappeared by the time of Columbo's voyage -- although legends and rumors of them still existed in Scandinavia. But more important than the Vikings, scores of Western fishermen – Basque, English, Irish, French, and perhaps even Portuguese – probably frequented the cold, fertile waters off the northeastern coast of North America before 1492. Driven ever further out to sea looking for food to feed the West's hungry masses, aided in their search by compasses and astrolabes, the canny captains of Europe's ever-expanding fishing fleets would have had little reason to publicize their voyages or give away the locations of their secret fishing grounds.

---

[81] University of Calgary Applied History Group; Parry, *Age of Reconnaisssance*, 153-158.
[82] Charles Corn, *The Scents of Eden: A History of the Spice Trade* (1998), 3-23; Parry, *Age of Reconnaissance*, 158-162.

Thinking he was in the East Indies (it was really the West Indies), Columbo claimed all the islands he saw for Spain by "right of discovery." He also insisted on renaming them. The second-largest and most populous island he named "Espanola" ("Hispaniola" in English), or "Little Spain." The fact that several million people already lived there – and that these people had their own towns, farms, governments, customs, laws, and their own name for the island, Haiti – does not seem to have mattered.

From the time of Columbo's voyage until the 1700s, several thousand Spanish colonists, the self-styled *conquistadors* ("conquerors"), carved out a vast new empire in America – which they New Spain – that ultimately stretched from Florida, New Mexico, and California in the north to the stormy southern tip of South America in the south, excluding Portuguese Brazil. The colonists forced the Native Americans to work for them, first as slaves and later – after Spain's King Carlos I (r. 1516-56) (the grandson of Ysabel and Fernando) outlawed Indian slavery – as *peons*, or peasants. They were the diggers in the Spaniards' gold and silver mines, the field hands on the Spaniards' sprawling sugarcane plantations, and the *llaneros* (cowboys) on the Spaniards' cattle ranches. Vast quantities of gold, silver, sugar, leather, and other products were brought back to Europe. Spain became rich and powerful. When 75 to 95 percent of the Native Americans died (mostly from diseases accidentally introduced from Europe, such as smallpox, chicken pox, influenza, and measles), the Spanish imported slaves from Africa to take their place.[83]

Other Western Countries Expand Overseas

In the 1600s and early 1700s England, France, and the Netherlands joined the scramble for colonies and created their own overseas empires, similar in form if not in size to those of Portugal and Spain. England's chief colonies lay on the North American mainland and in the West Indies, forming a long, serpentine arc that stretched from the icy, fog-bound fishing colony of Newfoundland in the north to the lush, tropical plantation colony of Guiana (GUY-anna) on the south. France established the fur colony of New France (now Canada) on the North American mainland and the sweltering sugarcane colonies of Saint Domingue (San Doh-MING) (now Haiti), Guadeloupe (Gwad-ah-LOOP-ay), and Martinique (Mar-tahn-EEK) in the West Indies. The Netherlands colonized New Netherlands (now New York), Cape Colony (now South Africa), Java (now Indonesia), and several sugar islands in the West Indies. In the 1700s Britain expanded its empire by conquering Australia (from the native Aborigines), New Zealand (from the native Maoris), and parts of India (from the native Indians), and taking over the French colony of New France (1763) and the Dutch colonies of New Netherlands (1664) and Cape Colony (1795).[84]

God, Gold, Glory, and Grub

Why did the West suddenly expand? There were several reasons. For one thing, the 1310-1850 climatic minimum and fourteenth-century ecological crisis had by the mid-1400s created acute food shortages in Europe, as well as an increased reliance on preserved (i.e., salted) meat and (especially) fish, leading to an increased demand for new fishing grounds (especially after the climatic minimum altered the spawning runs of the herring in the Baltic Sea in northern Europe), additional land to grow crops and raise livestock, and Asian and African spices like pepper, nutmeg, cloves, cinnamon, mace, and curry, which were used to preserve meat and fish, disguise the rancid taste of semi-rotten meat and fish, and (most important) counteract the overwhelming saltiness of all of the salt that Westerners used as their principal preservative. The Black Death added to the West's hunger for spices, especially nutmeg, which doctors considered an herbal medicine as well as a food preservative.

There was also the hunger for wealth, a constant in almost any era. Westerners looked for gold and silver, of course (one group of Native Americans grew so tired of the Spaniards' all-consuming "gold fever" that they captured some of them and poured molten gold down their throats), but what they really sought was trade. Cotton, silk, porcelain, and other fine Asian goods were popular in a Europe, where people had long dressed in uncomfortable wool and linen (or a combination of the two, known as linsey-woolsey) and eaten from plates made of wood, pottery, or pewter. The new Asian imports brought high prices. For its part, Africa proved a ready source of pepper, salt, and cheap slave labor. America turned out to have furs, gold, and silver, and a climate that was favorable for sugarcane, tobacco, and cacao, which soon became enormously popular – in part because sugar, nicotine, and caffeine were addictive substances. Moreover, population growth in Europe stimulated a desire for more land, which in turn helped fuel colonization. Between 1500 and 1800 approximately two-and-a-half million Europeans moved to America. Some of them came looking for religious freedom, but most simply sought farmland. Some hoped to acquire vast plantations and become rich, but most merely wanted enough land to establish modest family farms.

---

[83] John Merriman, *A History of Modern Europe, from the Renaissance to the Present* (1996), 39-45.
[84] Kenneth R. Andrews, *Trade, Plunder, and Settlement: Maritime Enterprise and the Genesis of the British Empire, 1480-1630* (1984), passim.

Others sought glory. With the Crusades over and feudalism on the wane, knights looked to overseas adventures to exhibit their courage and daring, to "win their spurs" by braving the seas and the elements, and finding new foes to fight. It wasn't for nothing that Spanish colonists in the Americas called themselves "conquistadors."

God, too, was a motive. Religious leaders wanted to expand the base of Christianity by winning new converts. Monarchs hoped to find new allies in their long struggle against the Muslims. The Church dispatched hundred of priests and friars overseas to find new souls for Christ.

Other factors beside God, gold, glory, and grub contributed to the expansion. New technologies brought from Asia during the Renaissance – astrolabes, magnetic compasses, lateen sails, and sternpost rudders – made long-distance seafaring possible. The fact that Asian ships were lightly armed made conquest possible. And a fifth "g" also played a major role: germs.

The Columbian Exchange

The consequences of expansion were many and profound, for Western Europe as well as for the rest of the world. For one thing, the West now had plenty of gold, glory, and grub. The environmental historian Alfred Crosby writes that the chronic food shortages that had plagued Western Civilization since the 1300s finally eased, thanks to the introduction of new, nutritious Native American "miracle crops" like maize, potatoes, sweet potatoes, and manioc, all of which had hitherto been unknown in Europe, but which produced far more calories per acre than the old staples of wheat, barley, and oats. Maize (the English called it "Indian corn") produces 7.3 million calories per hectare, potatoes 7.5 million, sweet potatoes 7.1 million, and manioc (from which tapioca is made) 9.9 million. On the other hand, wheat produces only 4.2 million calories per hectare, barley 5.1 million, and oats 5.5 million. In addition, Western fishermen – English, French, Basque, and Portuguese – harvested immense quantities of fish from the chill, shallow, nutrient-rich waters of the Grand Banks off of the coast of Newfoundland, the most fruitful fishery the world has ever known. As a consequence of all this new food, Crosby writes, the population of Europe exploded, from 103 million in 1650, to 144 million in 1750, to 274 million in 1850, to 593 million in 1950. The West had become the world's demographic powerhouse.

Many Western Europeans migrated to the new lands. Between 1500 and 1800 approximately 2.4 million Europeans moved to overseas colonies, mostly in the Americas. The largest colonial empire was New Spain, which featured a six-tiered class system. At the top were the *penninsulares* (pen-in-soo-LAHR-ays), men and women who had been born in Spain. Next were the *Creoles* (KREE-ohls), born in the Americas but of Spanish descent. Third were the *mestizos* (mess-TEETS-ohs), or people of mixed Spanish and Native-American ancestry. Fourth were the Native Americans, fifth were people of mixed native-American and African ancestry, and sixth were the black slaves. However, more British (English, Scottish, Welsh, and Irish) than Spanish colonists migrated to the Americas; most of them settled in England's Thirteen Colonies on the North American mainland. About 8.4 million slaves were exported from Africa, again mostly to the Americas. Tragically, slavery once again became a central feature of Western culture. Many of the American colonies – the various islands of the West Indies, the Portuguese colony of Brazil, and the English colony of South Carolina are examples – ended up with far more African "colonists" than Europeans. These places experienced "Africanization" as much or more than they did "Westernization."

Crosby refers to this mass movement of crops, weeds, animals, pests, germs, people, and other biological organisms back and forth across the Atlantic in the years following Columbo's voyage as "the Columbian Exchange." In essence, after 1492 Europeans, Africans, Native Americans, Asians, Aborigines, and Pacific Islanders exchanged germs, foodstuffs, weeds, and animals, as well as trade goods, on an unprecedented scale. Maize, potatoes, tomatoes, squashes, beans, and pumpkins were transplanted to Europe; wheat, oats, rye, barley, grapes, apples, peaches, oranges, sugarcane, coffee, rice, and other European and African crops were transplanted to the Americas. The Europeans also brought their weeds: daisies, dandelions, Queen Anne's lace, bluegrass, clover, crabgrass, ragweed, and others. And they brought their livestock, introducing cows, sheep, horses, honeybees, and other animals into an environment where they had never before existed. (The only Native American animals to make the return trip were turkeys and guinea pigs.) They also introduced their rats, dogs, housecats, and insect pests, including Hessian flies and wheat midges. European germs (smallpox, bubonic plague, chicken pox, measles, and influenza) and African diseases (malaria, yellow fever) arrived for the first time in the Americas, killing millions of Native Americans. Only one Native American disease (syphilis) traveled to Europe, Asia, and Africa. According to Crosby, the Europeans got by far the best of this uneven "exchange," for it was they who acquired the new miracle foods, vast riches, and immense new lands upon which they could settle their surplus population. In return, the Native Americans received only deadly new germs, horses, cattle, and the dubious benefits of Western culture, and were overwhelmed by an invading phalanx of European and African people, plants, and animals. For their part, the Africans, too, suffered, acquiring only guns, rum, maize, potatoes, and manioc, but in return were subjected to the horrors of the Atlantic slave trade.[85]

---

[85] Alfred W. Crosby, *The Columbian Exchange: Biological and Cultural Consequences of 1492* (1972), passim.

The Triangular Trades and the Rise of Corporations

The Expansion of the West speeded up the development of capitalism, which had already gotten underway in the High Middle Ages. In order to acquire the massive amounts of capital needed to outfit fleets of trading ships and establish far-flung empires, European entrepreneurs formed corporations. Corporations were new. Hitherto, business had operated either as sole proprietorships, partnerships, or (in most cases) family-owned enterprises. It was the sheer size of all the post-Henrican trade that made the corporations necessary, for unlike previous forms of business, corporations had the built-in ability to pool large amounts of capital. One corporation, the London-based Virginia Company, undertook no less a project than the settlement of England's most populous colony, Virginia – although truth-to-tell, the Company lost so much money on the venture (and managed the colony so atrociously) that the English government was reluctantly forced to assume control of the colony after less than two decades of operation.[86] More successful was the less ambitious but better-run Hudson's Bay Company (HBC), which traded English cloth, alcohol, and metal goods to Cree hunters for furs in what is now northern Canada. Unlike the Virginia Company, the HBC still exists, in the form of the Canadian department store chain, The Bay – so venerable that Canadians occasionally joke that HBC stands for "Here Before Christ."[87]

But according to the historian Kenneth Andrews, the real corporate giants were the British East India Company and the Dutch East India Company, mammoth conglomerations of capital and the prototypes for today's mega-corporations. By the late 1700s the British East India Company was the world's largest corporation, the Exxon of its age. From its corporate headquarters in London and huge factory complex at Calcutta (a city in India that the Company built from the ground up), the Company ruled a quarter of South Asia and dominated the tea, silk, ceramics, and opium trades.[88]

The British historian Giles Milton describes the founding of the British East India Company:

> On the evening of 24 September 1599, a loud cheer was heard coming from the half-timbered Founders Hall in London's Lothbury Street. For much of the day the city's merchant adventurers had been deep in discussion about sending a new fleet of ships to the East Indies. Now they had at last reached a decision. With a unanimous show of hands and a roar of excitement it was decided to apply to Queen Elizabeth I for her assent to a project "intended for the honour of our native country and for the advancement of trade of merchandise within this realm of England."
>
> No painting survives to record the scene behind the mullioned windows of Founders Hall on that September evening but with the Company scribe recording every last detail for posterity it is not hard to assemble a picture of the historic events unfolding. Some fourscore men had gathered to discuss the practicalities of the intended voyage. These were not aristocrats nor landowners, nor were they members of the courtly circle; most were merchants and burghers, men who made their living by speculating on trading ventures.
>
> Some of the leading lights of this new enterprise had considerable experience of international trade. Richard Staper and Thomas Smythe, for example, had been principal founders of the Levant Company [an earlier corporation] and had helped to build a successful business in the eastern Mediterranean. Others, like Sir John Hart and Richard Cockayne were well-known faces in City of London. Three of the men had held office as Lord Mayor of London and the chairman of the meeting, splendidly dressed in wig and robes, was Sir Stephen Soane, the present occupant of the Lord Mayorship....
>
> When everyone had had the chance to speak Sir Stephen Soane called the meeting to order. There were important matters to be settled, not least of which was to prevent the large sum of money which had been subscribed just two days earlier from being contributed in any form other than cash. It was also decided to entrust the day-to-day running of the Company to fifteen directors.[89]

Besides the Asia trade, corporations also came to control the more lucrative "triangular trades" that formed the core of the emerging new world economy. Western merchant ships carried cargoes "finished goods" (guns, gunpowder, rum, tools, furniture, cloth, paper, etc.), along with Asian imports (silk, spices, porcelain, etc.), from Europe to Africa, the first leg of the triangle. In Africa, they traded guns, gunpowder, rum, and Asian goods for slaves, gold, salt, and pepper. They transported the slaves across the Atlantic to the Americas in the so-called "middle passage" of the triangular trades, where they exchanged them (along with finished goods and Asian imports) for sugar, molasses, tobacco, hides, furs, wood, grain, gold, and silver. These cargoes (along

---

[86] Andrews, *Trade, Plunder, and Settlement*, 304-340.
[87] Peter C. Newman, *Empire of the Bay: The Company of Adventurers that Seized a Continent* (1998), passim.
[88] Andrews, *Trade, Plunder, and Settlement*, 256-279.
[89] Giles Milton, *Nathaniel's Nutmeg: Or, the True and Incredible Adventures of the Spice Trader who Changed the Course of History* (1999), 66-67.

with the salt, pepper, and gold from Africa) they brought back to Europe in the final leg of the triangular trades, where they sold them for cash.[90]

The vast amounts of gold, silver, and other wealth imported into Europe from the Asian and triangular trades triggered a permanent inflation, still a fixture of Western Civilization. This in turn further stimulated capitalism, by making it easier to borrow money. Trade also transformed the balance of power in Europe, with Spain (which had by far the biggest colonial empire, especially after the mid-1500s, when it annexed Portugal) supplanting the declining Holy Roman Empire as the West's reigning superpower.[91]

Racism and Race Slavery

Another consequence of the Expansion of the West was the rapid rise of racism and race-based slavery. The two phenomena are inseparable, coiled together like two serpents.

Racism, writes Audrey Smedley, is not the same thing as ethnocentrism, although they are similar and both are bad. Ethnocentrism is the belief that one's own culture is inherently better than others, a foolish but nevertheless common viewpoint. Like most other people at the time, Westerners were highly ethnocentric. Medieval Europeans viewed members of other religions, especially Muslims and Jews, as enemies. They even disliked those Jews who had lived among them for generations, irrationally considering them as being not really Western, but rather an alien people living in their midst. But Medieval Westerners were not racist. They didn't view their enemies as being *physically* different from themselves, at least not in any major way, nor did they see them as being any less civilized or technologically inferior. Muslims could be either light-skinned or dark-skinned, almost all Jews were light-skinned, and both were thought to possess greater scientific, medical, and technical knowledge than Western Europeans. It was from the Muslims that the West had learned about Hindu-Arabic numerals, algebra, magnetic compasses, astrolabes, and lateen sails. The differences between Christians, Jews, and Muslims were cultural, not racial. The dislike – even hard hatred – that many Westerners had for non-Christians was ethnocentrism, not racism.[92]

Unlike ethnocentrism, Smedley says that racism is based on perceived biological rather than cultural differences. Racists are people who divide humankind into various groups ("races") based on what they perceive to be innate physiological characteristics, such as skin color, hair texture, eye shape, head shape, blood type, intelligence, or even personality. (Later, in the nineteenth century, racists claimed that such characteristics were "inbred," or genetic.) Racists also believe that some "races" are superior to others, in terms of their strength, stamina, ability to resist germs, ability to withstand extreme temperatures, intelligence, and moral character.[93]

Do races really exist? Today, many anthropologists and biologists don't think so. They argue that the world cannot be divided neatly into "whites," "blacks," "yellows," "reds," "browns," and "tans." Rather, they say that humans exist in a near-infinite combination of sizes, shapes, and colors, with almost as much diversity within each racial group as there is among the groups themselves. Perhaps races did exist once, in prehistoric times when small groups of Stone Age humans lived isolated in widely scattered locations, physiologically adapted to their specific local habitats. But centuries of population growth, migration, trade, raiding, and intermarriage have permanently blurred such distinctions. Moreover, no anthropologist or biologist today believes that any racial group is inherently superior or inferior to others.[94]

Even those scholars who believe that races do exist are highly critical of racial stereotypes. According to the anthropologist Marvin Harris:

> There is no doubt that the species Homo sapiens consists of different populations which can justifiably be labeled races. However, the races which most people distinguish, such as "blacks," "yellows," and "whites" (or "Negroids," "Mongoloids," and "Caucasoids"; or "Africans," "Asians," and "Europeans"), are not taxonomically valid categories..... The absurdity of trying to cram all populations into the mold of three or four racial categories is well illustrated by the system of racial identity currently employed in the United States. In the American folk taxonomy, if one parent is "black" and the other is "white," the child is "black" despite the fact that by the laws of genetics, half of the child's genes are from the black parent and half from the white. The practice of cramming people into racial pigeonholes becomes even more absurd when black ancestry is reduced to a single

---

[90] Ronald Bailey, "The Other Side of Slavery: Black Labor, Cotton, and Textile Industrialization in Great Britain and the United States," *Agricultural History*, 68 (1994): 40-43.

[91] Merriman, *History of Modern Europe*, 181-191.

[92] Audrey Smedley, *Race in North America: Origin and Evolution of a Worldview* (1999), 15.

[93] Ibid, 13-35.

[94] Ashley M. F. Morgenthau, *Man's Most Dangerous Myth: The Fallacy of Race* (1974), passim; T. Allen, *The Invention of the White Race* (1994, 1997), passim; I. Hannaford, *Race: The History of an Idea in the West* (1996), passim.

grandparent or great-grandparent. This produces the phenomenon of the "white" who is socially classified as "black."[95]

Of course, Western Europeans had long been aware that not everyone in the world looked like them. They knew, for example, that Sub-Saharan Africans had darker skin than they did. But before the Age of Expansion, they expressed no broad dislike of Africans, nor any belief that Africans were biologically inferior to Europeans. On the contrary, in the early 1400s Prince Henrique had hoped to form an alliance between his own "white" Christian kingdom of Portugal and the "black" Christian kingdom of Ethiopia against the "white" Muslim kingdom of Morocco – showing that Henrique, at least, thought religious fellowship outweighed physiological differences. In Henrique's mind, "white" Christians had more in common with "black" Christians than they did with "white" Muslims. Henrique was horribly ethnocentric, to be sure. But he was not racist.

Nor was he unique. According to the historian Kevin Reilly:

> Black people…were viewed favorably by the ancient Egyptians, Hebrews, Greeks, and Romans. The Africans from Nubia and Ethiopia were frequently praised for their beauty, fighting ability, and civilization. Moses married a Kushite woman (from Nubia), and "the anger of the Lord was roused" against those who objected. For the Nubian was to live with the Egyptian, Babylonian, Philistine, and Tyrian, and Zion was to "be called a mother in whom men of every race are born." [96]

Adds the historian Frank Snowden:

> It is important to emphasize that the overall, but especially Greco-Roman, view of blacks was highly positive. Initial, favorable impressions were not altered, in spite of later accounts of wild tribes in the far south and even after encounters with blacks had become more frequent. There was clear-cut respect among Mediterranean peoples for Ethiopians, and their way of life. And, above all, the ancients did not stereotype all blacks as primitives.[97]

So, if racism was not present in the West in Classical and Medieval times, where did it come from? Tzvetan Todorov, in his book *The Conquest of America*, advances one possibility. According to Todorov, racism originated in the 1400s and 1500s and developed out of the historical circumstances of the Expansion of the West. Todorov thinks it began with Columbo. He says that when Columbo first reached America, the explorer – happy and excited that he had apparently found Asia – wrote glowing entries in his log about the Tainos (Tie-EEN-ohs), the first people he met, declaring them, "The best people in the world, and the most peaceable." The Tainos were friendly, inquisitive, eager, graceful, kindly, and helpful. "I do not believe in all the world there are better men," gushed Columbo. Physically, he compared them to Spanish peasants, whose skin was burnished by the sun from working and living outdoors.[98] He was convinced that the Tainos were Asians (he called them "los Indios," or "the people of the Indies"), and was sure that he would find sophisticated, technologically advanced China and Japan just around the next headland. In his excitement he even imagined that he could distinguish Japanese and Chinese words in the Tainos' speech.[99]

However, as time went on and Columbo did not find China or Japan, he grew increasingly frustrated. Todorov believes that this caused him to gradually change his mind about the Tainos, to slowly convince himself not that they were not Asians (for that would have meant admitting that he had not reached Asia after all), but that they were not true people – that the reason that they were unable to tell him where to find China and Japan was because they did not have true language. Their "words" were mere jabber. It was a bizarre idea, and most other Westerners quickly rejected it.[100]

In Columbo's mind, Todorov says, true people possessed language; they also practiced a recognizable religion, wore lots of clothes, used gold and silver for money, fought wars, were repelled by cannibalism, and smelted iron and other metals. Such attributes characterized not just Westerners, but also the peoples of Arabia, the Ottoman Empire, Morocco, Russia, China, and Japan. But the Tainos did not wear clothes – at least not many of them. Nor did they use gold and silver for money, fight wars, or smelt iron. Columbo also believed (falsely) that they were cannibals, had no religion, and lacked language. So he concluded that they could not be true humans. But because they looked human, he was not willing to declare them mere animals. Rather, he came to view them as subhuman, demi-people who were innately inferior to true, full humans like himself. Todorov says that Columbo's view of the Tainos progressed through three stages: (1) at first he thought that they were people similar to Western Europeans, (2) then he thought that they were people who were dissimilar to Western Europeans, but who could be Westernized (made to be like Western Europeans), and (3) he finally concluded that they were not truly people at all and therefore incapable of being Westernized. When Columbo reached this last view, he decided that the best thing to do with the Tainos was to turn them into slaves.[101]

The Spanish colonists who followed Columbo to America readily accepted this view. Most of the early colonists were young knights or other ambitious men-on-the-make, gold-hungry status-seekers hoping to find

---

[95] Marvin Harris, *Culture, People, and Nature: An Introduction to General Anthropology* (1985), 94-95.
[96] Kevin Reilly, *The West and the World: A History of Civilization* (1989), 2: 45.
[97] Frank M. Snowden, *Before Color Prejudice: The Ancient View of Blacks* (1983), 2: 58-59.
[98] Tzvetlan Todorov, *The Conquest of America: The Question of the Other* (1982, 1992), 36.
[99] Ibid, 31.
[100] Ibid, 30.
[101] Ibid, 34-50.

their fortunes in the New World. They thirsted for gold and land, and they needed large numbers of Tainos and other Native-American slaves to work in the mines and on the plantations. If the Native Americans could be viewed as being something less than truly human, then surely it would be acceptable to seize their land, take their gold, eat their food, enslave them, rape them, or even kill them. Who would object?

But there were some in the West who did object. Queen Ysabel and King Fernando, for example, preferred turning the Indians into tax-paying subjects rather than subhuman slaves. Pope Paul III (r. 1534-49) wanted to convert them to Christianity, and so he insisted that they were humans with souls and should be treated as such. But the staunchest defender of Indian rights was a stubborn, idealistic Spanish priest named Bartolome de Las Casas, whose words you will read later in this chapter. In 1554, in a famous part-trial, part-debate in the Spanish city of Valladolid, Las Casas challenged the conquistadors. He succeeded in convincing Spain's King Carlos I (the grandson of Ysabel and Fernando) that Native Americans were fully human and should be accorded the same legal status as other Spanish subjects. The king duly ordered the colonists to stop enslaving and killing them.

But by that time the colonists had already moved on to a new group of victims: Africans. The reason was that by the mid-1500s millions of Indians had already died, felled by a combination of disease and ill treatment. There were no longer enough Tainos left to labor in the mines and plantations. Indeed, by 1550 they had virtually been wiped out. Moreover, it was perfectly legal to acquire slaves from Africa, because slave traders in their own countries had already enslaved them. As a result, in the three centuries between 1500 and 1800 approximately 8.4 million African slaves (two-thirds of them males between the ages of fifteen and forty) were transported across the Atlantic. Most were put to work as laborers on the colonists' sugarcane and tobacco plantations. By comparison, during that same period only about 2.4 million Europeans came to the Americas.

And as the African slave trade got into full swing, many Europeans came to view Africans, too, as subhuman. Indeed, in order to justify having enslaved Africans on such a massive scale, sixteenth-, seventeenth-, and eighteenth-century Europeans often cited the same "facts" about them that Columbo had used about the Tainos: they wore few or no clothes, they were "superstitious" rather than religious, they did not use gold and silver as money, they lived in tribes rather than in true states, they were cannibals, they did not smelt iron, they were "primitive," they practiced human sacrifice, they were promiscuous – in short, they were "savages" and slavery was the only thing they were good for. Of course, most of these "justifications" were patently false. Africans did wear clothes, although not the same style as Europeans. The majority of them lived in kingdoms and belonged to societies that smelted iron. They were no more promiscuous or cannibalistic than Europeans. And even when the "facts" were true (some Africans, for example, used cowry shells for money instead of gold or silver), well, so what? It was not because they were physiologically or even culturally inferior, but because their culture was adapted to a different environment (in some parts of Africa, cowry shells were rarer than gold) than the Europeans. Nonetheless, in their desire to justify the new, mass slavery of Africans, Westerners succeeded in convincing themselves that Africans were inferior savages. In the 1500s and 1600s the West's traditional ethnocentrism turned into modern racism, and slavery was the reason.

One transitional figure in the shift from ethnocentrism to racism was the famous sixteenth-century Portuguese poet Luis Vaz de Camoes (Cah-MOINSH), the "Shakespeare" of Portugal. In contrast to Prince Henrique, who had lived a century earlier and viewed Africans as equals, Camoes, in his great fictional epic *The Lusiads* (LOO-see-ads) described some (but not all) Africans as savage and uncivilized. When you read Camoes's description of the Koisian people of southern Africa later in this chapter, notice how closely it resembles the way that Todorov says Columbo characterized the Tainos.

Kevin Reilly points out that, by the 1400s, Europeans like Camoes were able to draw upon a long history of stereotyping certain groups of people as fit to be slaves. Reilly writes:

> In the Roman Empire, Roman slaves came from captured peoples of Africa, Asia, and Europe. Since slaves could not be identified as a single physical type, the Romans did not develop racist ideas about slavery. But in periods when the Romans enslaved a particular ethnic group in large numbers, they did tend to stereotype that group as slaves. Thus, after the Roman conquered and enslaved many of the light-skinned Scythians from Thrace (north of Greece), they thought of Thracians as slaves. Then a Roman actor would wear a red wig to play a slave because Thracians had red hair. Similarly, the Thracian name Rufus came to be regarded as a typical slave's name. Thracians were even depicted as lazy, called "boy," and considered inferior. Ethnic stereotypes changed as the Romans drew their slaves from different ethnic groups. With the Roman conquest of Gaul (France) and Britain in the first century B. C., the Roman stereotype of slaves more closely resembled the light-skinned, blond Gauls and Britons….. In the later Middle Ages, European slaves were taken increasingly from…the Slavic peoples of the Balkans and Southern Russia, [who] were pressed into slavery by Italian traders, while the Slavs of Central Europe fell victim to the German expansion eastward. Ever since, the word "Slav" has been synonymous with "slave" in European languages.[102]

But while Classical and Medieval people had used ethnic stereotypes to justify enslaving other people, modern people had switched to racial stereotypes. This change was significant, for unlike ethnocentrism, racism could be used to justify perpetual as well as temporary servitude. If the differences between masters and

---

[102] Reilly, *The West and the World*, 2: 45-46.

slaves were simply cultural, then the slaves could, in theory, have learned Western culture, become "civilized," and then demanded their freedom. Indeed, in earlier times something very much like that had occurred, when the children of slaves did not always become slaves themselves. Furthermore, many European countries had laws prohibiting the enslavement fellow Christians. But freeing Westernized slaves (or the Westernized children of slaves) would have created serious problems for the West, for by the 1600s the entire Western economy had become utterly dependent on the use of slave labor in the colonies. It wasn't only the colonists who depended on slavery. The triangular trades and the new corporations relied on it, too, although indirectly. As the historian Ronald Bailey writes, "Commodities produced by slave labor [in the Americas] played a vital role in [European] commerce, and all of this produced 'a golden harvest' of capital and laid the foundation for furthering economic and social investment.... The system of slavery and the slave trade which supplied Africans as its prime laborers was a central factor in the success of the rise of commerce and of industrial capitalism in Europe and [America]."[103] Racism provided an excuse for not freeing Westernized slaves – a hideous justification for keeping them and their children in perpetual bondage, generation after generation. If Africans could be defined as being racially (i.e., biologically) inferior to Europeans, then they could be viewed as being incapable of becoming Westernized and would never have to be freed.

Thus the new, modern slavery was different from earlier forms. It was based on race: only non-whites were enslaved. There were other differences, as well. The new slavery was more brutal than the old. Because slaves were now relatively inexpensive, masters were more likely to view them as "disposable commodities" – something to be used up, tossed aside, and easily replaced. Too, after 1500 slavery occurred on a scale far more massive than ever before. In Classical times, slaves normally made up no more than 25% of the population. In the Middle Ages they almost disappeared from northern Europe, and remained only a tiny proportion of the population in southern Europe. But in 1780 the majority of the people in Spain's American colonies of Cuba and Santo Domingo (Hispaniola), France's colonies of Guadeloupe, Martinique, and Saint Domingue (Haiti), Portugal's colony of Brazil, and the Netherlands' colony of Curacao were slaves. Slaves also formed large minorities (more than 25% of the population) in many other colonies. In 1780 in England's colonies, slaves and so-called "free blacks" combined to form 38.6% of the population of Virginia and Maryland, 42.0% of the population of the Carolinas and Georgia, and a whopping 91.1% of the population in the West Indies. Writes the historian Ronald Bailey: "Too few scholars have pointed to the reality which I have previously labeled the Africanization of the Americas: up until 1820, more than 8.4 million Africans had been imported into the Americas mainly to provide slave labor, as compared to 2.4 million Europeans who 'immigrated' to this region."[104]

This hardening and extension of slavery and its connection to racism can be seen in the history of England's oldest American colony, Virginia. Virginia was founded in 1607, utilizing not African slaves but English indentured servants as the primary labor force. Indentured servants were not slaves: they were legally defined as persons, they could own property, and they entered into their contracts (indentures) voluntarily and for fixed terms, normally only one year in England and four-to-seven years in Virginia, after which they were free to leave their masters and go elsewhere. Indentured servants were common in Europe in the 1600s, especially in the bourgs. Most journeymen were indentured servants. They were typically "white" and Christian.

The first Africans arrived in Virginia twelve years later, in 1619, when a Dutch ship appeared unexpectedly with a cargo of slaves they had been unable to sell in New Spain, where the supply was high and the price was low. Desperately short of labor, the Virginians bought the cargo. At first, the Virginia colonists viewed the Africans as a new type of indentured servant and treated them as such. They imagined that the Africans had been justly enslaved in their native lands according to African laws and customs – as prisoners of war, perhaps, or debtors. Those who survived their seven-year indentures (about half of them) were freed and, as with English indentured servants, received fifty acres of land each. They could legally own property, enter into contracts, join the militia, marry, and become Christians. Overall, in these early days of the colony, "blacks" were treated pretty much the same as the poor "whites."

But as the supply of English indentured servants declined over the course of the 1600s (because the English economy was on the upswing and fewer people were migrating), Virginia was forced to import more and more Africans. Moreover, as the number of Africans increased the colonists changed their status from indentured servants to slaves. In a parallel development, all the "blacks" in Virginia, whether slave or free, were legally ostracized and dehumanized, the victims of growing race prejudice. "In Virginia ... before 1660, it might have been difficult to distinguish race prejudice from class prejudice," writes the historian Edmund Morgan. "As long as slaves formed only an insignificant minority of the labor force, the community of interest between blacks and lower-class whites posed no social problem." As African slaves became more numerous, however, Virginia's laws became increasingly racist. "By a series of acts, the [Virginia] assembly deliberately did what it could to foster the contempt of whites for blacks," Morgan concludes.

In 1660 the colony extended the term of servitude for Africans in Virginia from seven years to life. In 1662 it made slavery hereditary, declaring, "The children of a Negro woman and an English father ... should be slave or free according to the condition of the mother." In 1667 the colony denied slaves Christian baptism. In 1670 it forbid free "blacks" from having "white" servants. In 1680 it prescribed a penalty of thirty lashes "if any Negro," slave or free, "shall presume to lift up his hand in opposition to any Christian [i.e., any white]." In 1691

---

[103] Bailey, "Other Side of Slavery," 36, 50.
[104] Bailey, "Other Side of Slavery," 36-37.

marriage between "whites" and "blacks" was outlawed because, Morgan says, "the result of such unions could be a blurring of the distinction between slave and free, black and white. The children would ultimately become free and might constitute an intermediate class, neither black nor white. By providing severe punishments for white women who gave themselves to blacks, the authorities not only discouraged fraternization of slaves and poor whites but also assisted white freemen to find wives." [105]

Moreover, Virginia was not the only European colony that adopted racist policies. Connecticut did so as well. Although the number of slaves in Connecticut was never as large as in Virginia, slavery nevertheless existed there, and the colony enacted similar laws. In 1660 Connecticut exempted slaves from military duty, so that they would not have access to guns. By 1690 the colony's so-called "black codes" required all "blacks" – slave or free – "to have passes when they traveled from their homes and prohibited their being sold intoxicating beverages." In 1708 "blacks were denied the privilege of selling goods to whites, were prohibited from striking or arguing with a white, and were prohibited from being out after 9:00 p.m." Even free "blacks" were forbidden from serving on juries, voting, or holding office – although they were required to pay taxes.[106]

-The Documents-

Bias in History

It is a truism that different people view the same historical events in different ways. For that reason, historical documents inevitably reflect the biases or viewpoints of whoever wrote them. "History is about evidence, and evidence flagrantly distorts," writes the British historian John Vincent. "There is a bias in the creation of evidence, and a bias in the survival of evidence. There may be a bias in access to what survives, too. There is a bias towards the important (and self-important), a political bias to winners against losers, a bias towards the stable and against the unstable, and perhaps a deliberate censorship of the past on top of that. Before we even get to modern historians, distortion is built into the very nature of history." [107]

For that reason, historians cannot accept documents uncritically. Another British historian, R. G. Collingwood, once used the derisive term "scissors-and-paste historian" to refer to someone who simply accepts as true whatever the sources say and copies it down, under the premise that, well, if it's in a document, it must be right. (Some of my students do the same thing, constructing papers by cutting and pasting material found on the Internet. These are not good papers and do not receive good grades.) Collingwood, an aficionado of English detective stories, maintained that historical documents should be approached in much the same way a police inspector approaches an eyewitness to a crime – with a healthy dose of skepticism, the application of logic, and a willingness to "torture" the evidence in order to bring out the underlying truth (the last bit a rather troubling analogy that creates a disturbing image of modern British police methods, but then Collingwood always was prone to carrying an analogy too far).[108]

In the following excerpt, two sixteenth-century writers – Luis Vaz de Camoes and Bartolome de Las Casas – give two very different versions of the Expansion of the West. Your job is to avoid the scissors-and-paste approach and, like Collingwood's police inspector, be skeptical, apply logic, and "torture" the evidence in order to figure out what really happened.

Camoes's account was fictional (although based on actual events), while Las Casas took pains to describe only things that he had actually seen. Does that make a difference? Both excerpts are biased, for each author was trying to persuade his readers that his interpretation – his viewpoint – was correct. Yet neither author was lying: each believed that what he said was true. What points do you think each was trying to get across? How did they slant the evidence to strengthen their cases? Finally, neither author told everything that he knew, not because he was being intentionally deceptive, but simply because, like all authors, he did not have the time or space to include everything that happened. What sorts of things do you think they might have left out? What further evidence do you think is necessary?

One final point to ponder: How do you think sixteenth-century readers would have responded to the two different accounts? Do you think that Spanish readers would have reacted differently to Las Casas than Portuguese readers reacted to Camoes? How about English readers? The American historian C. Vann Woodward, a specialist on the Civil War Era South, reminds us that it is not always the truest historical account that is most believed, but rather the one that seems to be the most "essential to the spiritual comfort of a people in time of stress." [109] What do you think he meant by that? Which of the two accounts – Camoes's or Las Casas's – do you think was more likely to become integrated into the popular "legend" of the Expansion of the West – that is to say, the version of the event that most people believed and accepted to be true, and was told and

---

[105] Edmund S. Morgan, *American Slavery, American Freedom: The Ordeal of Colonial Virginia* (1975), 316-337.
[106] David M. Roth, *Connecticut: A Bicentennial History* (1979), 46.
[107] John Vincent, *An Intelligent Person's Guide to History* (1995), 52.
[108] R. G. Collingwood, *The Idea of History* (1956), 249-280.
[109] C. Vann Woodward, 1-2.

retold by generations of Western historians? Do you think the legend would have been any different if Native Americans, Africans, or Asians were telling the story?

Interpretation One: the Expansion of the West as a Heroic Epic: Luis Vaz de Camoes

Luis Vaz de Camoes (c. 1524-1580) was a Portuguese traveler and poet. In 1572 he published *The Lusiads*, a long fictional poem about the Portuguese explorer, Vasco da Gama, who had reached India in 1498. Although Camoes lived after Gama, he viewed him as a great hero, and was proud of the accomplishments of the Portuguese explorers. The narrator in Camoes's story is a fictionalized version of Gama, describing his voyage. Although this is a work of fiction, it illustrates the way that many Europeans in the 1400s and 1500s viewed the expansion of the West.

A prolific writer of poetry and plays, Camoes[110] came from the lesser Portuguese nobility. His father was a captain who was shipwrecked and died off the coast of India when Camoes was still a baby. Through one of his grandmothers, Camoes was distantly related to Vasco da Gama, although Gama died long before he was born. Bright and inquisitive, when he was in his teens Camoes received a university education (universities were in those days rather like modern high schools), and when he completed his studies in 1542 or 1543, when he was eighteen or nineteen, he went to Lisbon, Portugal's capital, to serve as a minor courtier at the court of King Joao III. While he was there he had a disastrous love affair with a woman whose family regarded him as not good enough for her (she was from the greater nobility, while he was from the lesser) and wrote a smug, foolish play that appeared to be (and probably was) intended as criticism of the late King Manuel I. His enemies had him banished to Ceuta, where he fought in two battles against the Moroccans, losing his right eye in one of them. When he finally returned to Lisbon in his late twenties he was physically worn out from his hard military service, impoverished, disfigured, and embittered. Neither had he learned anything. He soon got into a quarrel with an important royal official, wounded the man on the head with a sword, and was tossed into prison. He was released nine months later under the condition that he would go to India as a factor. Banished again, he spent time in Goa, Malacca, Mozambique, Macao (Mah-COW), and other Asian and African factories. As a nobleman, he was a poor businessman, and failed to make much money. In 1570, sixteen years later, he returned to Portugal, almost penniless. He wrote most of his poems and plays while in Asia, including the first part of his masterpiece, *The Lusiads*, all the time pining for home. He perhaps owned Asian slaves, but was never wealthy enough to have many. He died in obscurity in Portugal in 1580. His work became well known only after his death.

At the time Camoes wrote, Portugal was in the final throes of a long, slow decline. Portugal had come under the control of its larger, more powerful neighbor, Spain, a process that had begun when Ysabel and Fernando had pressured Portugal's King Manuel I (r. 1495-1521) to follow Spain's example and expel all of his Jewish and Muslim subjects. Not wanting to comply, Manuel had tried to finesse the issue by instead converting all the Jews and Muslims to Christianity; however, the plan backfired when many of them chose not to convert and a Christian mob rioted through Lisbon, killing many of them. Tensions between the two kingdoms came to a head in 1555, about the time Camoes was banished to India, when young Dom Joao, the son of King Joao III and heir to the throne, died prematurely. When the king himself died two years later, the throne passed to his infant grandson, Sebastiao I. As he grew towards adulthood, Sebastiao became increasingly dogmatic and irrational, a mystic who spent long periods fasting and hunting. He envisaged himself as the "captain" of Christ, a semi-divine figure destined to lead a great Crusade against the Muslims in Africa. In 1578, just before his scheduled marriage to a Spanish princess, Sebastiao led a Portuguese army into Morocco. Against the advice of his generals, he took his knights deep into the interior. There, his force was trapped at Alcazarquivir by the wily Moroccan King Ahmed Mohammed and annihilated. Sebastiao disappeared in the battle, never to be seen again. His uncle, the aged Cardinal Henrique, succeeded to the throne. Nearly 80 and ailing, Henrique quickly renounced his priest's vows and married, hoping to father an heir before he died. He didn't make it. When Henrique died without issue in 1580 (also the year of Camoes's death), his closest living heir was none other than King Felipe II of Spain, who sent an army to Portugal to claim the throne by force and merge the two kingdoms. Spain would occupy Portugal until 1640. Three times pretenders claiming to be the legendary Sebastiao returned from Africa and led rebellions against Spanish rule, but each time failed. Portugal's great age was over.

When Camoes finished *The Lusiads* in 1572, the Portuguese Empire was in decline, the Crusading boy-king Sebastiao was on the throne, and relations with Spain were tense. Do you think these factors were related to the kind of story Camoes chose to write?

---

[110] Aubrey F. G. Bell, *Portuguese Literature* (1922), 174-179.

from *THE LUSIADS* [111]

CANTO I

[In Canto I Camoes introduced the subject of his epic poem, the voyage of Vasco da Gama, and explained why he thought it had been glorious. He compared Gama and the other Portuguese explorers to the great heroes of Classical antiquity, but argued that the Portuguese had accomplished even more wonderful feats.]

Arms, and the men heroic of the West,
Who from their native Lusitanian[112] shore,
By seas till then unnavigated pressed
Even beyond Taprobane,[113] and more
Than seemed of human force the hardest test,
Through wars and perils resolutely bore,
Raised a new empire in a distant clime,
And crowned it with a glory all sublime.

These, and the kings of memory dear to fame,
Who, widening out dominion, spread the Faith,
Afflicted Africa as a chastening flame,
And Asia, rank with the idolater's breath –
And many a warrior who redeemed his name
By deeds of prowess from the law of death –
These shall my song proclaim in every part,
If Genius aid me, and melodious Art.

Let wonder cease at voyages of old
By the wise Greek and by the Trojan made;
Let Ammon's son and Trajan[114] cease to hold
The palm for eastern victories displayed;
I sing the illustrious Lusian[115] heart so bold,
Whom Neptune's[116] self and stubborn Mars[117] obeyed.
Hushed be all praise that ancient Muses[118] sing,
For later valor soars on stronger wing!

And you, O nymphs[119] of Tagus[120] dear,
At this new ardor in my soul you raise,--
If still it was my delight from year to year,
In lowly verse to sing your river's praise,
A style now give me, stately, flowing, clear,
A voice which shall be heard in after-days;
For so may Phoebus[121] graciously ordain
That Tagus shall not envy Hippocerene.[122]

---

[111] Luis Vaz de Camoes, *The Lusiads of Luis de Camoens*, trans. Edward Quillinan (1853), 1-3, 158-163, 166-170, 178-179, 183, 186, 191.

[112] "Lusitania" was the old Roman name for the western half of the Iberian Peninsula. Camoes used the word to mean "Portugal." In was typical of Renaissance writers to make Classical references, and *The Lusiads* was full of them. Even the name of the poem – *The Lusiads* – was a play on the titles of two famous Classical epic poems, the *Iliad* by Homer and the *Aeniad* by Virgil. Camoes used these Classical references to suggest that the feats of the Portuguese were similar to those of the Classical Greeks and Romans, and to suggest that the Portuguese were just as deserving of glory as the famous heroes of Classical mythology.

[113] Sri Lanka (Ceylon), a large island off the coast of India.

[114] Trajan was a Roman emperor. This was another Classical reference.

[115] Portuguese.

[116] Neptune was the Roman sea god. As a Christian, Camoes did not actually believe that Neptune really existed. This was another Classical reference.

[117] Roman war god.

[118] Classical Greek goddesses who inspired artists, poets, and historians.

[119] Half-human undersea female creatures.

[120] Portugal's chief river.

[121] Greek sun god.

Give me that frenzy, give the passionate tone,
Not of agrarian reed or pastoral cane;
But of trumpet by the warrior blown,
That kindles up the heart and thrills the brain.
Teach me a paen worthy of your own
Famed people – Mars-befriended; such a strain
As though the world shall spread, resounded long,
If worth so great can be comprised in song.

And you, O timely born, the pledge secured
For ancient Lusitanian liberty;
Nor less to Christendom the hope assured
Of wider range and ampler boundary!
You, O new terror to the Paynim sword,
The wonder-fated of our age to be;
Unto the world by God, the All-ruler given,
To win large portion of the world for Heaven!

Young tender scion of a tree more blest,
In the dear love of the Redeemer [123] mild,
Than all that ever flourished in the West,
Whether most Christian or Imperial styled!
Behold the proof upon your shield impressed,
A victory past it shows you, royal child;
A day whereon He gave your ancestor
For arms the same that on the Cross He bore.

You, powerful King,[124] whose empire vast the sun
When drawing on the world the first descries,
And still surveys when half his course is run,
And leaves the last when he forsakes the skies:
You, as we trust, the yoke that shall anon
The false and stubborn Ishmaelite [125] chastise,
And oriental Muslim, and the heathen brood
That drank the water of the scared flood!

CANTO V

[In Canto V Camoes had Gama narrate his voyage around Africa. In the stanzas below, "Gama" describes the first part of the voyage, from Portugal to the southern tip of Africa.]

"The man of honored years in words like these
Yet stood declaiming, when we opened out
Our wings to the bland wafture of the breeze,
And left the much-loved harbor.[126] With devout
Observance of a custom of the seas,
At setting sail, to heaven we raised the shout
'God speed our voyage!' – Soon the masts confess
With creaking sway the wind's accustomed stress.

"The light of inextinguishable ray
The fierce Nemaean beast [127] was entering now;
Our timeworn planet, verging on decay,
Revolved in its sixth age, infirm and slow,
And fifteen hundred years, less three, [128] the day

---

[122] A fountain in central Greece, sacred to the Muses.
[123] Jesus.
[124] The King of Portugal.
[125] Arab.
[126] Lisbon, the capital of Portugal and Gama's home port.
[127] A mighty lion supposedly slain by the Classical hero Hercules as one of his twelve labors.
[128] 1497.

(Since Christ assumed the bonds of human woe)
Had traveled his ecliptic round
When sailed the fleet on this adventure bound.

"By little and by little, lost we sight
Of those loved hills that guard the parent strand,
And cherished Tagus, and the breezy height
Of Cintra, last dim presence fondly scanned.
We left behind, too, in that painful flight,
Our hearts, tenacious of their native land:
All dear familiar objects vanished fast,
Till nought we saw but sea and sky at last.

"Thus went we forth, developing a waste
Of seas to human enterprise unknown;
Breaking new airs from isles that idly graced
Blind ocean till by princely Henry [129] shown.
The Mauritanian regions[130], where the vast
Antaeus[131] held in days of old his throne,
Rose on our left; far on the right hand
Surmise conceives a continent of land.

"We glided by Madeira's stately shore
Which from its wealth of woods derived its name:
Famed isle! The first we colonized, and more
Surpassing in its beauty than its fame.
Nor let those Islands Venus [132] loved of yore,
Cythera, Cyprus, vaunt their elder claim:
The Paphian Queen would have forgotten them
Had this been hers, the Atlantic's latent gem.

"Massyla's coast, the dreary breadth between
The Berber land [133] and Ethiopia,[134] then we past;
There on a churlish soil, of pasture lean,
The lot of the lorn Azeneque is cast:
His herds a stingy thirsty nurture glean;
The desert pulse scarce yields him a repast;
The bird that swallows iron wanders there;
And there reigns Want, the brother of Despair.

"We crossed the northern limit where the sun
Back to the central girdle slopes his way.
Here man for Phoebus's promise rashly won,
Lost the serene complexion of the day.[135]
Here where the Senegal's [136] dark waters run
Are tribes ferocious as the beasts of prey.
Before us loomed the Cape we call 'de Verde,' [137]
Once Arsinarium, now a name unheard.

"The fair Canarian [138] cluster, named of yore

---

[129] Prince Henrique, or Henry the Navigator.
[130] A Roman term for that part of North Africa where the Sahara met the Atlantic Ocean, roughly the location of the modern country of Mauritania.
[131] A mythical giant from Classical times.
[132] Roman love goddess.
[133] Morocco.
[134] Throughout the poem, the term "Ethiopia" was used to refer to all of Subsaharan Africa.
[135] A Classical story told that Subsaharan Africans had accepted the sun god's promise of warm weather, but had to accept dark skin as a consequence. Camoes's language suggests that he viewed this as a bad bargain.
[136] The Senegal River.
[137] Cape Verde.
[138] The Canary Islands. Camoes had the order reversed. Gama would have encountered the Canaries before reaching Cape Verde, not after.

The Happy Islands, left so far behind –
Among the daughters now of Hesper [139] hoar,
The bright Hesperides,[140] a prosperous wind
Our navy wafted. On this pleasant shore,
Which our first crusiers in their joy to find
Had hailed as new-sprung wonders of the Waste,
We too were reluctant the sweets of land to taste.

"Under the shelter of that Isle [141] we moored,
Named for Iago, champion Saint of Spain,
The Warrior Saint whose visionary sword
So often made the Crescent's pride to wane;
But when consenting Boreas gave the word,
Thence to the illimitable Lake [142] again
We turned, resigning for the desert sea
A land of plenty and its sheltering lee.

"By sinuous course and long, we coasted then
Those shores of Africa that eastward swerve,
The Jaloff province, whence the black men,
To bondage scattered, divers nations serve;
And wide Mandinga, from whose marts we gain
The precious metal.[143] Here, with many a curve
Abrupt, and many a broad majestic sweep,
Flows wizard Gambia [144] to the Western deep.

"We passed those islands to which, forced to flee,
The Gorgons,[145] odious to light, retired.
One eye among them served the mystic Three;
One mind their evil sorceries inspired.
But you,[146] the fatal charmer of the sea,
For Neptune by your golden ringlets fired,
Were cursed the most with hideous change of form,
And hence the Libyan sands with vipers swarm.

Due south we now the beaked prows incline,
And many a winding league of shore escape,
Leaving the rugged Sierra Leone, [147]
And headland named by us the Palmy Cape.
Wide of Saint Thomas's Isle [148] we cross the line,[149]
And, still athwart the mighty gulf [150] to shape
Our course, far westward of that mouth we glide
Where the great river [151] meets the sounding tide.

"That lucid river, the long winding Zaire, [152]
Flood which the roving ancients never saw,

---

[139] Hesperus. According to Classical myth, Hesperus was a king in Africa who owned a garden where there grew golden apples, guarded by a dragon. Hercules slew the dragon as one of his twelve labors. The Portuguese thought that Hesperus's garden may have been in the Cape Verde Islands.
[140] The Cape Verde Islands.
[141] One of the Cape Verde Islands.
[142] The Atlantic Ocean.
[143] Gold.
[144] The Gambia River.
[145] Three female monsters from antiquity, Stheno, Euryale, and Medusa. This was another reference to the Cape Verde Islands. Some Portuguese thought the islands might once have been the home of the Gorgons, so they sometimes called them the Gorgonas.
[146] Medusa.
[147] The mountain of Sierra Leone ("Lion Mountain") in the modern country of Sierra Leone.
[148] Sao Tome.
[149] The equator.
[150] The Gulf of Guinea.
[151] The Niger River.
[152] The Congo River.

Through Congo runs, a realm extending far,
Where erst our nation sowed the Christian law. [153]
Thus from the seaman's friend, Calisto's star, [154]
Our northern guide, did I at last withdraw
Beyond the limit of the Western main
And burning line that parts the world in twain.

"And right before us gladly we descried
In a new hemisphere a pole-star new,
Unseen by our forefathers, and denied,
Or thought a dream that might be false or true;
We saw the firmament's Antarctic side
Less bright than ours, for here the stars are few:
And none can tell if underneath its pole
More land exists, or shoreless waters roll.

"Through storms, through calms, through many a brunt severe
Of that rough trident which the sea-god wields,
Thus traversing the regions where the year
Twice welcomes Summer, twice to Winter yields
(As rules the sun upon his swift career
Between either zone along his argent fields)
We saw Calisto Juno's anger brave
And dive in the forbidden ocean-wave.

* * * *

[In this next excerpt, Gama's crew lands near the southern tip of Africa and meets the Khoi Khoi people who lived there. Notice how closely Camoes's depiction of the Khoi Khoi resembled Columbo's characterization of the Taino.]

"Before long we landed at an open space:
And while my crews the neighboring hills explore,
Fond to discover novelties, and trace
Their way where stranger never trod before, --
I, with the pilots, in a chosen place,
Remained to take our bearings on the shore,
Fix the sun's altitude with careful art
And prick the painted geographic chart.

"We found that we had plied the canvas wing
Far southward of the goal of Capricorn;
Being now, between it and the frozen ring
Of Auster's univestigable borne.
But lo! Our rovers, now returning, bring
By law of force a naked wretch forlorn,
A Negro, captured as he roamed to seize
Among the hills, the treasure of the bees.

"Troubled he comes, quaking in every limb,
As one in trouble never so extreme,
His speech is dark to us, as ours to him,
A savage wilder than brute Polypheme. [155]
To feel our way into a sense so dim,
We show him, first, to metals the supreme, [156]
Then silver, pure; then, aromatic spice;
But none of these he turns to look on twice.

"The charm of meaner[157] objects then we try,

---

[153] Portuguese missionaries had converted many Congolese to Christianity.
[154] The North Star.
[155] A famous Cyclops from Classical mythology, a son of Neptune. He ate people.
[156] Gold.
[157] Less valuable.

Such trivial gauds as lucid beads of glass,
A red cap, whose color takes his eye,
And little tinkling playthings, bells of brass;
At once his nods and gestures testify
That these with him for more than baubles pass:

I bid him take them all, and set him free;
Off to his kraal[158] he speeds exultingly.
 "Next day, at dawn, his comrades came; a band
All nude and of the color of the night;
Their rugged hills descending, in demand
Of fortune such as his, an envied sight.
Won by their looks companionably bland,
Fernan Velasco, [159] like an errant knight,
Must needs to closer test the adventure push,
And see the life of dwellers in the bush.

"So forth he fared, with courage for his shield
And arrogance to friend. When hours had past,
And not a sign of Fernan from the field,
An anxious look towards the hills I cast,
And longed for his return, or sign revealed
That he was safe: our hero came at last;
Adown a rocky slope his course he bent,
Sea-ward, returning faster than he went.

 "Coelho's[160] boat was in an instant manned,
And hurried to receive him: before it made
The nearest beach, an Ethiopian's [161] daring hand
Had all but seized the fugitive; no aid
Had he but speed of foot; to stand
Were death; pursuers on his shadow tread.
While I approached, swift as my rowers the stroke
Could ply, a swarm of blacks from hiding broke.

"On our devoted crews there poured a rain
Of stones and arrows from that black cloud;
Nor were they hurtled through the air in vain,
As this limb witnessed, by an arrow plowed,
But we, thus outraged, leaping to the plain,
So sharp a volley sent among the crowd,
That they decamping bore away, perhaps,
Some blushing honors redder than their caps.

"Velasco rescued, to our ships we turn,
Nor waste more anger in an idle fray
With men in whose wild nature we discern
The stealthy fierceness of brutes of prey;
From whom, too, naught of India could we learn
Save that the land desired was far away:
So making sail before a gallant breeze,
Again we tried the fortune of the seas.

"To Fernan then a boon companion cried,
While rang the decks with laughter's merry chime,
'Ho, friend Velasco, yonder mountainside
Seems less laborious to descend than climb.'
'True,' unabashed the adventurer replied,
'But, when yon black pack hither trooped, it was time,
For your sake, as I thought, my pace to mend,

---

[158] African house.
[159] A member of Gama's crew.
[160] One of Gama's captains.
[161] Again, "Ethiopian" was used as a generic term for all Subsaharan Africans.

Remembering you were here without friend.'

"When they had crossed the ridge that fronts the bay,
His Negro convoy, as he now averred,
Made halt, and bade him back retrace his way,
Threatening to slay him there, if he demurred;
And when perforce he turned, they cowering lay
On watch till we should seek him, and prepared
By sudden massacre of all to seize
A fearful hour to plunder at their ease.

* * * *

[At this point Gama's ships round Africa and head north into the Indian Ocean. Several days later Camoes has them encounter another group of Africans, probably in the vicinity of Mozambique, which Camoes himself later visited.]

"A kindlier people than those Ethiopians were
Who last received us with such evil grace,
The men that dwell upon this coast appear,
Unlike in nature though alike in race.
With dance they welcomed us, and festal cheer,
In crowds assembling on the sandy space,
Their women with them, and the gentle droves[162]
They pasture in the grassy mountain coves.

"Strange songs singing in a language strange,
The black women on their oxen roade;
(They prize, beyond all beasts that herded range,
These beeves,[163] slow-paced and patient of their load)
They sang in concert, true to every change,
And tuned to pastoral reeds their voices flowed:
I thought, while listening to the rural strain,
The age of Tityrus was come again.

"A temper true to their ingenuous air,
By gentle deeds the harmless natives show,
Bringing us fowls and sheep, for which they share
Content the showy trifles we bestow.
But since to our interpreters they bear
No word of what it is my concern to know,
Nor yield a sign that might our quest avail,
We lift anchor and unreef the sail.

* * * *

[The fleet sails further north along the coast of Africa. In the excerpt below Camoes has them reach an African city, perhaps Mombasa, that traded with Arabs who came from the north. Camoes characterized these Africans as having become "civilized" by their contact with the Arabs, in contrast to the "savage" Africans he described earlier.]

"For lo, as we approach the coast, where plain
The strand and vales behind it we descry,
Upon a river running to the main
And barks [164] that stem the stream or outward lie.
Great is in sooth our happiness to gain
The haunts of men who know the sail to ply.
'Now shall we surely find some guiding clue!'
Whispered reviving Hope, and whispered true.

"All Ethiopians are they, but it seems

---

[162] Herds.
[163] Cattle.
[164] Ships.

That they commune with some superior race;
For in their speech intelligible gleams
Of meaning, phrases Arabic, we trace;
The snow-white turban on the brow redeems
The wild expression of the Kaffir face;
A light blue kilt that half invests the frame
Bespeaks them civilized to sense of shame.

"In tongue Arabian, which though ill they speak,
Yet well interprets Fernan Martinez,[165]
They say that ships as long from stern to beak
As ours, are wont to navigate their seas;
That they go forth from eastern shores to seek
The coasts that southward broaden, and from these
Back towards the birthplace of the sun they sail
Unto a land of men, like us, of feature pale.

* * * *

[In this next excerpt Camoes has "Gama" boast of his accomplishments and glory.]

"Judge now, O King, if ever course was run
Like this of ours by men of other race:
Think you Aeneas,[166] or Laertes's son[167]
Persuasive, over an unimagined space
Of waters stretched their flight as we have done?
Who howsoever the Muse his name may grace
He dared to do the deeds with which our name
Descending, leaves but as one-eighth his fame."

* * * *

[At the end of Canto V, Camoes has "Gama" cease his narration. The following stanzas are in Camoes's own voice, explaining why he thought Gama and the other Portuguese explorers deserved glory.]

Let Gama thank the Muses that their zeal
For Lusitania's honor bids them sound
His name, according to the just appeal
Of strenuous deeds that claim to be renowned.
For neither they of Pindus's echoing hill
Nor Tejo's nymphs in Vasco's race have found
Such friends, that these should leave their grottoes dim
And woofs of golden twine, to sing of him.

Love patriotic and the pure desire
That every Lusian feat should have it praise
Impel the Tagan sisters of the Lyre,
For that alone the plausive voice they raise:
And yet, if in one breast survive the fire
That prompts to undegenerate scorn of ease,
Let deeds attest it! Valor shall not lose
Its price, though slighted be the generous Muse.

---

[165] A member of Gama's crew who spoke Arabic.
[166] A Trojan hero, the founder of Rome, and the hero of the most admired Classical work, Virgil's *Aenead*, the model for Camoes's *Lusiads*.
[167] Ulysses, the hero of Homer's *Odyssey*.

Interpretation Two: the Expansion of the West as the Oppression of Innocents: Bartolome de Las Casas

In the National Palace of Mexico in Mexico City, there exists today a magnificent painting by the great twentieth-century Mexican muralist, Diego Rivera. In one part of the painting several sixteenth-century, grim-looking, scowling, bearded, burly Spanish soldiers, swords unsheathed and cannons blazing, advance on a group of small, slender, frightened, fleeing, dying Aztec Indians. In the center of the action, dwarfed by the mighty, muscled, mustachioed conquistadors, stands a short, thin, bald, beardless, swordless man in priests' robes. Unarmed but brave, he stands between the soldiers and the Indians, facing the conquistadors and holding up a crucifix, as to block them from coming further. And, miracle of miracles, the soldiers have stopped! [168]

The little priest in Rivera's brilliant painting is Bartolome de Las Casas (1474-1566), a hero today in most of Latin America. Las Casas came to the Americas in the early 1500s as a young man. He came with the Spanish soldiers, conquered with them, enslaved and killed Indians with them, and soon owned a prosperous sugar plantation. Then God spoke to Las Casas, and slowly he came to understand that killing and conquering, raping and pillaging were wrong. He was particularly moved by Ecclesiastes 34:21, "the bread of the needy is their life: he that defraudeth him thereof is a man of blood." Las Casas had never intended to be a "man of blood" – he was studying to be a priest – but he now realized that he had become one anyway. He gave away his plantation and his slaves, completed his studies, and devoted the rest of his life to protecting the Indians from the soldiers. He took to heart Pope Paul III's admonition that Indians were human beings, and should be treated as such. He lived among the Indians and preached the gospel to them. He even challenged the soldiers in a famous part-debate, part-trial, held in 1554 in the Spanish city of Valladolid, where he got a panel of judges and Spain's King Carlos I, the grandson of Ysabel and Fernando, to declare that Indians had a legal right to their lives and property, and should not be enslaved. In 1552 Las Casas published a book, *A Brief Account of the Devastation of the Indies*, which contained the evidence that he had submitted to the judges and king at the Valladolid debate. He later published a longer, more detailed work on the same subject. The deaths did not stop altogether, however, for the pope, king, and courts were far away on the other side of the Atlantic Ocean. But they decreased. Unlike Camoes, Las Casas was not proud of what the Europeans had done. He was ashamed.[169]

The excerpts below are from an English translation of *Devastation of the Indies* published in 1563. (The spelling, grammar, punctuation, and some of the vocabulary have been modernized to make it easier to read.) At the time the book came out, Spain and England were enemies and their ships battled each other in an undeclared Sea War. Anti-Spanish English readers accepted Las Casas's account uncritically as proof that the Spanish were really all a bunch of evil, rapacious thugs (historians call this biased viewpoint "the black legend"), which was not, of course, what Las Casas had intended. The English version even carried a new introduction written by the English publisher, which declared, "Spanish cruelties and tyrannies perpetrated in the West Indies," and, "Happy is he whom other men's harms do make to beware," and warned that, if they had the chance, the Spanish would do the same nasty things to the English that they had done to the Native Americans. Moreover, the translator made a significant change in Las Casas's text; where Las Casas blamed the West generally for the ill treatment of the Native Americans, writing, "The Christians did this," and, "The Christians did that," the translator changed the language so as to focus all criticism on the Spanish alone, writing, "The Spaniards did this," and, "The Spaniards did that." (To be fair, it must be acknowledged that Spain was the *only* Western country to conduct an official hearing on the status of Native Americans, the trial at Valladolid in 1542, which means that Spain was also the *only* Western country to declare officially that Indians were people who had rights under the law. Indeed, when the English founded their own colonies in America a half-century later in the early 1600s, their colonists generally treated Native Americans just as badly as the conquistadors had, and nobody in the English government said much about it.) Many Spaniards were angry with Las Casas, because they believed his book had made Spain look bad in a time of war (although in fact, the fighting did not begin in earnest until after he first published his book in Spain). Do you think that Las Casas should have kept silent? Is it possible to love your country and at the same time criticize it, or the actions of some of its officials? Should such criticism be restricted only to peacetime?

---

[168] Todorov, *Conquest of America*, 178.
[169] Ibid, 168-182; Bill M. Donovan, "Introduction," in Bartolome de Las Casas, *The Devastation of the Indies: A Brief Account*, trans. Herma Briffault (1974, 1992), 1-24.

from *THE DEVASTATION OF THE INDIES* [170]

PROLOGUE

Most high and mighty Lord [King Carlos I of Spain], as God by his providence has for the guiding and commodity of mankind in this world, in realms and provinces, appointed kings to be as fathers, and as Homer [the famous Classical Greek poet who wrote the Iliad] names them shepherds, and so consequently the most noble and principal members of commonwealths, so can we not justly doubt by reason of the good will that kings and princes have to minister justice, but that if there be anything amiss, either any violence or injuries committed, the only cause that they are not redressed is that you princes ["prince" was a generic term for any king, queen, emperor, duke, count, archbishop, pope, etc.] have no notice of it. For certainly if they knew of them, they would employ all diligence and endeavor in the remedy thereof. Whereof it seems that mention is made in the holy scripture in the Proverbs of Solomon, where it is said, "Rex qui sedet in solio. Iudici dissipat omne malum intuitu suo." For it is sufficiently to be presupposed even of the kindly and natural virtue of a king, that the only notice that he takes of any mischief tormenting his kingdom, is sufficient to procure him, if it be possible, to root out the same as being a thing that he cannot tolerate even one only moment of time.

Considering therefore with myself, most mighty Lord, the great mischief, damages, and losses (the like whereof it is not to be thought were ever committed by mankind) of so large and great kingdoms [and] of this so large new world of the Indies [by "Indies" Las Casas meant all of North and South America], which God and holy Church have committed and commended to the King of Castile [i.e., Spain], to the end [that] they [it was customary at the time, to referred to kings with the plural pronouns "they" and "we," instead of the singular pronouns "he," "she," and "I"; this is sometimes known as the "royal we"] might govern, convert, and procure their [i.e., the kings'] property as well temporally as spiritually. I therefore (I say) being a man of experience, and fifty years of age or more, considering these evils, as having seen them committed, at my being in those countries. Also that your Highness having information of some notable particularities, might be moved most earnestly to desire his Majesty not to grant or permit to those tyrants [i.e., the conquistadors] such consequences as they have found out [i.e., the things the conquistadors gained from exploiting the Native Americans], and which they do so name (whereinto if they might be suffered they would return), seeing that of themselves, and being made against this Indian, peaceable, lowly, and mild nation [i.e., the Americas] which offends no one, they [i.e., the conquistadors] be wicked [and] tyrannous, and by all laws either natural, humane, or divine, utterly condemned, detested and accursed.

* * * *

INTRODUCTION

The Indies were discovered [in] the year one thousand, four hundred, ninety-two, and inhabited by the Spanish the year after ensuing: so as it is about forty-nine years since that the Spaniards some of them went into those parts. And the first land that they entered to inhabit was the great and most fertile Isle of Hispaniola [i.e., Espanola, or Haiti], which contains five hundred leagues [i.e., 1500 miles] in compass. There are other great and infinite isles round about and in the confines on all sides: which I have seen the most peopled, and the fullest of their own native people, as any other country in the world may be. The firm land [i.e., the mainland of North and South America] lying off from this island two hundred and fifty leagues [i.e., 750 miles], and somewhat over at the most, contains in length on the seacoast more than ten thousand leagues [i.e., 30,000 miles] which are already discovered, and daily be discovered more and more, all full of people, as a hill of ants. Insomuch, as by that which since, unto the year the fortieth and one has been discovered, it seems that God has bestowed in that same country the greatest portion of mankind.

---

[170] Bartolome de Las Casas, *The Spanish Colonie, Or Briefe Chronicle of the Acts and Gestes of the Spaniards in the West Indies, Called the Newe World, for the Space of XL Yeeres*, trans. James Aliggrodo (1583, reprinted 1977), n. p.

God created all these innumerable multitudes [i.e., the Native Americans] in every sort, very simple, without subtlety or craft [i.e., sneakiness], without malice, very obedient, and very faithful to their natural liege lords, and to the Spaniards, whom they fear, very humble, very patient, very desirous of peace-making, and peaceful, without brawls and struggles, without quarrels, without strife, without rancor or hatred, by no means desirous of revenge.

They are also people very gentle, and very tender, and of an easy complexion, and which can sustain no travel, and do die very seldom of any disease whatsoever, in such sort as the very children of princes and noblemen brought up among us, in all commodities, ease, and delicateness are not more soft than those of that country, even though they be the children of laborers. They are also very poor folk who possess little, neither yet do so much as desire to have much worldly goods, and therefore neither are they proud [i.e., arrogant], ambitious, or covetous. Their diet is such (it seems) than that of the holy fathers [i.e., the early saints] in the desert had not been more scarce, nor less dainty, nor less sumptuous. Their apparel is commonly to go naked: all have their shameful parts alone covered. And when they be clothed, at the most it is but with a mantle of bombast [i.e., cotton cloth] of an ell [i.e., 45 inches] and a half, or two ells of linen square. Their lodging is upon a mat, and those that have the best sleep as it were upon a net fastened at the four corners, which they call in the language of the isle of Hispaniola, a hammock. They have their understanding very pure and quick, being teachable and capable of all good learning, very apt to receive our holy Catholic faith, and to be instructed in good and virtuous manners, having less encumbrances and disturbances to the attaining thereunto than all the [other] folk of the world besides, and are so enflamed, ardent, and importune to know and understand the matters of the faith after they have but begun once to take them, as likewise the exercise of the sacraments of the Church, and the divine service: that in truth, the religious men [i.e., the Spanish priests who came to preach to the Native Americans] have need of a singular patience to support them. Undoubtedly these folks should be the happiest in the world, if only they knew God.

Upon these lambs so meek, so qualified and endowed by their maker and creator, as has been said, entered the Spanish incontinent as they knew them, as wolves, as lions, and as tigers most cruel of long time famished; and have not done in those quarters these 40 years past, neither yet do at this present, ought else but tear them in pieces, kill them, martyr them, afflict them, torment them, and destroy them by strange sorts of cruelties never either seen, nor read, nor heard of the like (of which some shall be set down hereafter [in this book]) so, that from the ... three million souls that were on the island of Hispaniola ... there are not now two hundred natives in the country. The island of Cuba, which is in length as far as from Valladolid to Rome, is at this day as it were all empty. St. Johns Island [i.e., Puerto Rico], and that of Jamaica, the both of them very great, very fertile, and very fair, are desolate. Likewise the islands of Lucayos [i.e., the Bahamas], near to the island of Hispaniola, and of the north side unto that of Cuba, in number being above three score [i.e., 60] islands, together with those which they call the islands of Geante [i.e., the Lesser Antilles], one with another, great and little, whereof the very worst is more fertile than the King's garden at Seville, and the country the healthiest in the world; there were in these same islands more than five hundred thousand souls, and at this day there is not one only creature. For they have been all of them slain, after they had drawn them out from thence to labor in their minerals [i.e., to dig for gold] on the island of Hispaniola, where there were no more left of the original natives of that island. A ship riding for the space of three years between all these islands ... to glean and cull the remainder of these folk (for there was a good Christian moved with pity and compassion, to convert and win to Christ such as might be found), [but] there were not found but eleven persons whom I saw; other islands, [in number] more than thirty, near to the island of St. John, have likewise been depopulated and marred. All these islands contain above two thousand leagues of land, and are all depopulated and laid waste.

As touching the main firm land, I am certain that our Spaniards, by their cruelties and cursed doings have depopulated and made more desolate more than ten realms greater than all Spain, compiling also therewith Aragon and Portugal, and twice as much or more land than there is from Seville to Jerusalem, which is more than a thousand leagues [i.e., 3,000 miles]; which realms as yet unto this present day remain in a wilderness and utter desolation, having been before time as well peopled as was possible.

* * * *

[1] Those who have come from Spain into that country, bearing themselves as Christians, have kept two general and principal ways to eradicate and abolish from off the face of the earth those miserable nations. The one is their brutal, cruel, bloody, and tyrannical war. The other manner is that they have slain all those who could any kind of way so much as

gasp, breathe, or think to set themselves at liberty, or to withdraw themselves from the torments which they endure, as are all the natural lords and the men of valor and courage. For commonly they suffer not in the wars to live any, save women and children; oppressing also afterwards those very same with the most cruel, dreadful, and heinous thralldom [i.e., slavery] that ever has been laid upon men or beasts....

The cause why the Spanish have destroyed such an infinity of souls has been only that they have held it for their last scope and mark to get gold, and to enrich themselves in a short time, and to mount at one leap to very high estates, in no wise agreeable to their persons; or, for to say in a word, the cause hereof has been their avarice and ambition, which has seized them exceedingly in the world in consideration of those lands so happy and rich, and the people so humble, so patient, and so easy to be subdued.

* * * *

OF THE ISLAND OF HISPANIOLA

On the island of Hispaniola, which was the first (as I have said) where the Spaniards arrived, began the great slaughters and spoils of the people; the Spaniards having begun to take their wives and children of the Indies, for to serve their turn and to use them ill, and having begun to eat their victuals, gotten by their sweat and travail; not contenting themselves with that which the Indians gave them of their own good will, every one after their ability, which is always very small, forasmuch as they are accustomed to have no more store than they have ordinarily need of, and that such as they get with little travail; and that which might suffice for three [Native American] households, reckoning ten persons for each household, for a month's space, one Spaniard would eat and destroy in a day.

Now after sundry other forces, violences, and torments, which they wrought against them, the Indians began to perceive that these were not men descended from heaven. Some of them therefore hid their victuals; others hid their wives and children; some others fled into the mountains, to separate themselves afar off from a nation of so hard-natured and ghastly conversation. The Spaniards buffeted them with their fists and clubs, pressing also to lay hands upon the lords of the towns. And these cases ended in so great a hazard and desperateness, that a Spanish captain dared adventure to ravish forcibly the wife of the greatest king and lord of this island. Since which time, the Indians began to search for a means to cast the Spaniards out of their lands, and set themselves in arms; but what kind of arms; very feeble and weak to withstand or resist, and of less defense (wherefore all their wars are no more wars than the games of children, when as they play at Iago di Cannes or Reeves). The Spaniards with their horses, their spears and lances, began to commit murders and strange cruelties; they entered into towns, bourgs, and villages, sparing neither children, nor old men, nor women with child, nor them that lay in, but that they ripped their bellies and cut them in pieces, as if they had been opening of lambs shut up in their pen. They laid wagers with such as with one thrust of a sword would punch or disembowel a man in the middle, or with one blow of a sword would most readily and most easily cut off his head, or that would best pierce his entrails at one stroke. They took the little souls by the heels, ripping them from their mothers' hugs, and crushed their heads against the cliffs. Others they cast into the rivers, laughing and mocking, and when they tumbled into the water, they said, "Now shift for yourself, such-a-one's corpse." They put others, together with their mothers and all that they met, to the edge of the sword. They made certain gibbets [i.e., the scaffolds used for hangings] long and low, in such sort that the feet of the hanged barely touched the ground, every one enough for thirteen, in honor and worship of our Savior and his twelve apostles (as they used to speak) and setting to fire, burned them all quick that were fastened. Unto all others, whom they used to take and keep alive, cutting off their two hands as near as might be, and so letting them hang up [i.e., the Spaniards tied the victims' severed hands around their necks with a cord], they said, "Get you with these 'letters,' to carry tidings to those who fled into the mountains." They murdered commonly the lords and nobility in this fashion: They made certain grates of perches suspended on forks, and made a little fire underneath, to the intent, that by little and little, screaming and sweating in their torment, they might give up the ghost.

One time I saw four or five of the principal lords roasted and boiled upon these gridirons. Also I think that there were two or three of these gridirons, garnished with the like furniture, and for that they cried out piteously, which troubled the captain because he could not sleep; he commanded to strangle them. The sergeant, who was worse than the hangman who burned them (I know his name and friends in Seville) would not have them strangled, but himself putting bullets in their mouths, to the end that they should not be able to scream, put them to the fire until they were softly roasted according to his desire. I have seen all the aforesaid things and others infinite. And forasmuch, as all the people who could flee, hid themselves in the mountains, and mounted on the tops of them, fled from the men [i.e., fled from the Spaniards] who were without all manhood, empty of all pity, behaving as savage beasts, the slaughterers and deadly enemies of mankind; they [i.e., the Spaniards] taught their hounds, fierce dogs, to tear them [i.e., the Native Americans] in pieces, and in the space that one may say a Credo, assailed and devoured an Indian as if he had been a pig. These dogs wrought great destruction and slaughter. And forasmuch as sometimes, although seldom, when the Indians put to death some Spaniards upon good right and law of due justice, they [i.e., the Spaniards] made a law among them, that for [every] one Spaniard [killed], they had to slay a hundred Indians.

-CHAPTER IV-
THIS WORLD WITH DEVILS FILLED:
THE REFORMATION AND THE SUNDERING OF RELIGIOUS UNITY IN THE WEST
1517 - 1648

The Greater New Haven, Connecticut, telephone directory today contains 342 listings under "churches" and "synagogues." Forty-nine are Roman Catholic churches, corresponding to the region's forty-nine Roman Catholic parishes. Nineteen are Jewish synagogues. Eleven are non-Western churches, originally founded by people from outside the West; these include six Eastern Orthodox churches, three Islamic mosques, and two Buddhist temples. One is a meeting hall for Scientologists. Another 262 listings (77%) are for various Protestant churches, all Christian and all Western in origin. These Protestant churches exist because in the early 1500s the catholic ideal - the traditional desire for religious unity, or one church for all believers - disintegrated. Although most of the people in the West remained (and still are) Roman Catholic (as is the majority of Greater New Haven), during the Reformation of the 1500s and 1600s millions of people left Holy Mother Church to found various Protestant Christian churches, each with its own unique beliefs and theology. As a result, religion in some parts of the West became less of a community experience and more a matter of individual choice. Why did this happen? And why did it cause centuries of bitter warfare between Catholics and Protestants? The causes lay in a sixteenth-century backlash against Renaissance humanism known as the Reformation. Led by the German monk Martin Luther, Protestants left the Roman Catholic Church because they believed it had become too worldly. They founded new churches that they believed were more firmly rooted in what they considered traditional Christianity - churches that they believed would better help them navigate their way, in Luther's words, "through this world with devils filled." For their part, Catholics stuck with their own Church, but also reformed it, attempting to bring it, too, back to its traditional roots. Both sides struggled to rebuild traditional Christianity in a modernizing West.

This chapter will also examine the role of leaders in history. Do leaders shape history? Or is history shaped by large, impersonal forces beyond the leaders' control? The nineteenth-century German philosopher Georg Hegel thought that some leaders (only a few) *did* shape history, and he called them "world historical actors." This chapter will look at the actions of Protestant leaders Martin Luther, Jean Cauvin, England's King Henry VIII, and France's King Henri IV. It will also examine the actions of Catholic leaders like Pope Leo X, Pope Clement VI, Pope Paul III, Pope Paul IV, Pope Pius IV, and Kaiser Karl V of the Holy Roman Empire. It will also look at political leaders like England's Queen Mary I and Queen Elizabeth I, France's Queen Mother Marie de Medici, Spain's King Felipe II, and the Dutch staatholder Willem van Orange. Finally, it will look at some cultural leaders, including the New England poet Anne Bradstreet and the Spanish writer Miguel de Cervantes. To what extent do you think these people controlled or shaped events? To what extent do you think they were the pawns of forces beyond their control?

-The Background-

The Rebellious Monk

The Reformation ("restructuring") of Western Christendom began with Martin Luther (1483-1546), a German monk. According to the historian R. H. Bainton, from youth Luther, like many Westerners, had been preoccupied with salvation, his own sense of personal sinfulness, and an abiding fear of hell. His parents, prosperous German peasants who had moved up the social ladder to join the lesser bourgeoisie, had wanted him to study law, make money, and provide for them in their old age. Yet Luther spurned the law to become a Roman Catholic monk, taking the requisite vow of poverty. He later explained that his decision was the result of a terrifying incident that had occurred in Germany's Black Forest. While a student, he had been traveling through the Forest during a severe thunderstorm. Lightning flashed all around. Thunder boomed. Cowering behind a rock, the terrified young man had promised Saint Anne that, if he were spared, he would become a monk. The clouds parted and the storm abated. Luther kept his promise, although it meant a bitter quarrel with his parents. As a monk, Luther studied theology. Eventually, he became a professor of religion at the prestigious University of Wittenberg (VITT-en-burg) in the Holy Roman Empire.[171]

Yet Luther continued to feel unworthy of salvation. Like all mortals, writes Bainton, Luther continued to sin, even when he tried hard not to. In an attempt to sin less, he undertook severe penances, wearing hair shirts and flagellating himself. "I was a good monk," he later wrote, "and I kept the rule of my order so strictly that I may say that if ever a monk got to heaven by his monkery it was I." But it did no good; he continued to sin. Luther

---

[171] R. H. Bainton, *Here I Stand: A Life of Martin Luther* (1955), 15-26.

became depressed and believed he was going to hell.[172] Then, one day while studying the Bible, Luther came across Romans I: 17, "The just shall live by faith." Luther interpreted this passage to mean that the only thing necessary for salvation was faith – not baptism, not holy orders, not Holy Communion, not penance, not even the avoidance of sin – just faith. It was a radical idea, sharply at odds with Church doctrine. For a while, Luther kept silent, brooding.[173]

Like many other theologians of his era (including William Langland, the author of *Piers the Plowman*), Luther believed that Holy Mother Church had become corrupt. Indeed, in many ways the Renaissance was the Church's spiritual nadir, a time when it became too worldly and materialistic. The low point had been the pontificate of Pope Alexander VI (Rodrigo Borgia) who, according to the historian William Manchester, sponsored orgies, fathered several children, and even impregnated his own daughter. Other fifteenth-century popes were not as bad as Alexander (it is difficult to imagine how they could have been), but several took bribes and all were deeply involved in Italian politics. Luther visited Rome when he was young, and had been distressed to find that the Church was spending vast fortunes on the construction of elegant cathedrals and other buildings, instead of using the money to help the poor. Many of the Renaissance's lesser clergy were known to be sexually active, despite their vows of chastity, and to accept simony (payment for services), despite their vows of poverty – issues that Langland had complained about in *Piers the Plowman*.[174]

Furthermore, like many monks and priests, including Langland, Luther strongly objected to the Church's practice of selling indulgences, certificates that got the buyer out of purgatory relatively quickly. For Luther and many others, indulgences were symbolic of the corruption they saw strangling Holy Mother Church.

Thus it was that when a Church official arrived in Wittenberg in 1517 to sell indulgences, Luther reacted. He protested – hence the term, "Protestant." Following traditional Medieval academic practices, he wrote up his views (his famous Ninety-five Theses) and tacked them to the university's chapel door for everyone to see. If in the Ninety-Five Theses Luther had stuck simply to attacking indulgences, it would have been a minor affair. After all, many Western theologians agreed with Luther that indulgences were a bad idea. But Luther didn't stop there. He also now made public his radical idea that Christians needed only faith in order to be saved.[175]

In a subsequent debate on the subject, Luther explained his position. The Church had defended indulgences by citing the Doctrine of Good Works – the idea, accepted by almost everybody at the time, that good deeds were rewarded by God, if not with immediate entrance into heaven, at least with a shorter stay in purgatory. Giving money to the Church was clearly a good deed, Church officials reasoned. And buying an indulgence certainly required one to give money to the Church. Therefore, buying an indulgence must be a good deed, and would be rewarded by God. Besides, argued Church leaders, God had given the Church an untapped reservoir of grace (accumulated by the selfless acts of all the saints) to distribute as it saw fit.

Luther could have simply attacked the spurious logic of this argument by pointing out (as other theologians were also doing at the time) that deeds are not "good" if they are done for selfish reasons. But instead, he denounced the Doctrine of Good Works itself. It was not good deeds that got one into Heaven, Luther insisted, but faith and faith alone. Sinners or not, the faithful would be rewarded in the afterlife. Hell was reserved for non-believers only, Luther said, while purgatory did not exist at all. Furthermore, since faith was all that was necessary for salvation, Luther said, then one needn't be baptized, or attend Holy Communion, or do penance, or participate in any of the Church's sacraments, which Luther claimed were only symbolic ceremonies and not true sacraments at all. Indeed, since absolution came directly from God, Luther declared, even priests – even Holy Mother Church herself – were not necessary for salvation. All you had to do was believe.

About one quarter of the people in Western Europe followed Luther out of the Church and became Protestants. Why? There were many reasons. For one thing, Luther was a brilliant thinker and scholar, a gifted preacher and writer, and a persuasive orator. And he wrote and spoke not in Latin but in German, the most widely understood language in Western Europe.

But it wasn't just Luther. Many lords became Protestants for reasons of their own. Some of the German lords saw Protestantism as a vehicle for undermining the Holy Roman Emperor, Karl V (Charles V), who had remained loyal to the Church. (Karl was also King Carlos I of Spain, the very same grandson of Ysabel and Fernando whom we have already met. How he came to rule over both realms will be explained shortly.) Other lords in other countries saw Luther's movement as an opportunity to weaken the power and wealth of the First Estate, with the hoped-for result of increasing their own.[176]

Another factor underlying the rise of Protestantism was the emerging modern force of patriotism. Many people in northern Europe resented the fact that the Church was dominated by Italians and Spaniards, and saw the Reformation as a vehicle for voicing their own growing sense of national pride.[177]

Too, many people in the West were undergoing their own personal crises of faith in the 1500s. For many, the Black Death and the Hundred Years War had created an apocalyptic mood. The Great Schism had undermined confidence in the whole concept of religious universalism. There were many Europeans who objected to the

---

[172] Ibid, 29-34.
[173] Ibid, 39-50; William Manchester, *A World Lit Only By Fire: The Medieval Mind and the Renaissance – Portrait of an Age* (1993), 58.
[174] Bainton, *Here I Stand*, 36-38.
[175] Ibid, 51-63.
[176] John Merriman, *A History of Modern Europe, from the Renaissance to the Present* (1996), 103.
[177] Ibid, 95-97.

idea of indulgences, and saw the practice as evidence that the Roman Catholic Church had strayed from its original purity. And, like Langland, many others had come to see the Roman Catholic clergy as too sexually active, too quick to accept bribes, too poorly trained, and insufficiently pious.[178]

Thus Protestantism became popular with many Europeans for many reasons. Concludes the British historian C. V. Wedgwood:

> The Reformation happened when it did, not because the teaching of Luther was inherently more compelling than that of earlier reformers, but because it came at a moment when the aggressive European dynasties saw in ecclesiastical reform a means of consolidating their power and increasing their wealth, because the growing merchant and trading classes, who had no place in feudal Europe, found in it a faith more easily reconcilable with their outlook, because Europe was growing, economically and politically, so fast that the old structure of society had split. The old Church was built into that structure and split with it.[179]

The Earnest Young Kaiser

Luther demanded that the Church reform. Pope Leo X (r. 1513-21) refused, and in turn demanded that Luther recant his views. Luther refused. The pope excommunicated him.[180]

Accordingly, in 1521 Luther's lord, the young but earnest Holy Roman Kaiser Karl V (r. 1519-56), less than three years on the throne, ordered him to appear at the Diet of Worms (DEE-it of VAIRMS) (a hearing or trial to be held in the German city of Worms), to answer charges of heresy. In a dramatic confrontation, Luther again refused to recant, saying, "I cannot, I will not recant! Here I stand. I cannot do other. It is better that I should die a thousand times than retract one syllable of the condemned articles. And as they [the pope] excommunicated me for the sacrilege of heresy, so I excommunicate them in the name of the sacred truth of God. Christ will judge whose excommunication will stand. Amen." Feeling that Luther had given him no other choice, Karl placed the rebellious under the ban of the Reich, tantamount to a death sentence. Luther fled and was offered refuge by some German lords, including the powerful Elector of Saxony, Friedrich the Wise.[181]

It wasn't so much that Friedrich and the other German lords who aided Luther were enamored of the rebellious monk's religious views, but rather that they resented the young kaiser's growing power and saw the developing dispute over religion as an excuse to challenge him.

The truth was that Karl had a fair shot of restoring the power of the kaiser to what it had been before the Italian Revolts of the thirteenth and fourteenth centuries. Karl's crafty grandfather, Maximilian von Habsburg, who had been kaiser before Karl (as Maximilian I, r. 1493-1519), had also ben the powerful Duke of Austria, one of the largest of the 300-plus states (most of them quite small) that together comprised the sprawling, aging German Reich. Cleverly, Maximilian had married the heiress to the throne of Burgundy, part of which was in France and part of which was in the Reich, and through her controlled not only Burgundy proper, but also the Low Countries, a large swatch of prosperous territory lying at the mouth of the Rhine River, and which today comprises the countries of Belgium, Luxembourg, Netherlands, and adjacent parts of Germany and France, but which was then part of the Reich. Furthermore, Maximilian had arranged for Karl's father, Philip "the Fair" von Habsburg, to marry Juana "la Loca" ("the Crazy") de Aragon, the elder daughter of Ysabel and Fernando of Spain and heiress to thrones of Spain and Naples. Both Philip and Juana had had the good grace to die young, but not before producing two sons. As a result of this tangle of royal marriages, Karl, the elder son, had inherited Spain, Austria, the Low Countries, Burgundy, and Naples, along with Spain's huge empire in the Americas. It was a mammoth empire – the largest that the West had ever seen, larger even than the old Roman Empire of Classical times – and young Karl, barely into his twenties, was consequently the most powerful man in Europe. It is no surprise that he was able to use that power to get himself elected to succeed his grandfather as Holy Roman kaiser – especially since, as the new Duke of Austria, Karl was also one of the Reich's seven Electors. Many of the German lords began to worry that Karl was becoming too powerful.[182]

Thus when several of the German lords took Luther's side and protected him, it was perceived for what it was: a serious challenge to Karl's authority, and not something that he could let pass. The Reich quickly dissolved into a civil war from which it never recovered, with Karl and the loyal southern Catholic lords on one side and the rebellious northern Protestant lords on the other. Long, draining, and destructive, the struggle dragged on for three decades, finally sputtering to a stop in 1552. Thousands died on each side. Cities were destroyed. Trade was ruined. Finally, totally exhausted, the two sides met in the German city of Augsburg and hammered out a truce. With neither side able to win, they compromised, establishing within the Reich the principle of *cuius regio eius religio* – Latin for "whose the region, his the religion," meaning that, in each of the

---

[178] Ibid, 97-99; J. H. Hexter, Richard Pipes, and Anthony Molho, *Europe Since 1500* (1971), 179-185.
[179] C. V. Wedgwood, *William the Silent: William of Nassau, Prince of Orange, 1533-1584* (1968), 26.
[180] Merriman, *History of Modern Europe*, 103.
[181] Ibid, 103; Hexter, *Europe Since 1500*, 192-193.
[182] Merriman, *History of Modern Europe*, 188-194; Paul Kennedy, *The Rise and Fall of the Great Powers: Economic Change and Military Conflict from 1500 to 2000* (1987), 32-33.

Reich's 300-plus regions, the local lord would be the one to decide which religion – Roman Catholicism or Lutheranism – would prevail. Other than the 300 great lords, individuals had no say.[183]

The Self-Righteous Lawyer

Meanwhile, Protestantism spread from its homeland in the war-torn German Reich to other parts of Europe. In France the urbane, university-trained lawyer Jean Cauvin (Koh-VAHN) (John Calvin, 1509-64) advocated Calvinism, an even more radical Protestant theology than Lutheranism. Among other things, Cauvin expounded the Doctrine of Predestination – the idea that an omniscient God had known from the beginning of time exactly who was going to be saved and who was not, and that consequently the decision had already been made and there was nothing anyone could do about it. Cauvin believed that only a small minority of Christians (the so-called "visible saints") was destined for heaven, and that everybody else was doomed to writhe for all eternity in the fiery pits of hell. Ever hopeful, Calvinists continually looked for tangible evidence of God's favor, that they were part of the lucky minority that He had chosen to save – evidence like success in business, luck in marriage, or a long pattern of moral and upright behavior.

As it turned out, Calvinism had great appeal among the bourgeoisie, in part because Cauvin put the Third Estate on an equal footing with the First and Second Estates; in part because he insisted that all work was equally holy in God's eyes, including trade, commerce, and lending money at interest; and in part because the bourgeoisie had an easier time than peasants or workers of finding tangible evidence of success in their lives. Switzerland (because Cauvin moved there, to escape the French authorities, who were hot on his trail), the Low Countries (because they were highly urbanized and therefore had a lot of bourgeois), Scotland (because…well, because the inhabitants were Scots), and many of the urban areas in France and England swung towards Calvinism. In England, Calvinists were known as Puritans. Today's Congregationalist, Presbyterian, and Dutch Reformed churches (major denominations in the United States) are Calvinist in origin.[184]

The Unhappily Married King

In England, King Henry VIII (r. 1509-47), the learned but stubborn, headstrong, oversexed, overweight, and unhappy son of Henry VII (who had been the victor in the Wars of the Roses) turned to Protestantism for political reasons. At first, King Henry had opposed Luther's ideas so vehemently that a grateful pope had granted him the title, "Defender of the Faith." But the corpulent monarch had a serious problem, one that ultimately led him to break with the Church. He was married to Catherine of Aragon (1485-1536), a solemn, pious, intelligent, and loyal Spanish noblewoman who also happened to be the beloved aunt of the most powerful man in Europe: none other than the young Kaiser himself, Karl V of the Holy Roman Empire. (Catherine was the younger, saner sister of Karl's late mother, Juana la Loca.) Karl's grandmother, the redoubtable Queen Ysabel of Spain, had taught Catherine several languages, as well as history, geography, religion, and the proper role of a strong and determined queen.

The problem was not that Catherine was an unloving or fickle wife, for in most respects she was a model queen and devoted helpmeet. Rather, it was that she and Henry had had only one child who had lived to adulthood, Mary, who according to English law (and Henry's proclamation) was the heir to the throne. But Henry, remembering the turmoil of the Wars of the Roses, feared that the notoriously strong-willed and patriarchal English lords would never accept a female monarch Before marrying Henry, Catherine had briefly been the wife of Henry's older brother Arthur, who had died soon after the marriage. Henry believed that his and Catherine's failure to produce a son had been because his decision to marry his brother's widow had been a sin, and that he was reaping God's punishment as a result. Besides, Catherine had grown older and decidedly rounder, and Henry was deeply smitten with a beautiful young courtesan, the fiery, auburn-haired, dark-eyed Anne Boleyn (1507-36) (Henry's eyes tended to wander, and marital fidelity was never one of his virtues). Much to Henry's dismay, Anne refused to have sex with him unless he agreed to marry her.

Henry, who unlike his cautious father tended to be hotheaded and impulsive, decided to solve his several dilemmas by asking Pope Clement VII (r. 1523-34) to grant him an annulment, on the grounds that because Catherine was his brother's widow he never should have married her in the first place. That way, he would be free to marry Anne, and if Anne became pregnant and gave birth to a boy, the child would vault ahead of Mary and become heir to the throne. Unfortunately for Henry, however, Clement was deeply beholden to Catherine's nephew, the mighty German kaiser and Spanish king. Religious civil war was still raging in the Holy Roman Empire, Karl's troops were in Italy, and without the kaiser's support the Reich and Holy Mother Church might fall to the Lutherans. Clement said, "No."

---

[183] Merriman, *History of Modern Europe*, 107-112.
[184] Ibid, 116-121; Hexter, *Europe Since 1500*, 212-219. (The connection between Calvinism and the business class was first expounded by the German pioneer sociologist Max Weber. See for example, Max Weber, "The Protestant Sects and the Spirit of Capitalism," in Max Weber, *From Max Weber: Essays in Sociology*, trans. And ed. H. H. Gerth and C. Wright Mills (1946), 302-322.)

Furious, in 1534 Henry bullied the English Parliament into declaring *him*, not the pope, the "supreme head of the Church of England" – henceforth to be known as the Anglican (or Episcopal) Church. He then annulled his marriage to Catherine himself and wed Anne, who was pregnant. However, much to the Henry's dismay, his new queen gave birth not to the boy he wanted, but to a red-haired, dark-eyed girl, named Elizabeth after Henry's mother. Still, what was done was done. England was now officially Protestant. And where once there had been only one church in Western Europe, there now existed several: the Roman Catholic Church, the Lutheran Church, the various Calvinist churches, the Anglican Church, and a small and persecuted offshoot of the Lutherans known as the Anabaptists.

Meanwhile, in 1536 Henry divorced and executed Anne (the reasons were complicated and the charge of treason largely trumped up) and wed the quiet, loyal, demure, colorless Jane Seymour, who gave him at last the son he craved, the sickly Edward. Altogether, Henry would have six wives (and innumerable mistresses) before he finally died in 1547. But infected with syphilis by one of his many mistresses, he managed to leave only three legal heirs: the sickly Edward, the neurotic Mary, and the clever Elizabeth. [185]

The Church Strikes Back

Ironically, Luther's religious revolt caused leaders within the Roman Catholic Church to implement certain reforms of their own, collectively known as the Catholic (or Counter) Reformation, an effort to win back many of those people who had left the Church. Indulgences were dropped. The clergy were better trained. With the blessing of Clement's successor, Pope Paul III (r. 1534-49), Ignatius of Loyola, a Spanish soldier-turned-monk, organized a new order of friars, the Jesuits, and sent them out into the world to do good works and seek converts. (We have already met Paul, in Chapter Three, when he declared that Native Americans were human beings with souls.) The Church also clamped down on dissent. Protestant books were banned, first by Pope Paul IV (1555-59) and then by Pope Pius IV (1559-65). This was something new, for never before had the Church attempted widespread censorship. Indeed, in the Middle Ages it had preserved books, not destroyed them. In Catholic strongholds like Spain and Italy, Paul III authorized the dreaded Inquisition rooted out heretics. Some Protestants were even burned at the stake.

The West thus was divided into a Catholic south, east, and west (Spain, Portugal, France, the Italian city-states, the southern half of the Holy Roman Empire, Poland, and Ireland) and Protestant north-center (Switzerland, the Netherlands, England, Scotland, the northern half of the Holy Roman Empire, Sweden, Denmark, and Norway). For several centuries the two sides battled each other in a deadly series of religious wars. Implacable hatred abounded. Outside of Elizabethan England, compromise seemed impossible. The Medieval ideal of religious universalism – one church of all believers – was dead.[186]

The Wars of Religion

The worst of the Wars of Religion were fought not by the generation that made the Reformation – the generation of Martin Luther, Pope Leo X, Kaiser Karl V, Jean Cauvin, Pope Clement VII, Pope Paul III, and King Henry VIII – but later, during the late 1500s and early 1600s. It was, ironically, the children of the Reformation, not its founders, who seemed the most determined to annihilate each other.

In the decades after Luther nailed his Ninety-Five Theses to the chapel door at the University of Wittenberg, Catholics and Protestants accused each other of all sorts of ridiculous things, in the process building up a massive reservoir of mutual hatred and intolerance. Catholics said that Protestants engaged in orgies. Protestants accused Catholics of worshipping idols and being in league with the devil. Death squads on each side roamed about, murdering religious rivals. Repression became the order of the day. By the late sixteenth century the reservoir of hate was overflowing its banks, and the two sides were again ready for war.

The bloodiest of the Wars of Religion occurred in England (under the reigns of Edward VI and "Bloody" Mary I, 1547-58), on the seas (the Sea War between Spain and England, c. 1560-1603), in France (the War of the Three Henrys, 1588-94), in the Low Countries (the Dutch War of Independence, or Eighty Years War, 1567-1648), in the Holy Roman Empire (the Thirty Years War, 1618-48), and then in England again (the English Civil War (1642-49). But at the center of all of these conflicts was Spain.

---

[185] Merriman, *History of Modern Europe*, 121-125; Hexter, *Europe Since 1500*, 207-212.
[186] Merriman, *History of Modern Europe*, 125-129; Hexter, *Europe Since 1500*, 221-227.

The Most Catholic King of Spain

In the early 1500s, thanks in large part to its lucrative colonies in America, Spain had emerged as the West's first modern superpower. Its rulers, Queen Ysabel and King Fernando, had used the tax revenues generated by the trade and commerce between Spain and its colonies (along with the "royal fifth," the monarchs' right to 20% of all the gold and silver mined in the Americas) to construct a large, powerful army and navy that would dominate the West for the next century and a half.

Yet Ysabel and Fernando had no sons to inherit their kingdom. The legal successor to the Spanish throne was their elder daughter, Juana la Loca. It would have been better if Juana's younger sister, the intelligent, steely, well-educated, cool-headed Catharine of Aragon – the well-polished apple of her mother's eye – could have inherited the throne instead. But the law was the law. Juana was older, the dynastic principle must be upheld, and competent or not, the throne would be hers. Ysabel and Fernando married Catharine off to a promising young English prince. We have already seen how that marriage turned out.

To ensure stable rule after their deaths, Ysabel and Fernando arranged for Juana to marry a handsome and powerful German lord, Philip "the Fair" von Habsburg, the son of the Holy Roman Kaiser Maximilian I and the heir to the thrones of both Austria and the Low Countries. The marriage took place in 1496, and when Ysabel and Fernando died in the early 1500s, Juana and Philip duly ascended to the Spanish throne as Queen Juana I and King Felipe I. Neither lived long, but they managed to produce two sons, Carlos and Fernando, the eldest of which in 1516 became King Carlos I of Spain (r. 1516-58). In 1519 Carlos was elected Karl V, Holy Roman Emperor, succeeding his paternal grandfather, Maximilian I. A strong ally of the Church, Carlos / Karl would – as we have seen – side with Pope Leo X against Martin Luther, agree with Pope Paul III that Native Americans were fully human, and at the behest of Pope Clement VII fight a long civil war in the Holy Roman Empire against rebellious Protestant lords.

In 1555-58 Carlos / Karl, now grown old and having recently made peace with his rebellious Protestant lords in the Holy Roman Empire, abdicated his several thrones and retired to a monastery. His younger brother succeeded him as Ferdinand I (r. 1558-64), Duke of Austria and Holy Roman Emperor. His moody, temperamental, idealistic, and radically Catholic son became King Felipe II (r. 1558-98) of Spain and Duke of Burgundy. Ferdinand usually followed his aggressive nephew's lead in religious affairs and foreign policy, and Spain and Austria thus continued to function as a single, united Habsburg Empire, with Spain the senior partner. The Habsburg coat of arms fittingly featured a two-headed black eagle, one head facing east towards Austria, the other west towards Spain and America.

For more than thirteen decades, from 1516 until 1648, the Habsburg Empire functioned as the leading power in the West. At its height, it included Spain; Portugal; the Italian city-states of Naples and Milan; Hungary; Austria, the Low Countries, Bohemia, Silesia, Saxony, Tyrol, and Franche-Comte in the Holy Roman Empire; and Spain and Portugal's vast overseas empires. It was the first modern superpower. It would not be the last.

Both Carlos / Karl and Felipe continued Ysabel and Fernando's policy of maintaining a powerful Spanish army and navy. With both economic and military muscle at their command, the two monarchs were able to control the Spanish lords and build an efficient, centralized, and loyal bureaucracy. Each regarded himself as a staunch defender of Holy Mother Church, protector of – to use a twenty-first-century phrase – the Western "way of life." Consequently, they engaged in a series of long, costly, and draining wars against what they viewed as the Church's many enemies: the Muslim Ottoman Turks, Protestant northern Europeans, and animist Native Americans. The father, cooler and more moderate than the son, eventually learned to compromise, agreeing in 1552 to the Treaty of Augsburg that saved the Holy Roman Empire from ruin. But Felipe, haughty, arrogant, close-minded, convinced that he alone was right, that God was on his side, that what he regarded as "evil" must be stopped at all costs, stubbornly kept on fighting, even when it was no longer expedient. As a result, his country weakened, convulsed, and crumbled about him

Eventually, all of Felipe's long, difficult struggles – each of them undertaken in the name of "good" – proved too costly for even the rich and powerful Habsburgs to sustain. Under Felipe, Spain fought too many wars on too many fronts. The historian Paul Kennedy calls this phenomenon "strategic overstretch." He points out that no Western superpower has ever lasted long. Inevitably, the other powers come to fear it and conspire against it. Surrounded by enemies, preoccupied with military matters, its leaders neglect the economy. The combination of the two – inattention to economic issues and the vast expenses incurred in keeping armies in the field for long periods of time – eventually bankrupt the superpower, and it falls. So it was with Spain. By 1648 the once-mighty Habsburg Empire was broke and exhausted, worn out by a century and a half of conflict. Spain not only became the first modern superpower, it also became the first modern superpower to fall, the victim of its own strategic overstretch.[187]

The Ordeal of Bloody Mary

The Wars of Religion began in England. When Henry VIII died in 1547, he was succeeded by his teenage son, the sickly Boy King Edward VI (r. 1547-53). Taking advantage of Edward's youth and ill health, radical English

---

[187] Kennedy, *Rise and Fall of the Great Powers*, 31-72; Merriman, *History of Modern Europe*, 187-197.

Protestants took control of the government and exultantly persecuted English Catholics. But when Edward died in 1553, the throne passed to his Catholic sister, "Bloody" Mary I (r. 1553-58), the daughter of the discarded Catharine of Aragon, who now turned the tables and persecuted the Protestants. Mary's husband – the driving force behind the persecutions – was none other than her cousin Felipe, the King of Spain. Mary died without children in 1558, thus ending Felipe's influence in England.

But he soon became embroiled in a bitter conflict with Mary's successor, the Protestant Elizabeth I (r. 1558-1603). Shrewd and decisive, Elizabeth was a strong and capable ruler. Calling herself "my father's daughter," she had little choice but to swing England back to Protestantism. According to Catholic doctrine, she was a bastard (the Church had never recognized Henry VIII's marriage to Elizabeth's mother, Anne Boleyn), and therefore was ineligible to be queen. Only if England remained Protestant would she continue to rule. Yet Elizabeth also proclaimed the famous Elizabethan Compromise, under which Anglicanism became the official religion of England, but Catholics and Calvinists (Puritans) were peaceably permitted to follow their own beliefs, as long as they were not too open about it. It was, in many ways, a sixteenth-century version of "don't ask, don't tell." It was not religious toleration (such a thing did not exist in the sixteenth century), but it was as close to it as the West would come. It was not what Felipe wanted, however, and he plotted against his Protestant former sister-in-law – after she rejected his offer of marriage. Soon Spain and England were engaged in a bitter Sea War that would last until Elizabeth's death in 1603.[188]

The Compromise of Henri the Politique

Meanwhile, the scene of religious conflict shifted to France. When Felipe became king of Spain, he went to Paris to meet with the French King Henri (EHN-ree) II, a loyal Catholic. Felipe knew that most of the inhabitants of the Low Countries (which was Spanish territory) were Protestants. He proposed that the Spanish and French armies jointly invade the region and root out the Protestant leaders. Henri agreed, but died in an accident (he was struck with a lance while jousting) before the plan could be carried out.

Over the next several years, Henri's three sickly teenage sons (Francois II, Charles IX, and Henri III) each reigned in turn, but the real ruler was their mother, Catherine de Medici (MED-i-chee), the shrewd and decisive daughter of Lorenzo de Medici, a rich Florentine merchant, banker, and associate of that unscrupulous Renaissance cynic, Niccolo Machiavelli. A foreigner, a woman, a bourgeoise, and an associate of Machiavelli: Catherine was everything the French lords despised, and so they conspired against her.

France was also riven by deep religious differences. On one side of the brewing religious struggle were the Protestants – Calvinists known as Huguenots (HEW-gah-noh). On the other were the Catholics, organized into the vocal Catholic League and led by the brutal, querulous Henri, Duke of Guise (GEEZ). In the middle were the moderates of both religions, known as the *politiques* (pahl-ee-TEEKS). Vainly, the *politiques* sought a compromise. Among the *politiques* was Henri de Bourbon (Bor-BOHN), the King of Navarre (a region in southern France), a political and religious chameleon who blithely switched back and forth between religions and sides based on expedience. Catherine de Medici also swung back and forth – not between Catholicism and Protestantism like Henri (she remained a Catholic), but between the radical Catholic League and the moderate *politiques*. Spain, too, was involved, with Felipe doing whatever he could to undermine the *politiques* and the Huguenots and to support the Catholic League – including a public defense of the infamous Saint Bartholomew's Day Massacre, in which armed Catholic Leaguers murdered hundreds of unsuspecting Huguenots.

By 1588 the situation had dissolved into a three-way civil war – the War of the Three Henrys – pitting the Catholic League (led by Henri de Guise), against the *politiques* and Huguenots (led by Henri de Bourbon), against the young King Henri III and his mother Catherine de Medici.

Felipe, of course, supported Henri de Guise and the Catholic League, but in 1588 Spain was preoccupied with a war in the Low Countries and a planned invasion of England. As a result, the struggle took place mostly among the French themselves. In the end it was the *politiques* who won, and in 1594 the chameleon Henri de Bourbon ascended the throne as King Henri IV. However, to win the support of the French lords, he had been required to switch religions (again) and convert to Catholicism. "Paris," he quipped cynically, "is worth a mass." Henri declared Catholicism France's official religion, but granted the Huguenots limited religious freedom similar to what Catholics had in England. For the moment, an uneasy truce prevailed.[189]

The Revolt of Willem the Silent

As France spiraled into its religious civil war, Felipe II was busy deciding to bring the Low Countries to heel, with or without French aid. The Low Countries were small, disunited, but densely populated, highly urbanized, and wealthy. Located in the delta of the Rhine River in the Holy Roman Empire, they sat at the nexus of several important maritime and riverine trade routes – up the Rhine into the heart of the Reich, down

---

[188] Merriman, *History of Modern Europe*, 197-203.
[189] Ibid, 139-155.

the English Channel to northern France, across the Channel to England, up the Meuse River to Champagne and the rest of central France, and over the North Sea to coastal Germany, Denmark, and Sweden. As a result, they had developed a sophisticated mercantile and maritime culture. More than anyplace else in the West except northern Italy, it was the Low Countries that had experienced the rise of the bourgeoisie. Merchants, traders, bankers, and master craftsmen had long governed on the local level. The high taxes they paid greatly enriched Spanish coffers. But the majority of the bourgeoisie were Calvinists, a situation Felipe decided he could not tolerate.

Felipe would have been better off leaving well enough alone. But that wasn't his way. In 1567 he unleashed the Spanish army and the Inquisition on the Low Countries, dispatching 10,000 crack Spanish troops under the Duke of Alba to pacify the region. Felipe had discussed his plans for the invasion with the region's canny, taciturn staatholder (governor), Prince Willem "the Silent" of Orange (1533-84). Although Willem opposed Felipe's plans, he wisely held his tongue, knowing that the stubborn Felipe would never listen to his objections. Instead, he organized a revolt.

The rebels succeeded in capturing the northern provinces, which was the most heavily Protestant, most Dutch-speaking, and most low-lying part of the country. This last factor was important, for the rebels cut the dikes and flooded the countryside, stymieing the vaunted Spanish cavalry (it was, they soon discovered, very difficult to execute cavalry charges in twelve feet of standing water and a thick gumbo of mud) and facilitating their own movements in small boats captained by experienced mariners known as the Sea Beggars. Felipe's army held most of the southern part of the country – the present Belgium – which was mostly Catholic, French-speaking, and dry. Although the struggle quickly dissolved into a no-win stalemate, Felipe stubbornly sent battalion after battalion into the morass of the delta, where the Sea Beggars chewed them up.

Despite appalling losses, Felipe refused to give up, even when it was apparent to everyone else that Spain could not possibly win. The costly war was still going on when Felipe died in 1598, and would not end until eleven years after that, when Felipe's son and successor, Felipe III (r. 1598-1621), finally agreed to a truce. Even then it wasn't really over. In 1621 the fighting started up again, this time begun by Willem's son and successor, Prince Maurice. Not until 1648 did Spain finally recognize Dutch independence.

In the end, Spain kept the southern, majority-Catholic, French-speaking half of the Low Countries as the Province of the Spanish Netherlands, today called Belgium. But the northern, majority-Protestant, Dutch-speaking part became an independent country, officially called the United Provinces of the Netherlands, but generally referred to in its day as the Dutch Republic. Governed by an oligarchy of wealthy Calvinist bourgeois, the Republic soon became a leading force in Western commerce.[190]

The Revenge of Good Queen Bess

In 1588, after thirty years on the throne, Felipe II was deeply frustrated. True, he had enjoyed many successes, and his country was the most powerful in the West. His navy had defeated the Muslim Ottomans and controlled the Mediterranean Sea. His armies ruled the Americas. His military might had allowed him to annex Portugal. In France, his allies, the Catholic League, were temporarily on the ascendant. The Holy Roman Empire generally did his bidding. The pope was his staunch ally.

Yet the Low Countries and England – those pestholes of Protestantism – still vexed him. Spain had poured vast amounts of resources – tens of thousands of soldiers, guns, swords, horses, ships, and golden *reals* – into the Dutch War for Independence and the Sea War with England, but had gotten precisely nowhere. Dutch rebels still held the soggy Rhine delta. And on the sea buccaneering Dutch Sea Beggars and dashing English Sea Dogs pirated Spanish shipping with impunity. The English captain Sir Francis Drake had even taken a squadron of his warships into Spain's busy Cadiz (Kah-DEEZ) harbor, looted the city, and sailed away, boasting that he had "singed the beard of the king of Spain." Furious, Felipe had reinforced his army in the Low Countries, increasing it to 60,000 men. But in the 1570s Felipe had run out of money to pay them, and they had mutinied. By 1577 the Spanish army in the Low Countries had dwindled to 8,000, the rebels were winning, Spanish seaports were in flames, and Felipe was nearly bankrupt. Something drastic had to be done.

In hindsight, it is obvious that what Felipe should have done was admit defeat and make peace. He should have granted the Dutch their independence, recognized Elizabeth as the rightful monarch of England, accepted the fact that northern Europe was Protestant, and given up on the old, traditional ideal of one church of all believers. But Felipe was an idealist, a true believer, a man who was intellectually incapable of giving up on a cause. So what he did instead was launch the worst naval disaster in history until Pearl Harbor, and in the process so weaken Spain as to condemn it to centuries as a second-rate power. He sent the so-called "invincible" Spanish Armada to its doom in the narrow waters of the English Channel.

On paper, the Armada did indeed look invincible. The Spanish vessels were larger and more numerous than their English and Dutch counterparts. The plan was to sail the Armada into the English Channel, defeat the smaller English and Dutch fleets, and then land armies in England and the Low Countries, conquering both. But, as Felipe's admirals well knew, the Protestants had certain advantages of their own. The English and Dutch ships were smaller, it is true, but they were also faster. They could maneuver better in shallow water.

---

[190] Ibid, 219-222, Wedgwood, *William the Silent*, passim.

Their longer cannon had greater range. Their captains were battle-tested, highly skilled in the art of fighting ship-to-ship. And they would be fighting in familiar home waters. Yet, the Spanish were confident of success. As one of Felipe's advisors told him, "It would seem to be God's obvious design to bestow upon Your Majesty the crowns of these two kingdoms." God, they were convinced, was on their side.[191]

And so the Armada sailed. Desperately, Elizabeth assembled every ship she had to meet it. At the English port town of Tilbury "Good Queen Bess" addressed her captains, showing them that she had steel in her spine. She urged them to victory, not for her sake only, but also for honor, glory, religion, and country. It was a masterpiece of oratory.

"My loving people," she told the Sea Dogs, referring to herself in the customary third person:

> we have been persuaded by some that are careful for our safety, to take heed how we commit ourselves to armed multitudes, for fear of treachery. But I assure you, I do not desire to live to distrust my faithful and loving people. Let tyrants fear. I have always so behaved myself that, under God, I have placed my chiefest strength and safeguard in the loyal heart and good will of my subjects; and therefore I am come amongst you as you see, at this time, not for my recreation and disport, but being resolved, in the midst and heat of battle, to live or die amongst you all, and to lay down for my God and for my kingdom and for my people, my honor and my blood, even in the dust. I know I have the body of a weak and feeble woman, but I have the heart and stomach of a king, and of a king of England too, and I think foul scorn that Parma [Felipe's chief military commander] or Spain, or any prince of Europe should dare to invade the borders of my realm; to which, rather than any dishonor shall grow by me, I myself will take up arms, I myself will be your general judge, and rewarder of every one of your virtues in the field. I know already for your forwardness you deserve rewards and crowns; and we do assure you, in the word of a prince, they shall be duly paid you.

In the words of the historian Garret Mattingly, "The shout of applause was tremendous."[192]

And they won. The smaller English ships stayed in shallow waters, where the larger Spanish ships couldn't reach them, and peppered the Armada with their long-range cannon. That night the English sent a flotilla of fire ships careening into the Spanish fleet. Inexplicably, the experienced Spanish captains panicked, ramming each other in the confusion. Attempting to reorganize, the next day the Armada stood off into the North Sea, but a storm blew up and scattered the Spanish fleet. The remnants limped back to Spain, defeated.

When Elizabeth died without children in 1603 (she was, after all, the "Virgin Queen"), her Protestant cousin, James Stuart (who was also the king of Scotland), took over as King James I. James made peace with Spain, maintained the Elizabethan Compromise, and appointed a committee of English scholars to translate the Bible into English. The famous King James Version (KJV) is still used today by most English-speaking Protestants. But he also started a chain of events that would lead to the bloody English Civil War of the 1640s, which we will examine in Chapter Five.

Conclusion

Spain's navy was virtually destroyed in 1588. After that the English Sea Dogs and Dutch Sea Beggars could raid Spanish shipping and ports almost at will. Worse, Spain's army was also severely weakened. Thousands of soldiers – the cream of Spanish manhood – had been loaded onto the Armada's transport ships and went to watery graves when the doomed ships went down. Moreover, Spain had gone deeply into debt to pay for the Armada. The treasury was bare.

Weak and broke, Spain was no longer a superpower. It could no longer keep the English, Dutch, and French from establishing colonies in the Americas. England was now smugly safe from invasion and knew it, protected by its mighty fleet. England's greatest writer, William Shakespeare, boasted that his country was now:

> This royal throne of kings, this scept'red isle,
> This earth of majesty, this seat of Mars,
> This other Eden, demi-paradise,
> This fortress built by Nature for herself
> Against infection and the hand of war,
> This happy breed of men, this little world,
> This precious stone set in the silver sea,
> Which serves it in the office of a wall
> Or as a moat defensive to a house,
> Against the envy of less happier lands,
> This blessed plot, this earth, this realm, this England.[193]

---

[191] Garret Mattingly, *The Armada* (1959), 81.
[192] Ibid, 349-350.
[193] From *Richard II*. While the play was set earlier, during the Hundred Years War, the lines were an obvious reference to the more recent defeat of the Spanish Armada.

Sea power had trumped land power. With Spain declining, England, France, and the Netherlands each plotted how they could rise to take its place.

The Wars of Religion were not yet over. The Thirty Years War (1618-48), a German civil war, would soon wreck the Holy Roman Empire, dooming it, like Spain, to inevitable decline. It would also weaken Spain further, because Spain became involved in it on the Catholic side. In the 1640s England, too, would be rent by a religious civil war.

By the mid-1600s the West had been truly reshaped. The old reality of one church of all believers was gone. The West was now irretrievably diverse, with several new Protestant churches existing alongside the old, Roman Catholic Church. Yet, if the reality of religious universalism had vanished, the ideal had not. Each group – Roman Catholics, Lutherans, Calvinists, and Anglicans – still dreamed of one church of all believers. But each side wanted unity on its own terms only, to be the last church left standing. Unable to shake the old ideal of one church of all believers, unable to accept the new reality of religious diversity, unable to achieve true religious toleration, for the next few decades Westerners could only eye each other warily, longing for a unity that would never come.

Furthermore, the religious struggles of the sixteenth and seventeenth centuries had brought down the West's old superpower, Spain, and several ambitious, hungry, upstart countries now looked to take its place. The Spanish and Portuguese monopoly on overseas trade and colonization ended. Catholic France, Anglican-Calvinist England, Calvinist Netherlands, and Lutheran Sweden now moved to establish colonies of their own. The fires of patriotism had been stoked in England and the Netherlands, which further contributed to the growth of the bourgeois ideal. A new age was dawning.[194]

-The Documents-

"Our Way of Life"

The history of Western Civilization is filled with tales of people who fought heroically for what they perceived as "their way of life" – the values and beliefs that they held sacred and dear, ideals for which they were willing to suffer and die, or force others to suffer and die. The participants in these intense conflicts generally viewed them as titanic death struggles between good and evil, upon which rested the fate of civilization itself. And as you well know, such conflicts are not merely the stuff of history. They continue to occur even today.

Historians approach such conflicts warily. One way to look at them is through the lens of what is sometimes called "cultural relativism." Historians who follow this approach acknowledge that the people involved truly believed that they were fighting the good fight for all that was just and true, but refuse to take sides. Cultural relativists would regard neither Roman Catholicism nor Protestantism, Felipe's idealism nor Elizabeth's pragmatism, Henri de Guise's piety nor Henri de Bourbon's cynicism, the doctrine of good works nor the doctrine of salvation by faith alone, as intrinsically good or evil, right or wrong. While such historians remain aloof from the issues about which people fought, they generally regard the struggles themselves as tragic. Like Paul Kennedy, they wonder how the wars, the deaths, the suffering could have been avoided. Usually, they conclude that intolerance was to blame, that the lesson of history is that unless we are willing to allow the other fellows their point of view, we will all suffer needlessly.

But some historians are suspicious of cultural relativism. Sometimes, they believe, such struggles *are* about good versus evil. They argue that certain cultural absolutes do exist – great moral truths that must be defended at all costs. Not many historians today would argue that either Roman Catholicism or Protestantism was evil (although I have encountered a few who do), but there are some (mostly Dutch or English) who view Anglo-Dutch constitutionalism as morally superior to Spanish absolutism.

What actions can people justify when they perceive themselves as defending their "way of life" against an attack of "evildoers"? Is censorship justifiable? War? Torture? Murder? Dishonesty? In times of such intense struggle, is compromise justifiable? Is it even possible? Was the Roman Catholic Church justified in censoring Protestant books? Were Puritans like Anne Bradstreet justified in their desire to create a "New England" in America (and in the process seize the land from its previous occupants, the Wampanoag, Massachusetts, Pequot, Mohegan, and other Algonkian peoples) so that there would be a safe haven for Puritans? If you were the President of the United States, what measures would you undertake if you believed that the American "way of life" was under siege?

Finally, is it possible to defend a "way of life" if that very culture is itself in the process of changing, of metamorphosing into something else?

---

[194] Hexter, *Europe Since 1500*, 245-257.

The Reformation as Good versus Evil: Martin Luther

Following the Diet of Worms, Martin Luther worked to rally Westerners to his cause. He translated the Bible into German, wrote and published numerous religious and political essays, and penned several hymns (religious songs) to be sung in church. He wrote the following hymn, "Ein Feste Burg" ("A Mighty Bourg" or "A Mighty Fortress") in 1529. The hymn reflects Luther's belief that a titanic battle between good and evil was being waged. The "ancient foe" mentioned in the first stanza was Satan. The following is a well-known English translation of the hymn.

"EIN FESTE BURG"[195]

A mighty fortress is our God,
   A bulwark never failing;
Our helper he amid the flood
   Of mortal ills prevailing:
For still our ancient foe
Doth seek to work us woe;
His craft and power are great,
And, armed with cruel hate,
   On earth is not his equal.

Did we in our own strength confide,
   Our striving would be losing;
Were not the right man on our side,
   The man of God's own choosing:
Dost ask who that might be?
Christ Jesus, it is he;
Lord Saboath his Name,
From age to age the same,
   And he must win the battle.
And though this world, with devils filled,
   Should threaten to undo us;
We should not fear, for God hath willed
   His truth to triumph through us:
The prince of darkness grim,
We tremble not for him;
His rage we can endure,
For lo! His doom is sure,
   Our little word shall fell him.

That word above all earthly powers,
   No thanks to them, abideth;
The Spirit and the gifts are ours
   Through him who with us sideth:
Let goods and kindred go,
This mortal life also;
The body they may kill:
God's truth abideth still,
   His kingdom is forever.

The Reformation as a War of Words: The Council of Trent

Between 1545 and 1563, during the height of the Reformation, at the direction of Pope Paul III (the same pope who declared that Native Americans were fully human, authorized Ignatius of Loyola to found the Jesuit Order, and authorized the Roman Inquisition), the leaders of the Roman Catholic Church met in the city of Trento (Trent), in the Alps Mountains on the border between Italy and the

---

[195] Martin Luther, "Ein Feste Burg" (1529), from an early English translation reprinted in *The Hymnal of the Protestant Episcopal Church in the United States of America* (1940), hymn no. 551.

Holy Roman Empire. The Council of Trent worked out many of the reforms of the Catholic (or Counter) Reformation. It forcefully defended the traditional doctrines of the Church. The Council also codified Church policy on the censorship of dangerous books, a practice that had first begun in 1559 under Paul III's successor, Pope Paul IV, who published *Index Auctorum et Librorum Prohibitorum*, usually referred to as the Pauline Index. By the time the Council had completed its work, Paul IV had died, but his successor, Pope Pius IV, accepted the Council's report. The new index was published in 1564 as *Index Librorum Prohibitorum* (*Index of Prohibited Books*), and was somewhat less strict than the earlier Pauline Index. Over the years, various popes expanded the list of prohibited books, and it was not until 1966 that the Church finally eliminated the *Index*. Among the works censored were everything written by Martin Luther, including "Ein Feste Burg." What do these rules tell us about the Council's state of mind? Do you think censorship was a reasonable response to the Protestant challenge? Why would the Council want to censor "Ein Feste Burg"? Try to develop arguments both for and against censorship.

from INDEX OF PROHIBITED BOOKS [196]

The holy Council [of Trent] in the second session, celebrated under our most holy Lord, [Pope] Pius IV, commissioned some fathers to consider what ought to be done concerning various . . . books either suspected or pernicious and to report to this holy Council.

1. All books which have been condemned either by the supreme pontiffs or by ecumenical councils before the year 1515 and are not contained on this list, shall be considered condemned in the same manner as they were formerly condemned.

2. The books of those heresiarchs, who after the aforesaid year originated or revived heresies, as well as those who are or have been the heads or leaders of heretics, as Luther, Zwingli, Calvin, Balthasar Friedberg, Schwenkfeld, and others like these, whatever may be their name, title or nature of their heresy, are absolutely forbidden. The books of other heretics, moreover, which deal professedly with religion are absolutely condemned. Those on the other hand, which do not deal with religion and have by order of the bishops and inquisitors been examined by [Roman] Catholic theologians and approved by them, are permitted. Likewise, [Roman] Catholic books written by those who afterward fell into heresy, as well as by those who after their fall returned to the bosom of the Church, may be permitted if they have been approved by the theological faculty of a [Roman] Catholic university or by the general Inquisition.

3. The translations of writers, also ecclesiastical, which have until now been edited by condemned authors, are permitted provided they contain nothing contrary to sound doctrine. Translations of the books of the Old Testament may be in the judgment of the bishop permitted to learned and pious men only.... Translations of the New Testament made by authors of the first group of this list shall be permitted to no one, since great danger and little usefulness usually results to readers from their perusal.

4. Since it is clear from experience that if the Sacred Books are permitted everywhere and without discrimination in the vernacular, there will by reason of the boldness of men arise therefrom more harm than good, the matter is in this respect left to the judgment of the bishop or inquisitor, who may with the advice of the pastor or confessor permit the reading of the Sacred Books translated into the vernacular by [Roman] Catholic authors to those who they know will derive from such reading no harm but rather an increase of faith and piety, which permission they must have in writing. Those, however, who presume to read or possess them without such permission, may not receive absolution from their sins until they have handed them over to the authorities.

* * * *

7. Books which professedly deal with, narrate or teach things lascivious or obscene are absolutely prohibited, since not only the matter of faith but also that of morals, which are usually easily corrupted through the reading of such books,

---

[196] J. Waterworth, trans., *The Cannons and Decrees of the Sacred and Oecumenical Council of Trent* (1848), reprinted in Eugen Weber, ed, *The Western Tradition* (1995), 1: 408-417.

must be taken into consideration, and those who possess them are to be severely punished by the bishops. Ancient books written by heathens may by reason of their elegance and quality of style be permitted, but may by no means be read to children.

Finally, all the faithful are commanded not to presume to read or possess any books contrary to the prescriptions of these rules or the prohibition of this list. And if anyone should read or possess books by heretics or writings by any author condemned and prohibited by reason of heresy or suspicion of false teaching, he incurs immediately the sentence of excommunication.

Establishing an Ideologically "Pure" Community in America: Anne Bradstreet

Anne Dudley Bradstreet (1612-72) emigrated from England to New England in 1630. She was part of the Great Migration, a mass movement of thousands of radical, Calvinist English Protestants, known as Puritans, to North America in the decade of the 1630s. Puritans feared that England was headed for disaster, and they didn't want to be around when it happened. In England, the royal government under the new Stuart dynasty had been attempting gradually to reform the country's official, government-sponsored church, the Church of England (Anglican Church), to make it closer to the Roman Catholic Church in its liturgy, organization, and practices. In the 1620s and 1630s, under King Charles I, Anglican Church leaders proposed a return to celebrating the mass in Latin (a language the average Englishman and Englishwoman did not understand), strengthening the authority of the bishops, and making the parish priests more independent of their congregations. Those who supported the changes were known as High Church Anglicans or Episcopalians (so-called because they believed the Church should be managed by the bishops). Those who opposed them were known variously as Low Church Anglicans, Congregationalists (because they believed that parish priests should be partly responsible to their congregations), Presbyterians (because they believed the Church should be managed not by bishops but by "presbyteries," or councils composed mainly of "teaching priests" and learned laymen), or Puritans (because they wanted to "purify" the Church, taking it back to its Old Testament roots).

Radical Puritans like Anne Bradstreet rejected the idea of bishops altogether and wanted to replace them completely with presbyteries. They believed that the bishops were corrupt men who put their own prestige, political power, and financial well being ahead of religious principles and piety. They also viewed bishops as a leftover relic of Roman Catholicism, and opposed the practice as a sinful return to the old Church. They feared that if the bishops remained in power, an angry and righteous God would exact a just punishment on England, causing great suffering. Believing that England was backsliding into Catholicism and thus might be nearly destroyed, they decided to create an ideal Puritan colony in North America, which would serve as a model "commonweal" that the surviving English could follow when, in the future, they rebuilt their shattered nation. It would also serve as a safe haven for Calvinists at a time when they felt themselves under increasing attack. When the English Civil War broke out in the 1640s, pitting High Church Anglicans and the king on the one hand and Puritans and Parliament on the other, the New England Puritans saw it as evidence that their predictions of disaster had come true.

Anne Bradstreet's relatives were all active Puritans. Her father, the former steward to the Earl of Lincoln, was a governor and assistant governor of the Puritan colony of Massachusetts Bay. Her husband, Simon Bradstreet, a Puritan minister, was another governor. Married when she was only sixteen, Anne came with her husband and parents to America two years later. Nervous about starting life over in what she at first viewed as a wilderness, her "heart rose" (i.e., was in her throat) when she first saw the thickly forested New England coast from the deck of the ship *Arbella*. But she also supported the idea of creating a Puritan utopian community in North America, and listened in rapt attention as the Puritan leader John Winthrop addressed the passengers, telling them that God commanded them to "build a city on a hill" – a new, Protestant society that would be watched by the whole world.

While raising her eight children, Bradstreet also managed to write poems. Neighbor women chided her for spending too much time writing, and not enough keeping house. But her family was proud of her poems. In 1650, when the English Civil War was over, Anne's brother-in-law, on a visit to England, had some of her poems published, which made her the first published poet in English America. Most of Anne's poems are warm, gentle pieces about family life. For example, in a moving love poem about her husband, she wrote:

> If ever two were one, then surely we.
> If ever man were loved by wife, then thee;
> If ever wife was happy in a man,
> Compare with me ye women if you can.

Like most seventeenth-century Europeans, Anne loved puns. She crammed several into another love poem, which she wrote to her husband when he was away on business. (A hind is a female deer, while a hart is a male deer.)

> As loving hind that (hartless) wants her deer,
> Scuds through the woods and ferns with harkening ear,
> Perplexed, in every bush and nook does pry,

Her dearest deer, might answer ear or eye;
So does my anxious soul, which now does miss,
A dearer dear (far dearer heart) than this.

Bradstreet also wrote poems in which she struggled to reconcile her Christian duty to God to keep her eyes firmly on heaven with her human desire for material things. In a sad, haunting poem, "Upon the Burning of Our House," she reflected that, after her house burned in a fire, she should be grateful that no one was hurt. She knew she should view the fire as God's way of strengthening her, of turning her eyes away from her "things" and towards heaven. And yet,

Here stood that trunk, and there that chest;
There lay that store I counted best:
My pleasant things in ashes lie,
And them behold no more shall I.

Being "heavenly," she confessed, was tough.

As warm, human, and funny as Bradstreet seemed in most her poems, she had another, darker side. In some of her poems – ones where she discussed the reasons the Puritans had migrated to America – Bradstreet seethed with bitter anger, most of which was directed at Roman Catholics and High Church Anglicans, whom she believed had conspired with Satan to destroy her beloved England. These political poems roiled with righteous indignation, religious intolerance, and political vituperation. They were a window into the Puritan psyche, and explained what the Puritans saw as the purpose of their colony in America: to preserve what they considered traditional religious values. Interestingly, Bradstreet saw England as a beloved but imperiled "mother" and the colonies in America as loving "daughters." She wrote the poem excerpted below in 1642, after the English Civil War had begun. Her spelling, phrasing, and grammar – which were very proper for the 1600s – have been modernized for clarity.

from "A DIALOGE BETWEEN OLD ENGLAND AND NEW;
CONCERNING THEIR PRESENT TROUBLES, ANNO 1642"[197]

[New England:]

Alas, dear mother, fairest queen and best,
With honor, wealth and peace, happy and blessed;
What ails you? Why do you hang your head and cross your arms?
Why do you sit in the dust and sigh such sad alarms?
What deluge of new woes could thus overwhelm
The glories of your famous realm?
What means your wailing tone, your mournful guise?
Ah, tell your daughter, so that she may sympathize.

[Old England:]

Are you ignorant indeed of these, my woes?
Must my forced tongue these griefs disclose?
Must I dissect my tarred state,
Which amazed Christendom stands wondering at?
And you, my child, my limb, don't you feel
My fainting, weakened body begin to reel?
This physick purging potion I have taken,
Will bring consumption, or an ague quaking,
Unless some cordial you fetch from high,
And give to me to ease my malady.
If I decease, do you think you can survive?
Or by my wasting state do you think to thrive?
Then weigh our case, if it be not justly sad;
Let me lament alone, while you are glad.

---

[197] Anne Bradstreet, "A Dialogue Between Old England and New; Concerning Their Present Troubles, Anno, 1642," in Anne Bradstreet, *The Tenth Muse, Lately Sprung Up in America* (1650), and reprinted in Anne Bradstreet, *To My Husband and Other Poems* (2000), 52-61.

[New England:]

And thus (alas) your state you much deplore
In general terms, but will not say why:
What medicine shall I seek to cure this woe?
If the wound's so dangerous, I may not know.
What is the storm from Earth or Heaven above?
Is it drought, is it famine, or is it pestilence?
Do you feel the sting, or fear the consequence?
Your humble child entreats you, show your grief,
Though weapons, nor money, she has for your relief,
Such is her poverty: yet you shall find
A suppliant for your help, as she is bound.

[Old England:]

I must confess some of these sores you name,
My beauteous body at this present time maim.
For wants, sure some I feel, but more I fear.
As for the pestilence, who knows how near.
Famine and plague, two sisters of the sword,
Destruction to a land, do soon afford.
They're for my punishment ordained on high,
Unless our tears prevent it speedily.
But yet I answer not what you demand,
To show you the grievance of my troubled land?
But before I tell the effect, I'll show the cause,
Which are my sins: the breach of sacred laws.
Idolatry, supplanter of a nation
With foolish superstitious adoration,
Is liked and countenanced by men of might.
The Gospel is trodden down and has no right.
Church offices were sold and bought for gain,
That the Pope hoped to find Rome here again.
Oaths and Blasphemies: one did never
From Belzebub himself such language hear.
What scorning of the Saints of the most high!
What injuries did daily on them lie!
What false reports, what disrespectful names did they take,
Not for their own, but for their Master's sake?
And you poor soul, were jeered among the rest,
Your flying for the truth was made a jest.
For Sabbath-breaking, and for drunkenness,
Did ever a land such profaneness more express?
Well to the matter then, there's grown of late
'Twixt King and Parliament a question of State:
Which is the chief, the law or else the King?
One said, "It's he." The other, "No such thing."
'Tis said, the better part in Parliament
To ease my groaning land, showed their intent
To crush the proud, and right to each man deal,
To help the Church and save the commonweal.
But now I come to speak of my disaster,
Contention grown, 'twixt the people and the king, their master;
They argued so long, they fell to blows.
Thousands lay in heaps. Here bleeds my woes.
I that no wars so many years have known,
Am now destroyed and slaughtered by my own.
Oh, pity me in this sad perturbation!
My towns are plundered. My houses are devastated.
My young women are weeping, and my young men are slain.
My wealthy trading has fallen. I have a dearth of grain.
The seedtime comes, but the plowman has no hope,
Because he knows not who shall buy his crop.
The poor lack their pay, and their children lack bread.

Their woeful mothers' tears are unpittied.

[New England:]

Dear mother, cease your complaints and wipe your eyes.
Shake off your dust, cheer up, and now arise.
You are my mother, m nurse, and I am your flesh.
Your sunken bowels gladly would I refresh.
Your griefs I pity, but soon hope to see,
Out of your troubles much good fruit to be.
To see those later days of hoped for good,
Though now beclouded all with tears and blood.
After dark Popery the day did clear,
But now the Sun in it's brightness shall appear.
These are the days the Church's foes to crush,
To root out Popelings head, tail, branch and rush.
Let's bring Baal's vestments forth to make a fire,
Of their miters, surplices, and all their attire,
Copes, rotchets, crosiers, and such empty trash,
And let their names be consumed, but let the flash
Light Christendom, and all the world to see
We hate Rome's whore, with all her trumpery
So shall your happy nation ever flourish,
When truth and righteousness they thus shall nourish.
When thus in peace, your armies brave send out,
To sack proud Rome, and all her Vassals rout;
There let your name, your fame, and glory shine,
As did your ancestors in Palestine.
And let Rome's spoils full pay, with interest, be
Of what unjustly once she taxed from you.
Of all the woes you can, let Rome be sped,
And on her pour the vengeance threatened.
Bring forth the beast that ruled the world with it's beck,
And tear its flesh, and set your feet on its neck.
And make its filthy den desolate,
To the astonishment of all that knew its state.

The Decline of a Superpower: Miguel de Cervantes

In *Piers the Plowman* and *Divine Comedy* William Langland and Dante Alighieri described Western Civilization as a traditional society based on the four pillars of manorialism, feudalism, Roman Catholicism, and trifunctionalism. But beginning in the mid-1300s, as we have seen, Western Civilization slowly began to modernize. "Modernization" is the process whereby a society or culture is transformed from traditional to modern. The events of the Reformation speeded up that process.

The increased literacy and emphasis on formal education that were hallmarks of the 1300s and 1400s led to a huge increase in the quantity of literature produced in the 1500s and 1600s. The new literature mirrored the many deep and vital changes going on in at the time, including modernization, and contained many modern elements. For example, some of the writers, such as Spain's Miguel de Cervantes (1547-1615), took advantage of rising literacy rates to write novels (a "new," individualistic form of literature designed to be read silently, to oneself) rather than epic poems (an older, communalistic form of literature designed to be memorized and recited aloud). Similarly, France's Michel de Montaigne (1533-1592) invented the essay as a literary form. England's William Shakespeare (1564-1616) explored several new, modern themes, such as religious toleration, business relationships, the nature of civic humanism, and the tension between communalism and individualism. Most of the new writers wrote not in the Medieval Latin used by the clergy, but in the various new national languages – Spanish, English, French, Italian, German, Dutch, and Swedish – favored by the up-and-coming bourgeoisie. Among them, these writers created the basis for modern Western literature.

Miguel de Cervantes Saavedra (1547-1615) was the son of a middle-class Spanish doctor. When he was 21, he left home, joined the Spanish army, and saw service in Italy, where Spain was fighting another one of those long, draining wars that so weakened the country in the 1500s. After seven years of fighting, Cervantes boarded a ship returning to Spain, only to be captured by Muslim pirates. Taken to Algiers, a Muslim kingdom in North Africa, Cervantes was sold as a slave. He failed in three escape attempts, but was finally ransomed after five years of captivity. Returning to Spain, Cervantes moved from job to job, barely eked out a living, and spent several years in debtors' prison. He wrote numerous plays and a novel, but none of them were successful.

Finally, in 1604, when he was 57 years old, Cervantes published part one of his masterpiece, *Don Quixote*. It was immediately popular. In 1613 he published a book of short stories. In 1614 came part two of *Don Quixote*. Cervantes died the following year.

Written in Castilian (a dialect of Spanish) rather than in Latin, *Don Quixote* established modern Spanish literature. Essentially a parody of Medieval ballads, *Don Quixote* satirized traditional notions of chivalry, knights errant, ladies fair, mighty dragons, and other aspects of Medieval culture and lore that Cervantes believed had no place in the modern world. Cervantes had seen real war close up, and he knew that it had nothing to do with chivalry and knights in shining armor. In his image of the aging, deluded Don Quixote, Cervantes portrayed an aspect of early 1600s Spain itself – a creaking empire, once a mighty superpower but now weakened by strategic overstretch, seeking to recapture its former greatness and hiding the truth of its decline in fine-sounding talk of God, gold, and glory.

The two protagonists of the novel were traditional figures struggling to make sense of the modern world: the insane nobleman, Don Quixote, who imagined himself a gallant knight of olden times, and his faithful squire, the common-sense peasant Sancho Panza. Modern machines like windmills (in fact, windmills were a Medieval invention, but Cervantes did not know that) didn't fit into the traditional world of the crazy old knight, so he perceived them as mythical giants instead. "The adventures of these two are the core of the book," writes one scholar of Spanish literature, "and several modern writers have reminded us that the two of them stand for opposing forces that have been active in Spain ever since the book was written: the spirit of Quixote, living in the mind, oblivious to the successive defeats his country has sustained, master of the huge ramshackle Spanish Empire, whose riches invariably drained into foreign hands, a poor gentleman concerned more with his title to nobility than with the bareness of his larder; and the spirit of Sancho, the shrewd peasant whose simplicity was forever exploited, and whose poverty has never diminished." The opposite of William Langland the traditionalist, Cervantes the modernist warned that Spain could only re-achieve greatness if it shucked the traditional mentality of Quixote and embraced the modern world.

To what extent was Cervantes a Spanish patriot? To what extent was he a social critic? Is it possible to be both? Is decline inevitable for all superpowers? How might it be avoided?

from *DON QUIXOTE* [198]

CHAPTER VIII

At that moment they caught sight of some thirty or forty windmills, which stand on that plain, and as soon as Don Quixote saw them he said to his squire: "Fortune is guiding our affairs better than we could have wished. Look over there, friend Sancho Panza, where more than thirty monstrous giants appear. I intend to do battle with them and take all their lives. With their spoils we will begin to get rich, for this is a fair war, and it is a great service to God to wipe such a wicked brood from the face of the earth."

"What giants?" asked Sancho Panza.

"Those you see there," replied his master, "with their long arms. Some giants have them about six miles long."

"Take care, your worship," said Sancho; "those things over there are not giants but windmills, and what seem to be their arms are the sails, which are whirled round in the wind and make the millstone turn."

"It is quite clear," replied Don Quixote, "that you are not experienced in this matter of adventures. They are giants, and if you are afraid, go away and say your prayers, whilst I advance and engage them in fierce and unequal battle."

As he spoke, he dug his spurs into his steed Rocinante, paying no attention to his squire's shouted warning that beyond all doubt they were windmills and not giants he was advancing to attack. But he went on, so positive that they were giants that he neither listened to Sancho's cries nor noticed what they were, even when he got near them. Instead he went on shouting in a loud voice: "Do not fly, cowards, vile creatures, for it is one knight alone who assails you."

At that moment a slight wind arose, and the great sails began to move. At the sight of which Don Quixote shouted: "Though you wield more arms than the giant Briareus, you shall pay for it!" Saying this, he commended himself with all his soul to his Lady Dulcinea, beseeching her aid in his great peril. Then, covering himself with his shield and putting his lance in the rest, he urged Rocinante forward at a full gallop and attacked the nearest

---

[198] Miguel de Cervantes Saavedra, *Don Quixote: The Ingenious Gentleman of La Mancha*, trans. John Ormsby (n. d.), 83-87.

windmill, thrusting his lance into the sail. But the wind turned it with such violence that it shivered his weapon in pieces, dragging the horse and his rider with it, and sent the knight rolling badly injured across the plain. Sancho Panza rushed to his assistance as fast as his donkey could trot, but when he came up he found that the knight could not stir. Such a shock Rocinante had given him in their fall.

"Oh my goodness!" cried Sancho. "Didn't I tell your worship to look what you were doing, for they were only windmills? Nobody could mistake them, unless he had windmills on the brain."

"Silence, friend Sancho," replied Don Quixote. "Matters of war are more subject than most to continual change. What is more, I think – and that is the truth – that the same sage Friston who robbed me of my room and my books has turned those giants into windmills, to cheat me of the glory of conquering them. Such is the enmity he bears me; but in the very end his evil arts shall avail him little against the goodness of my sword."

"God send it as He will," replied Sancho Panza, helping the knight to get up and remount Rocinante, whose shoulders were half dislocated.

-CHAPTER V-
AND ALL WAS LIGHT:
SCIENCE, CONSTITUTIONALISM, AND THE AGE OF REASON
1543 - 1789

Thomas Paine would later dub the period from the mid-1500s to the mid-1700s "the Age of Reason." He called it that because he believed that it had been a time when people turned away from faith and towards science and logic, a transformation that he heartily approved. Historians agree that "reason" did become more central to Western culture during this time. In particular, three major historical phenomena occurred during the Age of Reason: the Scientific Revolution, the advent of absolutism and constitutionalism as new forms of government, and the Enlightenment.

Two main aspects marked the Scientific Revolution of the 1500s and 1600s. One was the appearance in the West of Asian technology, imported from the Middle East, India, and China. Among these new technologies were magnetic compasses, caravels and galleons with lateen sails, gunpowder and cannon, printing presses, and telescopes – all of which had a major impact on the history of Western Civilization, which we examined in Chapter Three. The second aspect of the Scientific Revolution, which in the long run was more important than the first, was the arrival of a new way of thinking about science: the scientific method. This chapter will examine the shift from scholasticism (Medieval science) to modern science based on the scientific method.

In the 1600s the shape and form of government in Western Civilization also began to change. Medieval government had been based on feudalism, and was characteristically small, weak, and local. But after 1500 in several countries – Portugal, Spain, France, England, the Netherlands, and Sweden – larger, more powerful, more centralized governments first appeared. Historians call these new systems "centralized nation-states," or "the new monarchies." Each of the new states followed one of two new theories of government that had originated in the seventeenth century, absolutism and constitutionalism. Seventeenth- and eighteenth-century political philosophers used "scientific" evidence and reason to support one or the other of these new systems.

The 1700s saw the advent of the Enlightenment, a movement for political, social, and economic reform led by intellectuals known as philosophes. Impressed by the rationalism and seeming certainty of the Scientific Revolution, appalled at the death and destruction of the Wars of Religion, repelled by the rigid authoritarianism of absolutism, and drawn to the respect for individual liberty they saw as inherent in constitutionalism, these philosophes sought and attempted to apply "natural laws" of human behavior to design more efficient and more humane systems of government and business. In the process, they designed the basic systems of government (liberal democracy) and economy (capitalism) that characterize the West today. We will read excerpts from the works of one of these Enlightenment philosophes, England's John Locke, as well as an account of how Locke's words were interpreted by the former slave, Olaudah Equiano.

"Reason" was the catchword of the age, so much so that the eighteenth-century English political philosopher Thomas Paine would dub the seventeenth and eighteenth centuries "the Age of Reason." It was a time of optimism, when scientific and social progress seemed well within the grasp of the West. Lauding both the era's greatest scientist and reason itself, the eighteenth-century English poet Alexander Pope concluded:
> Nature and Nature's laws lay hid in night:
> God said, "Let Newton be!" and all was light.

It was a fitting epitaph for an Age of Reason.

-The Background-

Medieval Science

Medieval science – known as scholasticism – had four basic characteristics.

First of all, it was deductive, which is to say that Medieval scientists reasoned from the top down, seeking to answer specific questions by appealing to a core group of widely accepted general principles, which were assumed to be true and never questioned. A good example of deductive reasoning is plane geometry, developed during Classical times but accepted by Medieval thinkers. Plane geometry begins with seven general axioms and then proceeds by deductive reasoning to prove several hundred specific theorems. The axioms themselves are never questioned.

In addition to being deductive, Medieval science was also theocentric, or God-centered. Medieval thinkers accepted Christianity as true and considered the Bible a perfect source of knowledge. Consequently, they believed that they could deduce scientific truth directly from scripture. For example, when Medieval scientists wanted to calculate the age of the earth, they consulted chronologies contained in the Old Testament of the Bible. When they pondered the wonders of the universe, their first question was always, "How would God have arranged things? What makes the most sense from God's point of view?" They believed that heaven, hell, purgatory, and Eden were real places, located somewhere in the universe.

Third, Medieval science was authoritative. It relied on certain widely accepted Classical texts that had been passed down through the ages, especially the works of Aristotle (384-322 BCE), Archimedes (c. 287-212 BCE), and Ptolemy (c. 85-165 CE).

Fourth, Medieval scientists saw nature as God's will, and thus viewed it as essentially immutable and unknowable. People, they believed, could no more understand or control nature than they could understand or control God.

Guided by these four characteristics, Medieval scientists accepted a geocentric (earth-centered) model of the universe, a view first proposed by Aristotle and later refined by Ptolemy and others. This was the cosmology that Dante used in his famous Medieval epic poem, *Divine Comedy*, excerpts of which we read in Chapter One. According to this view, the earth (which Medieval scientists knew to be spherical) lay at the center of the universe. Hell, a real place, was at the center of earth (which was why Dante believed that it might be possible to get there by climbing down the crater of a volcano). Purgatory was somewhere on the earth's surface, possibly in the southern hemisphere. Eden was also on earth, probably in Asia. Since heaven was the opposite of hell, it must be located at the far edge of the universe, somewhere beyond the stars (or, as Dante depicted it, the planets and stars might be part of heaven). The various "heavenly objects" – the moon, sun, planets, asteroids, comets, and stars – were thought to be embedded in gigantic crystal spheres that rotated around the earth: the moon was in the closest sphere, then the sun, then the various planets, asteroids, and comets. The stars were in the last sphere. Although invisible, the spheres were solid. They held everything in place and kept the heavenly bodies from falling to earth. Because the spheres were close to heaven (or perhaps part of it), they and the bodies embedded in them must be perfect – perfectly spherical, with no mountains, valleys, volcanoes, or craters. Earth itself was imperfect, of course, but that was because it was close to hell.[199]

The Copernican Revolution in Astronomy

In the mid-1500s Mikolaj Kopernik (Nicholas Copernicus in Latinized English) (1473-1543), a studious Polish monk, challenged this view of the universe. Thanks to a wealthy uncle, Kopernik had been educated in medicine and law at the University of Padua in Italy, and had then become a professor at Poland's University of Krakow. Interested in astronomy, Kopernik read widely on the subject. With the naked eye – telescopes did not yet exist west of China – he watched the movements of the various heavenly bodies. He became intrigued by an old problem: why do the plants move across the night sky in such eccentric patterns? One day it dawned on him that the "orbits" of the planets appeared odd only if you accepted that they orbited the earth. If you believed instead that they orbited the sun, their paths did not seem strange at all. In 1543 Kopernik published *Concerning the Revolutions of the Celestial Spheres,* in which he challenged the old geocentric model of the universe. He proposed instead that it was the sun that lay at the center, and the earth was but one of several planets orbiting it. This new view came to be known as the heliocentric (sun-centered) model of the universe.

Kopernik's book unleashed a firestorm of controversy. The Roman Catholic Church, the most important institution in the West, had long accepted the older, geocentric view as true, and had even made it part of official church doctrine. Thus Kopernik challenged not only prevailing scientific wisdom, but also seemed to be challenging Holy Mother Church herself. Moreover, the controversy occurred in the 1500s, the very time that the Church was fighting for its life against a rising tide of Protestantism. It is entirely possible that if Kopernik had written his book in 1443 rather than 1543, there would have been far less controversy. But under the stress of the Reformation, Church leaders were in no mood for another challenge. Ironically, neither were Protestants; Martin Luther's comment on Kopernik was, "This fool wants to turn the whole of astronomy upside down!" Catholic, Protestant, and even Jewish leaders roundly condemned heliocentrism as anti-religious.

The story now shifted to Bohemia (today's Czech Republic). There, the eccentric, colorful Tycho Brahe (TIE-koh BRAH-hee) (1546-1601), a Danish lord who wore a prosthetic gold nose because he lost his real one in a swordfight – and who would eventually die of a burst bladder during an all-night drinking binge with his younger, hardier students – constructed an astronomical observatory at the University of Prague. Although still without the aid of a telescope, Tycho and his students charted the movements of the stars and planets, keeping careful measurements. Tycho never did agree with Kopernik's views, but he nevertheless passed his voluminous data on to his best student, the German Johannes Kepler (1571-1630). Applying careful mathematical analysis to Tycho's measurements, Kepler concluded that Copernicus had been right.

In 1609 the Italian astronomer Galileo Galilei (1564-1642), perhaps the greatest scientific mind of his era, heard that a tinker in the Netherlands had constructed a telescope, a gadget first invented in China. Galileo acquired a description of the device and soon constructed a hand-held telescope of his own. He trained it on the skies. What he saw astounded him. The sun was not perfect – it had sunspots. Neither was the moon, which was

---

[199] John Merriman, *A History of Modern Europe, from the Renaissance to the Present* (1996), 329-331; Richard E. Sullivan, Dennis Sherman, and John B. Harrison, *A Short History of Western Civilization* (1994), 458; J. H. Hexter, Richard Pipes, and Anthony Molho, *Europe Since 1500* (1971), 433-439.

studded with mountains and craters. But when Galileo turned his telescope on Jupiter and Saturn he was even more amazed. Rings encircled Saturn. And Jupiter had . . . moons!

This last fact had the greatest significance. It was empirical evidence that Kopernik had been on the right track. Galileo could now see for himself that not all heavenly bodies orbited the earth. Based on Kepler's mathematics and his own keen observations, Galileo concluded that Kopernik had been right, that the sun really was the center of the universe.

Church leaders were not pleased. It was all well and good for Kepler, who lived far away in the northern (Protestant) part of the Holy Roman Empire, to challenge Church doctrine. But Galileo lived in Italy, where the Church had its headquarters. He was hauled up before the Inquisition and forced to recant. But the word was out. Across Europe, scientists converted to heliocentrism.[200]

The Scientific Method

Science thus entered a new era, an age where mathematics and observation were considered stronger evidence of Truth than were Classical texts, the Bible, or deductive reasoning. The English philosopher Francis Bacon (1561-1626) and French philosopher and mathematician Rene Descartes (Day-KART) (1596-1650) argued that the debate over heliocentrism had generated a new way of doing science: the scientific method. The scientific method, Bacon and Descartes agreed, was based on inductive rather than deductive reasoning. Deduction is reasoning from top down, from the general to the specific; induction is reasoning from the bottom up, from the specific to the general. According to Bacon and Descartes, scientists like Kopernik, Tycho, Kepler, and Galileo begin by observing a phenomenon. Based on these observations, they induce a hypothesis, or plausible explanation for the phenomenon. That was what Kopernik had done. Then, the scientist tests that hypothesis by collecting data through direct observation, mathematics, or experimentation, as Tycho, Kepler, and Galileo had done. The third step was to refine the hypothesis, using the observations, mathematics, and experiments, into a theory – a detailed explanation of the phenomenon that was supported by the best available data. Heliocentrism was the hypothesis. Tycho, Kepler, and Galileo had collected the empirical data. But what was the theory?

The one thing that Kopernik, Kepler, and Galileo had not been able to explain was, why? Why did the planets and earth revolve around the sun? Why did moons revolve around planets? What kept all those heavenly bodies in place? What made them move? Why didn't everything fall into the sun? Obviously, the answer could not be crystal spheres, for the solar system was so complex and the planetary and lunar orbits so eccentric that the spheres would keep bumping into each other. It was the English mathematician and physicist Isaac Newton (1642-1727) who came up with the answer: gravity. Newton's theory of gravity (it is a misnomer to call it a "law"), a refinement of Kopernik's hypothesis of heliocentrism, explained why the solar system moved the way it did. Newton's theory of gravity became the foundation of Western physics until the twentieth century, when it was superceded by Albert Einstein's theory of relativity.[201]

A New Paradigm of Nature

The Scientific Revolution thus was not, at its core, really about new technology, although new inventions were involved in the form of telescopes, microscopes, printing presses, and other devices. Nor was it really about the switch from geocentrism to heliocentrism. It wasn't even essentially about Newton's theory of gravity. Rather, the real change – the real Scientific Revolution – was the decline of Medieval scholasticism and the rise of a new, modern science based on the scientific method. While Medieval science was deductive, theocentric, and authoritative, modern science was rooted in induction, observation, mathematics, and experimentation.[202]

With this change came two new and revolutionary attitudes about nature. The first was the realization that nature was not immutable, that in fact it changed over time. God's universe did not stand still. The second was the growing conviction that the universe was like a machine, something that could be studied, understood, mastered, and controlled. This second conclusion is sometimes referred to as the mechanistic view of nature. It would, as we will see, be fraught with danger.[203]

---

[200] Herbert Butterfield, *The Origins of Modern Science, 1300-1800* (1957), 29-48; Merriman, *History of Modern Europe*, 331-340; Sullivan, *Short History of Western Civilization*, 459-461; Hexter, *Europe Since 1500*, 439-451; Dava Sobel, *Galileo's Daughter: A Historical Memoir of Science, Faith, and Love* (1999), passim; Stillman Drake, *Galileo* (1980), passim.

[201] Butterfield, *Origins of Modern Science*, 89-128; Franklin Le Van Baumer, "The Scientific Revolution in the West," in *Main Currents of Western Thought*, ed. Franklin Le Van Baumer (1978), passim; Merriman, *History of Modern Europe*, 337, 340-353; Sullivan, *Short History of Western Civilization*, 461-463; Hexter, *Europe Since 1500*, 453-461; Sobel, *Galileo's Daughter*, 7-8; Drake, *Galileo*, passim.

[202] J. M. Roberts, *The Penguin History of the World* (1995), 654.

[203] Carolyn Merchant, *The Death of Nature: Women, Ecology, and the Scientific Revolution* (1980), passim.

> *Some Key Scientists of*
> *the Scientific Revolution:*
> *A Checklist*
>
> ✓ Gabriello Fallopio (Fah-LOH-pee-oh) (1523-62). Italian biologist. Dissected corpses. Developed theory of sexual reproduction.
>
> ✓ Andries van Wesele (Andreas Vesalius in Latinized English) (Vess-AIL-ee-us) (1514-64). Dutch physician. Court physician to Kaiser Karl V of the Holy Roman Empire. Dissected corpses to better understand how humans and other animals functioned. Founder of the modern science of biology.
>
> ✓ William Harvey (1578-1657). English physician. Dissected corpses. Developed theory of blood circulation.
>
> ✓ Anton van Leeuwenhoek (LEE-wen-hook) (1632-1723). Dutch merchant. Invented microscope and observed microscopic organisms.
>
> ✓ Margaret Cavendish, Duchess of Newcastle (1632-1723). English lady. Argued that there were limits to the ability of humans to control nature.
>
> ✓ Mikolaj Kopernik (Nicholas Copernicus in Latinized English) (1473-1543). Polish monk and teacher. Founder of the modern science of astronomy. See above.
>
> ✓ Tycho Brahe (1546-1601). Danish lord and astronomer. See above.
>
> ✓ Johannes Kepler (1571-1630). German astronomer and physicist. See above.
> ✓ Galileo Galilei (1564-1642). Italian astronomer and physicist. See above.
>
> ✓ Edmund Halley (1656-1742). English astronomer.
>
> ✓ Isaac Newton (1642-1727). English astronomer, mathematician, and physicist. The leading scientist of the Scientific Revolution. Founder of modern physics. Along with Leibniz, invented calculus. See above.
>
> ✓ Francis Bacon (1561-1626). English philosopher of science.
>
> ✓ Baruch Spinoza (1632-77). Spanish Jewish merchant and philosopher of science living in the Netherlands. Argued that matter and thought were two categories of reality and that freedom of thought (and toleration) were essential to scientific progress.
>
> ✓ Rene Descartes (1596-1650). French mathematician and philosopher of science. Invented analytic geometry. See above.
>
> ✓ Blaise Pascal (1623-62). French mathematician and physicist. Invented science of probability. Constructed the first calculating machine.
>
> ✓ Gottfried Leibniz (LIBE-nitz) (1646-1716). German mathematician and philosopher. Along with Newton, invented calculus.
>
> ✓ Robert Boyle (1627-91). Irish lord. Founder of the modern science of chemistry.
>
> ✓ Carl Linnaeus (Linn-AY-us) (1707-78). Swedish physician. Invented the taxonomic system in biology.

French Absolutism

As Spain declined, its neighbor France rose, and in the 1600s took Spain's place as the West's dominant superpower. France's American empire was smaller than Spain's, but almost as profitable – especially the sugar colony of Saint Domingue (Haiti), which in the 1700s was Europe's richest colony. France was also the second most populous country in the West (after the weakened Holy Roman Empire), and it had a strong agricultural base.

The rise of France was paralleled by the rise of an energetic new royal dynasty, the Bourbons, founded in 1594 by Henri IV (r. 1594-1610). However, the chief architect of Bourbon power had been Louis XIII's (r. 1610-43) chief minister (advisor), Cardinal Armand Jean du Plessis de Richelieu (REESH-lew) (1585-1642). Richelieu worked tirelessly to strengthen the monarchy, using tax revenues to finance an expanding army and navy. Louis XIV's (r. 1643-1715) chief minister, Cardinal Jules Mazarin (Mahz-ah-RAHN) (1602-1666) continued Richelieu's policies, as did Louis himself when he decided to become his own first minister.

The Bourbons based their power on several things: controlling the military, appointing bourgeois (who they could fire at will, and thus keep loyal) to key government posts, appointing bourgeois *intendents* (ahn-tahn-DAHNTS) to oversee the various provinces, censoring the press, spying on their critics, and in 1669-86 building an elegant new royal palace at Versailles (Vair-SIGH), just outside of Paris. The Bourbon kings invited lords to come reside at Versailles, where frequent parties and spirited gambling provided much more fun and excitement than life in the provinces. When lords lost their money at the gaming tables, or spent it on *cognac, coquetterie, et chansons,* the king was only too happy to lend them more – a strategy that put the lords firmly in his debt and under his thumb.

To justify their power, the Bourbons invoked an ideology known as absolutism, a term coined a century earlier by the French political philosopher Jean Bodin (Boh-DAHN) (1530-96). Appalled by the senseless, vicious religious wars and riots of the sixteenth-century Reformation – events he had witnessed firsthand – the anguished Bodin had advocated a political system in which wise, compassionate, patriotic, monarchs would rule with absolute power in order to promote justice, mercy, and peace. "Seeing that nothing upon earth is greater or higher, next to God, than the majesty of kings," Bodin reasoned in 1576, the "principal point of sovereign majesty and absolute power is to consist principally in giving laws unto the subjects in general, without their consent." Later, the English philosopher Thomas Hobbes (1588-1679) expressed the same sentiments. So did Louis XIV's tutor, Bishop Jacques Bossuet (Boss-WAY) (1627-1704), who claimed that kings were responsible only to God, and therefore ruled by "divine right." Significantly, no one – not Bodin, nor Hobbes, nor Bossuet, nor Louis – ever advocated misrule or arbitrary government. On the contrary, they believed that kings had a solemn duty to govern wisely and well, with justice and mercy, and in the best interest of the nation as a whole. Louis took his responsibilities seriously and strove to be a good king. But by putting their faith in "divine right," they proclaimed that it was God – not lords, nor Church, nor people – who would make sure the kings did a good job. Although based in part upon traditional theocentrism, absolutism was nevertheless a modern viewpoint, because it was used to justify large, centralized, bureaucratic nation-states like Bourbon France and Habsburg Spain.[204]

English Constitutionalism

England and the Netherlands went in a different direction. Following the Dutch War of Independence (1567-1648), the victorious Dutch bourgeoisie decided to form a republic. They organized their new country as a confederation of seven provinces, bound together by a federal legislature known as the States General. Lords received automatic representation in the States General, but were outnumbered by the bourgeoisie. The Princes of Orange (the heirs of Willem the Silent) served as the hereditary staatholders (chief administrative officers) of the Republic, but their authority was limited. Real power lay neither with the States General or the staatholders, but with the provinces. There, local courts enforced basic civil rights and administered local laws, mostly at the behest of the local bourgeoisie. Several times the staatholder attempted to increase his power, but each time the bourgeoisie managed to check him. The Republic was not a democracy where the people ruled; rather, it was an oligarchy where a minority – in this case, the bourgeoisie – was in charge. But if it wasn't democratic, neither was it absolutist. Instead, the Dutch developed a series of rules – some written, some unwritten – for governing the country. This system, where the country is governed according an agreed-on set of rules and procedures that are binding on the rulers as well as on the people, is known as constitutionalism.[205]

In England, constitutionalism developed slowly, over the course of the 1600s, out of a power struggle that pitted the kings on one side and the House of Commons on the other. It began when Queen Elizabeth I died in 1603. Her cousin and successor James I (r. 1603-1625) was a shy and scholarly man, and his reign was generally peaceful. But he nevertheless had a different view of monarchy than Elizabeth. Expressing a preference for absolutism, he asserted, "Kings are compared to fathers in families: for a king is truly *parens patriae*, the politic father of his people."[206]

James's son and successor, the dashing, elegant, ambitious, supremely self-confident Charles I (r. 1625-49), went further. A true absolutist, he embroiled England in a long and costly war with France, proposed changing the Anglican liturgy and church structure in order to make it more "Catholic," and more openly expressed his

---

[204] Merriman, *History of Modern Europe*, 274-299; Sullivan, *Short History of Western Civilization*, 420-425; Hexter, *Europe Since 1500*, 268-285.
[205] Merriman, *History of Modern Europe*, 260-262; Sullivan, *Short History of Western Civilization*, 441-443; Hexter, *Europe Since 1500*, 285-287.
[206] Merchant, *Death of Nature*, 173.

desire to rule as an absolute monarch. It was to escape Charles's religious reforms that Anne Bradstreet and other radical Puritans fled to New England in the 1630s.

In his drive for power, Charles enjoyed the support of many of the lords, the of majority of whom were High Church Anglicans, but he quarreled bitterly with the House of Commons, the elected branch of Parliament (England's chief legislative body), which represented the third estate and was dominated by the largely Puritan bourgeoisie. Charles desperately wanted a tax increase, especially after Scotland invaded England in 1639, but Commons replied that he could have one only if he renounced absolutism and abandoned his attempts to "episcopalize" the Anglican Church. Tempers flared. In 1642 Charles ordered his troops into Commons to arrest his critics, but someone tipped them off, and they fled before the soldiers arrived. Led by the charismatic, stubborn, self-righteous Puritan Oliver Cromwell (1599-1658), Commons organized a rebellion, known as the English Civil War.

In the conflict, Cromwell's loyal "New Model Army" (nicknamed the Roundheads because of their bad haircuts) defeated the forces of the king (dubbed the Cavaliers, from the French word *chevaliers*, meaning "knights"). Charles was captured and beheaded.

Commons now attempted to govern England by itself, without a monarch, England's first (and only) attempt at creating a republic, a government where the leaders are elected. But it turned out that the English were not yet ready to give up monarchy. Styling himself "Lord Protector," Cromwell ruled England as a virtual military dictator for ten years, as powerful and authoritarian as any absolute monarch, his power resting on the might of the New Model Army. He abrogated the Elizabethan Compromise and persecuted non-Puritans. He raised taxes to finance the conquest of Catholic Ireland. When he died in 1658, just like a king he was succeeded as Lord Protector by his son, the ineffective "Tumbledown Dick" Cromwell, who was even less popular than his father.

In 1660 Commons tired of the Cromwells and invited Charles I's son, Charles II (r. 1660-85), to assume the throne – provided that he agree to share power with Parliament and not seek to be an absolute monarch as his father had done. Charles readily agreed, and as the "Merry Monarch" spent most of his time partying and avoiding politics. Power thus passed to Parliament, which quickly divided into two competing political parties, the Tories (generally lords and other supporters of the king, who normally controlled Parliament's House of Lords) and the Whigs (mostly bourgeois who controlled the House of Commons). Although the two parties quarreled incessantly, for fifteen years there was peace.

However, when Charles died in 1685, another crisis arose. His younger brother and successor, James II (r. 1685-88), was reputed to be a closet Catholic (by now most English people were Protestants) and a secret advocate of absolutism (most of the English people supported constitutionalism). Parliament was worried about what James might do, but not overly so. After all, the new king was fifty-two and a widower. It was unlikely that he would live much longer. His adult children and heirs, his daughters Mary and Anne, were both Protestants and opponents of absolutism. But James confounded everyone. He remarried, choosing as his bride a young French (i.e., Catholic) princess. The new royal couple soon had a son, and decided that the boy – as a male, he was now the legal heir, before his older half-sisters – would be raised as a Catholic. Once again, England was thrown into turmoil.

Acting quickly, Parliament deposed James in the bloodless Glorious Revolution of 1688, which was supported by the Whigs and Tories alike. Parliament then invited Mary – witless, easily manipulated, but safely Protestant – to reign as Mary II (r. 1688-94), along with her Protestant husband William III (r. 1688-1702), the staatholder of the Dutch Republic. That the new king (everyone understood that William would be the actual monarch, not his weak-minded wife) had had plenty of experience working with constitutional government in the Netherlands was considered a plus.[207]

Still, it was thought best to get something in writing, just in case. Several new acts of Parliament, combined with some old acts and a number of unwritten "understandings," now established a new set of rules for governing the country. Collectively, these rules (along with others added since then) are known as the English Constitution. They included the newly enacted English Bill of Rights (1689), which reasserted that only Parliament could establish taxes, granted all members of Parliament freedom of speech, barred royal troops from entering Commons (as Charles I had once ordered them to do), mandated that Parliamentary elections be held at least every five years (so as not to have any more Cromwells), and provided for religious freedom for all Protestants (Catholics and Jews, however, still faced discrimination, and for many decades were barred not only from the throne, but from all government offices).

England thus became a constitutional monarchy, where an elected House of Commons held most of the power and the monarch was little more than an expensive figurehead. The office of Prime Minister, the actual head of government, who today is chosen by the majority party in Commons, would be created only slowly, over the next few decades. The first true British Prime Minister was Robert Walpole (1676-1745), who served during the reign of Mary's younger sister and successor, Queen Anne (1665-1714). The opposite of absolutism,

---

[207] Merriman, *History of Modern Europe*, 233-260; Sullivan, *Short History of Western Civilization*, 434-441; Hexter, *Europe Since 1500*, 306-329.

the British system – in which the rulers are bound by an agreed-upon set of rules and laws that apply to everyone – is known as constitutionalism. Because, like absolutism, it was used to justify large, centralized, state governments, it too is considered modern.

The Enlightenment of the Eighteenth-Century Philosophes

The 1700s saw the advent of something that the shy, bookish, misogynistic Prussian philosopher and university professor Immanuel Kant (1724-1804) would term the Enlightenment, an intellectual movement in which educated people throughout the West advocated a broad range of political, economic, and social reforms. Inspired by the logic and rationalism of the Scientific Revolution, repelled by the senseless brutality of the Wars of Religion, appalled by the intellectual narrowness and lack of freedom that they saw in absolutism, and attracted by the respect for individual liberties that underlay constitutionalism, the philosophes (FEEL-oh-sahfs) (intellectuals) of the Enlightenment strove to harness the scientific method to understand, explain, and improve Western Civilization.

Glib, well educated, and supremely confident of their own ideas, the philosophes were not really philosophers – not all of them, anyway. Rather, they were more analogous to the phalanx of "talking heads" that appear regularly on today's television talk shows, the eighteenth-century equivalent of Bill O'Reilly, George Will, Pat Buchanan, Rush Limbaugh, Anne Coulter, and Dr. Phil, alike in style, influence, and manner, although not in substance. According to the historian Peter Gay, they were "a loose, informal, wholly unorganized coalition of cultural critics, religious skeptics, and political reformers from Edinburgh to Naples, Paris to Berlin, Boston to Philadelphia, [who] made up a clamorous chorus" for reform. Although "there were some discordant voices among them,...what is striking is their general harmony, not their occasional discord. The men of the Enlightenment united on a vastly ambitious program, a program of secularism, humanity, cosmopolitanism, and freedom, above all, freedom in its many forms – freedom of arbitrary power, freedom of speech, freedom of trade, freedom to realize one's talents, freedom of aesthetic response, freedom, in a word, of moral man to make his own way in the world."[208]

The philosophes reasoned that if natural phenomena could be explained by "natural laws" (such as Newton's theory of gravity), then cultural phenomena could similarly be explained by "natural laws" (like Adam Smith's theory of supply and demand). Their use of the word "law" is important. What we today think of as theories (the best explanation available based on current empirical evidence), the philosophes viewed as immutable, ironclad laws. To them, Newton's explanation of gravity was more than a theory. Theories are subject to change as new evidence becomes available. Laws last forever. They are "Truth" with a capital "T." Theories are induced. Laws are "discovered."

To discover what the laws governing social phenomena were, the philosophes employed the scientific method: observe a problem, use inductive reasoning to develop a hypothesis, test the hypothesis by applying it to numerous case studies, and based on all the relevant data refine the hypothesis into a well-thought-out theory – except that, in their case, they viewed the end result as an immutable law rather than a theory. Once discovered, these social laws could not rationally be challenged. They could not be changed or altered, any more than gravity could be abrogated. Societies were machines, and the philosophes of the Enlightenment (like the scientists of the Scientific Revolution) took a very mechanistic view of the universe. No legislature, they believed, could possibly repeal the law of supply and demand. The most efficient and just societies, they insisted, were those based on natural laws.

The philosophes of the Enlightenment not only viewed knowledge in a different way than we do today, but also in a different way than people had before. Earlier, in the fourteenth and fifteenth centuries, the humanist philosophers of the Renaissance had divided knowledge into two broad categories, theology (the study of spiritual things such as religion) and humanism (the study of earthly things, such as philosophy, history, literature, art, music, mathematics, and science).

But the philosophes now subdivided humanism into three major sub-fields. The first of these sub-fields, which they dubbed "natural history," consisted of the study of those things that existed in nature, such as plants (botany), animals (zoology), rocks (geology), stars (astronomy), chemicals (chemistry), forces (physics), etc. – in other words, what we today think of as science. The second sub-field, which the philosophes called "civil history," was comprised of the study of those things that had been created by humans, such as governments, economies, societies, literature, art, philosophy, history, architecture, music, etc. – in other words, what we think of today as social science and the humanities. The third sub-field was mathematics, which provided scholars with the essential tools they needed in order to understand the other two fields. Keenly interested in all three sub-fields – natural history, civil history, and mathematics – the philosophes applied the same sorts of methods (observation, measurement, induction, application of empirical logic, the search for natural laws, etc.) to each.[209]

---

[208] Peter Gay, *The Enlightenment: An Interpretation* (1967-69), 1: 3.
[209] Butterfield, *Origins of Modern Science*, 171-186; Sullivan, *Short History of Western Civilization*, 466-475; Hexter, *Europe Since 1500*, 474-519; Carl L. Becker, *The Heavenly City of the Eighteenth-Century Philosophers* (1932), passim.

Benjamin Franklin

Typical of the philosophes of the Enlightenment was the American merchant Benjamin Franklin (1706-90), who lived most of his life in the British colonies of Massachusetts and Pennsylvania. Born in 1706 in Boston, Massachusetts (which had been founded only a little more than seventy years previously by Anne Bradstreet and the other Puritan refugees), Franklin was the tenth son of a candle maker. His father had more debts than money, but nevertheless owned his own business and was a respected member of the colony's lesser bourgeoisie. Franklin grew up in Boston, a middle-sized bourg of about 16,000 inhabitants. His father was able to provide him with basic schooling, although when he was in his early 'teens tight finances forced Franklin to leave school to become an apprentice to his older brother, who owned a print shop.

Despite his humble upbringing, Franklin had the same basic background as most of the philosophes. He was intelligent, bourgeois, urban, and (at least in part) formally educated. And his apprenticeship to his brother gave him access to a large amount of printed material, which he read voraciously. A virtual information sponge, the young Franklin absorbed works on natural history, civil history, and mathematics.

Moreover, Franklin was cosmopolitan. While still in his teens, he ran away from home (his brother used to beat him) and made his way to Philadelphia, the capital of the large, prosperous colony of Pennsylvania. With 30,000 inhabitants, Philadelphia was twice the size of Boston, and far more cosmopolitan. The largest bourg in the British colonies, it trailed only Mexico City and Lima, Peru in all the Americas. Unlike parochial, Puritan Boston, Philadelphia was a diverse community. It contained colonists who had come from a variety of places: England, Wales, Scotland, Ireland, Germany, Scandinavia, the Netherlands, France, Switzerland, and Africa. The laws of Pennsylvania granted Philadelphia residents a great deal of religious freedom, and the city consequently boasted a variety of different faiths: Quakers, Presbyterians, Anglicans, Lutherans, Anabaptists, Huguenots, and even some Jews and Catholics.

Once in Philadelphia Franklin discarded the strict Calvinism of his forbears for a new, more open philosophy known as deism (DEE-ism). Deism was not a particular sect. Deists did not have a church or dogma of their own, but rather attended whatever church they wanted (or, like Franklin, did not attend any church at all), as their own individual consciences dictated. They were united only by the belief that God was no longer actively involved in the matters of this world. Deists accepted that God had created the universe at some point in the past, but they also believed that He had wisely organized it so that it would operate by itself, according to various natural laws. God, deists said, was like a clockmaker. He had built the universe, wound it up, put it on a shelf, and then sat back to enjoy watching it tick. He never found need to touch it again. If any progress was to occur in this world, deists like Franklin believed, it had to come from humans. We could not count on God to bail us out.

Although of humble birth, Franklin became affluent. Philadelphia was growing rapidly, emerging as the third-largest city in the British Empire after London and Edinburgh. It was, as a result, chock full of good business opportunities. Although when Franklin arrived he was young and relatively inexperienced (he had never completed his apprenticeship with his brother), he also was shrewd, energetic, abstemious, and had good business sense. He soon found himself a business partner whose father had some money to invest (Franklin himself had barely enough capital to purchase two loaves of bread), and together the two men opened a print shop. It began a smashing success, in no small part because Franklin was a champion schmoozer who chatted up the local politicians and managed to secure the contract for all of the colony's official printing. By the time he was in his forties Franklin was retired and rich.

Franklin was also well traveled. Twice, he journeyed to London, the capital of the English Empire, and lived there for extended periods. He spoke French and German as well as English, traveled around Europe, attended plays and operas, and hobnobbed with various European scientists and philosophers.

Like most other philosophes, Franklin's two great passions in life were science and politics, and after his retirement he indulged in both. As a self-trained natural historian, he studied the behavior of lightning and, in a famous experiment, flew a kite in a lightning storm (a risky business, for a French scientist who tried the same experiment had managed to electrocute himself) to prove that lightning and static electricity were the same thing. He published an article on the experiment in a leading European scientific journal and became famous, after which he began calling himself "Doctor" Franklin. Seeking practical applications for scientific knowledge, he designed lightning rods for his neighbors' barns and a scientific cast iron fireplace, the famous Franklin stove, which functioned more efficiently than old-fashioned masonry fireplaces.

In politics, Franklin was for several years a member of the Pennsylvania legislature (a miniature version of England's House of Commons), organized numerous community betterment projects (paved streets, a volunteer fire department, the American Philosophical Society, a lending library, the University of Pennsylvania), and on his second sojourn in London, he acted as Pennsylvania's unofficial representative to the English government. To Franklin, business and politics were every bit as scientific as the study of electricity.[210]

---

[210] Edmund S. Morgan, *Benjamin Franklin* (2002), passim; Benjamin Franklin, *The Autobiography* (1788, 1990), passim.

What the Philosophes Believed

Like most philosophes of the Enlightenment, Franklin agreed with the following conclusions about politics, society, and economics:[211]

- Rational thought and action is better than irrational thought and action.
- All people have common sense and are capable of rational thought.
- Therefore, all people are basically equal. No one is any "better" than anyone else.
- Most political, economic, and social relationships can and should be based on rational behavior and enlightened self-interest. (Franklin said that he was a good person not because he was afraid that God would punish him for being bad, but because it was in his best interest to be virtuous. If he cheated his customers, they would take their business elsewhere. If he gossiped about his friends, they would desert him. If he boasted about his political accomplishments – he preferred working quietly, behind the scenes – he would become less effective. If he drank on the job, he would mess up his business. If he left his tools in disarray, his business would suffer. If he spent too much money on frivolous things, he would not have enough left for important things.)
- God does not intervene directly in human affairs. (As a deist, Franklin did not believe in miracles. Nor did they believe that any one group of people could ever truthfully claim that "God was on their side.")
- People can make the world a better place if they are willing to work at it. They should not expect God to do it for them.
- Knowledge is better than ignorance.
- Constitutionalism is better than absolutism.
- Toleration is better than prejudice.
- Religion is essentially a private matter between the individual believer and God, and people generally should not interfere with other people's religious beliefs.
- All people are born with certain "natural rights," including freedom of thought, freedom of religion, freedom of speech, freedom of the press, and the freedom to own property.
- The chief purpose of government is to protect these "natural rights."
- Government is responsible directly to the people, not to God.
- Free trade is better than monopoly.[212]

Some Key Philosophes of
The Enlightenment:
A Checklist

✓ John Locke (1632-1704). English. "Father of the Enlightenment." Argued that, since all people are capable of rational thought (i.e., have common sense), then all people are equal, without regard for class or gender. Argued that, since all people are equal, then all people have certain "natural rights" (human rights), including life (not to be killed), liberty (not to be enslaved), and property (not to have their stuff taken). Argued that the true purpose of government is to protect these rights; ergo, the only true government is constitutional government. See below for more.

✓ Immanuel Kant (KAHNT) (1724-1804). German (Prussian). Argued, along with Spinoza, that freedom of thought (freedom of conscience, freedom of religion) is vital for progress. Argued that freedom of thought requires freedom of speech, freedom of the press, and freedom of assembly. Argued that the main opponents of freedom were the military, the state, and the church.

✓ David Hume (1711-76). Scottish. Argued that it is possible to create large republics. Coined the term "Enlightenment." Referred to civil history as the "science of man."

✓ Adam Smith (1723-90). Scottish. Developed the basic principles of economics.

---

[211] Gay, *Enlightenment*, 1: 3-19.
[212] Merriman, *History of Modern Europe*, 399-440; Sullivan, *Short History of Western Civilization*, 466-475; Hexter, *Europe Since 1500*, 474-519.

> ✓ Charles-Louis de Secondat, Baron de Montesquieu (Mahn-tess-CUE) (1689-1755). French. Argued that well-constructed governments should be divided into three co-equal branches, so that no one branch can dominate.
>
> ✓ Francois-Marie Arouet Voltaire (Vohl-TAIR) (1694-1778). French. The quintessential Enlightenment philosophe, there was almost no aspect of the Enlightenment that Voltaire did not represent.
>
> ✓ Benjamin Franklin (1706-90). American. See above.
>
> ✓ Denis Diderot (Deed-ah-ROH) (1713-84). French. Created the first encyclopedia.
>
> ✓ Jean-Jacques Rousseau (Rue-SOH) (1712-78). French. In some ways the anti-philosophe. Embraced emotion as well as reason. Denigrated women. Exalted nature over civilization. But like the other philosophes, supported the social contract theory of government.
>
> ✓ Mary Wollstonecraft (1759-97). English. Argued for the equality of women, in opposition to Rousseau.

-The Documents-

Constitutionalism and Human Rights: John Locke

John Locke (1632-1704) is probably the most important political thinker in the history of Western Civilization. An English physician of bourgeois background and good education, the tall, gaunt Locke became the personal doctor and secretary to the Earl of Shaftsbury. Although a lord, Shaftsbury was active in the Whig Party and an opponent of absolutism. Banished from England in 1683 for attempting to prevent James II from coming to the throne, Shaftsbury fled to safety in the Dutch Republic, taking Locke along with him. Five years later both Shaftsbury and Locke returned to England in triumph in the Glorious Revolution of 1688 that overthrew James II and made England a constitutional monarchy.

During his exile in the Netherlands, Locke wrote his masterpiece, *Of Civil Government*, a long book of political theory that attacked absolutism and advocated constitutionalism. Influenced by the Scientific Revolution, Locke agreed with Descartes that all people were capable of rational thought. That being the case, Locke argued, it was also true that all people could be properly educated. And once they were educated, he concluded, they should also be able to participate in government – an idea that obviously had much appeal to members of England's House of Commons. Holding that all people were created equal by nature, Locke condemned the old idea of the "divine right of kings," which held that kings and lords were wiser than commoners and ruled by the grace of God. Instead, Locke argued, rulers only ruled with the consent of the governed, and could be replaced if they did a bad job.

Locke also argued that all people were born with what he called "natural rights," and which we today call "human rights." Human rights differ from civil rights, which the individual acquires as a result of his or her membership in a civil society. Unlike civil rights, human rights belong to everyone, regardless of citizenship, and cannot be alienated (taken away) by the government. The chief job of government, Locke argued, was to protect the people's human rights. Any government that failed to do, he said, was a tyranny, and the people were justified in overthrowing it. According to Locke, the chief human rights were life (the right not to be killed), liberty (the right not to be enslaved), and property (the right not to have your stuff taken away from you). (Locke defined property narrowly as those things that the individual had either created, traded for, or otherwise legitimately acquired, and which the individual actually used.)

Published in the early 1690s, after Locke's return from exile, *Of Civil Government* quickly became the classic defense of constitutional government, as well as the first exposition of what, a century later, would come to be called liberalism. So strong was Locke's influence that today both liberals and conservatives claim him as their ideological "parent." Locke is also known as "the father of the Enlightenment," because his ideas about reason, equality, individual liberty, education, constitutional government, and republican institutions would become the basis for most of the proposals made by the philosophes of the 18th-century Enlightenment.

from *TREATISE ON GOVERNMENT* [213]

OF THE STATE OF NATURE

To understand political power right we must consider what state all men are naturally in, and that is, a state of perfect freedom to order their actions and dispose of their possessions and persons, as they think fit, within the bounds of the law of nature; without asking leave, or depending upon the will of any man.

A state also of equality, wherein all the power and jurisdiction is reciprocal, no one having more than another; there being nothing more evident, than that creatures of the same species and rank, born to the same advantages of nature, and the use of the same faculties [i.e., the same ability to use reason], should also be equal one amongst the other without subordination or subjection.

But though this be a state of liberty, yet it is not a state of license. The state of nature has a law of nature to govern it, which obliges every one: and reason, which is that law, teaches all mankind that being all equal and independent, no one ought to harm another in his life, health, liberty, or possessions.

OF THE STATE OF WAR
[AND THE STATE OF SLAVERY]

The state of war is a state of enmity and destruction. [When one person attempts to deprive another person of his life or property without his consent, it is a state of war. But anyone may defend himself when attacked, because] it [is] reasonable and just [that] I should have a right to destroy that which threatens me with destruction for, by the fundamental law of nature, man being to be preserved as much as possible, when all cannot be preserved, the safety of the innocent is to be preferred: and one may destroy a man who makes war upon him.

And hence it is, that he who attempts to get another man in to his absolute power, does thereby put himself into a state of war with him; it being to be understood as a declaration of a design upon his life. He who would get me into his power without my consent, would use me as he pleased when he got me there, and destroy me too when he had a fancy to it; for nobody can desire to have me in his absolute power, unless it be to compel me by force to that which is against the right of my freedom, i.e., make me a slave.

OF PROPERTY

The earth, and all that is therein, is given to men for the support and comfort of their being. And though all the fruits it naturally produces, and beasts it feeds, belong to mankind in common, yet being given for the use of men, there must of necessity be a means to appropriate them in some way or other, before they can be of any use, or at all beneficial to any particular man.

Every man has a property in his own person: this nobody has any right to but himself. The labour of his body, and the work of his hands, we may say, are properly his. Whatsoever then he removes out of the state that nature hath provided, and left it in, he hath mixed his labour with, and joined it to something that is his own, and thereby makes it his property.

[But] the same law of nature, that does by this means give us property, does also bound [i.e., limit] this [right of] property too. As much as any one can make use of to any advantage of life before it spoils, so much he may by his labour fix a property in: whatever is beyond this is more than his share, and belongs to others. Nothing was made by God for man to spoil or destroy.

As much land as a man tills, plants, improves, cultivates, and can use the product of, so much is his property.

---

[213] John Locke, *Treatise on Government* (1690), v. 2, exerpted in John L. Beatty and Oliver A. Johnson, eds, *Heritage of Western Civilization* (1995), 65-75.

OF CIVIL SOCIETY

Whenever any number of men are so united into one society, as to quit everyone his executive power of the law of nature, and to resign it to the public, there and there only is a civil society.

It is evident, that absolute monarchy is indeed inconsistent with civil society. The [goal] of civil society [is] to avoid and remedy these inconveniences of the state of nature, which necessarily follow from every man being judge in his own case, by setting up a known authority, to which every one of that society may appeal upon any injury received, or controversy that may arise, and which every one of the society ought to obey. [But in an absolute monarchy, everyone becomes the] slave of an absolute prince. Whenever his property is invaded by the will and order of his monarch, [a subject of an absolute monarch] has not only no appeal, as those in [a civil] society [do], but, as if he were degraded from the common state of rational creatures, is denied a liberty to judge of, or to defend his right.

Men being, as has been said, by nature, all free, equal, and independent, no one can be subjected to the political power of another, without his own consent. The only way, whereby any one divests himself of his natural liberty, and puts on the bonds of civil society, is by agreeing with other men to join and unite into a community, for their comfortable, safe, and peaceable living one amongst another, in a secure enjoyment of their properties, and a greater security against any, that are not of it. [In such a civil society] the majority have a right to act and conclude [for] the rest.

[People voluntarily agree to leave a state of nature and join a civil society only] for the mutual preservation of their lives, liberties, and property.

The great and chief end of men's uniting into [civil societies], and putting themselves under government, is the preservation of their property.

[OF REVOLUTION]

There remains still in the people a supreme power to remove or alter the [government] when they find [its actions] contrary to the trust reposed in [it].

Whenever the legislators endeavor to take away and destroy the property of the people, or to reduce them to slavery under arbitrary power, they put themselves into a state of war with the people, who are thereupon absolved from any farther obedience.

If a long train of abuses, prevarications, and artifices, all tending the same way, make the design [of the government to enslave the people] visible to the people, and they cannot but feel what they lie under, and see whither they are going; it is not to be wondered, that they should then rouse themselves, and endeavor to put the rule into such hands which may secure to them the ends for which government was at first erected.

Everyone has a right to defend himself, and to resist the aggressor.

Slavery and Human Rights: Olaudah Equiano

According to his memoirs, Olaudah Equiano was born in c. 1745 in what is now Nigeria in western Africa. The Igbo – his people – were prosperous farmers who lived inland, in a wide swatch of self-governing agricultural villages set like straw-colored patches in the dark green of the tropical rain forest. Olaudah recalled that raiders from a neighboring people captured him from his village when he was a boy, marched him to a large city on the coast, and sold him to English slavers, who took him across the Atlantic Ocean to the British colony of Barbados, where they resold him at auction to a planter from Virginia. Soon, he was sold again, this time to Michael Pascal, a young lieutenant in the British Royal Navy, who wanted him as a personal servant. Pascal renamed his teenaged captive Gustavus Vasa, the name of a famous Swedish king. This "slave name" was a cruel joke, an ironic reminder that slaves were not kings, and Olaudah resented it. From 1756 to 1762 he accompanied Pascal on a series of military postings in Europe and North America. Although still only a teen, he had in essence become a sailor in the Royal Navy. Working as a gunner's mate, he saw action in several engagements during the bloody Seven Years War between Britain and France. He learned to speak English, curse, load a cannon, read, write, and cipher, and (believing that it might help him earn his freedom) became a nominal Christian. (A more sincere conversion to Christianity came later, in the 1770s, when Olaudah became a devout Anglican.) Unhappy as a slave, at the end of the war Olaudah told Pascal that he desired his freedom. He believed his religious conversion and military service entitled him to it, and he hoped to live in London as a free man. Furious, Pascal vindictively sold the eighteen-year-old Olaudah to a British merchant captain, who carried him off to the West Indies and sold him to Robert King, a wealthy planter in the British colony of Montserrat. It was the lowest moment of his life.

Slowly, Olaudah began to turn things around. It helped that King was a kind master. But just as important, King was also a canny businessman who appreciated his good fortune at having acquired so cheaply a valuable slave who could read, write, cipher, and navigate ships – vital but unusual skills that Olaudah had picked up in the Royal Navy. King owned several small merchant ships that he used to carry goods from his plantation on Montserrat to his home colony of Pennsylvania and to other British colonies in the Americas. He quickly put Olaudah to work as a seaman, often as a first mate. He also gave him small amounts of money to meet expenses while traveling. Olaudah saved the money and used it to purchase small quantities of goods in the various ports he visited, which he resold at profit at other ports. Sometimes his customers were whites, but they sometimes cheated him (as a slave, he had no legal recourse when they did), so more frequently he sold small amounts of coffee, yams, rice, and other "African goods" to free blacks, who made up about a tenth of the population of the West Indies. A clever capitalist, by 1766 Olaudah had saved forty pounds sterling (a substantial sum) – enough to purchase his freedom, which a stunned King reluctantly agreed to sell to him after being cajoled into it by one of Olaudah's white friends.

In 1767 Olaudah – now calling himself Olaudah Equiano (meaning "equal") – returned to London, where he worked as a hairdresser. For financial reasons, from time to time he returned to sea as a seaman on merchant ships. He visited Italy, Turkey (where he was impressed by the lack of racial prejudice among the Muslims), Greece, and Portugal. In 1773 he sailed on an expedition to explore the Arctic, and in 1775 he joined a British group attempting to plant a colony in Central America. During this last adventure he acted as an overseer, supervising the colony's slaves, whom the expedition's leaders had purchased in the West Indies. Convinced that West Indian slavery was a moral evil, Olaudah returned to England in 1777 when the colony failed and became an abolitionist, or anti-slavery advocate, as well as a born again Christian. He became active in the effort to found the British colony of Sierra Leone in Africa as a home for emancipated slaves (the colony's capital was the new city of Freetown, the first culturally Western city in Africa), although he himself remained in London, his adopted city. He published his memoirs in 1789 and died in 1797.

Recently, several historians have maintained that not all of the material in Olaudah's memoir actually happened to him. Rather, they say, the book was a synthesis of Olaudah's own experiences and those of several other former slaves. These "revisionists" argue that Olaudah was not born in Africa, but instead in Virginia or Carolina to slave parents, and that he gave himself African origins because he wanted to make himself the personal embodiment of the entire slave experience. Just as he fashioned the "free" name Equiano, the revisionists say, he also invented the "African" name Olaudah – and the identities that went with it – to erase the hated slave name and his own humble origins. If this interpretation is true, then Olaudah's chief motive for publishing his memoirs was probably to indict slavery – in other words, he reshaped his own autobiography so as to include important aspects of the slave experience (a childhood in Africa, capture by slavers, transport to the Americas, sale at an auction) that were absent from his own life in order to make readers in Britain understand the full range of the slave experience. This reinterpretation of Olaudah remains only a hypothesis, however, and it may yet be disproved.[214]

In the following excerpt from his memoirs, Olaudah arrives at Montserrat and is sold to King, events that even the revisionist historians agree actually occurred. He accurately describes slavery in the West Indies and delivers an impassioned plea for its abolition. Notice how similar his argument is to Locke's. Clearly, Olaudah Equiano was a man of the Enlightenment.

from *THE INTERESTING NARRATIVE OF THE LIFE OF
OLAUDAH EQUIANO, OR GUSTAVUS VASA, THE AFRICAN* [215]

CHAPTER FIVE

III

On the 13th of February 1763, from the mast-head, we descried our destined island, Montserrat, and soon after I beheld those
> Regions of sorrow, doleful shades, where peace
> And rest can rarely dwell. Hope never comes
> That comes to all, but torture without end
> Still urges.

At the sight of this land of bondage, a fresh horror ran through all my frame, and chilled me to the heart. My former slavery now rose in dreadful review to my mind, and displayed nothing but misery, stripes, and chains; and in the first paroxysm of my grief, I called upon

---

[214] Angelo Costanzo, *Surprizing Narrative: Olaudah Equiano and the Beginnings of Black Autobiography* (New York: 1987); Vincent Carretta, "Olaudah Equiano or Gustavus Vassa? New Light on an Eighteenth-Century Question of Identity," *Slavery and Abolition*, 20 (1999), 73-86.

[215] Olaudah Equiano, *The Interesting Narrative of the Life of Olaudah Equiano, or Gustavus Vasa, the African* (London: 1814 [1789]), reprinted in Henry Louis Gates, ed., *The Classic Slave Narratives* (New York: 1987), 69-80.

God's thunder, and his avenging power, to direct the stroke of death to me, rather than permit me to become a slave, and to be sold from lord to lord.

In this state of my mind our ship came to an anchor, and soon after discharged her cargo. I now knew what it was to work hard; I was made to help to unload and load the ship. And to comfort me in my distress, at that time two of the sailors robbed me of all my money, and ran away from the ship. I had been so long used to a European climate, that at first I felt the scorching West-India sun very painful, while the dashing surf would toss the boat and the people in it, frequently above high-water mark. Sometimes our limbs were broken with this, or even attended with instant death, and I was day by day mangled and torn.

IV

About the middle of May, when the ship was got ready to sail for England, I all the time believing that fate's blackest clouds were gathering over my head, and expecting that their bursting would mix me with the dead, Captain Doran sent for me on shore one morning; and I was told by the messenger that my fate was determined. With trembling steps and a fluttering heart I came to the captain, and found with him one Mr. Robert King, a Quaker, and the first merchant in the place. The captain then told me my former master had sent me there to be sold; but that he had desired him to get me the best master he could, as he told him I was a very deserving boy, which Captain Doran said he found to be true, and if he were to stay in the West-Indies he would be glad to keep me himself; but he could not venture to take me to London, for he was very sure that when I came there, I would leave him. I at that instant burst out a crying, and begged much of him to take me with him to England, but all to no purpose. He told me he had got me the very best master in the whole island, with whom I should be happy as if I were in England, and for that reason he chose to let him have me, though he could sell me to his own brother-in-law for a great deal more money than what he got from that gentleman. My new master, Mr. King, then made a reply, and said the reason he had bought me was on account of my good character; and, as he had not the least doubt of my good behavior, I should be very well off with him. He also told me he did not live in the West-Indies, but at Philadelphia, where he was soon going; and, as I understood something of the rules of arithmetic, when we got there he would put me to school, and fit me for a clerk. This conversation relieved my mind a little, and I left those gentlemen considerably more at ease in myself than when I came to them; and I was very thankful to Captain Doran, and even to my old master, for the character they had given me; a character which I afterwards found of infinite service to me.

I went on board again, and took leave of all my shipmates, and the next day the ship sailed. When she weighed anchor I went to the waterside, and looked at her with a very wishful and aching heart, following her with my eyes until she was totally out of sight. I was so bowed down with grief that I could not hold up my head for many months; and if my new master had not been kind to me, I believe I should have died under it at last. And indeed I soon found that he fully deserved the good character which Capt. Doran had given me of him; for he possessed a most amiable disposition and temper, and was very charitable and humane. If any of his slaves behaved amiss, he did not beat or use them ill, but parted with them. This made them afraid of disobliging him; and as he treated his slaves better than any other man on the island, so he was better and more faithfully served by them in return. By this kind treatment I did at last endeavor to compose myself; and with fortitude, though moneyless, determined to face whatever fate had decreed for me. Mr. King soon asked me what I could do; and at the same time said he did not mean to treat me as a common slave. I told him I knew something of seamanship, and could shave and dress hair pretty well; I could refine wines, which I had learned on shipboard, where I had often done it; and that I could write, and understood arithmetic tolerably well as far as the Rule of Three. He then asked me if I knew anything of gauging; and, on my answering that I did not, he said one of his clerks should teach me to gauge.

V

Mr. King dealt in all manner of merchandize, and kept from one to six clerks. He loaded many vessels in one year; particularly to Philadelphia, where he was born, and was connected with a great mercantile house in that city. He had besides many vessels and doggers, of different sizes, which used to go about the island; and others to collect rum, sugar, and other goods. I understood pulling and managing those boats very well; and this hard work, which was the first that he set me to, in the sugar seasons used to be my constant employment. I have rowed the boat and slaved at the oars, from one hour to sixteen in the twenty-four; during which I had fifteen pence sterling per day to live on, though sometimes only ten pence. However, this was much more than was allowed to other slaves that used to work often with me, and belonged to other gentlemen on the island; these poor souls had never more than ninepence a day, and seldom more than sixpence, from their masters or owners, though they earned them three or four pisterines. For it is a common practice in the West-Indies for men to purchase slaves, though they have not plantations themselves, in order to let them out to planters and merchants, at so much a piece by the day, and they give what they choose, out of this produce of their daily work; to their slaves for subsistence. This allowance is often very scanty.

My master often gave the owners of these slaves two and a half pieces per day, and found the poor fellows in victuals himself, because he thought their owners did not feed them well enough, according to the work they did. The slaves used to like this very well; and, as they knew my master to be a man of feeling, they were always glad to work for him in preference to any other gentleman; some of whom, after they had been paid for these poor people's labors, would not give them their allowance out of it. Many times have I seen these unfortunate wretches beaten for asking for their pay; and often severely flogged by their owners, if they did not bring them their daily or weekly money exactly to the time; though the poor creatures were obliged to wait on the gentlemen they had worked for, sometimes more than half the day before they could get their pay, and this generally on Sundays, when they wanted the time for themselves. In particular, I knew a countryman of mine, who once did not bring the weekly money directly that it was earned; and though he brought it the same day to his master, yet he was staked to the ground for his pretended negligence, and was just going to receive a hundred lashes, but for a gentleman who begged him off fifty.

This poor man was very industrious, and by his frugality had saved so much money, by working on shipboard, that he had got a white man to buy him a boat, unknown to his master. Some time after he had this little estate, the governor wanted a boat to bring his sugar from different parts of the island; and, knowing this to be a negro-man's boat, he seized upon it for himself, and would not pay the owner a farthing. The man on this went to his master, and complained to him of this act of the governor; but the only satisfaction he received was to be damned very heartily by his master, who asked him how dared any of his negroes to have a boat…. Such treatment as this often drives these miserable wretches to despair, and they run away from their masters at the hazard of their lives. Many of them, in this place, unable to get their pay when they have earned it, and fearing to be flogged, as usual, if they return home without it, run away where they can for shelter, and a reward is offered to bring them in dead or alive….

* * * *

VI

I had the good fortune to please my master in every department in which he employed me; and there was scarcely any part of his business, or household affairs, in which I was not occasionally engaged. I often supplied the place of a clerk, in receiving and delivering cargoes to his ships, in tending stores, and delivering goods; and, besides this, I used to shave and dress my master, when convenient, and take care of his horse; and when it was necessary, which was very often, I worked likewise on board of his different vessels. By these means I became very useful to my master, and saved him, as he used to acknowledge, above a hundred pounds a year. Nor did he scruple to say I was of more advantage to him than any of his clerks; tho' their usual wages in the West-Indies are from sixty to a hundred pounds current a year.

I have sometimes heard it asserted that a negro cannot earn his master the first cost; but nothing can be further from the truth. I suppose nine-tenths of the mechanics throughout the West-Indies are negro slaves; and I well know the coopers among them earn two dollars a day; the carpenters the same, and oftentimes more; also the masons, smiths, and fishermen, &c. and I have known many slaves whose masters would not take a thousand pounds current for them. But surely this assertion refutes itself: for, if it be true, why do the planters and merchants pay such a price for slaves? And, above all, why do those, who make this assertion, exclaim the most loudly against the abolition of the slave trade? So much are men blinded, and to such inconsistent arguments are they driven by mistaken interest! I grant, indeed, that slaves are sometimes, by half-feeding, half-clothing, over-working, and stripes, reduced so low, that they are turned out as unfit for service, and left to perish in the woods, or to expire on a dunghill.

* * * *

While I was thus employed by my master, I was often a witness to cruelties of every kind, which were exercised on my unhappy fellow slaves. I used frequently to have different cargoes of new slaves in my care for sale; and it was almost a constant practice with our clerks, and other whites to commit violent depredations on the chastity of the female slaves; and to these atrocities I was, though with reluctance, obliged to submit at all times, being unable to help them. When we have had some of these slaves on board my master's vessels to carry them to other islands, or to America, I have known our mates commit these acts most shamefully, to the disgrace not of Christians only, but of men. I have even known them gratify their brutal passion with females not ten years old; and these abominations some of them practiced to such a scandalous excess, that one of our captains discharged the mate and others on that account. And yet in Montserrat I have seen a negro-man staked to the ground, and cut most shockingly, and then his ears cut off, bit by bit, because he had been connected with a white woman, who was a common prostitute! As if it were no crime in the whites to rob an innocent African girl of her virtue; but most heinous in a black man only to gratify a passion of nature, where the temptation was offered by one of a different color, though the most abandoned woman of her species.

VII

Once Mr. D----- told me he had sold 41,000 negroes, and he once cut off a negro-man's leg for running away. I asked him if the man had died in the operation, how he, as a Christian, could answer, for the horrid act, before God. And he told me, answering was a thing of another world; what he thought and did were policy. I told him that the Christian doctrine taught us "to do unto others as we would that others should do unto us." He then said that his scheme had the desired effect – it cured that man and some others of running away.

Another negro-man was half hanged, and then burnt, for attempting to poison a cruel overseer. Thus, by repeated cruelties, are the wretched first urged to despair, and then murdered, because they still retain so much human nature about them as to wish to put an end to their misery, and to retaliate on their tyrants! These overseers are, indeed, for the most part, persons of the worst character of any denomination of men in the West-Indies. Unfortunately, many humane gentlemen, by not residing on their estates, are obliged to leave the management of them in the hands of these human butchers, who cut and mangle the slaves in a shocking manner, on the most trivial occasions, and altogether treat them, in every respect, like brutes. They pay no regard to the situation of pregnant women, nor the least attention to the lodging of the field negroes. Their huts, which ought to be well covered, and the place dry where they take their short repose, are often open sheds, built in damp places; so that, when the poor creatures return tired from the toils of the field, they contract many disorders, from being exposed to the damp air in this uncomfortable state, while they are heated, and their pores are open.

The neglect certainly conspires with many others to cause a decrease in births, as well as in the lives of the grown negroes.... For want, therefore, of such care and attention to the poor negroes, and otherwise oppressed as they are, it is no wonder that the decrease should require 20,000 new negroes annually to fill up the vacant places of the dead.

Even ... Barbados ... requires 1,000 negroes annually to keep up the original stock, which is only 80,000. So that the whole term of a negro's life may be said to be there, but sixteen years!

VIII

While I was in Montserrat I knew a negro-man, one Emanuel Sankey, who endeavored to escape from his miserable bondage, by concealing himself on board of a London ship. But fate did not favor the poor oppressed man; for, being discovered when the vessel was under sail, he was delivered up again to his master. This Christian master immediately pinned the wretch to the ground, at each wrist and ankle, and then took some sticks of sealing wax, lighted them, and dropped it all over his back. There was another master noted for cruelty: -- I believe he had not a slave but had been cut, and pieces fairly taken out of the flesh: and after they had been punished thus, he used to make them get into a long wooden box, or case, he had for that purpose, and shut them up during pleasure. It was just about the height and breadth of man; and the poor wretches had no room when in the case to move.

It was very common in several of the islands, particularly in St. Kitt's, for the slaves to be branded with the initial letters of their master's name, and a load of heavy iron hooks hung about their necks. Indeed on the most trivial occasions they were loaded with chains, and often instruments of torture were added. The iron muzzle, thumb-screws, &c. are so well known as not to need a description, and were sometimes applied for the slightest faults. I have seen a negro beaten till some of his bones were broken, for only letting a pot boil over....

* * * *

X

Nor was such usage as this confined to particular places or individuals; for, in all the different islands in which I have been (and I have visited no less than fifteen) the treatment of the slaves was nearly the same; so nearly, indeed, that the history of an island, or even a plantation, with a few exceptions as I have mentioned, might serve for a history of the whole. Such a tendency has the slave-trade to debauch men's minds, and harden them to every feeling of humanity! For I will not suppose that the dealers in slaves are born worse than other men. No; it is the fatality of this mistaken avarice, that it corrupts the milk of human kindness and turns it into gall. And, had the pursuits of those men been different, they might have been as generous, as tender-hearted, and just, as they are unfeeling, rapacious and cruel. Surely this traffic cannot be good, which spreads like a pestilence, and taints what it touches! Which violates that first natural right of mankind, equality, and independency; and gives one man a dominion over his fellows which God could never intend! For it raises the owner to a state as far above man as it depresses the slave below it; and, with all the presumption of human pride, sets distinction between them, immeasurable in extent, and endless in duration! Yet how mistaken is the avarice even of the planters. Are slaves more useful by being thus humbled to the condition of brutes, than they would be if suffered to enjoy the privileges of men? The freedom which diffuses health and prosperity throughout Britain answers you – "No." When you make men slaves, you deprive them of half their virtue, you set them, in your own conduct, an example of fraud, rapine, and cruelty, and compel them to live with you in a state of war....

-CHAPTER VI-
LIBERTY! EQUALITY! FRATERNITY!
LIBERALISM, CAPITALISM, AND THE WEST'S AGE OF REVOLUTION
c. 1750 - c. 1850

In 1789 the French people did just what John Locke had suggested they (or anyone else) should do: they "rouse[d] themselves, and endeavor[ed] to put the rule into such hands which may secure to them the ends for which government was at first erected." In other words, they revolted, stripped the hapless King Louis XVI of his absolutist powers, and proclaimed a constitutional monarchy – and a few years later, a republic. Outlining their goals in the famous Declaration of the Rights of Man and Citizen, the French revolutionaries explained that they had been motivated by the desire to achieve human rights, constitutionalism, individualism, elected government, and popular sovereignty – in short, liberal democracy – and that they were prepared to fight for "the maintenance of the constitution and the welfare of all." A popular slogan of the day summed it up a bit more dramatically: "Liberty! Equality! Fraternity!"

Like the English Glorious Revolution of 1688 and the American Revolution of 1763-87, the French Revolution of 1789-99 was an important milestone in the history of constitutional government. But the Glorious Revolution had stopped far short of either creating a republic or extending human rights to the majority. And while the new United States had gone further, it was underdeveloped, underpopulated, located hundreds of miles from the centers of Western Civilization, and a country whose people were notoriously eccentric. France, however, was the most populous country in the West, and its capital, Paris, was the West's largest city and intellectual center. Too big to ignore, the French Revolution sent shock waves throughout the West. It spawned similar revolutions in Haiti, the Spanish colonies in the Americas, and elsewhere – all of which invoked the ideas of Locke, Voltaire, and the other philosophes of the Enlightenment. Far more than either the Glorious Revolution or the American Revolution, the French Revolution made the possibility of achieving dramatic change seem both real and imminent.

At the same time that people throughout the West took to the streets and back roads demanding new, more enlightened governments, another kind of revolution also occurred: the Industrial Revolution. More gradual, less dramatic, and certainly less exciting than the political revolutions in America, France, and elsewhere, the Industrial Revolution – the shift from a traditional agrarian to a modern industrial economy – nevertheless had just as great an impact on the course of Western history.

This chapter focuses on three of the revolutions that occurred the Age of Revolution: the French Revolution, the Haitian Revolution, and the Industrial Revolution, and the new political and economic systems – liberal democracy and capitalism – that they unleashed.

-The Background-

Introduction

From the mid-1700s to the mid-1800s, the West found itself in tremendous flux. So many political and economic revolutions occurred during those years that the British economic and social historian Eric Hobsbawn has dubbed it the Age of Revolution.[216] Some of these revolutions were:

- The American Revolution (1763-87)
- The French Revolution (1789-99)
- The Haitian Revolution (1791-1804)
- The Mexican Revolution (1810-21)
- The Venezuelan Revolution (1810-19)
- The Argentine Revolution (1810-16)
- The Chilean Revolution (1810-17)
- The Spanish Revolution of 1820-22 (failed)
- The French Revolution of 1830
- The Belgian Revolution (1831)
- The Polish Uprising (1830-31) (failed)
- The Lower Canada Uprising (1837) (failed)
- The Upper Canada Uprising (1837) (failed)
- The Revolutions of 1848
- The First Industrial Revolution (c. 1750 – c. 1850)

---

[216] Eric J. Hobsbawm, *The Age of Revolution, 1789-1848* (1962), passim.

Failed revolutions also occurred in Portugal, several of the Italian city-states, and some of the German principalities. The years 1763-1848 also witnessed another kind of revolution: the Industrial Revolution. Together, these revolutions fundamentally transformed the West, ushering in a new age of constitutionalism, republicanism, liberalism, and capitalism.

A Theory of Revolutions

Revolutions seem chaotic, but according to the political historian Crane Brinton, they actually follow discernable patterns. Since Brinton wrote only about political revolutions (which can be defined as movements to overthrow existing governments and replace them with new types or systems of government, such as replacing a monarchy with a republic, or a republic with a dictatorship), for the moment we will set aside the Industrial Revolution (which was an economic and social revolution, not a political revolution) and focus on those political transformations that occurred during the Age of Revolution.

First, writes Brinton, political revolutions usually are led not by the poor, nor by the rich, but by one of the middle classes. While it might *seem* that revolutions would be most likely to be begun by the most oppressed and exploited members of society – those who suffer the most under what the French call the *ancient regime*, or the old order – in fact, such rarely turns out to be the case. Normally, the poor and downtrodden are too busy figuring out where their next meal is coming from, or how to pay their rent, to find the time to meet in dimly lit revolutionary cafes, read and write revolutionary pamphlets, post revolutionary placards, carefully study revolutionary theory, heatedly discuss revolutionary tactics, and plot revolutionary mass movements. Neither are revolutions likely to be led by the elite – those people who are at the top of the social order – for such individuals have too much invested in the prevailing system to desire any kind of meaningful change. Rather, revolutions are usually led by people with just enough wealth, education, and leisure time to organize a revolt, but who also have something to gain by changing the system. The American Revolution was led not by the people who existed at the very bottom of the colonial social system (the slaves, Indians, and poor farmers), nor by the elite of the British Empire (the lords and gentry who lived in Britain), but by a middle group (the colonial planters and bourgeois like Benjamin Franklin, George Washington, Thomas Jefferson, Patrick Henry, John Adams, Samuel Adams, and John Hancock).

Second, most revolutions are what Brinton called "revolutions of rising expectations." Revolutions do not normally occur when things are really bad, for during truly terrible times people tend to hunker down and live day-by-day. Rather revolutions usually occur when things seem to be getting better for the middle classes – either when the economy seems to be improving, or when upward social mobility seems to be becoming more possible. The middle classes develop "rising expectations," which is to say that they expect conditions to continue to improve, often more quickly than is actually possible. And if things don't improve as quickly as they expect them to, or if there is a sudden and unexpected decline in the economy, or the possibility of upward social mobility is suddenly and unexpectedly foreclosed, and the "rising expectations" are not met, the middle classes grow restive, sullen, and angry, and begin to agitate for change. Conditions become ripe for a revolution.

In Britain's American colonies, the end of the French and Indian Wars in 1760 had caused rising expectations. The colonial planters and bourgeois expected there to occur what we in the twenty-first century call a "peace dividend" – that with the war over at last, taxes would go down, new lands would be opened up for settlement (thus creating new opportunities for investment and profit), colonial populations would continue to grow (thus creating even more opportunities for investment and profit), British officials and soldiers would no longer be needed and so would be recalled to Britain (thus leaving the colonial planters and bourgeois in charge of the colonies), and British lords and gentry would come to accept the colonial planters and bourgeois as their equals. When Parliament instead increased taxes, closed the interior of the continent to settlement, and kept British officials and soldiers stationed in the colonies, and when the British elite continued to look down on the colonial leaders as unsophisticated provincials, those expectations were cruelly dashed.

Third, according to Brinton, revolutions require the formation of revolutionary coalitions. The middle classes quickly discover that they can't carry off everything by themselves. They are not numerous enough, nor – in many cases – are they willing to get their hands dirty passing out leaflets, marching through the streets, rioting, or fighting as ordinary soldiers in revolutionary armies. Consequently, they are forced to organize coalitions, bringing together various "out groups," such as city workers, artisans, the poor, peasants, slaves, or even women, in a larger movement for change. In the case of the American Revolution, the colonial planters and bourgeois had soon found it necessary to bring colonial women, small farmers, and city workers into their movement for change.

Fourth, Brinton writes that the revolutionaries usually find it necessary to invoke some sort of ideology as a justification for their actions. In order to appeal to the other groups in the coalition, the middle classes have to offer them something, some kind of vision of a better way of life, or the promise of a more just socio-economic or political order. In short, they find that they need to couch their plans for reform in the context of a potent and appealing ideology or "ism," be it liberalism, nationalism, socialism, or something else. They do not always do this cynically, for in most cases the middle classes truly believe in the ideologies they invoke. The trick is to convince the other groups in the coalition to believe in them, too. Revolutionary ideologies thus do not actually cause revolutions to occur. The rising expectations of the middle classes are the cause. Revolutionary ideologies are consequences of revolutions. Nevertheless, they are very real, for the revolutionaries – middle and lower classes alike – come fervently to believe in them. In the case of the American Revolution, the revolutionary ideology was something the Americans thought of as "republicanism," but which historians have come to know as "liberalism." Whatever its name, it was in essence the ideas of the philosophes of the Enlightenment.

Fifth, Brinton argues that revolutions tend to occur in three stages, a reform (or moderate) stage, a radical stage, and a reactionary stage (or counterrevolution). In the reform stage, the middle classes demand modest reforms, but stop short of advocating the complete overthrow of the old order. If the middle classes get what they want (or if the government responds with such brutal force that it immediately puts down the movement), the uprising ends there, without a real revolution occurring. But if the government resists change (and also hesitates to respond immediately with severe force), the middle classes conclude bitterly that the old system cannot be changed from within and decide instead to overthrow it and put a new system in its place. This is the radical stage. Frequently, however, the radical stage goes too far for many people – it either becomes too violent, or brings about deeper changes than most people desire – and so is followed by a reactionary stage (or counterrevolution) in which people back away from some (but not all) of the radical changes and restore some (but not all) of the elements of the old order. In the case of the American Revolution, the 1763-75 protests leading up to the War for Independence comprised the reform stage (when the goal was to give the colonists control over colonial taxes), the War for Independence (1775-83) and Confederation Period (1783-87) together formed the radical stage (when the goals were independence from Britain, a republican system of government, direct democracy, and a major shift of political power almost completely to the local level), and the Constitutional Convention of 1787 was the reactionary stage, or counterrevolution (when independence and republicanism were retained, but direct democracy and local government were replaced by indirect democracy and federalism).

Finally, Brinton says that although revolutions normally begin over limited, concrete political issues like taxes, they almost always expand to have enormous social and economic consequences. Making major changes in the government usually results in making major changes in the social and economic structure as well, whether intended or not. For example, the decision to abolish a monarchy and replace it with a republic – a change in the type of government – is usually accompanied by a move from aristocracy to democracy – a social change. In the case of the American Revolution, the major unintended social and economic consequences included a rapid expansion of capitalism, industrialization, the development of an anti-slavery movement, the emergence of a women's rights movement, and the creation of a movement to expand the rights of propertyless males, none of which the original revolutionaries had foreseen.[217]

The French Revolution: the Reform Stage

By 1788, after years of debilitating wars and foolish overstretch under the absolutist Bourbon dynasty, the French government was broke. The government of King Louis XVI (r. 1774-92) was forced to borrow and spend enormous sums simply to pay the country's massive debts. In addition, many of the lords were bitter at their loss of power to the monarchy, the bourgeois and peasants were unhappy about the high taxes they paid, and the city workers of Paris – the so-called *sans culottes* (SAHNS koo-LOHT, literally, "without knee pants") who paid half their income for bread alone – stood starving and sullen on street corners. Desperate for increased taxes to replenish the royal treasury and unsure how to handle the crisis, the king reluctantly ordered the Estates-General (*Etats-General* in French) to convene the next year.

The Estates-General was an assembly of the French people, roughly analogous to the English Parliament, created in the Middle Ages to advise the king during times of crisis. It had played a major role in the 1300s and 1400s, rallying support for France's embattled monarchs during the Hundred Years War. It had calmed the country after the brutal assassination of King Henri IV in 1614, and helped ensure a peaceful succession. But after 1614, Louis XIII, Louis XIV, Louis XV, and Louis XVI had ruled as absolute monarchs. They did not wish to share power with anyone, not even an advisory body like the Estates-General. Thus it had not been since 1614 had a king called the assembly into session. For more than 150 years it had not met ... until now.

According to tradition, the Estates-General was composed of three branches or houses: the First Estate (representing the first estate, or clergy), the Second Estate (representing the second estate, or lords), and the Third Estate (representing the third estate, or commoners). In the past, the number of delegates in each house had varied, depending on what had seemed expedient. This time, acting on the advice of his bourgeois Minister of Finance, Jacques Necker, Louis decided that there would be 1,200 total delegates – 300 from the First Estate, 300 from the Second Estate, and 600 from the Third Estate. Traditionally, each of the branches voted separately, and any action required a majority vote in at least two of the three branches in order to pass – a system known as "voting by estate." Louis intended to maintain that tradition.

---

[217] Crane Brinton, *Anatomy of Revolution* (1952), passim; James DeFronzo, *Revolutions and Revolutionary Movements* (1991), 7-26.

The representatives were elected. Louis divided France into 250 election districts. Each district was to have at least four representatives, one chosen by the clergy, one by the lords, and two by the commoners. Large cities like Paris were allowed larger delegations. Wealthy men dominated. Although the Third Estate supposedly represented all commoners (who included not only the upper bourgeoisie, but also the lower bourgeoisie, small artisans, peasants, servants, and city workers, who collectively comprised 95% of the French population), and although all the men over the age of twenty-five who owned property and paid taxes were permitted to vote, as a practical matter, only men who possessed sufficient wealth to leave their businesses and come to Versailles for several months could afford to serve. Women were permitted neither to vote nor to sit in the assembly. As a result, the upper bourgeoisie held most of the seats in the Third Estate. Indeed, the majority of the house's delegates turned out to be lawyers.

During the elections, several reform-minded men who were committed to transforming France from an absolutist monarchy into a constitutional monarchy won seats. Quickly, they became the leaders of a reform bloc. One of the men was the young, thin, idealistic Marquis de La Fayette (1757-1834), just thirty-two years old, an extremely wealthy lord who had fought alongside the Americans in the American Revolution (France had been an American ally in the struggle, to revenge itself on Britain for defeating it in the French and Indian War of 1754-61), and idolized the American revolutionary leader George Washington as his ideological father. Another was the serious, intense Abbe Emmanuel-Joseph Sieyes (See-EHZ) (1748-1836), forty-one, an abbot whose parents had been commoners. Although Sieyes was part of the first estate, the commoners of Paris liked him so much that they elected him to represent them in the Third Estate. A third reformer was the rotund, pockmarked, amorous Count de Mirabeau (Meer-ah-BOH) (1749-91), forty. In his youth Mirabeau's own father, embarrassed at his son's torrid love affairs, had imprisoned him in a vain attempt to cool him off. Mirabeau had also spent time in England and the Netherlands, partly to escape jealous husbands, and had come to support those country's constitutional systems of government. Like Sieyes, Mirabeau was elected to represent the Third Estate. A fourth reformer was the moody, mercurial young lawyer Maximillien Robespierre (Robes-pee-AIR) (1758-94), thirty-one, elected to the Third Estate from his home city of Arras. A fifth was Charles-Maurice Talleyrand (1754-1838), forty-five, the wily Bishop of Autun, disinherited by his noble father because of a birth defect and now a member of the First Estate.

The elections for the Estates-General created rising expectations throughout the French kingdom. Peasants, bourgeois, artisans, city workers, and others all hoped that the Estates-General would lead to reform. Because he had been the one who had called the elections, Louis was for the moment lauded as a wise and great king. In public hearings all across France, commoners turned out to voice their displeasure not with the king himself, but with the old system of absolutism. Delegates to the Estates-General recorded these complaints in large notebooks, known as *cahiers de dolerances* (kai-YAY deh doh-lair-AHNCE) ("notebooks of grievances"). The cahiers reveal what the French people wanted the Estates-General to do. Yes, they expected that it would solve the current fiscal crisis. But they also hoped for more. Peasants also wanted their *droits* (DWAH) (the old manorial boons they had to pay to their lords) reduced, as well as their taxes cut. City workers wanted price controls for bread. The bourgeoisie wanted capitalism, and equal access to the good government jobs that normally went to lords. But the chief expectation of everyone was that the Estates-General would end absolutism and establish a constitutional monarchy.

On May 5 the Estates-General met at the royal palace at Versailles, a few miles outside of Paris. The members of the Third Estate immediately signaled their opposition to absolutism by wearing their hats in the presence of the king. Soon, they also revealed their first demand: that the Estates-General vote not by estate, as was traditional, but by head – in other words, that each representative should have one vote, regardless of his estate, with a simple majority of all the representatives needed to pass any law. With 50% of the representatives – and support from a few reform-minded delegates from the First and Second Estates like La Fayette and Talleyrand – the Third Estate knew that if the Estates-General voted by head, they would have enough votes to reform the system. Louis, however, declared their demand invalid. Then, on June 20, the Third Estate found itself locked out of its meeting chamber. Led by Mirabeau, they moved to the king's sumptuous indoor tennis court and swore their famous Tennis Court Oath – that they would stick together in their demand for voting by head, no matter the consequences. When Louis's worried advisors suggested that they leave the tennis court, Mirabeau replied coldly, "If you have orders to remove us from this hall, you must also get authority to use force, for we shall yield to nothing but to bayonets." In Paris, thousands of protesters, most of them lowly *sans culottes* fired up by Sieve's pro-reform pamphlet, *What Is the Third Estate?* took to the streets to support the Third Estate. Seven days later, Louis gave in. The Estates-General, now renamed the National Assembly, would vote by head. Reform seemed possible.

However, rumors soon spread that Louis had summoned the royal army to surround Versailles, to quash the movement for constitutionalism. In response, on July 14 a furious Paris mob stormed the Bastille (Bass-TEEL), a large stone structure in Paris that had once served as a political prison and now was used as an arsenal. In the ensuing fight more than 200 of the attackers died, but the soldiers defending it were overwhelmed and killed. Then, with their bare hands, the frenzied mob tore the hated building down. Now armed, the Parisians formed the National Guard, a military unit led by La Fayette.

The Storming of the Bastille was a tocsin that sounded throughout France. Emboldened by the Parisians' example, in the Great Fear (it was the lords who were afraid) rural peasants similarly attacked the lords' châteaux (manor houses), looting and destroying records. On the night of August 4 a worried National Assembly responded to the deteriorating situation by outlawing manorialism, feudalism, and absolutism. The old order was thus dead. Two weeks later, on August 26 the National Assembly passed the Declaration of the Rights of Man and Citizen, which provided the framework for the new order the reformers hoped to raise on the ashes of the old.

Still, Louis controlled the army, and as long as the government sat at rural Versailles, it was vulnerable. Therefore, on October 5, in what came to be called the March on Versailles and the October Days, about 10,000 Parisians, most of them women, accompanied by La Fayette's National Guard, marched the few miles from Paris to Versailles. They demanded that Louis, the National Assembly, and the rest of the government move to Paris, to the Tuileries (Twee-lair-EE), the old royal palace, where the National Guard would be able to protect the National Assembly from the army. Reluctantly, Louis agreed. He also agreed to accept the vote of August 4 and the Declaration of the Rights of Man and Citizen. France was now a constitutional monarchy. Absolutism was gone. The reformers had won.[218]

The French Revolution: the Radical Stage

Or so they thought. Two years later, in June 1791, in the so-called Flight to Varennes (Vah-RAHN), Louis and his family and advisors attempted to flee France. However, the National Guard caught them in Varennes, near the border with the Austrian Netherlands (today's Belgium), which at the time was ruled by the absolutist Austrian Habsburg dynasty, the family of Louis's wife, Marie Antoinette (1755-93). The French had never liked their queen. They viewed her as a symbol of absolutism, a foreign interloper, and a dangerously forceful and beautiful woman whose sexuality was beyond their control and thus suspect. About the nicest thing they called her was "the Austrian bitch." They were sure that she was up to no good. Their suspicions aroused, the leaders of the National Assembly rifled the royal correspondence and discovered to their shock that Louis had written to his in-laws in Austria, urging them to invade France and restore absolutism. It was not the queen who was the enemy of reform. It was the king.

And in April 1792 war came, with France on one side and absolutist Austria and Prussia on the other. Because most of the officers in the French army had been lords who were opposed to reform and who had left France after 1789 (many of them deserting to the Austrians), the army was at first nearly leaderless. As a result, it lost a series of decisive battles to the more experienced, better-led Austrian and Prussian forces. The enemy closed in on Paris. However, with each defeat the army's new, young, inexperienced, bourgeois officers learned more and more about soldiering, and finally, on September 20, at the Battle of Valmy (Vahl-MEE), they at last defeated the invaders. The war continued on, but Paris was safe. But the fate of the nation still hung in the balance, for now Britain, the Netherlands, Russia, and Spain joined Austria and Prussia in the war against France.

In the National Assembly, sentiment turned strongly against the disgraced Louis. Those representatives who sat on the "left" now clamored for a republic, while those who sat on the "right" still supported a constitutional monarchy. Mirabeau, once the leader of the moderates, and who might have calmed the waters, had died. As the war raged on, more and more of the representatives switched to the "left." In the summer of 1792 the "left" – also known as the Jacobins (JACK-oh-bins) – became the majority. They voted out the monarchy and declared a republic. Led by radical republicans like Robespierre, Georges-Jacques Danton, and Jean-Paul Marat, they launched the so-called Reign of Terror, in which hundreds of monarchists and moderates were rounded up, imprisoned, and executed. Louis himself was tried for treason, and on January 21, 1793, was executed. Marie Antoinette soon followed. Fearful lest they be next, moderates like La Fayette and Sieyes fled the country or went into hiding.

Once in power, the Jacobins initiated numerous radical changes. They passed a new constitution, one that proclaimed France a republic and renamed the National Assembly the National Convention. The new constitution didn't provide for a separate executive branch – that would smack too much of monarchy – and so the National Convention acted as both executive and legislature. A Committee of Public Safety, headed by Robespierre, oversaw day-to-day operations. The Jacobins outlawed slavery in all of France's colonies, instituted a military draft (the *levee en masse*), and replaced the old French flag, the royal *fleur-de-lis*, with a new standard, the republican *tricoleur*. They established a national anthem, the stirring *Marseillaise*, the first of its kind. They confiscated church property and appointed church officials. They dropped the old "monsieur" and "madame" (which meant "my lord" and "my lady") and in the spirit of equality substituted the more democratic word "citizen." They proclaimed a new, more rational calendar, with 1789 designated Year I, and with 10-month years and 10-day weeks. They brought in the newly invented, rational metric system and printed paper money. They confiscated the property of some of the lords.[219]

---

[218] Crane Brinton, *A Decade of Revolution, 1789-1799* (1963), 1-63; Hobsbawm, *Age of Revolution*, 74-86; John Merriman, *A History of Modern Europe* (1996), 496-520; Richard E. Sullivan, Dennis Sherman, and John B. Harrison, *A Short History of Western Civilization* (1994), 493-500; J. H. Hexter, Richard Pipes, and Anthony Molho, *Europe Since 1500* (1971), 562-570.

[219] Brinton, *Decade of Revolution*, 64-189; Hobsbawm, *Age of Revolution*, 86-95; Merriman, *History of Modern Europe*, 520-537; Sullivan, *Short History of Western Civilization*, 500-503; Hexter, *Europe Since 1500*, 570-574.

The French Revolution: the Reactionary Stage, or Counterrevolution

By 1794, however, public sentiment had turned against the Jacobins. The lords, the clergy, and even the moderate bourgeoisie believed the revolution had gone too far. Danton and Marat were both dead – Marat murdered in his bathtub – and Robespierre had become drunk with power. Shouting "Down with the tyrant!" the National Convention now demanded his ouster. Robespierre fled, was cornered, attempted suicide, failed, was arrested, and was executed. In the ensuing turmoil, the moderate leader Sieyes returned and took control.

At Sieyes's urging, the National Convention passed yet a third constitution, this time creating a strong executive branch called the Directory, composed of five Directors appointed by the National Convention. Sieyes was appointed one of the Directors. Another was a brilliant young general who had risen rapidly in the French army – Napoleon Bonaparte (1769-1821).

Sieyes believed he could control Bonaparte, and through him the army, but he was wrong. In 1799 Sieyes tried to seize power in a *coup d'etat* (KEW day-TAH) ("strike against the state"), but the young general stopped him and took control himself, making himself dictator. Thus it was that three heroes of the revolution – first Robespierre, then Sieyes, and now Bonaparte – in the end betrayed it. La Fayette still languished in an Austrian prison. Mirabeau, Danton, and the hard-working Marat were dead. Everything had come apart.

Bonaparte did not take France completely back to the way things had been before 1789. He left in place some of the elements of the reform and radical stages – the *tricoleur*, the *Marseillaise*, promotion by merit rather than birth, the *levee en masse*, the abolition of manorialism and feudalism, and the metric system. But he dropped the radical new calendar, mostly restored the position of the Roman Catholic Church, reinstated slavery in the colonies, returned the lords' estates to them, and did away with the republic. In 1804 he crowned himself Emperor Napoleon I, and remained in power until 1812.[220]

The Haitian Revolution

But in one small corner of the sprawling French Empire, writes the West Indian Marxist philosopher and political essayist C. L. R. James, the Revolution lived on. Back in 1789, when everything had started, France's richest colony – indeed, the richest of all the European colonies – had been the West Indian island of Saint Domingue (SAHN DOH-ming), today called Haiti. Founded in the 1600s, Saint Domingue's rich volcanic soil and mammoth plantations produced enormous crops of sugar, coffee, cocoa, indigo, and cotton.

Only a few thousand French colonists lived in Saint Domingue. The majority of the population consisted of tens of thousands of black slaves, brought from Africa to labor under the island's hot, tropical sun. To keep the slaves in line, the colonists used brutal measures – whipping, mutilation, torture, and murder. Disobedient slaves were buried up to their necks in insect hills, or blown up with gunpowder that had been inserted into their rectums. The slaves longed to be free, and according to James their favorite song was "Eh! Eh! Bomba! Heu! Heu! / Canga, bafio te! / Canga, moune de le! / Canga, do ki la! / Canga, li!" ("We swear to destroy the whites and all that they possess; let us die rather than fail to keep this vow.") In addition to the whites and the slaves, Saint Domingue's population also included a few thousand free blacks and mulattoes (people of mixed race). But the slaves were the majority.

During the first, reform stage of the French Revolution, most of Saint Domingue's whites had supported it, mainly because they thought that ending absolutism in France would lower their taxes in San Domingue and make them equal to the lords and upper bourgeoisie back in France. But the blacks overheard all the fine talk about *"liberte, egalite, et fraternite,"* and so thought, "why not us, too?" Some of the free blacks and mulattoes went to Paris to lobby the National Assembly for equal rights, regardless of race, and for an end to slavery.

In the colony, the slaves revolted against their masters. Toussaint Breda (Tew-SAHNT BRAY-dah) (1743-1803), a fifty-seven year old slave, led the uprising. Discarding the surname "Breda" (it was his master's name), Toussaint renamed himself "L'Ouverture" (Lew-ver-TUR) ("the Opening") because, it is sometimes said, he hoped to open a doorway for his people to freedom. The ex-slaves formed an army in the mountains and received some weapons from Spain, France's enemy. When the French government finally outlawed slavery during the radical stage of the French Revolution, Toussaint and the other slaves were overjoyed. Their goal achieved, they now supported both the Revolution and the new French Republic. It was the whites in the colony who now grimly opposed both. Thus it was that the colony's blacks and mulattoes, writes James, became Haiti's true Jacobins, supporters of revolutionary republicanism, with its emphasis on equality, human rights, and patriotism. Toussaint, he maintains, would always remain a Jacobin.

In 1794 France's enemy, Britain, slyly took advantage of the war in Europe to invade Saint Domingue, declare it a henceforth to be a British colony, and order slavery reinstated. The colony's whites were pleased to have their slaves back, and so collaborated with the British. But Toussaint, now sixty-one and holding a temporary commission as a brigadier general in the new, revolutionary French army, led the slaves, free blacks, and mulattoes in a long and bitter war against the British and the whites. During three years of brutal guerilla

---

[220] Brinton, *Decade of Revolution*, 190-245; Hobsbawm, *Age of Revolution*, 95-100; Merriman, *History of Modern Europe*, 537-565; Sullivan, *Short History of Western Civilization*, 503-512; Hexter, *Europe Since 1500*, 574-603.

combat, the redcoated invaders lost 80,000 soldiers and millions of pounds sterling. It was too much. In early 1797 Britain – the West's military superpower – realized that for the second time in two decades it had been defeated by a bunch of ragtag colonials – this time a group ex-slaves who had received no outside assistance. The British withdrew. In panic, many of the whites also fled, a substantial number of them taking refuge in the new United States, where slavery was still legal. But others stayed, joining Toussaint and the ex-slaves in rebuilding the colony. Always the Jacobin, Toussaint resisted demands by radical blacks to subjugate the whites, seize their property, and redistribute it among the ex-slaves; equality, human rights for whites as well as blacks, and the sanctity of private property, Toussaint insisted, were what the French Revolution had been about, and would thus be the cornerstones of the new Saint Domingue as well.

Later in 1797 the now sixty-four year old Toussaint received word from France that the Directory was considering reinstating slavery in the colony. The radical stage of the French Revolution had passed, the democratic Jacobins had been toppled, and a new, reactionary government was in power in Paris. The new French government was less committed to equality than the Jacobins had been. Toussaint responded to the news by writing a long, passionate letter to the Directory, pointing out that the colony's former slaves were now loyal, patriotic citizens of the French Republic. The letter was polite, but alongside Toussaint's words of praise for the "wisdom" of the Directors there was also a cold threat. If the Directory tried to reinstate slavery in Saint Domingue, Toussaint and the other ex-slaves would fight them. And they would win, just as they had defeated the British.

For a while, nothing happened. But when Napoleon Bonaparte consolidated his power in France in 1799, he was determined to reinstate slavery throughout the French Empire. Partly this was because he was a racist who believed that blacks were inferior to whites. But it was also because he wanted the money from the plantations to finance his wars. In 1800 a French army led by Napoleon's brother-in-law invaded Saint Domingue, for the express purpose of restoring slavery.

As Toussaint had promised, the ex-slaves fought back. Toussaint himself, now sixty-seven years old, was captured and carried back to France in chains. Bonaparte tossed the proud old man into a cold, dank dungeon where he slowly starved and froze, dying in 1803 at the age of seventy. But to Napoleon's surprise, the struggle in Haiti continued on without him. Led by another ex-slave – the bitter, angry, vengeful Jean-Jacques ("the Tiger") Dessalines (Dess-ah-LEEN) (1758-1806), Toussaint's best general and closest ally – the ex-slaves declared the colony to be an independent republic, which they renamed Haiti. Dessalines's soldiers used guerilla warfare. Moreover, they were aided by an outbreak of yellow fever among the French troops. A virulent tropical disease of African origin, yellow fever was more deadly to the Europeans than it was to the Haitians who, as the consequence of generations of exposure, had developed a partial immunity to it. By 1804 the French army was destroyed, with tens of thousands of casualties. In a rage, the defeated Bonaparte called what was left of his army home. Haiti was free, the second independent country in the Americas, and the first to be governed by former slaves. Amazingly, the impoverished, ill-armed, mostly illiterate, but determined Haitians had taken on the West's two greatest military powers – Britain and France – and beaten them both. It was a tremendous achievement.

But the long, exhausting Haitian War for Independence had embittered both Dessalines and his followers. Angrily, they turned their backs on the West and on Jacobinism, which they (unlike the French) decided was not radical enough. Although Toussaint had tried to win over the white plantation owners, the vengeful Dessalines decided to kill them instead. Most of the whites managed to escape, either to France or the United States, but hundreds died. Dessalines broke up their plantations and redistributed their lands to the ex-slaves, free blacks, and mulattoes as small family farms. In a fury, he tore down the Catholic churches and melted their bells into scrap metal. Rejecting Western-style republicanism, he declared Haiti an African-style monarchy, with himself Emperor Jean-Jacques I (r. 1804-06). He wanted nothing to do with Western Civilization – with its religion, its philosophy, its economy, or its politics – which he considered hopelessly corrupted and thoroughly suffused with the white men's evil. Unlike Toussaint, Dessalines was no Jacobin. He was something more radical: a black nationalist. For the time being, Haiti would go it alone.[221]

The Industrial Revolution

Not all revolutions are political. Some are economic and social. In addition to the American Revolution, the French Revolution, the Haitian Revolution, and the various other political revolutions of the late 1700s and early 1800s, the Age of Revolution also witnessed the Industrial Revolution, an economic and social revolution that began in England in the mid-1700s.

According to the social historians Louise Tilly and Joan Scott, "industrialization [was] the movement of labor and resources away from primary production (agriculture, fishing, forestry) toward manufacturing and commercial and service activities." They continue, "The scale of production increased and the factory replaced the household as the center of productive activity.... The industrial mode of production replaced the domestic mode of production.... Over the long run, the decline of small units of production meant a decline in the

---

[221] C. L. R. James, *The Black Jacobins: Toussaint L'Ouverture and the San Domingo Revolution* (1963, 1989), passim.

numbers of propertied peasants and craftsmen and an increase in proletarians, propertyless people working for wages."[222]

So far, three stages of industrialization have occurred, and in all likelihood the process will continue and other stages will occur in the future. The first stage, called the First Industrial Revolution, began in England around 1750, was based on the mass production of cheap textiles (cloth) using new technologies, and used falling water as the main power source. The second stage, known as the Second Industrial Revolution, also began in England, around 1850. It was based on the mass production of cheap steel using new technologies, and used coal and other fossil fuels as the chief source of power. The third stage, the Third Industrial Revolution, is still underway. It began in the United States around 1950, is based on microtechnology ("high-tech"), and uses electricity as the principal power source.

Industrialization, says the economic historian Phyllis Dean, is a complex process in which numerous elements must be present or nothing will happen. According to Dean, the main ingredients for the First Industrial Revolution were:

Raw materials. With the decline of manorialism, many English lords had slowly converted their manors to sheep ranches, which required less peasant labor and thus were cheaper to maintain than traditional family tenant farms. By 1500 wool was abundant in England and the country's chief export. Wheat was imported from England's "colony" of Ireland, and later from North America. The evicted peasants moved to the cities looking for work.

Labor. The introduction of American crop plants like maize and potatoes after 1600 triggered long-term population increase throughout Europe, including England. Known as the demographic revolution, this growth combined with the large number of impoverished ex-peasants streaming into the English cities to provide a large potential (and cheap) work force by about 1650.

Markets. The demographic revolution also created a large potential market for cheap woolens by about 1650.

Transportation. The cheapest way to transport goods in bulk is by water. And England had good access to water-borne transportation. After the defeat of the Spanish Armada in 1588, Britain had become an important sea power, along with Spain, Portugal, France, and the Netherlands. With the British victory over France in 1761 in the French and Indian Wars, it dominated the oceans. Moreover, the island nation's numerous harbors, large fleet of merchant ships, and ready supply of trained sailors provided plenty of transportation, all under the protection of the heavily armed royal navy. Too, by the mid-1700s the British had completed an efficient network of canals and canalized rivers that crisscrossed the island.

Capital. Starting with the British East India Company in the Age of Expansion, British merchants (like their counterparts in France, Spain, Portugal, and the Netherlands) had developed large corporations and pooled large quantities of capital, produced by the spice trade, the slave trade, and the profits of the slave colonies. The first banks opened their doors in the early 1700s. Some historians also argue that, without cheap slave labor in the 1600s and early 1700s to generate this capital, industrialization could not have occurred. By 1700 England had plenty of slave colonies and more than enough capital for industrialization.

Energy. England's hilly topography, rainy climate, and numerous smallish rivers produced an abundance of middle-sized waterfalls, just right for powering the early textile factories.

Social capital. The term "social capital" refers to schools, universities, hospitals, money, sewers, public water supplies, and other things provided by the state that encourage industrial development. In the case of the First Industrial Revolution, the most important of elements of social capital were money (which most countries had), schools, and universities. Unlike Medieval villeins, modern industrial workers need to be educated. They need to be able to read and write, do basic math, and tell time. And factories need engineers with even more advanced educations. And here was Britain's chief weakness, for in 1750 its literacy rate among males was less than 50% -- probably just barely enough to trigger industrialization. Still, only two other places in the entire world could boast higher male literacy rates in the 1700s: China and Britain's New England colonies in North America.

Technology. The final ingredient consisted of several new technologies – the spinning jenny, the power loom, the steam engine, the cotton gin, the idea of the assembly line, the notion of hiring women and children as workers – which were not invented until the late 1700s. Although the cotton gin was an American invention and the assembly line was Chinese, the others were British in origin.[223]

There is one final factor to consider: necessity. According to the economic historian Lynda Shaffer, England *needed* to industrialize its textile production, in order to continue doing business on the world market. Most people quite naturally preferred Chinese silk and Indian and African cotton to English (and other European) wool and linen. Silk and cotton are softer, lighter, and more comfortable, especially in warm climates. In order to compete with the Chinese and Indian textile merchants on the world market, British merchants had to find some way to make their own products more desirable.

That was easier said than done. They couldn't grow cotton in England (it's a semitropical plant), and silk technology proved difficult to master. They couldn't make wool or linen any softer or lighter. The only other option was to lower their prices, and the only way to do that was to increase their productivity. The invention of the spinning jenny and power loom boosted productivity by an estimated 1,000%. In other words, a single worker with a spinning jenny and a power loom could produce a hundred times as much cloth in a day as that

---

[222] Louise A. Tilly and Joan W. Scott, *Women, Work, and Family* (1987), 63.
[223] Phyllis Deane, *The First Industrial Revolution* (1979), passim.

same worker could using only an old-fashioned spinning wheel and handloom. Increased productivity led to lower prices, which in turn led to an increased market share.

Conversely, it would have been economic suicide for China and India to industrialize. In 1700 China and India combined to produce over half of the textiles sold on the world market. (By contrast, England produced less than ten percent.) If China and India had industrialized and, like England, increased their productivity by 1,000%, they would have glutted the world market, driving prices so far down that they would have put themselves out of business.[224]

-The Documents-

The French Revolution: The National Assembly

DECLARATION OF THE RIGHTS OF MAN AND CITIZEN[225]

The representatives of the French people, organized in National Assembly, considering that ignorance, forgetfulness, or contempt of the rights of man are the sole causes of public misfortunes and the corruption of governments, have resolved to set forth in a solemn declaration the natural, inalienable, and sacred rights of man, in order that such declaration, continually before all members of the social body, may be a perpetual reminder of their rights and duties; in order that the acts of the legislative power and those of the executive power may constantly be compared with the aim of every political institution and may accordingly be more respected; in order that the demands of the citizens, founded henceforth upon simple and incontestable principles, may always be directed towards the maintenance of the Constitution and the welfare of all.

Accordingly, the National Assembly recognizes and proclaims, in the presence and under the auspices of the Supreme Being, the following rights of man and citizen.

1. Men are born and remain free and equal in rights; social distinctions may be based only upon general usefulness.
2. The aim of every political association is the preservation of the natural and inalienable rights of man; these rights are liberty, property, security, and resistance to oppression.
3. The source of all sovereignty resides essentially in the nation; no group, no individual may exercise authority not emanating expressly therefrom.
4. Liberty consists of the power to do whatever is not injurious to others; thus the enjoyment of the natural rights of every man has for its limits only those that assure other members of society the enjoyment of those same rights; such limits may be determined only by law.
5. The law has the right to forbid only actions which are injurious to society. Whatever is not forbidden by law may not be prevented, and no one may be constrained to do what it does not prescribe.
6. Law is the expression of the general will; all citizens have the right to concur personally, or through their representatives, in its formation; it must be the same for all, whether it protects or punishes. All citizens, being equal before it, are equally admissible to all public offices, positions, and employments, according to their capacity, and without other distinction than that of virtues and talents.
7. No man may be accused, arrested, or detained except in the cases determined by law, and according to the forms prescribed thereby. Whoever solicit, expedite, or execute arbitrary orders, or have them executed, must be punished; but every citizen summoned or apprehended in pursuance of the law must obey immediately; he renders himself culpable by resistance.
8. The law is to establish only penalties that are absolutely and obviously necessary; and no one may be punished except by virtue of a law established and promulgated prior to the offense and legally applied.
9. Since every man is presumed innocent until declared guilty, if arrest be deemed indispensable, all unnecessary severity for securing the person of the accused must be severely repressed by law.

---

[224] Lynda Shaffer, "China, Technology, and Change," *World History Bulletin*, 4 (1986-87): 1-5.
[225] Ministere de la Justice de la Republique Francaise, "Declaration of the Rights of Man and Citizen, 26 August 1789," www.justice.gouv.fr/anglain/europe/addhc.htm, retrieved 23 June 2004.

10. No one is to be disquieted because of his opinions, even religious, provided their manifestation does not disturb the public order established by law.

11. Free communication of ideas and opinions is one of the most precious of the rights of man. Consequently, every citizen may speak, write, and print freely, subject to responsibility for the abuse of such liberty in the cases determined by law.

12. The guarantee of the rights of man and citizen necessitates a public force; such a force, therefore, is instituted for the advantage of all and not for the particular benefit of those to whom it is entrusted.

13. For the maintenance of the public force and for expenses of administration a common tax is indispensable; it must be assessed equally on all citizens in proportion to their means.

14. Citizens have the right to ascertain, by themselves or through their representatives, the necessity of the public tax, to consent to it freely, to supervise its use, and to determine its quota, assessment, payment, and duration.

15. Society has the right to require of every public agent an accounting of his administration.

16. Every society in which the guarantee of rights is not assured or the separation of powers not determined has no constitution at all.

17. Since property is a sacred and inviolate right, no one may be deprived thereof unless a legally established public necessity obviously requires it, and upon condition of a just and previous indemnity.

The Haitian Revolution: Toussaint L'Ouverture

In 1797 Toussaint L'Ouverture, the ex-slave, soldier, and acting governor of the French colony of Saint Domingue (Haiti), received word that in France the Directory was thinking about reinstating slavery, which had been outlawed several years earlier during the radical stage of the French Revolution. Toussaint wrote the following letter to the Directory warning them not to do it. Notice that the letter is unfailingly polite. Toussaint supported the French Revolution because it had outlawed slavery, considered himself a patriotic French citizen, and was loyal to the Republic. He also knew that you cannot persuade people to do what you want by using insulting language. But beneath the politeness was a cold, hard threat. "You will not do this," he was telling the Directors. "You will not restore slavery. If you try, I and the other ex-slaves will stop you. We beat the British, and we can defeat you, too." Notice also that Toussaint's phrasing was different from the previous two documents. He was a part of Western Civilization – he was born in a French colony, spoke French, and was a devout Roman Catholic. But unlike Jefferson and La Fayette, he had read very little of the literature of the Enlightenment, and there was little of the philosophe about him. But he had read a French translation of Julius Caesar's *Commentaries*, and there seems to be some of Caesar's personality in his words. They glint with fire, steel, and self-confidence. They are the words of a man who was a soldier as well as a politician. Do you think the ex-slave Toussaint would have understood the word "liberty" the same way as the slave owner Jefferson, or the young, idealistic aristocrat La Fayette? How would you define "liberty"? Do you think that Toussaint would have cared much about the argument over whether constitutionalism was better form of government than absolutism? Would he have defined "State of Slavery" the same way as John Locke? Do you think he would have been interested in preserving property rights? Why or why not?

from TOUSSAINT L'OUVERTURE'S LETTER TO THE DIRECTORY [226]

The impolitic and incendiary discourse of Vaublanc [a white plantation owner, who was then in Paris lobbying the French government to reinstate slavery in the colony] has not affected the blacks nearly so much as their certainty of the projects which the proprietors [i.e., the white plantation owners] of Saint Domingue are planning: insidious declarations should not have any effect in the eyes of wise legislators [here Toussaint is politely telling the Directors that he believes them to be wise men] who have decreed liberty for the nations. But the attempts on that liberty which the colonists [i.e., the white plantation owners] propose are all the more to be feared because it is with the veil of patriotism that they cover their detestable plans. We know that they seek to impose some of them on you by illusory and specious promises [Toussaint is telling the Directors not to be tricked by the planters], in order to see renewed in this colony its former scenes of horror. Already

---

[226] Letter, Toussaint L'Ouverture to the Directory of France, 1797, reprinted in James, *Black Jacobins*, 195-197.

perfidious emissaries have stepped in among us to ferment the destructive leaven prepared by the hands of liberticides [i.e., killers of liberty]. But they will not succeed. I swear it by all that liberty holds most sacred. My attachment to France, my knowledge of the blacks, make it my duty not to leave you ignorant either of the crimes which they mediate or the oath that we renew, to bury ourselves under the ruins of a country revived by liberty rather than suffer the return of slavery.

It is for you, Citizens Directors, to turn from over our heads the storm which the eternal enemies of our liberty are preparing in the shades of silence. It is for you to enlighten the legislature, it is for you to prevent the enemies of the present system from spreading themselves on our unfortunate shores to sully it with new crimes. Do not allow our brothers, our friends, to be sacrificed to men who wish to reign over the ruins of the human species. But no, your wisdom will enable you to avoid the dangerous snares which our common enemies hold out for you....

I send you with this letter a declaration which will acquaint you with the unity that exists between the proprietors of Saint Domingue who are in France, those in the United States, and those who serve under the English banner [here Toussaint is arguing that many of the white planters have either fled to the United States or, worse, collaborated with France's enemy, Britain]. You will see there a resolution, unequivocal and carefully constructed, for the restoration of slavery; you will see there that their determination to succeed has led them to envelop themselves in the mantle of liberty in order to strike it more deadly blows. You will see that they are counting heavily on my complacency in lending myself to their perfidious views by my fear for my children [Toussaint's sons were living in France, where he could not protect them]. It is not astonishing that these men who sacrifice their country to their interests are unable to conceive how many sacrifices a true love of country can support in a better father than they, since I unhesitatingly base the happiness of my grandchildren on that of my country, which they and they alone wish to destroy.

I shall never hesitate between the safety of Saint Domingue and my personal happiness; but I have nothing to fear. It is to the solicitude of the French Government that I have confided my children.... I would tremble with horror if it was into the hands of the colonists that I had sent them as hostages; but even if it were so, let them know that in punishing them for the fidelity of their father, they would only add one degree more to their barbarism, without any hope of ever making me fail in my duty.... Blind as they are! They cannot see how this odious conduct on their part can become the signal of new disasters and irreparable misfortunes, and that far from making them regain what in their eyes liberty for all has made them lose, they expose themselves to a total ruin and the colony to its inevitable destruction. Do they think that men who have been able to enjoy the blessing of liberty will calmly see it snatched away? They supported their chains only so long as they did not know any condition of life more happy than that of slavery. But today when they have left it, if they had a thousand lives they would sacrifice them all rather than be forced into slavery again. But no, the same hand which has broken our chains will not enslave us anew. France will not revoke her principles, she will not withdraw from us the greatest of her benefits. She will protect us against all our enemies; she will not permit her sublime morality to be perverted, those principles which do her most honor to be destroyed, her most beautiful achievement to be degraded, and her Decree of 16 Pluviose [the law that made slavery illegal] which so honors humanity to be revoked. But if, to reestablish slavery in Saint Domingue, this was done, then I declare to you if you would attempt the impossible: we have known how to face dangers to obtain our liberty, we shall know how to brave death to maintain it.

This, Citizens Directors, is the morale of the people of Saint Domingue, those are the principles that they transmit to you by me.

My own you know. It is sufficient to renew, my hand in yours, the oath that I have made, to cease to live before gratitude dies in my heart, before I cease to be faithful to France and to my duty, before the god of liberty is profaned and sullied by the liberticides, before they can snatch from my hands that sword, those arms, which France confided to me for the defense of its rights and those of humanity, for the triumph of liberty and equality.

The Industrial Revolution: Harriet Hanson Robinson

The new factories of the Industrial Revolution were often dangerous, dirty, and noisy. By today's standards, the work hours were long – normally fourteen hours a day, six days a week. And by today's standards, the pay was pitifully low, barely enough to survive on, and often not even that. The leading economists of the nineteenth century claimed that the "Iron Law of Wages" required all prudent businesspeople to keep wages low, hours long, and conditions dismal. Yet thousands of men, women, and children gladly accepted these jobs.

Among them was eleven-year-old Harriet Hanson (1825-1911) of Boston, Massachusetts. Harriet was born in 1825, the daughter of a poor carpenter. Her father died in 1831, when she was only six years old, leaving his wife and four young children destitute. For a while, Harriet's mother tried running "a little shop," but she was unable to make a go of it. Harriet's widowed aunt advised her to move the family to Lowell, a new factory city recently sprung up just a few miles north of Boston, where she worked as a boardinghouse keeper. Nicknamed the "City of Spindles," by 1835 Lowell had become the center of textile manufacturing in the United States. Rows of large brick-and-stone factories lined the banks of the Merrimack River, which provided the energy for hundreds of spinning frames (more advanced versions of spinning jennies) and power looms. Hundreds of modest brick houses provided homes for thousands of workers. Most of the young, single workers lived in large boardinghouses owned by the mills, which routinely hired widows like Harriet's mother and aunt to work as housekeepers. Harriet's mother secured a job as a housekeeper, and in 1832 she moved the family to Lowell. Four years later in 1836, Harriet went to work in the mills. She was only eleven years old. She remained in the mills for twelve years, until 1848, when aged twenty-three, she left to marry William Stevens Robinson (1818-76), a poorly paid abolitionist newspaper reporter.

While at the mills, Harriet had written for *The Lowell Offering*, a literary magazine founded and managed by the "mill girls" themselves. She wrote poetry, short stories, and essays on the abolition of slavery and women's rights. It was through the *Offering* that she met her husband; he had admired her writing ability and dedication to the abolition of slavery, and sought her out. After marriage, she continued to write, acting as William's "silent partner." They had no children. When William died in 1876, leaving Harriet a fifty-one-year-old widow, she supported herself by writing, mostly children's stories, eking out a modest existence. In 1898, aged seventy-three, she wrote *Loom and Spindle*, a memoir of her years at the factory. She was probably inspired by the recent publication in 1889 of another mill girl memoir, *A New England Girlhood* by Lucy Larcom (b. 1824), her coworker at the Lowell mills and fellow contributor to *The Lowell Offering*.[227]

In *Loom and Spindle* Harriet not only described the working conditions at the mills, she also explained why she and so many other women and girls gladly took jobs there. Contrary to what we might expect, she viewed her experience in the factory positively. As a child, she had pestered her mother to be allowed to work there, and was proud to be able to contribute to the family economy. The hours were too long for her liking, but the pay and amount of work was acceptable, especially when compared to the few other jobs available to women at the time. Her tone suggests that she believed that she was participating in something important, making a major contribution to the further modernization of Western Civilization.

from LOOM AND SPINDLE [228]

CHAPTER II
CHILD-LIFE IN THE LOWELL COTTON-MILLS

In attempting to describe the life and times of the early mill-girls, it has seemed best for me to write my story in the first person; not so much because my own experience is of importance, as that it is, in some respects, typical of that of many others who lived and worked with me.

* * * *

I had been to school constantly until I was about ten years of age, when my mother, feeling obliged to have help in her work besides what I could give, and also needing the money which I could earn, allowed me, at my urgent request (for I wanted to earn money like the other little girls), to go to work in the mill. I worked first in the spinning-room as a "doffer." The doffers were the very youngest girls, whose work was to doff, or take off, the full bobbins, and replace them with the empty ones.

I can see myself now, racing down the alley, between the spinning-frames, carrying in front of me a bobbin-box bigger than I was. These mites had to be very swift in their movements, so as not to keep the spinning-frames stopped long, and they worked only about fifteen minutes in every hour. The rest of the time was their own, and when the overseer was kind they were allowed to read, knit, or even to go outside the mill-yard to play.

Some of us learned to embroider in crewels, and I still have a lamb worked on cloth, a relic of those early days, when I was first taught to improve my time in the good old New England fashion. When not doffing, we were often allowed to go home, for a time, and thus we were able to help our mothers in their housework. We were paid two dollars a

---

[227] Jane Wilkins Pultz, "Introduction," in Harriet H. Robinson, *Loom and Spindle, or, Life Among the Early Mill Girls* (1898, 1976), ix-xii; Claudia L. Bushman, "After the Mills: A Biographical Sketch of Harriet H. Robinson," in Robinson, *Loom and Spindle*, 127-133.

[228] Harriet H. Robinson, *Loom and Spindle, or, Life Among the Early Mill Girls* (1898, 1976), 16, 18-20, 24-27, 37-42.

week; and how proud I was when my turn came to stand up on the bobbin-box, and write my name in the paymaster's book, and how indignant I was when he asked me if I could "write." "Of course I can," said I, and he smiled as he looked down on me.

The working-hours of all the girls extended from five o'clock in the morning until seven in the evening, with one-half hour for breakfast and for dinner. Even the doffers were forced to be on duty nearly fourteen hours a day, and this was the greatest hardship in the lives of these children. For it was not until 1842 that the hours of labor for children under twelve years of age were limited to ten per day [by an act of the Massachusetts legislature]; but the "ten-hour law" itself was not passed until long after some of these little doffers were old enough to appear before the legislative committee on the subject, and plead, by their presence, for a reduction of the hours of labor.

I do not recall any particular hardship connected with this life, except getting up so early in the morning, and to this habit, I never was, and never shall be, reconciled, for it has taken nearly a lifetime for me to make up the sleep lost at that early age. But in every other respect it was a pleasant life. We were not hurried any more than was for our good, and no more work was required of us than we were able easily to do.

* * * *

I was a "little doffer" until I became old enough to earn more money; then I tended a spinning-frame for a little while; and after that I learned, on the Merrimack corporation, to be a drawing-in girl, which was considered one of the most desirable employments, as about only a dozen girls were needed in each mill. We drew in, one by one, the threads of the warp, through the harness and the reed, and so made the beams ready for the weaver's loom. I still have the two hooks I used so long, companions of many a dreaming hour, and preserve them as the "badge of all my tribe" of drawing-in girls.

It may be well to add that, although so many changes have been made in mill-work, during the last fifty years, by the introduction of machinery, this part of it still continues to be done by hand, and the drawing-in girl – I saw her last winter, as in my time – still sits on her high stool, and with her little hook patiently draws in the thousands of threads, one by one.

CHAPTER III
THE LITTLE MILL-GIRL'S ALMA MATER

The education of a child is an all-around process, and he or she owes only a part of it to school or college training. The child to whom neither college nor school is open must find his whole education in his surroundings, and in the life he is forced to lead. As the cotton-factory was the means of the early schooling of so large a number of men and women, who, without the opportunity thus afforded, could not have been mentally so well developed, I love to call it their Alma Mater. For, without this incentive to labor, this chance to earn extra money and to use it in their own way, their influence on the times, and also, to a certain extent, on modern civilization, would certainly have been lost.

I had been to school quite constantly until I was nearly eleven years of age, and then, after going into the mill, I went to some of the evening schools that had been established, and which were always well filled with those who desired to improve their scant education, or to supplement what they had learned in the village school or academy.

* * * *

And so the process of education went on, and I, with many another "little doffer," had more than one chance to nibble at the root of knowledge. I had been to school for three months in each year, until I was about thirteen years old, when my mother, who was now a little better able to do without my earnings, sent me to the Lowell High School regularly for two years, adding her constant injunction, "Improve your mind, try and be somebody." There I was taught a little of everything, including French and Latin....

I left the high school when fifteen years of age, my school education completed....

Lucy Larcom, in her "New England Girlhood," speaks of the windows in the mill on whose sides were pasted newspaper clippings, which she calls "window gems." It was very common for the spinners and weavers to do this, as they were not allowed to read books openly in the mill; but they brought their favorite "pieces" of poetry, hymns, and extracts, and pasted them up over their looms or frames, so that they could glance at them, and commit them to memory. We little girls were fond of reading these clippings, and no doubt they were an incentive to our thoughts as well as to those of the older girls, who went to "The Improvement Circle," and wrote compositions.

A year or two after this I attempted poetry, and my verses began to appear in the newspapers, in one or two Annuals, and later in The Lowell Offering.

CHAPTER IV
THE CHARACTERISTICS OF THE EARLY FACTORY GIRLS

When I look back into the factory life of fifty or sixty years ago, I do not see what is called "a class" of young men and women going to and from their daily work, like so many ants that cannot be distinguished one from another; I see them as individuals, with personalities of their own....

Yet they were a class of factory operatives, and were spoken of (as the same class is spoken of now) as a set of persons who earned their daily bread, whose condition was fixed, and who must continue to spin and to weave to the end of their natural existence. Nothing but this was expected of them, and they were not supposed to be capable of social or mental improvement. That they could be educated and developed into something more than mere work-people, was an idea that had not yet entered the public mind. So little does one class of persons really know about the thoughts and aspirations of another!

* * * *

In 1831 Lowell was little more than a factory village. Several corporations were started, and the cotton-mills belonging to them were building. Help was a great demand; and stories were told all over the country of the new factory town, and the high wages that were offered to all classes of work-people – stories that reached the ears of mechanics' [i.e., artisans'] and farmers' sons, and gave new life to lonely and dependent women in distant towns and farmhouses. Into this Yankee El Dorado, these needy people began to pour by the various modes of travel known to those slow old days. The stage-coach and the canal-boat came every day, always filled with new recruits for this army of useful people. The mechanic and machinist came, each with his home-made chest of tools, and often-times with his wife and little ones. The widow came with her little flock and her scanty housekeeping goods to open a boarding-house or variety store, and so provided a home for her fatherless children. Many farmers' daughters came to earn money to complete their wedding outfit, or buy the bride's share of housekeeping articles.

Women with past histories came, to hide their griefs and their identity, and to earn an honest living in the "sweat of their brow." Single young men came, full of hope and life, to get money for an education, or to lift the mortgage from the home-farm. Troops of young girls came by stages and baggage-wagons, men often being employed to go to other States and to Canada, to collect them at so much a head, and deliver them at the factories.

A very curious sight these country girls presented.... When the large covered baggage-wagon arrived in front of a block on the corporation, they would descend from it, dressed in various and outlandish fashions, and with their arms brimful of bandboxes containing all their worldly goods.... And sorrowful enough they looked ...; for they had all left their pleasant country homes to try their fortunes in a great manufacturing town, and they were homesick even before they landed at the doors of their boarding-houses.

* * * *

Their dialect was ... very peculiar.... But the severe discipline and ridicule which met them was as good as a school education, and they were soon taught the "city way of speaking."

Their dress was also peculiar, and was of the plainest homespun, cut in such an old-fashioned style that each young girl looked as if she had borrowed her grandmother's gown. Their only head-covering was a shawl, which was pinned under the chin; but after the first payday, a "shaker" (or "scooter") sunbonnet usually replaced this primitive head-gear of their rural life.

But the early factory girls were not all country girls. There were others also, who had been taught that "work is no disgrace." There were some who came to Lowell solely on account of the social or literary advantages to be found there. They lived in secluded parts of New England, where books were scarce, and there was no cultivated society. They had comfortable homes, and did not perhaps need the money they would earn; but they longed to see this new "City of Spindles," of which they had heard so much from their neighbors and friends, who had gone there to work.

* * * *

The laws relating to women were such, that a husband could claim his wife wherever he found her, and also the children she was trying to shield from his influence; and I have seen more than one poor woman skulk behind her loom or her frame when visitors were approaching the end of the aisle where she worked. Some of these were known under assumed names, to prevent their husbands from trusteeing their wages. It was a very common thing for a male person of a certain kind to do this, thus depriving his wife of all her wages, perhaps, month after month. The wages of minor children could be trusteed, unless the children (being fourteen years of age) were given their time [i.e., had been emancipated by their fathers]. Women's wages were also trusteed for the debts of their husbands, and children's for the debts of their parents.

* * * *

It must be remembered that at this date woman had no property rights. A widow could be left without her share of her husband's (or the family) property, a legal "encumbrance" to his estate. A father could make his will without reference to his daughter's share of the inheritance. He usually left her a home on the farm as long as she remained single. A woman was not supposed to be capable of spending her own or of using other people's money. In Massachusetts, before 1840, a woman could not legally be treasurer of her own sewing-society, unless some man was responsible for her.

The law took no cognizance of woman as a money-spender. She was a ward, an appendage, a relict. Thus it happened, that if a woman did not choose to marry, or, when left a widow, to re-marry, she had no choice but to enter one of the few employments open to her, or to become a burden on the charity of some relative.

In almost every New England home could be found one or more of these women, sometimes welcome, more often unwelcome, and leading joyless, and in many instances unsatisfactory, lives. The cotton-factory was a great opening to these lonely and dependent women. From a condition approaching pauperism they were at once placed above want; they could earn money, and spend it as they pleased; and could gratify their tastes and desires without restraint, and without rendering an account to anybody. At last they had found a place in the universe; they were no longer obliged to finish out their faded lives mere burdens to male relatives. Even the time of these women was their own, on Sundays and in the evening after the day's work was done. For the first time in this country woman's labor had a money value. She had become not only an earner and a producer, but also a spender of money, a recognized factor in the political economy of her time. And thus a long upward step in our material civilization was taken; woman had begun to earn and hold her own money, and through its aid had learned to think and act for herself.

Understanding Historical Actors

DECLARATION OF THE RIGHTS OF MAN & CITIZEN
ROLE-PLAYING EXERCISE

It is August 27, 1789. France's National Assembly is debating the Declaration of the Rights of Man and Citizen. You are a member of the National Assembly, one of the individuals profiled below. Playing the role assigned to you, you and your discussion group (acting like a miniature National Assembly) will also consider and vote on the Declaration. But there is a catch. Your group will treat the 17 sections of the Declaration as separate proposals, to be voted on individually. You cannot amend (change) any of them; you can only vote "oui" or "non" on each of the 17 sections. In addition, your group may only adopt FIVE of the 17 sections. Your task is to try to understand why different people in the National Assembly would have voted different ways. It is important that you try to understand your character and play your role accurately. (The characters in this game were all real members of the National Assembly.)

FIRST ESTATE (CLERGY):

The Abbe Richard Maury (1746-91). You are forty-three years old. You are a priest. You are by birth a commoner, the son of a cobbler, and consider yourself a self-made man. You despise your origins and admire the lords. You are a strong royalist. You figure that if you could succeed in absolutist France, then any other hard-working, pious, virtuous man should be able to make something of himself as well. You believe that the bourgeois, peasants, and *sans culottes* who are complaining about things are really just a bunch of lazy sinners who are not willing to work as hard as you did, or give up their pleasures the way you did, or perhaps are not as smart as you are. Such people certainly should not be allowed to run the country. You are a gifted orator, the leading spokesman for the king in the First Estate. You support absolutism and have long believed that the king rules by the will of God. You believe in the idea of a state-supported Church, and believe that all men and women in France should be members of the same (Catholic) Church. Fearing that God will punish a blasphemous society, you oppose freedom of speech and the press, for that would only allow Protestantism (which you view as devil worship) to gain a foothold. You believe nobles are, as a group, more virtuous, better educated, and more fit to rule than most commoners. You believe capitalism (lending money at interest) is a sin. You oppose science – and the whole idea of natural rights – as anti-Catholic. You do not believe that either the church or the nobles should be taxed.

The Bishop Charles-Maurice de Talleyrand-Perigord (1754-1838). You are thirty-five. You are a moderate reformer. Although you are a priest, you are a supporter of the ideas of John Locke. Your parents were lords, but you were disinherited in favor of your younger brother because of a birth defect, and now you dislike and are jealous of those lords who lead such "perfect," idle lives. You wish to end absolutism and *droits*, and increase personal freedoms. You want to tax the nobles, who you believe are not paying their fair share. However, you want to protect the Church, and although you agree that it should be taxed, you don't want the government to control the appointment of its priests or bishops. You are wily and cautious, and don't believe in letting your true feelings show if you can help it. Your motto is "live, and let live." Although you are a Catholic, you are tolerant of Protestants. You incline towards compromise, and you tend to vote with the majority. If the reformers seem to be in the majority, that is good, you are quite prepared to support them; otherwise, however, you will not go out on a limb on their behalf.

SECOND ESTATE (LORDS):

Andre Boniface Louis Riqueti, Viscount de Mirabeau (1754-92). You are thirty-five. You are a strong royalist. You are the straight-laced younger brother of that pockmarked, loudmouth, liberal womanizer, the Count de Mirabeau. You are the good brother. You led a virtuous life, obeyed your father, and never fooled around – well, hardly ever, anyway. You are so rotund that certain members of the Third Estate (instigated, no doubt, by your no-account brother) have nicknamed you "Barrel Mirabeau." You love nothing better than to challenge your brother. You despise peasants, and don't think much of merchants, either. You wish to maintain *droits*. You strongly object to taxing nobles, but would like to increase taxes on merchants. You support the king and absolutism, and are one of Louis's foremost advocates in the Second Estate.

Marie Joseph Paul Yves Roch Gilbert du Motier, Marquis de La Fayette (1757-1834). You are thirty-two. You are a moderate reformer. A volunteer in the army of George Washington a few years earlier, you yearn to end absolutism and turn France into a constitutional monarchy. You are the principal author of the Declaration of the Rights of Man and Citizen, which you have modeled on the American Declaration of Independence. You believe in the right to a fair trial, religious toleration, representative government, freedom of the press, abolition of noble titles, fair taxes, and elimination of *droits*. Most of the other lords consider you a traitor to your estate. You believe in the sanctity of private property.

THIRD ESTATE (COMMONERS):

Honore Gabriel Riqueti, Count de Mirabeau (1749-91). You are forty years old. You are a moderate reformer. Although you are a lord, you have been elected by the commoners to represent them in the Third Estate. You are a supporter of constitutionalism. Along with the Abbe Sieyes, you led the movement to merge the three houses of the Estates-General into one National Assembly. Having been jailed by your own father, you oppose punishing people without due process of law. You believe that many of the lords (especially your younger brother, the Viscount de Mirabeau) are self-righteous twits who lack good sense. You believe in the fundamental equality of all people, regardless of estate. But at the same time you do not want to take reform too far. You do not oppose the Declaration of the Rights of Man and Citizen per se, but you strongly believe that it is premature – that a new constitution must be written first. Otherwise, each person will interpret the Declaration in his own way, and it will have the effect of splintering the country and make drafting a working constitution much more difficult. (As it turns out, you will be right.)

The Abbe Emmanuel-Joseph Sieyes (1748-1836). You are forty-one. You are a moderate reformer, although some people view you as a radical reformer. Although you are a priest, you have been elected by the commoners of Paris to elect them in the Third Estate. You are a strong supporter of the ideas of John Locke and the other philosophes. You believe in constitutionalism and human rights. Along with the Count de Mirabeau, you led the movement to merge the three houses of the Estates-General into one National Assembly. Your parents were commoners, and you dislike the lords' sons who seem to run the Church. You wish to end absolutism and *droits*, and increase personal freedoms. You want to tax the lords, who you believe are not paying their fair share. However, you have reservations about taxing the Church, and you are not a believer in deism or the separation of Church and state.

Maximillien Robespierre (1758-94). You are thirty-one. You are a radical reformer, and in time you will help organize and lead the Jacobins. You are a deist and a lawyer. You are a strong supporter of constitutionalism, human rights, and capitalism. You dislike the lords and the Church, and do not believe that they should have any special privileges. You support all of the major ideals of the Enlightenment. Secretly, you would like to see France become a republic. Unlike the Count de Mirabeau, you believe that it is necessary to have a Declaration of the Rights of man and Citizen first, before a constitution, because you believe that no constitution can be valid unless it is based on the idea of human rights.

Antoine Pierre Joseph Marie Barnave (1761-93). You are twenty-seven. You are a radical reformer, and in time you will help organize and lead the Jacobins. You are a lawyer (like your father), and are considered the best orator among the radical reformers. Unlike most people in France, you are a Protestant. Your mother is well educated, and indeed she was your primary teacher, since as a Protestant you were not permitted to attend school (the schools are run by the Catholic Church). You have worked closely with Abbe Sieyes ever since you arrived in Versailles. You are a passionate lover of liberty. You are especially angry at the privileges enjoyed by the lords and the Catholic Church, and would like to make everyone equal. You support a constitutional monarchy. You think taxes are too high, and you want the lords and the Church to pay their fair share.

-CHAPTER VII-
LIVES OF QUIET DESPERATION:
WESTERN IDEOLOGY IN THE AGE OF "ISMS"
c. 1790 - c. 1870

Commenting on the rise of modern middle-class materialism that he believed had resulted from the Industrial and Market Revolutions of the late 1700s and early 1800s (we know that it actually had begun earlier), the nineteenth-century American philosopher Henry David Thoreau shook his head ruefully and observed sadly, "The mass of men lead lives of quiet desperation." In their drive to succeed, Thoreau believed, middle-class farmers and tradesmen had exhausted themselves with overwork, lost touch with nature, lost sight of "higher laws," and lost contact with the things that really make them happy. The values of the Enlightenment and the Age of Revolution - individualism, mastering nature, capitalism, acquisitiveness, materialism, cold rationalism, and cutthroat competition - seemed to Thoreau to have done the West more harm than good, and so he challenged his fellow Westerners to question them. In their place he advocated a new value system: transcendentalism.

One important consequence of the culture-churning revolutions of the late eighteenth and early nineteenth centuries was that people had become politicized. A whole new series of political, economic, and social ideologies, or "isms," emerged, as women and men like Thoreau reacted to the revolutions either by embracing them or, as Thoreau did, by challenging them. The isms that they came up with - classical liberalism, classical conservatism, early feminism, early socialism, transcendentalism, nationalism, and others - lasted. They have remained the basis of Western political, social, and economic thought ever since. So important were these new ideologies that some historians refer to the Age of Revolution as the Age of Isms.

The first and most important of the Western isms was classical liberalism, which accepted and even celebrated the changes brought by the various revolutions of 1763-1848. For good or ill, classical liberalism emerged triumphant as the dominant Western ism of the nineteenth and twentieth centuries. Basing their views on the philosophies of John Locke, Immanuel Kant, Benjamin Franklin, and the other philosophes of the Enlightenment, classical liberals like the political writers Thomas Paine (1737-1809), Mary Wollstonecraft (1759-97), Jeremy Bentham (1748-1832), and John Stuart Mill (1806-73), and the political leaders Alexander Hamilton (1755-1804) of the United States, William Ewart Gladstone (1809-98) of Britain, and John A. Macdonald (1815-91) of Canada viewed the Enlightenment, American Revolution, French Revolution, and Industrial Revolution as great leaps forward - "progress," as they saw it.

On the other hand, classical conservatives like Britain's Edmund Burke (1729-97) and Austria's Klemens von Metternich (MET-er-nick) (1773-1859), early socialists like Germany's Karl Marx (1818-83) and France's Charles Fourier (For-NYAY) (1772-1837), early nationalists like Italy's Giuseppe Mazzini (Mahts-EE-nee) (1805-72) and Giuseppe Garibaldi (Gair-eh-BALD-ee) (1807-82), early environmentalists like Thoreau (1817-62), Ralph Waldo Emerson (1803-82), and Canada's Catharine Parr Traill (1802-99), anarchists, syndicalists, romantics, and others opposed certain aspects of these revolutions. As a result, conservatism, socialism, nationalism, and environmentalism challenged the dominant ideology of classical liberalism, although from different directions. For its part, early feminism grew out of classical liberalism, seeking to expand the "rights of man" into the "rights of man and woman."

Only slowly did the terms liberalism, conservatism, feminism, socialism, nationalism, and environmentalism come into common usage, which meant that most early nineteenth-century thinkers and politicians did not call themselves by these names - a fact that sometimes confuses people learning about them for the first time. In their own time, classical liberals were known variously as republicans, Jacobins, Whigs, reds (or, in French, *rouges*), or democrats; classical conservatives as Tories, blues (or, in French, *bleus*), blacks (or, in French, *noirs*), whites (or, in French, *blancs*), or royalists; socialists as Fourierists, Marxists, reds, *rouges*, chartists, or communists (the distinction between socialism and communism did not emerge until later, in the twentieth century); and environmentalists as transcendentalists, conservationists, or romantics.

The following readings are intended to introduce you to the isms as they first emerged at the dawn of the nineteenth century. As you read the following documents, think about what connections - if any - exist between the isms of today and the way they were two centuries ago. How much, and in what ways have they changed? How much, and in what ways, have they stayed the same? Which perspectives seem to you to be modern? Which perspectives seem to you to be traditional?

-The Documents-

Differing Points of View

Different people can experience the exact same events and yet view them very differently. All seven of the writers excerpted below lived during the Age of Revolution. Yet each of them came up with a markedly different interpretation of it. Three – Thomas Paine, Edmund Burke, and Mary Wollstonecraft – lived in the middle of the era, during the heady days of the French Revolution. Paine supported the French Revolution, Burke opposed it, and Wollstonecraft supported it but wanted it to go further, to liberate women as well as men. Henry David Thoreau, Karl Marx, Friedrich Engels, and Giuseppe Mazzini lived later, at the end of the Age of Revolution. Unlike Paine, Burke, and Wollstonecraft, they had the time to see how the French Revolution turned out, and also to witness the full impact of the Industrial Revolution. Thoreau opposed many of the consequences of industrialization. Marx and Engels approved of the new machinery and material goods, but disapproved of the way that factory workers were treated. Mazzini thought of change and revolution as good things, but only if duty tempered individualism and each national group was permitted to control its own destiny. Paine became a classical liberal, Burke a classical conservative, Wollstonecraft an early feminist, Thoreau an early environmentalist, Marx and Engels early socialists, and Mazzini an early nationalist.

How could seven good, intelligent, well-meaning, perceptive people interpret the same events so differently? Did different aspects of their backgrounds give them different perspectives on the Age of Revolution? Was it significant that Wollstonecraft was female, and the other six were all male? Did socio-economic class play a role? None of the seven were lords or clergy; none were peasants or, with the possible exception of Paine, workers; all (again, with the possible exception of Paine) were from the bourgeoisie. Yet Burke and Engels came from wealthy families; Marx, Mazzini, and Thoreau from upper middle-class families; and Wollstonecraft and (possibly) Paine from lower middle-class families. All seven were highly educated. Wollstonecraft came from a dysfunctional family and had been unlucky in love, but found happiness near the end of her life. The only woman Thoreau ever courted rejected him, and he never married, which gave rise to (probably false) rumors that he was gay. Marx and Burke, on the other hand, had stable, loving families. Thoreau and Wollstonecraft died young. Marx and Paine lived to ripe old ages. Mazzini, Marx, Engels, and Paine spent much of their lives in exile from their native lands. Of the seven, only Burke ever held significant political office. Burke was Protestant, but came from a religiously mixed family. Paine and Wollstonecraft were deists. Thoreau was raised a Protestant, but became a transcendentalist. Mazzini was a Roman Catholic. Marx was an atheist of Jewish descent. As you read about each thinker, think about what aspects of their lives led them to the "ism" they espoused. Why do people become liberals, conservatives, feminists, environmentalists, socialists, and nationalists, then and now? Which ism do you support? Can you think of any events in your own life that have led you there?

Classical Liberalism: Thomas Paine

Thomas Paine (1737-1809) was born and raised in London, the son of a poor craftsman and devout Quaker. When he was thirteen, he was apprenticed to his father's trade, and eventually became a craftsman himself. Concerned with the plight of the working person and strongly influenced by Lockean rationalism, Paine became involved with various radical reform movements in London, read political pamphlets voraciously, wrote some himself, concluded that monarchical government was hopelessly corrupt and oppressive, and devoted his life to republicanism. In 1774, when he was thirty-seven, Paine met Benjamin Franklin, who was in London negotiating on behalf of the colonies in their growing dispute with Parliament over taxes. Impressed by the young man's powerful writing style and zeal for reform, Franklin suggested that Paine go to Philadelphia and become a printer.

Taking Franklin's advice, Paine crossed the Atlantic later that year. He quickly became a proponent of American independence. His 1776 pamphlet, *Common Sense*, urged the Continental Congress to pass the Declaration of Independence. Paine's argument was not just that Americans would be better off economically if they formed their own country (although he believed that such was true), but also that a full-scale revolution would give the Americans the opportunity to replace the old aristocratic monarchy with a new democratic republic – a form of government in which all citizens would be equal and possess human rights, regardless of their class. Later, Paine traveled with George Washington's Continental Army, writing a series of pamphlets, collectively called *The Crisis*, which whipped up public support for the war effort. (One of these pamphlets began, "These are the times that try men's souls," one of the most famous lines in Western literature.) Paine remained in America after the war ended in 1783. He did not return to Britain until 1787, when he was fifty.

He didn't stay there long. When the French Revolution began two years later, Paine – who believed fervently in ideas expressed in the Declaration of the Rights of Man and Citizen – went to Paris to aid a second revolution. When Edmund Burke, a member of the British Parliament and the founder of classical conservatism, wrote a book in 1790 attacking the French Revolution as too radical, Paine rose to defend it in a powerful, sarcastic, and acerbic book, *The Rights of Man*, published in 1791. A ringing statement of what would later be called classical liberalism (Paine himself used the term republicanism), the book was just as critical of the British monarchy as it was of the French king, and therefore was deemed treasonous by the British government. Remaining in France, Paine was tried in absentia in Britain and banished from the British Empire. Later, Paine himself was a victim of the French Revolution, spending time in prison during the Reign of Terror. While in prison he wrote *The Age of Reason*, his last book, a defense of the Enlightenment and an attack on organized religion.

Paine returned to America in 1802, only to find himself shunned by his old comrades as a hopeless radical (which was true) and an atheist (which was not quite true). He lived in poverty and obscurity in the country for whose cause he had labored so mightily until his death in 1809 at the age of seventy-two.[229]

from THE RIGHTS OF MAN [230]

[The Right Not to be Bound by the Past]

[Edmund Burke saw the English constitution as permanent, the achievement of an especially wise group of venerated founders. However, Paine believed that the founders were no wiser than anyone else, and maintained that each generation of English men and women had the option of making any changes it wished.]

Every age and generation must be free to act for itself, in all cases, as the ages and generations which preceded it [were also free to act]. The vanity and presumption of governing beyond the grave [by establishing laws or constitutions that cannot be altered by future generations], is the most ridiculous and insolent of all tyrannies.

Man has no property in man; neither has any generation a property in the generations which are to follow. The Parliament or the people of 1688 [the time of the Glorious Revolution, which established the English constitution as it existed in Paine's day], or of any other period, had no more right to dispose of the people of the present day, or to bind or control them in any shape whatever, than the Parliament or people of the present day have to dispose of, bind, or control those who are to live a hundred or a thousand years hence.

Every generation is, and must be, competent to all the purposes which its occasions require. It is the living, and not the dead, that are to be accommodated. When [a] man [dies], his power and his wants [die] with him; and having no longer any participation in the concerns of this world, he has no longer any authority in directing who shall be its governors, or how its government shall be organized, or how administered.

* * * *

The circumstances of the world are continually changing, and the opinions of men change also; and as government is for the living, and not the dead, it is the living only that has any right in it. That which may be thought right and found convenient in one age, may be thought wrong and found inconvenient in another.

[The Right to Equality of Opportunity]

[Burke defended aristocrats as well-trained, public-spirited, unbiased men who constituted a vital link to Europe's cherished past. Paine, however, denounced them as a privileged, pampered minority. He thought all people deserved the opportunity to succeed based on their merits, not on the accident of their birth.]

The French Constitution says, there shall be no titles; and of consequence, all that class of equivocal generation, which in some countries as called "aristocracy," and in others "nobility," is done away [with], and the peer [i.e., lord] is exalted into man.

* * * *

It is, properly, from the elevated mind of France, that the folly of titles has been abolished, [France] has outgrown the baby-clothes of count and duke, and breeched itself in manhood [i.e., put on adult trousers]. France has not leveled [i.e., brought everyone down to the level of peasant], it has exalted [i.e., brought everyone up to the level of citizen]. It has put down the dwarf to set up the man.

* * * *

The patriots of France have discovered in good time, that rank and dignity in society must take a new ground. The old one has fallen through. It must now take the substantial ground of character, instead of the chimerical ground of tithes; and they have brought their titles to the altar, and made of them a burnt-offering to Reason.

* * * *

---

[229] I. Kramnick, "Editor's Introduction," in Thomas Paine, *Thomas Paine's Common Sense*, ed. I. Kramnick (1976), 25-37.
[230] Thomas Paine, *The Rights of Man* (1791, 1961), passim.

That...which is called aristocracy in some countries, and nobility in others, arose out of the governments founded upon conquest. It was originally a military order [i.e., Medieval knights], for the purpose of supporting military government (for such were the governments founded in conquest); and to keep up a succession of this order for the purpose for which it was established, all the younger branches of those families were disinherited, and the law of primogenitureship set up. [Primogeniture required that all property and titles pass to a single heir, usually the oldest son. Paine ignored the fact that primogeniture was not universal in Medieval Europe, nor in the West of his own day.]

The nature and character of aristocracy shows itself to us in this law. It is a law against every law of nature, and nature herself calls for its destruction. Establish family justice, and aristocracy fails. By the aristocratical law of primogenitureship, in a family of six children, five are exposed. Aristocracy never has more than one child. The rest are begotten to be devoured. They are thrown to the cannibal for prey, and the natural parent prepares the repast.

[The Right to Personal Liberty, or Individualism]

[Burke denied the existence of all natural rights and stressed membership in the group. Paine, however, argued that all people possessed individual rights guaranteed by nature. Among these rights, Paine believed, were freedom of conscience, freedom of religion, freedom of speech, freedom of the press, the right to own property, the right to security, the right to a fair trial, and the right to resist oppression, all listed in the French Declaration of the Rights of Man and Citizen.]

The French Constitution...hath established [a] UNIVERSAL RIGHT OF CONSCIENCE.

* * * *

Who...art thou, vain dust and ashes! By whatever name thou art called, whether a king, a bishop, a church or a state, a parliament or any thing else, that obtrudest thine insignificance between the soul of man and his Maker? Mind thine own concerns. If he believes not as thou believest, it is proof that thou believest not as he believeth, and there is no earthly power can determine between you.

* * * *

With respect to what are called denominations of religion, if every one is left to judge of his own religion, there is no such thing as a religion that is wrong; but if they are to judge of each other's religion, there is no such thing as a religion that is right.

But with respect to religion itself, without regard to names, and as directing itself from the universal family of mankind to the divine object of all adoration, it is man bringing to his Maker the fruits of his heart; and though these fruits may differ from each other like the fruits of the earth, the grateful tribute of every one is accepted [by God].

[Unity Through Diversity.]

Made up, as [America] is, of people from different nations [here Paine uses the word "nation" to mean "ethnic group"], accustomed to different forms and habits of government, speaking different languages, and more different in their modes of worship, it would appear that the union of such a people was impracticable; but by the single operation of constructing government on the principles of society and the rights of man, every difficulty retires, and all the parts are brought into cordial union.

[The Right to Own Property,
or Economic Individualism.]

Government is nothing more than a national association [here Paine uses the word "nation" to mean "country"]; and the object of this association is the good of all, as well individually as collectively. Every man wishes to pursue his occupation, and enjoy the fruits of his labors, and the produce of his property, in peace and safety, and with the least possible expense. When these things are accomplished, all the objects for which government ought to be established are answered.

[The Right to a Republican Government]

[Burke defended monarchy as a "contrivance of human wisdom." Paine despised it as foolish and oppressive, advocating a republic instead. Burke argued that good government required well-trained, virtuous, unbiased leaders. Paine maintained that it required public servants instead.]

What is a monarchy? Is it a thing, or is it a name, or is it a fraud? Is it a "contrivance of human wisdom," or human craft [i.e., sneaky trick], to obtain money from a nation [here Paine uses the word "nation" to mean "country"] under specious pretenses? Is it a thing necessary to a nation? If it is, in what does that necessity consist, what service does it perform, what is its business, and what are its merits?

* * * *

[Monarchy] appears to be a something going much out of fashion, falling into ridicule, and rejected in some countries both as unnecessary and expensive. In America it is considered as an absurdity, and in France it has so far declined, that the goodness of [Louis XVI], and the respect for his personal character are the only things that preserve the appearance of its existence. [Paine obviously wrote this passage before Louis was executed for treason.]

Hereditary succession is a burlesque [i.e., bad joke] upon monarchy. It puts it in the most ridiculous light, by presenting it as an office, which any child or idiot may fill. It requires some talents to be a common mechanic [i.e., craftsperson]; but to be a king, requires only the animal [i.e., biological] figure of a man – a sort of breathing automaton. [At this point, Paine went on to describe several of the bad kings, child kings, foreign kings, and insane kings in English history.]

* * * *

If a country does not understand its own affairs, how is a foreigner [here Paine takes jabs at several of England's kings, including William I, who was Norman, Henry II, who was French, James I and Charles I, who were Scottish, and George I and George II, who were German] to understand them, who knows neither its laws, its manners, nor its language? If there existed a man so transcendently wise above all others, that his wisdom was necessary to instruct a nation, some reason might be offered for monarchy; but when we cast our eyes about a country, and observe how every part understands its own affairs; and when we look around the world, and see that of all men in it, the race of kings are the most insignificant in capacity, our reason cannot fail to ask us – What are those men kept for?

* * * *

I see in America, a government extending over a country ten times as large as England, and conducted with regularity for a fortieth part of the expense which government costs in England. If I ask a man in America, if he wants a king, he retorts, and asks me if I take him for an idiot.... I see in America, the generality of the people living in a style of plenty unknown in monarchial countries; and I see that the principle of its government, which is that of the equal Rights of Man, is making a rapid progress in the world.

If monarchy is a useless thing, why is it kept up any where? And if a necessary thing, how can it be dispensed with [in America]? That civil government is necessary, all civilized nations will agree; but civil government is republican government.

* * * *

It is easy to conceive, that a band of interested man [i.e., members of special interest groups] such as placemen [i.e., office holders and bureaucrats], pensioners, lords of the bed-chamber, lords of the kitchen, lords of the necessary-house, and Lord knows what besides, can find as many reasons for monarchy as their salaries, paid at the expense of the country, amount to; but if I ask the farmer, the manufacturer, the merchant, the tradesman, and down through all the occupations of life to the common laborer, what service monarchy is to him? He can give me no answer.

* * * *

The two modes of government which prevail in the world are, First, government by election and representation: Second, government by hereditary succession. The former is generally known by the name of republic; the latter by that of monarchy and aristocracy.

These two distinct and opposite forms, erect themselves on the two distinct and opposite bases of Reason and Ignorance. As the exercise of government requires talents and abilities, and as talents and abilities cannot have hereditary descent, it is evident that hereditary succession requires a belief [i.e., faith] from man, to which his reason cannot subscribe, and which can only be established upon his ignorance; and the more ignorant any country is, the better it is fitted for this species of government.

[However], government in a well constituted republic requires no belief from man beyond what his reason can give. He sees the rationale of the whole system, its origin and its operation; and as it is best supported when best understood, the human faculties act with boldness, and acquire, under this form of government, a gigantic manliness.

* * * *

And the representative system takes society and civilization for its basis; nature, reason, and experience for its guide.

* * * *

As the republic of letters [i.e., the collegial community of scholars and artists upon which modern universities are based] brings forward the best literary productions, by giving to genius a fair and universal chance; so the representative system of government is calculated to produce the wisest laws, by collecting wisdom where it can be found.

* * * *

There is existing in man, a mass of sense lying in a dormant state, and which, unless something excites it to action, will descend with him, in that condition, to the grave. As it is to the advantage of society that the whole of its faculties should be employed, the construction of government ought to be such as to bring forward, by a quiet and regular operation, all that extent of capacity.

* * * *

In the representative system, the reason for everything must publicly appear. Every man is a proprietor in government and considers it a necessary part of his business to understand. It concerns his interest, because it affects his property. He examines the cost, and compares it with the advantages; and above all, he does not adopt the slavish custom of following what in other governments are called LEADERS.

[The Right to Free Trade]

[Burke supported mercantilism, an economic system in which the government undertook to regulate commerce with other countries in such a way as to promote a positive balance of trade and, presumably, economic growth. The key features of mercantilism were protective tariffs (taxes on foreign imports, designed to stimulate consumers to purchase domestically produced goods), colonies (as producers of needed raw materials and as markets for domestic manufactures), wage and price controls (to ensure that wages and prices were "fair"), government expenditures on transportation (harbor facilities, canals, roads, etc.), government-granted monopolies for certain businesses, such as mining, colonizing, or overseas trade (to encourage businesspeople to undertake risky ventures), and the maintenance of a large and powerful navy (to protect commercial shipping from pirates and from other countries). Paine, however, supported Adam Smith's view, soon to be called laissez-faire or free trade, that the government should take a "hands-off" position on commerce, and allow the "natural law" of supply and demand to take its course.]

All the great laws of society are laws of nature. Those of trade and commerce, whether with respect to the intercourse of individuals, or of nations [i.e., countries], are laws of mutual and reciprocal interest. They are followed and obeyed because it is the interest of the parties so to do, and not on account of any formal laws their governments may impose or interpose.

Classical Conservatism: Edmund Burke

Edmund Burke (1729-1793) is sometimes called the father of British conservatism. Born in Ireland, Burke was the son of a Catholic mother and Protestant father. His parents decided to raise him as a Protestant and his sister as a Catholic. Although his family lived in Dublin where his father practiced law, as a sickly child Burke spent a great deal of his youth in the countryside, living with Catholic relatives and attending Catholic schools. He was attracted to traditional Catholic viewpoints, and held a deep and abiding affection for Ireland's traditional Catholic past. Yet as the son of a Protestant (his father had converted some time before Burke was born, possibly to increase his chances for upward mobility in an English-dominated society), Burke also loved the British Empire and viewed England and Ireland as a single, joined society with a common future in which Catholics and Protestants would be treated as equals. He was no believer in the equality of classes, however. As the son of a lawyer, son-in-law of a physician, and kin to wealthy landowners, Burke sympathized more with the gentry (landlord class) and upper bourgeoisie than with the poor peasants who made up the vast majority of the Irish people.[231]

After graduating from Dublin's Trinity College, Burke moved to London, the capital of the British Empire. He loved the bustling metropolis and all its intense political activity. He practiced law briefly, hated it, and quit to become a politician. He took a job as private secretary to a powerful member of the Whig Party, and eventually settled in as a key political advisor to Charles Wentworth, the Marquis of Rockingham, one of the Whig leaders. (It is ironic that the father of British conservatism was a Whig rather than a Tory.) Although remaining a resident of London, Burke was elected to Parliament as the representative of Wendover, a "pocket borough" or "rotten borough," a largely unpopulated rural district controlled by the local landlord, who in this case was Burke's patron Rockingham. Although the Whigs came to power briefly in the 1760s (with Rockingham as Prime Minister), for most of Burke's thirty-plus years in politics they remained in opposition to the ruling Tory Party. Under Britain's largely unwritten constitution, the party with the majority in Commons chooses the Prime Minister and Cabinet, with the "loyal opposition" organizing what is today known as a "Shadow Cabinet" (the term had not yet been invented in Burke's day), with each member acting as the chief critic of a particular member of the real Cabinet. Burke spent most of his political career in the Whig Shadow Cabinet, his party's foremost expert on colonial affairs and imperial trade. He also took a job as a paid lobbyist for the British colony of New York. He bought a large estate in the country and lived the life of an English gentleman.

As a politician and political thinker, Burke was associated with several ideas that became central to conservatism. Among these were:

> - *National unity.* Burke believed that societies were organic wholes, composed of several parts working together for the common good of all. He dissented from the Enlightenment view that people were separate individuals. Comments the historian J. R. Green, "A nation was to him a great living society, so complex in its relationships, and whose institutions were so interwoven with glorious events in the past, that to touch it rudely was a sacrilege. Its constitution was no artificial scheme of government, but an exquisite balance of its history and development." [232] Burke himself compared societies to families. His own family had both Protestant and Catholic members, was both Irish and British, yet still functioned as one. (Notice that Burke used the word "nation" in the same sense that Paine usually did – to mean a country, rather than a group of people sharing a common ethnicity or nationality.)
> - *Law and order.* Burke believed that tranquility was the natural state of mankind.
> - *Virtuous leadership.* Burke believed that "magistrates" (the eighteenth-century term for government officials) should not be viewed as public servants (people who managed the government the way the voters wanted them to), but as wise and virtuous leaders, people who possessed qualities above those of ordinary people, and who would always do right thing rather than the popular thing. "Liberty without wisdom and without virtue," he wrote in *Reflections on the Revolution in France* in 1790, "is folly, vice, and madness." "Parliament," he once said in a speech to the voters in his district, "is not a congress of ambassadors from different and hostile interests; which interests each must maintain, as an agent and advocate, against other agents and advocates; but Parliament is a deliberative assembly of one nation, with one interest, that of the whole." [233]
> - *The sanctity of property.* Although generally a mercantilist, Burke nevertheless argued that the chief job of government was to protect private property. "Property," he said in a 1779 speech in Parliament, "was not made by government, but government by and for it." [234]
> - *Reverence for tradition.*

Burke also championed equal rights for Irish Catholics, railed at political corruption, denounced special interest groups, supported both monarchy and aristocracy, advocated the economic interests of the gentry and bourgeoisie, worried that democracy was tantamount to mob rule, and warned against rapid change. He was sometimes inconsistent in his beliefs, and suspected that people with strong, dogmatic philosophies were either impractical or insane. As a Member of Parliament, he was often forced to compromise. Solutions, he believed, depended as much on the circumstances as on principles. Moderation and flexibility, he thought, were essential for good government. For example, although he opposed revolutions in general, Burke nevertheless supported

---

[231] J. Kirk, *Edmund Burke: A Genius Reconsidered* (1967), 32.
[232] J. R. Green, *History of the English People* (n. d.), 10: 59.
[233] Edmund Burke, "Speech to the Electors of Bristol" (1774), n. p.
[234] Edmund Burke, "Speech to Parliament" (1779), n. p.

the American colonists in their dispute with Parliament the 1760s and 1770s, partly because he was the paid agent of the colony of New York, but also because he believed the colonists were fighting for their "ancient [*traditional*] rights and liberties," and because giving the Americans what they wanted was the only practical way to hold the Empire together. The Americans' "ancient rights and liberties," Burke believed, included the right to local self-government and the right to establish their own taxes through their own elected legislatures. Such liberties, Burke believed, were the birthright of all the English people, guaranteed by the English constitution and British law, and the colonists had brought them with them from England to America.

However, Burke opposed the French Revolution of 1789. In his opinion the French, unlike the Americans, had long been the subjects of an absolute monarch, and thus had never had any "ancient rights and liberties" in the first place. Central to Burke's thinking was his conception of how rights and liberties were created. Unlike Paine and the other Enlightenment philosophes (who got the idea from John Locke), Burke rejected the notion that rights were "natural" – that they were created by nature and appertained to everyone, regardless of citizenship. There was, he believed, no such thing as "human rights." Remember that John Locke had argued that rights were universal – they had been created by nature and belonged to all people everywhere, who had the right to revolt in order to protect them. Burke, however, believed in the concept of "civil rights" – that rights were the benefit of citizenship in a particular country, and only citizens could claim them, not humans in general. True, he supported equal rights for Irish Catholics within the British Empire. But he sought to achieve this goal not by revolution or declarations of natural rights, but rather constitutionally, by working quietly, behind the scenes, to change British law. According to Burke, the British people enjoyed certain rights because those rights had been created slowly, over a long period of time, as part of the evolution of English constitutional law; they were, in a sense, the gift of English history. However, France had a different history, a different constitution, different laws, and consequently different civil rights. France had no parliament, no tradition of elected representation, and no experience with self-government. Burke believed that the French could – and should – emulate the British and, over time, create civil rights similar to those enjoyed by the British people. But that would require a protracted period of slow, incremental historical change. The French people would have to be trained in constitutional law, responsible voting, mercantilist economics, civic duty, public virtue, and other necessary skills and attitudes. To Burke, France in 1789 was where England had been in 1215, at the time of the Magna Charta. Rather than a quick revolution, it needed about six centuries of careful state building in order to catch up. Any attempt to use a revolution to shortcut history, Burke believed, could only lead to chaos and disaster.

Burke's book attacking the French Revolution, *Reflections on the Revolution in France* (1790), expressed these ideas and others that would become cornerstones of nineteenth- and twentieth-century conservatism. He demanded proper respect for tradition, defended monarchy and aristocracy, insisted that virtue and training more than "common sense" was necessary for proper statecraft, praised law and order, argued against rapid change, denied the existence of "natural rights," argued that faith and virtue superceded reason, believed that civic duty was more important than individualism, and exalted religion as the source of all morality.

from *REFLECTIONS ON THE REVOLUTION IN FRANCE* [235]

[Magistrates Should be Leaders,
not Public Servants]

It is not true that they [i.e., kings] are, in the ordinary sense, (by our [i.e., English] constitution at least), anything like servants, the essence of whose situation is to obey the commands of some other, and to be removable at pleasure. But the king of Great Britain obeys no other person; all other persons are individually, and collectively too, under him, and owe him a legal obedience. The law, which knows neither to flatter nor to insult, calls this high magistrate, not our servant, but "our sovereign Lord the king."...

As he is not to obey us, but as we are to obey the law in him, our constitution has made no sort of provision towards rendering him, as a servant, in any degree responsible. Our constitution knows nothing of...any court legally appointed, nor of any process legally settled, for submitting the king to the responsibility belonging to all servants.

* * * *

The ceremony of cashiering [i.e., removing] kings...can rarely, if ever, be performed without force. It then becomes a case of war, and not of constitution. Laws are commanded to hold their tongues amongst arms; and tribunals fall to the ground with the peace they are no longer able to uphold.... The question of dethroning...kings will always be, as it has always been, and extraordinary question of state, and wholly out of the law; a question

---

[235] Edmund Burke, *Reflections on the Revolution in France* (1790, 1967), passim.

(like all other questions of state) of dispositions, and of means, and of probable consequences, rather than of positive rights. As it was not made for common abuses, so it is not to be agitated by common minds.... A revolution will be the very last resource of the thinking and the good.

[Rights are not "Natural," but "Civil" –
Inheritances from our Ancestors that
Evolve Slowly over Time]

The [Glorious] Revolution [of 1688, which had dethroned the English king James II, but which Burke defended as having been justified by James's abridgement of traditional English liberties] was made to preserve our ancient, indisputable laws and liberties, and that ancient constitution of government which is our only security for law and liberty. If you are desirous of knowing the spirit of our [i.e., English] constitution, and the policy which predominated in that great period which has secured it to this hour [i.e., since 1688], pray look for both in our histories, in our records, in our acts of parliament, and not in...the after-dinner toasts of the Revolution Society [i.e., a group of English philosophes – including Thomas Paine and Mary Wollstonecraft – who supported the French Revolution on the grounds that it was based on John Locke's ideas about natural rights].... The very idea of the fabrication of a new government is enough to fill us with disgust and horror. We wished at the period of the [Glorious] Revolution, and do now wish, to derive all we possess as an inheritance from our forefathers. Upon that body and stock of inheritance we have taken care not to inoculate any scion alien to the nature of the original plant. All the reformations we have hitherto made proceeded upon the principle of reverence to antiquity: and I hope, nay I am persuaded, that all those which possibly may be made hereafter, will be carefully formed upon analogical precedent, authority, and example....

The same policy pervades all the laws which have since been made for the preservation of our liberties. In the 1st [year] of William and Mary [i.e., in 1689, the first year of the reign of William III and Mary II, immediately following the Glorious Revolution], in the famous statute, called the Declaration of Right [i.e., the English Bill of Rights], the two Houses [of Parliament] utter[ed] not a syllable of "a [natural] right to frame a government for themselves." You will see that their whole care was to secure the religion, laws, and liberties that had long been possessed, and had been lately endangered. "Taking into their most serious consideration the best means for making such an establishment, that their religion, laws, and liberties might not be in danger of being subverted," they auspicate[d] all their proceedings, by stating as some of those best means, "in the first place" to do "as their ancestors in like cases have usually done for vindicating their ancient rights and liberties, to declare"; -- and then they pray the king and queen, "that it may be declared and enacted, that all and singular rights and liberties asserted and declared are the true ancient and indubitable rights and liberties of the people of this kingdom."

You will observe that from Magna Charta to the Declaration of Right, it has been the uniform policy of our constitution to claim and assert our liberties, as an entailed inheritance derived to us from our forefathers, and to be transmitted to our posterity, as an estate specially belonging to the people of this kingdom, without reference whatever to any other more general or prior right. By this means our constitution preserves a unity in so great a diversity of its parts. We have an inheritable crown; an inheritable peerage; and a House of Commons and a people inheriting privileges, franchises, and liberties, from a long line of ancestors.

[Change is Best When it Occurs Slowly,
is Based on Lessons Learned from History,
and Occurs within the
Context of Traditional Values]

A spirit of innovation is generally the result of a selfish temper [i.e., self-righteous arrogance], and confined [i.e., narrow] views. People will not look forward to posterity, who never look backward to their ancestors. Besides, the people of England well know that the idea of inheritance furnishes a sure principle of conservation, and a sure principle of transmission; without at all excluding the principle of improvement. It leaves acquisition free; but it secures what it acquires. Whatever advantages are obtained by a state proceeding on these maxims, are locked fast as in a sort of family settlement; grasped as in a kind of mortmain forever. By a constitutional policy, working after the pattern of nature, we receive, we hold, we transmit our government and our privileges, in the same manner in which we enjoy and transmit property and our lives. The institutions of policy, the goods of fortune, the gifts of providence, are handed down to us, and from us, in the same course and order. Our political system is placed in a just correspondence and symmetry with the order of the world, and with the mode of existence decreed to a permanent body composed of transitory parts [i.e., Parliament]; wherein, by the disposition of a stupendous wisdom, molding together the great mysterious incorporation of the human race, the whole, at one time, is never old, or middle-aged, or young, but, in a condition of unchangeable constancy, moves on through the varied tenor of perpetual decay, fall, renovation, and progression. Thus, by preserving the method of nature in the conduct of the state, in what we improve, we are never wholly new; in what we retain, we are never wholly obsolete. By adhering in this manner and on those principles to our forefathers, we are guided not by the superstition of antiquarians, but by the spirit of philosophic analogy. In this choice of inheritance we have given to our frame of polity the image of a relation of blood; binding up the constitution of our country with our dearest domestic ties; adopting our fundamental laws into the bosom of our family affections; keeping inseparable, and cherishing with the warmth of all their combined and mutually reflected charities, our state, our hearts, our sepulchers, and our altars.

[In Government, Virtue and Tradition are
More Important than Individualism and Reason]

Through the same plan of a conformity to nature in our artificial institutions [i.e., in government], and by calling in the aid of her unerring and powerful instincts to fortify the fallible and feeble contrivances of our reason, we have derived several others, and those no small benefits, from considering our liberties in the light of an inheritance. Always acting as if in the presence of canonized forefathers, the spirit of freedom, leading in itself to misrule and excess, is tempered with an awful gravity. This idea of a liberal [i.e., broad] descent inspires us with a sense of habitual native dignity, which prevents that upstart insolence almost inevitably adhering to and disgracing those who are the first acquirers of any distinction [i.e., prevents upstarts from getting above their place]. By this means our liberty becomes a noble freedom. It carries an imposing and majestic aspect. It has a pedigree and illustrating ancestors. It has its bearings and its ensigns armorial. It has its gallery of portraits; its monumental inscriptions; its records, evidences, and titles. We procure reverence to our civil institutions on the principle upon which nature teaches us to revere individual men; on account of their age, and on account of those from whom they are descended. All your sophisters cannot produce anything better adapted to preserve a rational and manly freedom than the course that we [i.e., English people] have pursued, who have chosen our nature rather than our speculations, our breasts [i.e., our emotions] rather than our inventions [i.e., our minds], for the great conservatories and magazines [i.e., storehouses] of our rights and privileges.

[Law and Order]

France, by the perfidy of her [new revolutionary] leaders has utterly disgraced the tone of lenient council in the cabinets of princes.... She has sanctified the dark, suspicious maxims of tyrannous distrust; and taught kings to tremble at (what will hereafter be called) the delusive plausibilities of moral politicians.... They have seen the French rebel against a mild and lawful monarch, with more fury, outrage, and insult, than ever any people has been known to rise against the most illegal usurper, or the most sanguinary tyrant.... This was unnatural. The rest is in order. They [i.e., the French people] have found their punishment in their success. Laws overturned; tribunals subverted; industry without vigor; commerce expiring, the revenue unpaid, yet the people impoverished; a church pillaged, and a state not relieved; civil and military anarchy made the constitution of the kingdom; everything human and divine sacrificed to the idol of public credit, and national bankruptcy the consequence; and, to crown all, the paper securities of new, precarious, tottering power, the discredited paper securities of impoverished fraud and beggared rapine, held out as a currency for the support of an empire, in lieu of the two great recognized species [i.e., hard currencies, or gold and silver] that represent the lasting, conventional credit of mankind, which disappeared and hid themselves in the earth from whence they came, when the principle of property whose creatures and representatives they are, was systematically subverted.

[When Left Unchecked, Most Politicians
are Either Ill-trained, Foolish,
Demagogic, Self-Serving, or Corrupt]

After I have read over a list of the persons and descriptions elected into the [French Estates General], nothing which they afterwards did could appear astonishing. Among them, indeed, I saw some of known rank; some of shining talents; but of any practical experience in the state, not one man was to be found. The best were only men of theory. But whatever the distinguished few may have been, it is the substance, the mass of the body which constitutes its character, and must finally determine its direction.... The leaders will be obliged to bow to the ignorance of their followers.

* * * *

Nothing can secure a steady and moderate conduct in such assemblies, but that the body of them should be reasonably composed, in point of condition in life, of permanent property, of education, and of such habits as enlarge and liberalize [i.e., broaden] the understanding.

In the calling of the Estates-General of France, the first thing that struck me was a great departure from the ancient course. I found the representation for the third estate composed of six hundred persons. They were equal in number to the representatives of both the other orders. If the orders were to act separately, the number would not be of much consequence. But when it became apparent that the three were to be melted down into one, the policy and necessary effect of this numerous representation became obvious... In fact, the whole power of the state was soon resolved into that body [i.e., the Third Estate]....

Whenever the supreme authority is vested in a body so composed, it must evidently produce the consequences of supreme authority placed in the hands of men not taught habitually to respect themselves; who had no previous fortune in character at stake; who could not be expected to bear with moderation, or to conduct with discretion, a power, which they themselves, more than any others, must be surprised to find in their hands. Who could flatter himself that these men, suddenly, and, as it were, by enchantment, snatched from the humblest rank of subordination, would not be intoxicated with their unprepared greatness? Who could conceive that men, who are habitually meddling, daring, subtle, active, of litigious dispositions and unquiet minds, would easily fall back into their old condition of obscure contention, and laborious, low, and unprofitable chicane? Who could doubt but that, at any expense of the state, of which they understood nothing, they must pursue their private interests which they understood but too well?

Early Feminism: Mary Wollstonecraft

If Edmund Burke was the father of British conservatism, then Mary Wollstonecraft (1759-1797) was the mother of Western feminism. One of the most talented and prolific of the Enlightenment philosophes, Wollstonecraft was born in Britain, the second of seven children of Elizabeth and John Wollstonecraft, a tyrannical and abusive middle-class father who drank to excess, beat his wife, and squandered what little money the family had. Yet Wollstonecraft and one of her sisters both grew up to repeat their mother's experience, becoming involved with abusive men. Wollstonecraft's lover Gilbert Imlay (they were not married) abandoned her when she gave birth to their daughter, Fanny. Grief stricken, Wollstonecraft attempted suicide. Meanwhile, her sister Eliza married an abusive alcoholic, a marriage from which she escaped only with Wollstonecraft's help.

Although a brilliant thinker and skillful writer, like most unmarried women in eighteenth-century Europe Wollstonecraft had trouble finding work and spent most of her life in or near poverty. When she was eighteen she left home and worked for two years as a companion and housekeeper to a wealthy English lady. She returned home to nurse her dying mother, and then opened a private school with her friend Fanny Blood. But the next year Blood married and moved to Portugal with her husband. Wollstonecraft visited Blood to help with her pregnancy, only to witness the death of both mother and child. The following year Wollstonecraft's school closed. Suffering from depression, Wollstonecraft took a job as governess for the children of Lord Kingsborough, a wealthy Anglo-Irish lord. In 1787, still depressed, she left the Kingsboroughs, moved to London, and became a writer, publishing both fiction and nonfiction; translations of German, French, and Dutch works; an anthology; collected letters; and children's books. In London she hobnobbed with other philosophes of the English Enlightenment, including Samuel Johnson, Joseph Johnson, Thomas Paine, and William Godwin. This was a happy period in Wollstonecraft's life. A frequent participant in the intellectual debates of the age, she became one of England's leading philosophes. Unconventional, she refused to wear make-up, style her hair, or wear fancy clothes. Like most philosophes she espoused a philosophy that "experience was the basis of all knowledge, a confidence that environment produced character, a belief that men were innately good and potentially perfectible, and a faith that the truth would make them free."[236] She advocated republican government, argued for human rights, and defended the French Revolution.

Wollstonecraft's greatest book, *A Vindication of the Rights of Women*, appeared in 1792. Written in a defiant, often sarcastic tone (a writing style she shared with her friend Paine), the book was a spirited reply to the French philosophe Jean Jacques Rousseau, who had argued that women's primary role was to make men's lives more pleasurable, that women were not really capable of rational thought, and that women lacked real virtue. Convinced that women were the intellectual equals of men, Wollstonecraft is often considered the founder of feminism and women's rights. She argued that women's seeming lack of intellectual achievements was the consequence of poor education and stifled opportunity, not poor minds. She insisted that girls should receive the same schooling as boys, and that men and women should have equal rights under the law. She opposed the idea of "putting women on a pedestal" as degrading to both genders. In all things important, Wollstonecraft believed, men and women were fundamentally equal and thus should be treated the same.

In 1793 Wollstonecraft began her disastrous affair with Imlay, an American diplomat and writer she met in Paris. The next year she gave birth to a daughter, Fanny. When Imlay took another lover, Wollstonecraft again plunged into depression and attempted suicide. Recovering, she wrote *Letters from Sweden* in 1796 a romantic, autobiographical, and presumably cathartic work. When fellow philosophe Godwin read it, he fell in love with her from afar, commenting, "If ever there was a book calculated to make a man fall in love with its author, this appears to me to be the book."[237] He sought her out, they became lovers, and in 1797 they married. Godwin encouraged Wollstonecraft to write, and she began work on her final book, the semi-autobiographical novel *The Wrongs of Woman*.

But happiness was not to be. Wollstonecraft died of complications of childbirth in 1797, when she was only thirty-eight years old. The child, Mary Wollstonecraft Godwin, survived and later married the poet Percy Shelley and became Mary Wollstonecraft Shelley, the author of *Frankenstein* and other works.[238]

from *A VINDICATION OF THE RIGHTS OF WOMEN* [239]

Men complain, and with reason, of the follies and caprices of our sex, when they do not keenly satirize our headstrong passions and groveling vices. Behold, I should answer, the natural effect of ignorance [i.e., lack of education]! The mind will ever be unstable that has only prejudices [i.e., feelings, rather than actual knowledge] to rest on, and the current will run with destructive fury when there are no barriers to break its force. Women are told from their infancy, and taught by the example of their mothers, that a little knowledge of human weakness, justly termed cunning, softness of temper, outward obedience, and a scrupulous attention to a puerile kind of propriety, will obtain for them the protection of man; and should they be beautiful, everything else [i.e., education] is needless, for, at least, twenty years of their lives....

How grossly do they insult us who thus advise us only to render ourselves gentle, domestic brutes! For instance, the winning softness so warmly, and frequently, recommended, that governs by obeying. What childish expressions, and how insignificant is the being – can it be an immortal one? – who will condescend to govern by such sinister methods! [What Wollstonecraft is doing in this paragraph is attacking the idea that women can control men by so-called "feminine wiles," which she considers immoral and degrading to both genders.]

* * * *

I may be accused of arrogance; still I must declare what I firmly believe, that all the writers who have written on the subject of female education and manners from [Jean Jacques] Rousseau [in Emile, or a Treatise on Education] to Dr. [John] Gregory [in A Father's Legacy to his Daughters], have contributed to render women more artificial, weak characters, than they would otherwise have been; and, consequently, more useless members of society. I

---

[236] G. Kelly, "Introduction," in Mary Wollstonecraft, *Mary Wollstonecraft's* Mary *and* The Wrongs of Woman, ed. G. Kelly (1976), viii.
[237] Ibid, xiv-xv.
[238] Ibid, vi-xxviii.
[239] Mary Wollstonecraft, *A Vindication of the Rights of Women* (1792), chapter 9, passim.

might have expressed this conviction in a lower key; but I am afraid it would have been the whine of affectation, and not the faithful expression of my feelings, of the clear result, which experience and reflection have led me to draw.... In the works of the authors I have just alluded to...my objection extends to the whole purport of those books, which tend, in my opinion, to degrade one half of the human species, and render women pleasing at the expense of every solid virtue.

Though, to reason on Rousseau's ground, if man did attain a degree of perfection of mind when his body arrived at maturity, it might be proper, in order to make a man and his wife one, that she should rely entirely on his understanding; and the graceful ivy, clasping the oak that supported it, would form a whole in which strength and beauty would be equally conspicuous. But, alas! Husbands, as well as their helpmates, are often only overgrown children; nay, thanks to early debauchery, scarcely men in their outward form – and if the blind lead the blind, one need not come from heaven to tell us the consequence....

Rousseau declares that a woman should never, for a moment, feel herself independent, that she should be governed by fear to exercise her natural cunning, and made a coquettish slave in order to render her a more alluring object of desire, a sweeter companion to man, whenever he chooses to relax himself. He [i.e., Rousseau] carries the arguments, which he pretends to draw from the indications of nature, still further, and insinuates that truth and fortitude, the corner stones of all human virtue, should be cultivated [in women] with certain restrictions, because, with respect to the female character, obedience [to men] is the grand lesson which ought to be impressed with unrelenting rigor.

What nonsense! When will a great man arise with sufficient strength of mind to puff away the fumes which pride and sensuality [i.e., lust] have thus spread over the subject! [Even] if women are by nature inferior to men, their virtues must be the same in quality [i.e., of the same kind], if not in degree, or virtue is a relative idea; consequently, their conduct should be founded on the same principles [as that of men], and have the same aim.

Connected with man as daughters, wives, and mothers, [women's] moral character may be [but, in Wollstonecraft's view, should not be] estimated by their manner of fulfilling those simple duties; but the end, the grand end of [women's] exertions should be to unfold their own faculties and never to forget, in common with man, that life yields not the felicity [i.e., state of bliss] which can satisfy an immortal soul. I do not mean to insinuate that either sex should be so lost in abstract reflections or distant views, as to forget the affections and duties that lie before them, and are, in truth, the means appointed to produce the fruit of life; on the contrary, I would warmly recommend them, even while I assert, that they afford most satisfaction when they are considered in their true, sober light.

Probably the prevailing opinion, that woman was created for man, may have taken its rise from Moses's poetical story [i.e., the creation story from the Bible]; yet, as very few, it is presumed, who have bestowed any serious thought on the subject, ever supposed that Eve was, literally speaking, one of Adam's ribs, the deduction [that God intended women to serve men] must be allowed to fall to the ground; or, only be so far admitted as it proves that man, from the remotest antiquity, found it convenient to exert his strength to subjugate his companion, and his invention to show that she ought to have her neck bent under the yoke, because the whole creation was only created for his convenience or pleasure.

* * * *

To speak disrespectfully of love is, I know, high treason against sentiment and fine feelings; but I wish to speak the simple language of truth, and rather to address the head than the heart. To endeavor to reason love out of the world, would be to out Quixote Cervantes, and equally offend against common sense; but an endeavor to restrain this tumultuous passion, and to prove that it should not be allowed to dethrone superior powers, or to usurp the scepter which the understanding should ever coolly wield, appears less wild.

Youth is the season for love in both sexes; but in those days of thoughtless enjoyment provision should be made for the most important years of life, when reflection takes [the] place of sensation. But Rousseau, and most of the male writers who have followed his steps, have warmly inculcated that the whole tendency of female education ought to be directed to one point: -- to render [women] pleasing.

Let me reason with the supporters of this opinion who have any knowledge of human nature; do they imagine that marriage can eradicate the habitude of life? The woman who has only been taught to please will soon find that her charms are oblique sunbeams, and that they cannot have much effect on her husband's heart when they are seen every day, when the summer is passed and gone. [In other words, what will happen to a woman who relies on sexuality and good looks once she and her husband are no longer young, or once he is tired of her?] Will she then have sufficient native energy to look into herself for comfort, and cultivate her dormant faculties? [In other words, will she be able to take care of herself and acquire an education once she is older/] Or, is it not more rational to expect that she will try to please other men; and, in the emotions raised by the expectation of new conquests, endeavor to forget the mortification her love or pride has received? When the husband ceases to be a lover – and the time will inevitably come – her desire of pleasing will then grow languid, or become a spring of bitterness; and love, perhaps, the most evanescent of all passions, give place to jealousy or vanity. [Here Wollstonecraft is arguing that women who rely only on romance and sexuality to get along in the world, will become angry and bitter when their husbands finally grow tired of them. They may even seek solace in extra-marital affairs. Is that what their husbands really want?]

I now speak of women who are restrained [from having affairs] by principle or prejudice; such women, though they would shrink from an intrigue with real abhorrence, yet, nevertheless, wish to be convinced by the homage of gallantry that they are cruelly neglected by their husbands; or, days and weeks are spent in dreaming of the happiness enjoyed by congenial souls till their health is undermined and their spirits broken by discontent. How then can the great art of pleasing be such a necessary study? It is only useful to a mistress; the chaste wife, the serious mother, should only consider her power to please as the polish of her virtues [i.e., something else must lie deeper within her], and the affection of her husband as [only] one of the [many] comforts that render her task less difficult and her life happier. But, whether she is loved or neglected, her first wish should be to make herself respectable [i.e., to cultivate her own inner strengths and abilities], and not to rely for all her happiness on a being subject to like infirmities with herself [i.e., her husband].

****

If all the faculties of woman's mind are only to be cultivated as they respect her dependence on man; if, when a husband is obtained, she has arrived at her goal, and meanly proud rests satisfied with such a paltry crown, let her grovel contentedly, scarcely raised by her employments above the animal kingdom; but, if, struggling for the prize of her high calling, she looks beyond the present scene, let her cultivate her understanding without stooping to consider what character the husband may have whom she is destined to marry. Let her only determine, without being too anxious about present happiness, to acquire the qualities that ennoble a rational being, and a rough inelegant husband may shock her taste without destroying her peace of mind. She will not model her soul to suit the frailties of her companion, but to bear with them: his character may be a trial, but not an impediment to virtue.

****

That a proper education; or, to speak with more precision, a well stored mind, would enable a woman to support a single life with dignity, I grant; but that she should avoid cultivating her taste, lest her husband should occasionally shock it, is quitting a substance for a shadow. To say the truth, I do not know of what use is an improved taste, if the individual be not rendered more independent of the casualties of life; if new sources of employment, only dependent on the solitary operations of the mind, are not opened.

****

If...[women] be really capable of acting like rational creatures, let them not be treated like slaves; or, like the brutes who are dependant on the reason of man, when they associate with him; but cultivate their minds, give them the salutary, sublime curb or principle, and let them attain conscious dignity by feeling themselves only dependant on God. Teach them, in common with men, to submit to necessity, instead of giving, to render them more pleasing a sex, to morals.

****

These may be termed Utopian dreams. Thanks to that Being who impressed them on my soul, and gave me sufficient strength of mind to dare to exert my own reason, till, becoming dependant only on [H]im for the support of my virtue, I view, with indignation, the mistaken notions that enslave my sex.

I love man as my fellow; but his scepter, real or usurped, extends not to me, unless the reason of an individual demands my homage; and even then the submission is to reason, and not to man. In fact, the conduct of an accountable being must be regulated by the operations of its own reason; or on what foundation rests the throne of God?

It appears to me necessary to dwell on these obvious truths, because females have been insulated, as it were; and, while they have been stripped of the virtues that should clothe humanity, they have been decked with artificial graces that enable them to exercise a short-lived tyranny. Love, in their bosoms, taking place of every nobler passion, their sole ambition is to be fair, to raise emotion instead of inspiring respect; and this ignoble desire, like the servility in absolute monarchies, destroys all strength of character. Liberty is the mother of virtue, and if women be, by their very constitution, slaves, and not allowed to breathe the sharp invigorating air of freedom, they must ever languish like exotics, and be reckoned beautiful flaws in nature.

* * * *

Man, taking her body, the mind is left to rust; so that while physical love enervates man, as being his favorite recreation, he will endeavor to enslave woman; -- and, who can tell, how many generations may be necessary to give vigor to the virtue and talents of the freed posterity of abject slaves?

Early Environmentalism: Henry David Thoreau

In a cool September drizzle in 1853, Henry David Thoreau (1817-62), taking a vacation from writing *Walden*, boarded a steamer bound from Boston, Massachusetts, to Bangor, Maine. Nineteen hours later he arrived at the raw frontier community, lumber port, and gateway to the North Woods. The little city pulsed with activity. Each year more than 2,000 vessels crowded into its narrow, wedge-shaped harbor, surrounded by the rounded hills and granite bluffs of northern Maine. Most of the ships were coasters, small sailing vessels looking to take on cargoes of fresh-cut boards, deals, shingles, and firewood to sell in the fast-growing industrial cities of the eastern United States. So much timber bobbed in Bangor's great, looping booms that lumberjacks boasted of being able to cross the river by walking on the logs. Dozens of busy, barn-shaped sawmills lined the riverbanks, their screeching ripsaws churning out between 100,000,000 and 200,000,000 board feet of lumber each year. Freshly sawn boards sat in stacks on the wharves, ready for shipment. Behind the crowded docks and clattering mills, newly cobblestoned streets curled chaotically among the steep, rocky hills, framing the city's dozen or so blocks of taverns, grog shops, hotels, churches, artisans' shops, and storekeepers' establishments. From upper-story office windows, the powerful "lumber barons" who controlled the timber trade looked out on the city. On the streets below, farmers from outlying districts rumbled by in buckboards, on their way to sell their wares in West Market Square. Tough river drivers known as Bangor tigers, heavy-booted lumberjacks fresh from the forest, and wool-capped sailors lounged on the docks and street corners and in the dives and brothels that lined Exchange Street and Pickering Square. The acrid scents of sweat, horse dung, and animal urine hung heavily in the air.[240]

Landing at the large stone wharf used by the Boston steamers, Thoreau met his traveling companions for the rest of the trip – his cousin George A. Thatcher, a Bangor resident and businessman, and Joe Aitteon (Ah-TEEN), a Wabanaki Indian guide. The next morning Thoreau and Thatcher loaded their hunting and camping supplies into Thatcher's buckboard (Aitteon had already departed by stagecoach, his birch bark canoe lashed to the roof) and struck out for Moosehead Lake, more than sixty miles to the northwest, deep in the North Woods. Despite the gloomy weather, Thoreau was full of excitement, eager to be away from his writing desk and alive with the prospect of wilderness adventure. Traveling over rough, muddy roads, the two men soon entered a vast fir, spruce, and pine forest. It was the North Woods – America's northern frontier – thousands of square miles of evergreen forest sprawling across Maine, northern New Hampshire, Vermont, northern New York, parts of Michigan, Wisconsin, and Minnesota, as well as adjacent chunks of Canada.

For Thoreau, the North Woods was the perfect place for a vacation: quiet, peaceful, and wild. It was, he thought, a "primitive wilderness," fundamentally different from the tame, well-populated, work-a-day countryside of his native Massachusetts. Wide, blue Moosehead Lake, with only one tiny settlement at the south end, was "a suitably wild looking sheet of water, sprinkled with small low islands, which were covered with shaggy spruce and other wild wood." The shore was "an unbroken wilderness." Indeed, the whole region seemed an "endless forest," a "damp and shaggy wilderness," a land of "solitude and wildness" with "a peculiarly wild and primitive look." According to the environmental historian Roderick Nash, Thoreau was awestruck – unnerved and overwhelmed by the unexpectedly stark and primal wildness of the region. Indeed, accustomed as he was to the more settled countryside of Massachusetts, he actually found the North Woods a little too wild, too stark, and too raw for comfort. "It was a relief," he confessed later, "to get back home to [the] smooth, but still varied landscape" of Massachusetts. "For a permanent residence, it seemed to me that there could be no comparison between [Massachusetts] and the wilderness." Massachusetts was a comfortable land of "parks and groves, gardens, arbors, paths, vistas, and landscapes." By contrast, the North Woods was "simple almost to barrenness." "The civilized man," Thoreau mused soberly, "must at length pine there, like a cultivated plant, which clasps its fibers about a crude and undissolved mass of peat."[241]

---

[240] Robert D. Richardson, *Henry Thoreau: A Life of the Mind* (1986), 300-305; David C. Smith, "Lumbering and Shipping in Bangor Port," *Maine Historical Society Quarterly* (1976), 3: 29-38; Edward D. Ives, "Argyle Boom," *Northeast Folklore* (1976), 1: 15-134.

[241] Henry David Thoreau, *The Maine Woods* (1864, 1974), 84-85, 89, 92-93, 100, 102-103, 155-156; Roderick Nash, *Wilderness and the American Mind* (1982), 90-93.

Between busy, industrial Bangor and the quiet wilderness around Moosehead Lake lay a broad transitional countryside of newly settled frontier farms, similar to the other frontier regions of nineteenth-century North America. Here Thoreau saw scattered houses, villages, and fields. "We went...through more than a dozen flourishing towns," he wrote, "not one...on my general atlas published, alas! in 1824; so much are they before the age, or I behind it." Yet even this area seemed more like a wilderness than civilization. "We had hardly got out of the streets of Bangor," he wrote, "before I began to be exhilarated by the sight of the wild fir and spruce tops, and those of other primitive evergreens, peering through the mist in the horizon." Here "the prevailing fences were log ones," as opposed to the more permanent stone and board fences of Massachusetts. The "houses were far apart, commonly small and of one story." Although the settlers had cleared a few patches of land, most of the fields were bare of crops. Gaunt stumps, "frequently as high as one's head, showing the depth of the [winter] snows," still peppered the clearings. Wild animals abounded. Thoreau saw numerous partridges and "large flocks of [passenger] pigeons," a now-extinct bird. The plant life, too, had a wild, primal character to it. Primitive-looking ferns, "which in older countries are commonly confined to wet ground," filled entire fields. Many of the plants appeared alien and unfamiliar. Thoreau saw "very few flowers, even allowing for the lateness of the season," and noticed almost none of the familiar asters or buttercups, "though they were so abundant then in Massachusetts." Instead, densely packed stands of fir and spruce predominated, and oozing peat bogs lay all around. When Thoreau and Thatcher stopped at mid-afternoon at a roadside tavern in the frontier hamlet of East Sangerville, the tavern keeper – probably Benjamin Lane – boasted that only a few years previously "he had found a wilderness where we found him."[242]

Still, Thoreau realized that people like Lane were already beginning to transform the North Woods into a settled farm country. Soon, it might be just another Massachusetts. Already the settlers had felled enough trees so that "the forest did not often border the road." They had hunted and killed many of the wild animals, and the number of moose, caribou, lynx, and black bear had already declined sharply. Thoreau noticed with grim distaste that, in the frontier town of Monson, someone had fashioned a grisly road sign from a pair of moose antlers, and some settlers – possibly including Lane – used antlers as hat racks. "I trust," Thoreau sniffed, "that I shall have a better excuse for killing a moose, than that I may hang my hat on his horns." Thoreau also saw several non-native plants sprouting in the settlers' clearings and along the roadside, introduced into the region by the settlers. These included not only crop plants like maize, beans, and timothy, but also several weeds. "The Canada thistle, an introduced plant, was the prevailing weed all the way to the lake, the road-side in many places and fields not long cleared being densely filled with it...to the exclusion of everything else." Furthermore, by clearing the land, the settlers had also inadvertently created new niches for some of the region's native plants, including "the two fire-weeds...commonly where there had been a burning."[243]

Thoreau worried about the long-term impact of human activity on wilderness areas like the North Woods. He feared that some day wilderness might vanish entirely. This would be a tragedy, he believed, for wilderness seemed to him to be essential to civilization. Like most transcendentalists, Thoreau believed that something wild and primal existed somewhere deep within the human psyche, and that to destroy wilderness was to consequently destroy humanity. In the words of his biographer Robert Richardson, Thoreau believed that by its very existence wilderness encouraged "the impulse to recognize and act on what is wild within us" – or, as Thoreau himself put it, "in wildness is the preservation of the world." Wilderness inspired poets, artists, and philosophers, crucial to any well-ordered society. It provided homes for certain plants, animals, and even people – Indians, lumberjacks, and hunters – that could not survive in places overcrowded with civilization. Thoreau wanted always to be able to visit the wilderness, to touch it, in order to preserve his own mental well-being. "The poet must," he wrote, "from time to time, travel the logger's path and the Indian's trail, to drink at some new and more bracing fountain of the Muses, far in the recesses of the wilderness."[244]

For Thoreau, the two great symbols of the North Woods were evergreen trees and moose. Yet he feared that neither one of them would be around much longer. In an 1858 magazine article he wrote about his trip, he mentioned one or the other of them in almost every paragraph. "Spruce trees crowded to the track on each side." The countryside was "densely covered with white and black spruce, which I think must be the commonest trees thereabouts." Walls of "dense spruce and fir trees" surrounded his campsites. He slept at night on beds of fir boughs and stoked his campfires with dry spruce branches. The evergreens seemed to exude a powerful, almost primal fertility, a quality that made them symbolic of all living things. Thoreau marveled at a wind-fallen spruce, "with its rich burden of cones, [which] look[ed] still fuller of life than our [Massachusetts] trees in the most favorable positions." Especially at night, evergreens seemed to dominate the landscape. "The lofty spiring tops of the spruce and fir [were] very black against the sky, and more distinct than by day." Thoreau mentioned moose almost as frequently as evergreens. Although he actually saw only a few living moose on the trip, he seemed to find their cloven tracks and discarded antlers around every bend, and imagined that the rustling noises he heard in the woods were their furtive movements.[245]

But both the evergreen trees and the moose seemed to be threatened by encroaching civilization. While Thoreau had come to the North Woods to relax, camp, and gather wild plant specimens, Thatcher and Aitteon had come to hunt moose. And although they had no way to cart away all of the meat, hide, and antlers of even

---

[242] Thoreau, *Maine Woods*, 86-88.
[243] Ibid, 86-87.
[244] Richardson, *Henry Thoreau*, 288; Thoreau, *Maine Woods*, 155-156.
[245] Thoreau, *Maine Woods*, 89, 92-94, 96.

one animal, they planned to bag several. At first, Thoreau did not object to their plans. After all, many nineteenth-century North Americans supplemented their diets by hunting wild game, and Thoreau himself had hunted. "It is true," he admitted, "I came as near to being a hunter and miss it, as possible myself, and as it is, I think that I could spend a year in the woods fishing and hunting just enough to sustain myself, with satisfaction." But this was different. "The object," he realized with horror, was "to slay as many moose…as possible." Sickened by the gory spectacle of Aitteon skinning a cow moose – "to see that still warm and palpitating body pierced with a knife, to see the warm milk stream from the rent udder" – Thoreau reacted viscerally. "This hunting of the moose merely for the satisfaction of killing him," he wrote, "is too much like going out by night to some woodside pasture and shooting your neighbor's horses."[246]

Distraught, Thoreau declined to join the hunt. "When we reached our camping ground," he recalled, "I decided to leave my companions to continue moose hunting down the stream, while I prepared the camp." Wretched and guilty, he tried to ignore the hunt going on in the distance:

> In the midst of the damp fir wood, high on the mossy bank, about nine o'clock of this bright moonlight night, I kindled a fire, when they were gone, and sitting on the fir-twigs, within sound of the falls, examined by its light the botanical specimens which I had collected that afternoon, and wrote some of the reflections which I have here expanded; or I walked along the shore and gazed up the stream, where the whole space above the falls was filled with mellow light. As I sat before the fire on my fir twig-seat, without walls above or around me, I remembered how far on every hand that wilderness stretched, before you came to cleared or cultivated fields, and wondered if any bear or moose was watching the light of my fire, for nature looked sternly upon me on account of the murder of the moose.

Then, in a flash of raw emotional insight, Thoreau realized that it was not only moose that were endangered by human activity. All wild things were threatened. Recalling the millions of floating logs and piled boards that he had seen at Bangor, he suddenly knew that the evergreen trees were also under siege. "This afternoon's experiences suggested to me how base or coarse are the motives which commonly carry men into the wilderness," he concluded. "The explorers, and lumberers generally, are all hirelings, paid so much a day for their labor, and as such, they have no more love for wild nature, than wood-sawyers have for forests."[247]

It was an epiphany that took Thoreau from the transcendentalism of *Walden* to the early environmentalism of *The Maine Woods*. "Every creature is better alive than dead," he now realized, "men and moose, and pine-trees, and he who understands it aright will rather preserve its life than destroy it." Fired by this new realization, Thoreau became an outspoken advocate of wilderness preservation and the philosophical founder of environmentalism. He proposed creating wilderness parks, where wild environments like the North Woods could be preserved for future generations. Comparing such parks to the king's forests of Medieval England, he wrote, "Why should not we…have our national preserves, in which the bear and panther…may still exist, and not be 'civilized off the face of the earth,' – our forests, not to hold the king's game merely, but to hold and preserve the king himself also, the lord of creation, -- not for idle sport or food, but for inspiration and our own true recreation? Or shall we, like villains, grub them all up, poaching on our own national domains?"[248]

The bourgeois world of business held little attraction for Henry David Thoreau. Instead he sought Truth in nature and philosophy – at Walden Pond, in the North Woods, on Cape Cod, in the White Mountains, and (late in life) on the Great Plains. He also looked for Truth among the sacred Hindu writings of India, the myths of ancient Greece, and the moral teachings of Jesus of Nazareth. As a transcendentalist, he sought a Truth that would transcend the narrow confines of his own modern Western culture, a Truth that would synthesize the ideas and discoveries of all the world's peoples, past, present, and future.

Thoreau grew up in Concord, Massachusetts, the son of middle-class parents. His father owned a small pencil factory and was well enough off to send young Henry to Harvard, where he studied Latin, Greek, French, German, and Spanish literature. Upon graduation he became a schoolteacher in his native Concord. He resigned two weeks later rather than obey orders from the school board to discipline his students by beating them with sticks. Along with his brother, he opened a private school where he taught for several years. He also worked in the family pencil factory and as a surveyor. A thorough localist, he resided in Concord for the rest of his life. His neighbors considered him eccentric, but generally liked him. Most of them respected him for his honesty and strict moral standards. He was the kind of person you would trust to hold your money for you; you knew that it would never even occur to him to steal it.

Thoreau struck up a close friendship with his neighbor, the well-known philosopher Ralph Waldo Emerson. Emerson was the leader in America of a new philosophical movement, transcendentalism. According to the writer Walter Harding, transcendentalism was "a reaction against [John] Locke's theories…that averred that the infant is born without knowledge; his mind is a tabula rasa. All knowledge is gained directly through the senses – through touch, sight, hearing, taste, and smell." Transcendentalists like Emerson believed "that while Locke's ideas were valid as far as they went, there was [*also another*] body of knowledge innate within man and that this knowledge transcended the senses – thus the name 'transcendentalism.' This knowledge was the voice

---

[246] Ibid, 99-100.
[247] Ibid, 115-121.
[248] Ibid, 119, 121, 153, 156.

of God within man – his conscience, his moral sense, his inner light, his over-soul." Evil came when people no longer listened to their inner voice. "It was the duty, the obligation of the good citizen to return to a childish innocence and heed once more the voice of God within him."[249] Thoreau became a convert to transcendentalism, and remained a transcendentalist for the rest of his life. Like Emerson, he concluded that this "inner voice" was somehow connected to nature. He also found it reflected in all of the major world religions, and became a "pantheist," a spiritual person who believed in religion in general, but no one religion in particular. Instead, he looked for ideas common to all religions, under the assumption that these ideas were the most likely to be true.

In the 1840s Thoreau, at Emerson's urging, began to write short nature pieces and travel articles for various magazines. (He also wrote poetry, but truth to tell, as a poet he made a good philosopher.) *The Maine Woods*, published in book form only after his death, comprises three articles he wrote about three different camping trips in northern Maine. Although at first carried away with the romance of the northern wilderness and its seemingly self-reliant farmers, lumberjacks, and hunters, Thoreau was eventually repulsed by the wastefulness of hunting for sport, and of the lumber industry, which felled many acres of forest each year. His call for forest conservation and wilderness preservation was years ahead of the times.

It was while in Maine that Thoreau, ahead of his time as usual, intuited the central principle of the not-yet-invented science of ecology, that all living things are interrelated. People are part of nature, not separate from it, and humankind thus destroys nature only at its own peril.

In 1845 Thoreau built a cabin on some land that Emerson owned at Walden Pond in Concord. He resided at Walden for a little more than two years, seeking to live as simply as possible, to avoid the rat race of the business world that he believed was consuming civilization, and focus on reading, writing, and philosophy. He was not a hermit. He visited town frequently, and guests often visited him. His goal was not to set a blueprint for others to follow in detail, but to advance the general principle that people would be happier and better off if they simplified their lives.

In 1846, while on a trip into town, Thoreau was arrested for refusing to pay his poll tax. Although he scrupulously paid other taxes and did not object to the idea of taxes in general, he declined to pay the poll tax because the money was used to support both slavery and the Mexican-American War, both of which he considered immoral. An ardent abolitionist (a person who wanted to abolish slavery), Thoreau was quietly a conductor on the famous Underground Railroad, guiding escaped slaves from Concord to the next stop further north. Although he spent only one night in jail (someone anonymously paid the tax for him, much to his ire), Thoreau was galvanized to write his famous essay, "Civil Disobedience," in which he urged others to disobey immoral laws and go to jail as a form of protest. To do so, he believed, was to follow a higher law – the inner voice of his own conscience. Years later, both Mohandas Gandhi and Martin Luther King, Jr., would be profoundly influenced by the essay.

Thoreau died at the age of forty-four of lung disease. Considered an extreme radical in his own time, his elegant prose and firm convictions inspired later generations. Thoreau remains the West's first important environmentalist, associated with conservation, respect for nature, a fervent belief in the necessity of obeying higher laws (the inner voice of God), and a fierce longing for the simple life.

from *THE MAINE WOODS* [250]

II: CHESUNCOOK

[Living Things]

But on more accounts than one I had had enough of moose-hunting. I had not come to the woods for this purpose, nor had I foreseen it, though I had been willing to learn how the Indian maneuvered; but one moose killed was as good, if not as bad, as a dozen. The afternoon's tragedy, and my share in it, as it affected the innocence, destroyed the pleasure of my adventure. It is true, I came as near to being a hunter, and miss it, as possible myself, and as it is, I think that I could spend a year in the woods fishing and hunting just enough to sustain myself, with satisfaction. This would be next to living like a philosopher on the fruits of the earth which you had raised, which also attracts me. But this hunting of the moose merely for the satisfaction of killing him – not even for the sake of his hide, without making any extraordinary exertion or running any risk yourself, is too much like going out by night to some woodside pasture and shooting your neighbor's horse. These are God's own horses, poor timid creatures that will run fast enough as soon as they smell you though they are nine

---

[249] Walter Harding, *The Days of Henry Thoreau: A Biography* (1982), 62.
[250] Henry David Thoreau, *The Maine Woods* (1864, 1974), 110-121.

feet high. Joe [Aitteon, a Native American guide and hunter] told us of some hunters who a year or two before had shot down several oxen by night, somewhere in the Maine woods, mistaking them for moose. And so might any of the hunters; and what is the difference in the sport, but the name? In the former case, having killed one of God's and your own oxen, you strip off its hide, because that is the common trophy, and moreover you have heard that it may be sold for moccasins, cut a steak from its haunches, and leave the huge carcass to smell to heaven for you. It is no better, at least, than to assist at a slaughter house.

This afternoon's experience suggested to me how base or coarse are the motives which commonly carry men into the wilderness. The explorers, and lumberers generally, are all hirelings, paid so much a day for their labor, and as such, they have no more love for wild nature, than wood-sawyers have for forests. Other white men and Indians who come here are for the most part hunters, whose object is to slay as many moose and other wild animals as possible. But, pray, could not one spend some weeks or years in the solitude of this vast wilderness with other employments than these – employments perfectly sweet and innocent and ennobling? For one that comes with a pencil to sketch or sing, a thousand come with an axe or rifle. What a coarse and imperfect use Indians and hunters make of nature! No wonder that their race is so soon exterminated. I already and for weeks afterward felt my nature the coarser for this part of my woodland experience, and was reminded that our life should be lived as tenderly and daintily as one would pluck a flower.

With these thoughts, when we reached our camping ground I decided to leave my companions to continue moose hunting down the stream, while I prepared the camp, though they requested me not to chop much or make a large fire, for fear I should scare their game. In the midst of the damp fir wood, high on the mossy bank, about nine o'clock of this bright moonlight night, I kindled a fire, when they were gone, and sitting on the fir-twigs, within sound of the falls, examined by its light the botanical specimens which I had collected that afternoon, and wrote down some of the reflections which I have here expanded; or I walked along the shore and gazed up the stream, where the whole space above the falls was filled with mellow light. As I sat before the fire on my for-twig seat, without walls above or around me, I remembered how far on every hand that wilderness stretched, before you came to cleared or cultivated fields, and wondered if any bear or moose was watching the light of my fire, for nature looked sternly upon me on account of the murder of the moose.

[Higher Laws]

Strange that so few ever come to the woods to see how the pine lives and grows and spires, lifting its evergreen arms to the light – to see its perfect success, but most are content to behold it in the shape of many broad boards brought to market, and deem that its true success! But the pine is no more lumber than man is, and to be made into boards and houses is no more its true and highest use than the truest use of a man is to be cut down and made into manure. There is a higher law affecting our relation to pines as well as to men. A pine cut down, a dead pine, is no more a pine than a dead human carcass is a man. Can he who has discovered only some of the values of whalebone and whale oil be said to have discovered the true use of the whale? Can he who slays the elephant for his ivory be said to have "seen the elephant"? These are petty and accidental uses; just as if a stronger race were to kill us in order to make buttons and flageolets of our bones; for everything may serve a lower as well as a higher use. Every creature is better alive than dead, men and moose and pine-trees, and he who understands it aright will rather preserve its life than destroy it.

Is it the lumberman then who is the friend and lover of the pine – stands nearest to it and understands it best? Is it the tanner who has barked it, or he who has boxed it for turpentine, whom posterity will fable was changed into a pine at last? No! No! It is the poet; he it is who makes the truest use of the pine – who does not fondle it with an axe, nor tickle it with a saw, nor stroke it with a plane; who knows whether its heart is false without cutting into it; who has not bought the stumpage of the township on which it stands. All the pines shudder and heave a sigh when that man steps on the forest floor. No, it is the poet, who loves them as his own shadow in the air, and lets them stand. I have been into the lumber yard, and the carpenter's shop, and the tannery, and the lampblack factory, and the turpentine clearing; but when at length I saw the tops of the pines waving and reflecting the light at a distance high over all the rest of the forest, I realized that the former were not the highest use of the pine. It is not their bones or hide or tallow that I love most. It is the living spirit of the tree, not its spirit of turpentine, with which I sympathize, and which heals my cuts. It is as immortal as I am, and perchance will go to as high a heaven, there to tower above me still.

[Nature Preserves]

No one has yet described for me the difference between that wild forest which once occupied our oldest townships [in Massachusetts], and the tame one which I find there today. It is a difference that would be worth attending to. The civilized man not only clears the land permanently to a great extent, and cultivates open fields, but he tames and cultivates to a certain extent the forest itself. By his mere presence, almost he changes the nature of the trees as no other creature does. The sun and air, and perhaps fire, have been introduced, and grain raised where it stands. It has lost its wild, damp, and shaggy look, the countless fallen and decaying trees are gone, and consequently that thick coat of moss which lived on them is gone too. The earth is comparatively bare and smooth and dry. The most primitive places left with us are the swamps, where the spruce still grows shaggy.

Those Maine woods differ essentially from ours [in Massachusetts]. There you are never reminded that the wilderness which you are treading is, after all, some villager's familiar wood-lot, some widow's thirds, from which her ancestors have sledded fuel for generations, minutely described in some old deed which is recorded, of which the owner has got a plan too, and old bound-marks may be found every forty rods, if you will search. 'Tis true, the map may inform you that you stand on land granted by the State to some academy, or on Bingham's purchase; but these names do not impose on you, for you see nothing to remind you of the academy or of Bingham. What were the "forests" of [Medieval] England to these? One writer relates of the Isle of Wight [off the coast of England], that in Charles the Second's time [1660-86] "there were woods in the island so complete and extensive, that it is said a squirrel might have traveled in several parts many leagues together on the tops of the trees." If it were not for the rivers, (and he might go round their heads), a squirrel could here [in Maine] travel thus the whole breadth of the country.

We have as yet no adequate account of a primitive pine-forest. I have noticed that in a physical atlas lately published in Massachusetts, and used in our schools, the "wood land" of North America is limited almost solely to the valleys of the Ohio and some of the Great Lakes, and the great pine-forests of the globe are not represented. In our vicinity, for instance, New Brunswick [a province of Canada bordering on Maine] and Maine are exhibited as bare as Greenland. It may be that the children of Greenville, at the foot of [Maine's] Moosehead Lake, who surely are not likely to be scared by an owl, are referred to the valley of the Ohio to get an idea of a forest; but they would not know what to do with their moose, bear, caribou, beaver, etc., there. Shall we leave it to an Englishman to inform us, that "in North America, both in the United States and Canada, are the most extensive pine-forests in the world"? The greater part of New Brunswick, the northern half of Maine, and adjacent parts of Canada, not to mention the northeastern part of New York and other tracts further off, are still covered with an almost unbroken pine-forest.

But Maine, perhaps, will soon be where Massachusetts is. A good part of her territory is already as bare and common-place as much of our neighborhood, and her villages generally are not so well shaded as ours. We seem to think that the earth must go through the ordeal of sheep-pasturage before it is habitable by man....

But there are spirits...to whom simplicity is barren. There are not only stately pines, but fragile flowers, like the orchises, commonly described as too delicate for cultivation, which derive their nutriment from the crudest mass of peat. These remind us that, not only for strength but for beauty, the poet must, from time to time, travel the logger's path and the Indian's trail, to drink at some new and more bracing fountain of the Muses, far in the recesses of the wilderness.

The kings of England formerly had their [royal] forests "to hold the king's game," for sport or food, sometimes destroying villages to create or extend them; and I think that they were impelled by a true instinct. Why should not we [Americans], who have renounced the king's authority, have our [own] national preserves, where no villages need be destroyed, in which the bear and panther, and some even of the hunter race, may still exist, and not be "civilized off the face of the earth," – our forests, not to hold the king's game merely, but to hold and preserve the king himself also, the lord of creation, -- not for idle sport, but for inspiration and our own true recreation? Or shall we, like villains, grub them all up, poaching on our own national domains?

from *WALDEN* [251]

[Live Simply]

I have traveled a good deal in Concord [Massachusetts, Thoreau's hometown]; and everywhere, in shops and offices and fields, the inhabitants have appeared to me to be doing penance in a thousand remarkable ways. What I have heard of Brahmins [Hindu priests] sitting exposed to four fires and looking in the face of the sun; or hanging suspended, with their heads downward, over flames; or looking at the heavens over their shoulders "until it becomes impossible for them to resume their natural position, while from the twist of the neck nothing but liquids can pass into the stomach"; or dwelling, chained for life, at the foot of a tree; or measuring with their bodies, like caterpillars, the breadth of vast empires; or standing on one leg on the tops of pillars – even these forms of conscious penance are hardly more incredible and astonishing than the scenes which I daily witness. The twelve labors of Hercules were trifling in comparison with those which my neighbors have undertaken; for they were only twelve, and had an end; but I could never see that these men slew or captured any monster or finished any labor. They have no friend Iolaus to burn with a hot iron the root of the hydra's head, but as soon as one head is crushed, two spring up.

I see young men, my townsmen, whose misfortune it is to have inherited farms, houses, barns, cattle, and farming tools; for these are more easily acquired than got rid of. Better if they had been born in the open pasture and suckled by a wolf, that they might have seen with clearer eyes what field they were called to labor in. Who made them serfs of the soil? Why should they eat their sixty acres, when man is condemned to eat only his peck of dirt? Why should they begin digging their graves as soon as they are born? They have got to live a man's life, pushing all these things before them, and get on as well as they can. How many a poor immortal soul have I met well-nigh crushed and smothered under its load, creeping down the road of life, pushing before it a barn, seventy-five feet by forty, it Augean stables never cleansed, and one hundred acres of land, tillage, mowing, pasture, and wood lot!

* * * * *

The mass of men lead lives of quiet desperation. What is called resignation is confirmed desperation. From the desperate city you go into the desperate country…. A stereotyped but unconscious despair is concealed even under what are called the games and amusements of mankind. There is no play in them, for this comes after work. But it is a characteristic of wisdom not to do desperate things.

* * * * *

Most of the luxuries, and many of the so-called comforts of life, are not only not indispensable, but positive hindrances to the elevation of mankind. With respect to luxuries and comforts, the wisest have ever lived a more simple and meager life than the poor….

When [a person] has obtained those things which are necessary to life, there is another alternative than to obtain the superfluities; and that is, to adventure on life now, his vacation from humbler toil have commenced….

Most men appear never to have considered what a house is, and are actually though needlessly poor all their lives because they think that they must have such a one as their neighbors have. As if one were to wear any sort of coat the tailor might cut out for him, or, gradually leaving off palm leaf hat or cap of woodchuck skin, complain of hard times because he could not afford to buy him a crown! It is impossible to invent a house still more convenient and luxurious than we have, which yet all would admit that man could not afford to pay for. Shall we always study to obtain more of these things, and not sometimes be content with less?

It is the luxurious and dissipated who set the fashions which the herd so diligently follow…. Men have become tools of their tools.

* * * * *

If one would live simply and eat only the crop which he raised, and raise no more than he ate, and not exchange it for an insufficient quantity of more luxurious and expensive things, he would need to cultivate only a few rods of ground…. I was more independent than any farmer in Concord, for I was not anchored to a house or farm.

---

[251] Henry David Thoreau, *Walden* (1858, 1971), passim.

[The Interrelationship of Culture and Nature]

Our village life would stagnate if it were not for the unexplored forests and meadows which surround it. We need the tonic of wildness – to wade sometimes in marshes where the bittern and the meadow hen lurk, and hear the booming of the snipe; to smell the whispering sedge where only some wilder and more solitary fowl builds her nest, and the mink crawls with its belly close to the ground. At the same time we are earnest to explore and learn all things, we require that all things be mysterious and unexplorable, that land and sea be infinitely wild, unsurveyed and unfathomed by us because unfathomable. We can never have enough of Nature. We must be refreshed by the sight of inexhaustible vigor, vast and Titanic features, the seacoast with its wrecks, the wilderness with its living and its decaying trees, the thunder cloud, and the rain which lasts three weeks and produces freshets. We need to witness our own limits transgressed, and some life pasturing freely where we never wander. We are cheered when we observe the vulture feeding on the carrion, which disgusts and disheartens us, and deriving health and strength from the repast.

Early Socialism: Karl Marx

Karl Marx (1818-83), who wrote *The Communist Manifesto* in 1848 with his partner, Friedrich Engels (1820-95), did not invent socialism, but he did become its most famous proponent. Born in German-speaking Prussia, the son of a bourgeois lawyer of Jewish heritage, Marx studied law and philosophy before becoming a journalist. Moving first to France and then to Britain (he was fluently trilingual), he teamed up with Engels, the well-to-do immigrant son of a German textile tycoon. Despite their privileged backgrounds, Marx and Engels were both concerned with the plight of the industrial working class. Engels had managed his family's factory in Manchester, England, where he saw first-hand the hard lives of workers like Charles Dickens's Stephen Blackpool. After working for several years as a journalist (he was for a time a "foreign correspondent" for a British newspaper, stationed in the United States) Marx – more scholarly than Engels – became one of the West's leading economic theorists, completing most of his research at the esteemed British Museum. In 1847 both men joined the Communist League, a small secret society of socialist revolutionaries, many of them, like Marx and Engels, German-speaking immigrants living in Britain and allied with similar groups in France. It was for the League that Marx and Engels wrote *The Communist Manifesto*, originally published in French but later translated into English and other languages. The League soon collapsed, but Marx's interest in socialism did not. After years of intense research, in 1867 he published his most famous work, *Das Kapital* (*Capital*) – written in German – a powerful (and lengthy) argument for socialism.

At the heart of Marx's version of socialism was the concept of "dialectical materialism." In a nutshell (and it is always dangerous to cram Marx's complex ideas into anything as small as a nutshell), he argued that all of human history was a story of recurring class struggles. At any given time in history and in any given place, Marx believed that there had always been a ruling class. In the Middle Ages the ruling class had been the lords. A new rising class always opposed the ruling class, challenging it for power. In the Middle Ages the new rising class had been the bourgeoisie. During the Age of Revolution the bourgeoisie had successfully overcame the lords and established itself as the new ruling class. Marx argued that in past epochs, numerous other social classes had also existed, living alongside the ruling and rising classes: peasants, laborers, priests, etc. However, he believed that in his own times the Industrial Revolution had changed all that, that by the mid-1800s there were only two major classes left, that all the others were preindustrial classes in the process of withering away. The two classes left were the bourgeoisie (now the ruling class) and the "proletariat," or industrial workers (now the rising class). Marx predicted that the proletariat would eventually revolt, overthrow the bourgeoisie, and itself take control as the new ruling class. But since by then no other classes besides the bourgeoisie and proletariat would exist, no new rising class would emerge to challenge the proletariat. For a while, the proletariat would continue its struggle with the bourgeoisie, a time Marx called "the dictatorship of the proletariat." He didn't mean a real dictatorship, or rule by one person, but rather a time when the bourgeoisie would finally be driven out of existence. Once the bourgeoisie disappeared, the proletariat would be the only remaining class – creating what Marx envisioned as an essentially "classless society." Marx viewed such a state of affairs as the end of history, as there would no longer be any class struggle and all peoples would live in relative harmony.

Marx believed that, in all epochs, the ruling class controlled the government and used it as an instrument to enrich itself and oppress everyone else. However, once the proletariat took over and became the only class left, the process would stop. The proletariat would use the government to advance its own interests, to be sure, but since everyone was part of the proletariat to begin with, that meant the proletariat would be using government in the best interests of the entire population. In order to prevent a new bourgeoisie from forming, Marx believed that the proletarian government of the future must be socialist, not liberal. In other words, he thought that the government should actually own the "means of production" – Marx's term for all the factories, shops, railroads, banks, etc., that made the economy work. He did not intend to abolish all private property, for individuals would still retain their clothing, homes, and other personal possessions, but he did intend to abolish private capital. For Marx, socialism was supposed to be both democratic (majority-rule) and egalitarian (each worker would have one vote).

from THE COMMUNIST MANIFESTO [252]

I: BOURGEOIS AND PROLETARIANS

By bourgeoisie is meant the class of modern Capitalists, owners of the means of social production and employers of wage-labor. By proletariat the class of modern wage-laborers who, having no means of production of their own, are reduced to selling their labor-power in order to live.

The history of all hitherto existing society is the history of class struggles.

Freeman and slave, patrician and plebeian, lord and serf, guild master and journeyman, in a word, oppressor and oppressed, stood in constant opposition to one another, carried on an uninterrupted, now hidden, now open fight, that each time ended, either in a revolutionary reconstitution of society, or in the common ruin of the contending classes.

In the earlier epochs of history we find almost everywhere a complicated arrangement of society into various orders, a manifold gradation of social rank. In ancient Rome we have patricians, knights, plebeians, slaves; in the Middle Ages, feudal lords, vassals, guild masters, journeymen, apprentices, serfs; in almost all of these classes, again, subordinate gradations.

The modern bourgeois society has sprouted from the ruins of feudal society, but has not done away with class antagonisms. It has but established new forms of struggle in place of the old ones.

Our epoch, the epoch of the bourgeoisie, possesses, however, this distinctive feature: it has simplified the class antagonisms. Society as a whole is more and more splitting up into two great hostile camps, into two great classes directly facing each other: Bourgeoisie and Proletariat....

The bourgeoisie, wherever it got the upper hand, has put an end to all feudal, patriarchal, idyllic relations. It has pitilessly torn asunder the motley feudal ties that bound man to his "natural superiors," and has left remaining no other nexus between man and man than naked self-interest, than callous "cash payment."...

The bourgeoisie has stripped of its halo every occupation hitherto honored and looked up to with reverent awe. It has converted the physician, the lawyer, the priest, the poet, the man of science, into its paid wage laborers.

The bourgeoisie has torn away from the family its sentimental veil, and has reduced the family relation to a mere money relation....

The need of a constantly expanding market for its products chases the bourgeoisie over the whole surface of the globe....

The bourgeoisie has through its exploitation of the world's market given a cosmopolitan character to production and consumption in every country. To the great chagrin of [conservatives], it has drawn from under the feet of industry the national ground on which it stood. All old established national industries have been destroyed or are daily being destroyed. They are dislodged by new industries, whose introduction becomes a life and death question for all civilized nations, by industries that no longer work up indigenous raw material, but raw material drawn from the remotest zones, industries whose products are consumed, not only at home, but in every quarter of the globe. In place of the old wants, satisfied by the productions of the country, we find new wants, requiring for their satisfaction the products of distant lands and climes....

The bourgeoisie, by the rapid improvement of all instruments of production, by the immensely facilitated means of communication, draws all...nations into [the orbit of Western] civilization. The cheap prices of its commodities are the heavy artillery with which it batters down all Chinese walls.... It compels all nations, on pain of extinction, to adopt the bourgeois mode of production [i.e., to become capitalist]; it compels them to introduce what it calls civilization into their midst, to become bourgeois themselves. In one word, it creates a world after its own image.

The bourgeoisie has subjected the country to the rule of the towns. It has created enormous cities, has greatly increased urban population as compared with the rural....

---

[252] Karl Marx and Friedrich Engels, *The Communist Manifesto* (1848, 1955), passim.

The bourgeoisie...has agglomerated population, centralized the means of production, and has concentrated property in a few hands. The necessary consequence of this was political centralization....

{But] modern bourgeois society...is like the sorcerer, who is no longer able to control the powers of the nether world whom he has called up by his spells.... [T]here breaks out an epidemic... -- the epidemic of over-production....

The weapons with which the bourgeoisie felled feudalism to the ground are now turned against the bourgeoisie itself.

Not only has the bourgeoisie forged the weapons that bring death to itself; it has also called into existence the men who are to wield those weapons – the modern working class – the proletarians.

As the bourgeoisie...developed, [so too] the proletariat...developed; a class of laborers, who live only so long as they find work, and who find work only so long as their labor increases capital. These landless laborers, who must sell themselves piecemeal, are a commodity, like every other article of commerce, and are consequently exposed to all the vicissitudes of competition, to all the fluctuations of the market.

Owing to the extensive use of machinery and to division of labor, the work of the proletarians has lost all individual character, and consequently, all charm for the workman. He becomes an appendage of the machine, and it is only the most simple, most monotonous, and most easily acquired knack, that is required of him. Hence, the cost of production of a workman is restricted almost entirely to the means of subsistence that he requires for his maintenance....

The lower strata of the middle class – the small tradespeople, shopkeepers, and retired tradesmen generally, the handicraftsman and peasant – all sink gradually into the proletariat, partly because their diminutive capital does not suffice for the scale on which modern industry is carried on, and is swamped in the competition with the large capitalists, partly because their specialized skill is rendered worthless by new methods of production. Thus the proletariat is recruited from all classes of the population.

The proletariat goes through various stages of development. With its birth begins its struggle with the bourgeoisie. At first the contest is carried on by individual laborers, then by the workpeople of a factory, then by the operatives of one trade, in one locality, against the individual bourgeois who directly exploits them...

At this stage the laborers still form an incoherent mass scattered over the whole country, and broken up by their mutual competition...

But with the development of industry the proletariat not only increases in number, it becomes concentrated in greater masses, its strength grows and it feels that strength more....

This organization of the proletariat into a class, and consequently into a political party...ever rises up again; stronger, firmer, mightier....

II: PROLTARIANS AND COMMUNISTS

[Marx and Engel's "Communists" were members of the old Communist League they had joined, not communists in the twentieth-century sense. It was only later that the term "communist" came to be used to describe radical socialists like V. I. Lenin. What follows are planks from the 1848 platform of the Communist League.]

1. Abolition of property in land and application of all rents of land to public purposes.
2. A heavy progressive or graduated income tax.
3. Abolition of all rights of inheritance.
4. Confiscation of the property of all emigrants and rebels [i.e., those who would oppose the coming socialist revolution].
5. Centralization of credit in the hands of the State, by means of a national bank with State capital and an exclusive monopoly. [This would essentially eliminate all private banks.]
6. Centralization of the means of communication and transport in the hands of the State.
7. Extension of factories and instruments of production owned by the State; the bringing into cultivation of waste lands, and the improvement of the soil generally in accordance with a common plan.
8. Equal liability of all to labor [i.e., everyone must work]. Establishment of industrial armies, especially for agriculture.

9. Combination of agriculture with manufacturing industries; gradual abolition of the distinction between town and country, by a more equitable distribution of the population over the country.

10. Free education for all children in public schools. Abolition of children's factory labor in its present form. Combination of education with industrial production, etc., etc.

When, in the course of development, class distinctions have disappeared and all production has been concentrated in the hands of a vast association of the whole nation, the public power will lose its political character...

In place of the old bourgeois society with its classes and class antagonisms we shall have an association in which the free development of each is the condition for the free development of all.

Early Nationalism: Giuseppe Mazzini

An Italian nationalist, Giuseppe Mazzini (1805-72) nevertheless spent most of his adult life in exile in France and Britain. As a young man, Mazzini longed for Italy, which was divided into numerous small city-states and dominated by the powerful Austrian Empire, to be united and free of foreign influence. In 1831 he founded Young Italy, an organization devoted to his cause. After a failed attempt to overthrow the conservative government of the city-state of Piedmont, Mazzini fled to France. In exile, he published and edited *Young Italy* magazine, which he arranged to be smuggled into Italy. Influenced by Mazzini's ideas, nationalists in other countries formed similar groups, including Young Germany, Young America, Young Canada, and Young India, the latter organized in the early twentieth century by Mohandas Gandhi. Mazzini lived long enough to see Italy united in 1860 by Camillo Cavour, ironically the Prime Minister for King Victor Emmanuel II of Piedmont, the very monarch that Mazzini had once tried to overthrow as an impediment to Italian unification. In 1864 Mazzini joined with Karl Marx and others to organize the International Workingmen's Association, commonly called the First Communist International. Quarreling with Marx and the socialists, however, Mazzini and his nationalists soon left the organization.

Unlike Thomas Paine and the classical liberals, Mazzini rejected individualism. Instead, he sublimated the individual to the community, emphasizing duties over rights. Unlike Edmund Burke and the classical conservatives, he had no love for the old order of lords and monarchs, and preferred a republic. Unlike Karl Marx and the early socialists, he did not believe that one's primary duty was to one's class. A person's greatest duty, Mazzini wrote, was to God and humanity in general, but after that came duty to one's nation – ahead of duty to family, class, ancestors, or even self. Mazzini believed that membership in a nation was not a matter of legal citizenship, but of culture. For him, a nation was not the same thing as a state – although ideally the two could and should be combined as a nation-state. Italy was divided into many independent city-states, each with its own different laws and rules of citizenship. Moreover, many ethnic Italians lived in Tyrol, Milan, and Venice, areas under the control of Austria, a foreign and German-speaking country – or, like Mazzini himself, they lived in France, Britain, South America, or the United States. For Mazzini, a person was part of the Italian "nation" by being culturally and ethnically Italian – that is, by being born of Italian parents, speaking the Italian language, accepting the "Italian" religion (Roman Catholicism), holding "Italian" ideals and beliefs (whatever they were), and having an "Italian" personality (whatever that was). He did not consider the issue of ethnic minorities within Italy itself, a troublesome question in the twentieth century. Rather, Mazzini envisioned a utopian world where all countries would be ethnically homogeneous, politically united, and independent of foreign control – that is to say, a world composed of nation-states, where every nationality had its own country, which it controlled. This, he believed, would end oppression and exploitation and lead to global harmony.

from THE DUTIES OF MAN [253]

[Mazzini addresses this essay to his fellow ethnic Italians.]

Your first Duties – first, at least, in importance – are, as I have told you, to Humanity. You are men before you are citizens or fathers. If you do not embrace the whole human family in your love, if you do not confess your faith in its unity – consequent on the unity of God – and in the brotherhood of the Peoples who are appointed to reduce that unity to fact – if whatever one of your fellowmen groans, wherever the dignity of human nature is violated by falsehood or tyranny, you are not prompt, being able, to succor that wretched one, or do not feel yourself called, being able, to fight for the purpose of relieving the deceived or

---

[253] Giuseppe Mazzini, *The Duties of Man*, trans. Ella Noyes (1907), 51-59.

oppressed – you disobey your law of life, or do not comprehend the religion which will bless your future.

But what can each of you, with his isolated powers, do for the moral improvement, for the progress of Humanity? You can, from time to time, give sterile expression to your belief: you may, on some rare occasion, perform an act of charity to a brother not belonging to your own land, no more.... [Here Mazzini is saying that, yes, our first duty is to humanity, but as individuals we are too weak and small to help people not of our own nationality, except on rare occasions.]

The watchword of the future...is association, fraternal cooperation towards a common aim.... But divided as [people] are in language, tendencies, habits, and capacities, [they] cannot attempt this common work. The individual is too weak, and Humanity too vast.... But God gave you [a] means [to make the world better] when He gave you a Nation, when like a wise overseer of labor, who distributes the different parts of the work according to the capacity of the workmen, He divided Humanity into distinct groups upon the face of the globe, and thus planted the seeds of nations. Bad governments have disfigured the design of God, which you may [nevertheless]see, clearly marked out, as far, at least, as regards Europe, by the courses of the great rivers, by the lines of the lofty mountains, and by other geographical conditions; they [i.e., bad governments] have disfigured it [i.e., God's design of nations] by conquest, by greed, by jealousy of the just sovereignty [i.e., self-rule] of others; disfigured it so much that today there is perhaps no nation except England and France whose confines correspond to this design.... But the divine design will infallibly be fulfilled.... The map of Europe will be remade. The Nations of the People will rise, defined by the voice of the free, upon the ruins of the Countries of Kings and privileged castes. Between these Nations there will be harmony and brotherhood.... Then each of you, strong in the affections and in the aid of millions of men speaking the same language, endowed with the same tendencies, and educated by the same historic tradition, may hope by your personal effort to benefit the whole of Humanity.

In you, who have been born in Italy, God has allotted, as if favoring you specially, the best-defined country in Europe. [Mazzini goes on to argue that the Mediterranean Sea and Alps Mountains form "natural boundaries" for Italy. The idea of "natural boundaries" did not originate with Mazzini. Napoleon, for example, had claimed the Rhine River as the "natural boundary" of France on the east, a notion that the Dutch and Germans, who lived on both banks of the river, found particularly worrisome.] As far as this frontier your language is spoken; beyond this you have no rights.... [Mazzini here implies that Italian migrants to the United States, Canada, South America, France, or Britain could not expect to enjoy civil rights. Liberals like Paine believed that all people had human rights, because those rights came either from God or nature, not from nationality. Mazzini clearly disagreed.]

Without Country [by "Country," Mazzini here means all of Italy, not the independent city-state in which the reader happens to live], you have neither name, token, voice, nor rights; no admission as brothers into the fellowship of the Peoples. You are the bastards of Humanity.... [Mazzini next goes on to criticize socialism.] Do not beguile yourselves with the hope of emancipation from unjust social conditions if you do not first conquer a Country for yourselves; where there is no Country there is no common agreement to which you can appeal; the egoism of self-interest rules alone, and he who has the upper hand keeps it, since there is no common safeguard for the interests of all. Do not be led away by the idea of improving you material conditions without first solving the national question. You cannot do it. Your industrial associations [i.e., labor unions] and mutual help societies are useful as a means of educating and disciplining yourselves; as an economic fact they will remain barren until you have an [independent and united] Italy. The economic problem [i.e., the problems caused by industrialization] demands, first and foremost, an increase of capital and production; and while your Nation is dismembered into separate fragments – while shut off by the barrier of customs [i.e., local tariffs] and artificial difficulties [i.e., local laws] of every sort, you have only restricted markets open to you – you cannot hope for this increase. Today – do not delude yourselves – you are not the working class of Italy; you are only fractions of that class; powerless, unequal to the great task which you propose to yourselves. Your emancipation can have no special beginning until a National Government, understanding the signs of the times, shall, seated in Rome, formulate a Declaration of Principles to be the guide for Italian progress....

[Mazzini now goes on to criticize liberalism, arguing that rights do not come from God or nature, but are a reward for adherence to duty to the nation.] You cannot obtain your Rights except by obeying the commands of Duty. Be worthy of them, and you will have them. O my Brothers! Love your Country. Our Country is our home, the home which God has given us, placing therein a numerous family [i.e., ethnic Italians] which we love and are loved by, and which we have a more intimate and quicker communion of feeling and thought with than with others; a family which by its concentration upon a given spot, and by the homogenous nature of its elements, is destined for a special kind of activity.... Before associating ourselves with the [other] Nations which compose Humanity we [also] must exist as a Nation. There can be no association except among equals; and you [Italians do not yet] have [a] recognized collective existence....

[Next, Mazzini criticizes individualism.] May the constant thought of your soul be for Italy, may all the acts of your life be worthy of her, and may the standard beneath which you range yourselves to work for Humanity be Italy's. Do not say "I"; say "we." Be every one of you an incarnation of your Nation, and feel himself responsible for his fellow-countrymen; let each one of you learn to act in such a way that in him men shall respect and love his Nation.

Your Nation is one and indivisible....

A Nation must have, then, a single government...

[Mazzini also criticizes conservatism, with its reverence for the hierarchical societies of the past.] A Nation is a fellowship of free and equal men bound together in a brotherly concord of labor towards a single end.... A Nation is not an aggregation, it is an association. There is no true Nation without a uniform right. There is no true Nation without a uniform right. There is no true Nation when the uniformity of that right is violated by the existence of caste, privilege, and inequality.

A Nation is not a mere territory; the particular territory is only its foundation. The Nation is the idea which rises upon that foundation; it is the sentiment of love, the sense of fellowship which binds together all the sons of that territory.

Applying Ideology to Issues

MODERN ISMS ROLE-PLAYING EXERCISE

Based on the readings, indicate which of the six political theorists – Thomas Paine, Edmund Burke, Mary Wollstonecraft, Henry David Thoreau, Karl Marx, and Giuseppe Mazzini – would (if alive today) have *agreed* with the following statements, taken from newspaper stories and television shows over the last several years. You may select more than one choice for your answer. Then indicate whether or not *you* would agree with it. Based on your responses, do you consider yourself a classical liberal, classical conservative, early feminist, early environmentalist, early socialist, or early nationalist?

1. Each country should have one official language.

2. Each country should have one established religion.

3. Society has an obligation to censor material deemed offensive, obscene, or unpatriotic.

4. Women should have the same rights as men.

5. A free society must protect the rights of minorities.

6. Religion is the source of all morality; people who are not religious are therefore immoral.

7. Religion should be encouraged, because it brings morality to society.

8. The family is the cornerstone of society.

9. All adults should have the right to vote.

10. Stupid people should not be allowed to vote.

11. Outsiders should not be allowed to vote.

12. Immigration should be limited.

13. Abortion should be a matter of individual choice.

14. A landowner should be able to do whatever he wants with his own property.

15. The common good transcends individual rights.

16. Religion is a fundamental part of our culture.

17. The homeless have a right to shelter.

18. Labor unions are good because they help working people get a fair shake.

19. A strong military is essential to national security.

20. The chief job of a political leader is to be a role model for moral behavior.

21. The best way to prevent crime is to end poverty.

22. The needs of the many outweigh the needs of the few.

23. Infinite diversity in infinite combinations.

24. Big business is dangerous.

25. Big government is dangerous.

26. Big labor is dangerous.

27. The government should play a role in economic planning.

28. Anybody can make it if they work hard enough.

29. On the job, people should be promoted by merit, rather than birth or favoritism.

30. Affirmative action is the only way to ensure basic fairness and equality.

31. We must protect our markets from foreign imports.

32. Uneducated people should not be allowed to vote or hold office.

33. Our country should not get involved in foreign conflicts.

34. Our country should use its military power to ensure that we have access to abundant supplies of cheap oil and other vital resources.

35. Such-and-such a religion is a threat to our way of life.

-CHAPTER VIII-
THE GOLDEN AGE OF THE WEST?
PROSPERITY, POWER, AND DISAPPOINTMENT IN THE NINETEENTH CENTURY
1815-1914

The period from 1815 to 1914 is sometimes viewed as a kind of Golden Age in the West. The argument goes like this: There were no major wars in the West between 1815 and 1914 - well, at least none in Western Europe. There was political stability - except, of course, for a bloody civil war in the United States, labor unrest everywhere, major changes in the international balance of power, and continued revolution in France, but those are just minor details. There was unprecedented prosperity as industrialization continued - although the gap between rich and poor did widen rather alarmingly, but that was only a problem if you were poor. There was the conquest of glorious new empires in Asia and Africa - although it was true that the colonial peoples did revolt rather frequently, but that was only because they were irrationally ungrateful for all the good things the West had brought them. The nineteenth century witnessed the abolition of slavery, and that was good - although admittedly peonage and sharecropping continued, and racism somehow became worse than ever. There were new discoveries in science and new departures in art - although, truth to tell, not everyone was all that enamored with evolution, psychotherapy, and impressionism. There was a great drive for reform - but, then again, many of the proposed reforms never really got accomplished. A Golden Age? Well, maybe. But if it was, there was plenty of tarnish on the gold.

If the nineteenth century was the high water mark for modernity in the West, then the water never got as high as lot of people would have liked. Rationalism, industrialization, formal education, science, urban growth, individualism, capitalism, faith in progress - all of these things did seem to peak. But, as it turns out, that was precisely the problem. If the nineteenth century represented the pinnacle of modernity, the best that modern culture could do, some Westerners began to wonder if modernity was all that it was cracked up to be. A few even began to ask if at least a partial return to traditional values might be in order. This chapter considers the West in the golden, modern years of the nineteenth century, examining the era's successes and failures, defenders and critics.

-The Background-

The Congress of Vienna

In 1815 peace came to the West at long last, after more than a century of nearly nonstop bloodshed and struggle. Although the deadly Wars of Religion (see chapter four) had pretty much ended in 1648, it was only a scant half-century later that a new round of deadly conflict, the so-called Great Wars for Empire, had begun. The Great Wars for Empire lasted off-and-on from 1689 to 1815, always pitting Britain on one side against France on the other, with the various other Western powers (Spain, Portugal, Austria, the Netherlands, Sweden, Denmark, Prussia, and the United States) shifting sides depending on the issues. From 1689 to 1783 Britain and France fought five major wars, with the sixth and decisive struggle - the so-called Napoleonic Wars - occurring between 1794 and 1815. France turned Spain into a virtual puppet state. Britain countered by extending its own influence within the Holy Roman Empire, the Netherlands, and Portugal. Both countries sought to expand their empires in North America, but ironically each ended up losing the bulk of them. In 1763 France lost Canada to Britain in the Seven Years War, but in 1783 Britain's prized Thirteen Colonies revolted and, with French assistance, became the independent United States of America. There was an uneasy decade of peace from 1783 to 1794 that both sides knew could not last, and then they were at each other's throats again when, in 1794, Britain put settling old scores ahead of furthering its system of constitutionalism and joined the absolutist coalition of Austria, Prussia, and Spain against constitutionalist France. Old hatreds died hard.

It had been in the midst of this latest war that Napoleon Bonaparte had come to power in France. Indeed, it had been in large part *because* of the war that "Old Boney," as the British called him, had been able to make himself dictator. Without the opportunity to prove his mettle in battle, without the turmoil and fear that the war had engendered within the French population, Bonaparte might never have had the opportunity or support he needed to overthrow the civilian government. Once begun, the Napoleonic Wars dragged on, year after bloody year, until Old Boney was finally defeated in 1815. The casualties, property damage, political turmoil, civilian suffering, and government expenditures were unprecedented. At his height, Napoleon had defeated Austria and Prussia; conquered Spain, Portugal, the Netherlands, the Italian city-states, and most of the Holy Roman Empire, which became French puppet states; "freed" Poland from Prussian and Russian domination (although in reality making it another French puppet state); and had Britain at bay. Then, in 1812, he had made the fateful mistake of invading Russia. Although France's Grand Army had little trouble dispatching the Russian army, it had nevertheless become trapped in Russia in the middle of winter. Cold, starving (the Russian peasants had destroyed their crops in a "scorched earth" campaign), hounded by guerilla fighters, more dead than alive, the hitherto invincible Grand Army barely staggered into Moscow, only to find the city deserted and the food destroyed. By the time Napoleon had marched the Grand Army back to Poland, only about a tenth of his soldiers were still alive. Seizing the initiative, Prussia, Austria, and Britain counterattacked. Napoleon was defeated, captured, and exiled to the island of Elba off the coast of Italy. Two years later he escaped, returned to France, and raised a new army, only to be finally defeated by a combined British and Prussian force at Waterloo. This time he was exiled to an even more remote island, Saint Helena, in the middle of the South Atlantic Ocean, where his British warden slowly poisoned him to death.[254]

Victory assured at last, the leaders of the various Western countries (joined by their new ally, the tsar of Russia) met in Vienna, the capital of Austria, in 1814-15 in a famous meeting known as the Congress of Vienna, to hammer out a peace. The major powers were all represented – Britain, Austria, Prussia, and even France itself. Russia was there, too, and so were several of the lesser powers, such as Spain, Portugal, the Netherlands, some of the Italian city-states, and a number of the German principalities. But the chief architect was the ultra-conservative, brilliant, vain, and aristocratic forty-one-year-old Prince Klemens von Metternich (1773-1859) (MET-er-nick), the chief advisor to the Archduke of Austria (Marie Antoinette's brother) and staunch defender of absolutism. Metternich was determined, as much as possible, to return the West to the old order that had existed before the French Revolution. The peace, therefore, would be a conservative one.[255]

The Congress's chief goal was to ensure that France never again plunged the West into a terrible war. The historian Paul Kennedy provides some statistics that show why Metternich and the other Western leaders felt that way. From 1793 to 1815, in order to defeat France, Britain alone had had to spend a mind-staggering 1,657,854,518 pounds, 26.6% of which it had been forced to borrow, which meant that winning the Napoleonic Wars had left Britain 440,298,079 pounds in debt. Moreover, in order to match Napoleon's 600,000-strong Grand Army, Britain had had to increase its own forces to 250,000, while its ally Austria expanded its army to 250,000, Prussia to 270,000 (out of a total population of only 9.5 million), and Russia to 500,000. And Britain also had had to more than double its already formidable Royal Navy from 90 to 215 ships of the line, so as to be sure not only of defeating Napoleon's Franco-Spanish fleet of 105 ships, but also of controlling the shipment of trade goods into and out of France – for without supplies from Canada and other colonies, Britain most likely would have lost the war. Even the winners had been exhausted by the arms race.[256]

To achieve this goal, Metternich decided on a threefold strategy. First, the victors would offer France a lenient peace, under the assumption that a harsh peace would only make the French people angry, resentful, and more determined than ever to get revenge. France would be allowed to keep almost all of its prewar territory, although in return it would have to agree to restore the monarchy. Pleased to get off so lightly, the French Foreign Minister, the wily ex-revolutionary Talleyrand, quickly agreed to the condition, and Louis XVIII (r. 1815-24) (there was no Louis XVII, for the dauphin had perished during the Revolution) assumed the throne. Second, Metternich proposed that France be "contained" by a ring of several strong states – at least, states that were stronger than those that had surrounded it in 1793. Austria turned over the Austrian Netherlands (today's Belgium) to the new, larger Kingdom of the Netherlands (the Dutch, like the French, were required to establish a monarchy, but theirs, at least, would be a constitutional one), to create a theoretically stronger state on France's northeast border. Some territory along the Rhine River that had been part of the old Holy Roman Empire (the Congress of Vienna had decided not to restore the old Reich, which Napoleon had abolished, instead leaving a welter of small, independent principalities) was turned over to Prussia, which now bordered France on the east. Spain, of course, bordered France on the south. Finally, the old French province of Savoy was merged with of the three Italian city-states – Turin, Genoa, and Sardinia – to form the new Kingdom of Piedmont, ostensibly to block French expansion to the southeast. (To recompense Austria for giving up the Austrian Netherlands, the Congress gave it three Italian city-states of its own: Milan, Lombardy, and Venice. This move ended up backfiring on Austria, however, as it stirred up intense anti-Austrian sentiment among the Italian people, who now viewed the Austrians as foreign invaders – which, of course, they were.) The third part of Metternich's strategy was to create a conservative Concert of Europe in which the absolutist states would commit troops to put down any future constitutionalist revolutions that might occur anywhere in Europe. Britain and the Netherlands, both of them constitutionalist, of course declined to participate in the Concert, although absolutist Austria, Prussia, and Russia joined enthusiastically.[257]

With France now unlikely to start another major war, with absolute monarchs on every throne except those of Britain and the Netherlands, with four former republics eliminated (France, the Netherlands, Venice, and Genoa – leaving only Switzerland, Haiti, and the United States), the Congress disbanded. And for ninety-nine years the West knew relative peace and stability. Most historians consequently have pronounced the Congress of Vienna a success.[258]

---

[254] Erik Durschmied, *The Weather Factor: How Nature Has Changed History* (2000), 106-127.
[255] Richard E. Sullivan, Dennis Sherman, and John B. Harrison, *A Short History of Western Civilization* (1994), 540-541.
[256] Paul Kennedy, *The Rise and Fall of the Great Powers: Economic Change and Military Conflict from 1500 to 2000* (1987), 81, 99.
[257] Sullivan, *Short History of Western Civilization*, 542-545.
[258] Henry A. Kissinger, "The Congress of Vienna: A Reappraisal," *Politics* (1956), 7: 268-280.

Stability or Turmoil?

But was it? *"Relative peace and stability"* is, of course, a *relative* term. True, Europe managed to avoid a major, continent-wide war until 1914. But it did experience several smaller ones, including the Crimean War (1853-56) (Britain, France, Piedmont, Austria, and the Ottoman Empire vs. Russia) (600,000 deaths), the Risorgimento (wars for Italian unification) (1859-60) (Piedmont and France vs. Austria and the Papal States), two Polish revolts (1830-31 and 1863) (Polish revolutionaries vs. Russia), the Austro-Prussian War (1866) (79,000 soldiers and civilians killed), the Danish-Prussian War (1864), and the Franco-Prussian War (1870-71) (187,500 soldiers and 590,000 civilians killed), and these were bad enough. And if we look at the entire West, not just Europe, we also have the Mexican-American War (1845-48), American Civil War (1861-65) (620,000 soldiers and 50,000 civilians killed), the War of the Triple Alliance (1864-70) (Argentina, Brazil, and Uruguay vs. Paraguay) (610,000 deaths), various wars in the United States against Native-American tribes (19,000 "whites" and 50,000 "Indians" killed), numerous other wars in Latin America, and the Spanish-American War (1898) (9,303 direct deaths and 53,440 killed by war-related disease). There were also wars overseas, such as the Opium War (1840-42) between Britain and China, the Espy Revolt (1857) against British rule in India, the Boer War (1899-1902) between Britain and the Afrikaner republics of Transvaal and Orange Free State in southern Africa, the Anglo-Zulu War (1879) (1,430 British, 1,000 Xhosa, and 8,000 Zulus killed), the Ashanti War between Britain and the African Ashanti people, the Javanese War (1825-30) (an uprising of Javanese rebels against Dutch colonial rule) (200,000 Javanese and 15,000 Dutch killed), the "pacification" of the Congolese by the Belgians (1886-1908) (4.5 million deaths), etc. Indeed, hardly a year went by without a war or uprising taking place somewhere. By a very conservative estimate, wars involving Western countries killed at least 25 million people between 1815 and 1924, about a quarter of whom were Westerners – approximately the same number as the combined five million Westerners who died in the American Revolution, French Revolution, and Napoleonic Wars of 1775-1815.[259]

France and Belgium. Fifteen years after the Congress of Vienna, the French abrogated one of its achievements and cashiered the last Bourbon king, Charles X (r. 1824-30) in the largely bloodless Revolution of 1830. They replaced him with the pear-shaped, plain-dressed, bourgeois-minded Duke of Orleans, Louis-Philippe, who agreed to reign as a constitutional rather than absolutist monarch. Three centuries before, the first Bourbon monarch, Henri IV, had come to power by declaring that "Paris is worth a mass." Evidently, Louis-Philippe believed that it was also worth a parliament.

The next year, Belgium divorced the Netherlands, ending what had been an unnatural union, and proclaimed itself an independent constitutional monarchy.

In 1848 the French revolted again and deposed the hapless Louis-Philippe, who must have wondered what had happened to all those people who had cheered him just a few years earlier. This time the French eliminated the monarchy entirely and established the short-lived Second Republic. Unfortunately, as their new president they elected the colorful, charismatic, big-talking, remember-the-good-old-days, nationalistic, patriotic politician Louis Napoleon Bonaparte (r. 1852-70), the erstwhile nephew of Old Boney himself. Following in his uncle's monarchist footsteps, Bonaparte slyly overthrew the republic, proclaimed the Second Empire, and crowned himself Emperor Napoleon III. (There was no Napoleon II.)

The French people hoped that the boastful, impetuous, easy-answer-for-every-problem Bonaparte would bring them respect, power, peace, stability, and greatness after decades of revolutionary turmoil, but instead he brought dictatorship at home, blunders in foreign policy, and defeat in war. In 1859, in alliance with Piedmont, Napoleon III invaded northern Italy to fight Austria – certainly not the result that Metternich had hoped for when he had "contained" France in 1815. French troops forced Austria to surrender Milan and Lombardy to Piedmont (forming what now became the nucleus of a new, united Kingdom of Italy), in return for which Piedmont ceded France the small and relatively unimportant territories of Savoy and Nice. Napoleon pledged that his troops would remain in Italy only long enough to make sure that the Austrians didn't return and recapture Lombardy, but instead he garrisoned Rome and the Papal States for several years before the frustrated Italians finally convinced him to withdraw – a circumstance that served only to create unnecessary hard feeling between France and the Italian people, which otherwise might have viewed the French positively as their liberators and allies, but who now became increasingly francophobic. In the end, the only gains for France were the relatively unimportant Savoy and Nice, while its losses included the French soldiers who had died in the war, its former friendship with Austria, and the good will of the Italian people, which vanished when the French troops overstayed their welcome and remained in Italy too long. France now had a strong, resentful, new nation on its southern border.

As if his blundering in Italy had not been enough, Napoleon III also messed things up in Mexico, where his meddling toppled the Mexican Republic and placed his protégé Maximilian I (r. 1864-67) on the throne of a short-lived Mexican Empire. This needless and high-handed maneuver only served to outrage the Mexican people, who soon overthrew the inept Maximilian, and alarm the United States, which feared having a monarchy on its southern border and threatened military intervention unless France backed down – which it did. At the same time, Napoleon foolishly told the Prussian Chancellor Otto von Bismarck (see below) that

---

[259] Estimates of war dead are from Matthew White, "Statistics of Wars, Oppressions and Attrociities of the Nineteenth Century," users.erols.com/mwhite28/ wars19c.htm, retrieved 7/28/2004. Although not a professional historian, White gives good, credible sources for all of his data.

France would support the Prussian occupation of the German principality of Hanover (the ancestral home of the British monarchs) if Prussia would back French annexation of Belgium and Luxembourg (British allies). Bismarck wisely declined, but craftily informed the British and Belgians of the conversation, which drove a wedge between France and Britain, Belgium, and Luxembourg. Thus it was that by 1870 the inept Napoleon III had successfully alienated Austria, Italy, Mexico, the United States, Britain, and Belgium. France had no allies left.

Then, in a further fit of stupidity, in 1871 Napoleon III allowed France to be drawn into the disastrous Franco-Prussian War with Prussia. When the friendless French forces lost badly to the smaller but better-prepared army of Prussia (as a general, Napoleon III was no Napoleon I), the French people wised up and decided that they had finally had enough of Napoleon. They tossed him off his throne and proclaimed the Third Republic.

The Congress of Vienna had hoped to prevent further revolutions from occurring in France and stop megalomaniacal French leaders from making war with their neighbors. Clearly, it had not succeeded.[260]

Italy. During the nineteenth century the balance of economic power shifted away from some of the old powers like Austria, the Netherlands, Spain, and France and towards four young upstarts: the United States (not yet forty years old when the Congress of Vienna had met in 1814-15) and three newly created countries, a united Germany, a united Italy, and an independent and united Canada. (Britain, of course, remained the major economic power, not only in the West, but in the entire world.) Of the three new countries, Italy arrived first. With help from France's Napoleon III (see above), from 1859 to 1870 the canny, pragmatic Prime Minister of Piedmont, Count Camillo di Cavour (1810-61) (Kah-VOHR), the chief advisor to the Piedmontese King Victor Emmanuel II (r. 1849-78), and his successors succeeded in uniting the once-divided Italian city-states into the new Kingdom of Italy – omitting only the tiny, relatively unimportant city-state of San Marino and an even smaller enclave within the city of Rome, the Vatican, which remained under the direct rule of the pope. As we have already seen, in return for two relatively unimportant territories, France had joined with Piedmont to force Austria to surrender its rich Italian territories of Milan, Lombardy, and (eventually) Venice to the new united Italy, which was then established as a constitutional rather than an absolutist monarchy. Revolts in several other Italian city-states overthrew puppet governments that had been friendly to Austria and the pope, which brought these areas, too, into the new kingdom. The whole process was known as the Risorgimento. Italy had no experience as a unified country, however, and so it would take awhile for it to get its bearings. The visiting French writer Maxime du Camp told of witnessing a patriotic crowd surge ecstatically through the streets of Naples in 1860, shouting "Long Live Italy!" and then stop ask what the word "Italy" meant.[261]

Germany. Far more significant for the history of the West was the unification of most of Germany under the leadership of Prussia. In 1861 the pious, hardworking Prussian King Wilhelm I (1797-1888) (VILL-helm) appointed the iron-willed, archconservative Count Otto von Bismarck (1815-1898) as his Chancellor, or prime minister. Like the canny Cavour, the dyspeptic Bismarck was a pragmatist, an unsentimental practitioner of *realpolitik* (re-ahl-pahl-ah-TEEK) ("practical politics"). Bismarck set out to unite the various independent German principalities around Prussia, just as Cavour had united the several Italian city-states around Piedmont. (The old Holy Roman Empire, remember, had officially disbanded at the Congress of Vienna in 1815.) Knowing that Austria would oppose any unification that put Prussia, not it, in control of Germany (the Austrian ruling elite was comprised largely of ethnic Germans, and Austria was still ruled by the German-speaking Habsburg dynasty), Bismarck provoked the Austro-Prussian War in 1866 at a time when Austria was unready for battle. Prussia won easily. Reluctantly, Austria was forced to step aside as Prussia assumed the leadership of a new North German Confederation. Next, the cagey Bismarck goaded the witless Napoleon III into the Franco-Prussian War of 1871-72. Once again, Prussia won. Humiliated, France was forced to surrender two prosperous provinces, Alsace and Lorraine. Moreover, the small, defenseless German principalities, their vulnerability to "French aggression" now seemingly demonstrated by the recent war, agreed to join with mighty Prussia to form a new German Empire, the so-called Second Reich, with Wilhelm I as its autocratic Kaiser, Bismarck as Chancellor, and a relatively weak and powerless legislature known as the Reichstag that was dominated by delegates from Prussia. Far larger and more powerful than the Kingdom of Italy, the new German Empire, which was far more absolutist than it was constitutionalist, fundamentally altered the balance of power in the West. The old great powers – an aloof Britain, a weakened and defeated France, and an increasingly impotent Austria – now eyed it warily. So, too, did its large non-Western neighbor to the east, Russia.[262]

The United States. Unification occurred not just in Italy and Germany, but also across the Atlantic in North America. From its founding in the Age of Revolution, the United States had always been more of a loose, sprawling confederation of semi-sovereign province-states than a modern, unified, centralized nation-state like France or the new Germany. Indeed, when most Americans said the words "the United States of America," they used it as a plural noun, as in "*these* (not *this*) United States." But the American Civil War (1861-65) changed all that. It allowed the leaders of the victorious North to centralize political authority into the now powerful federal government, which they controlled, and away from the individual states. What's more, the desire of people on both sides of the conflict to get on with their lives led to a series of compromises between

---

[260] John Merriman, *A History of Modern Europe, from the Renaissance to the Present* (1996), 716-722, 731-733, 744-747, 819-843.
[261] Ibid, 754-765.
[262] Ibid, 765-778.

North and South. A new "Conservative Coalition" (a term invented by later historians, and not used by people at the time) of Southern Democrats and Northern Republicans came to control both Congress and the Presidency, frustrating the efforts of socialists, feminists, progressives, Northern Democrats, and Southern and Great Plains Populists to achieve deep and meaningful reforms. This Conservative Coalition was more pragmatic than it was ideological and more centrist than it was truly conservative. It had to be, for Northerners and Southerners, still deeply divided over the issues that had led to the war, were unable to agree on solutions to the country's deep, underlying issues, such as temperance, factory reform, or woman suffrage. But the Coalition enabled leaders to work together on the less divisive, surface issues. They authorized the construction of a vast national network of transcontinental railroads (to improve internal transportation), levied a series of stiff protective tariffs (to stimulate the growth of domestic businesses), allocated the profits from western land sales to endow state universities (to increase social capital), and passed racist and antiunion laws that retained the freed slaves (now mostly sharecroppers) and immigrant workers as submerged and easily controlled sources of cheap labor. The United States thus entered the Second Industrial Revolution only two decades behind Britain, gaining fast. Consequently, the balance of economic power in the West slowly began to change, to shift westward from Europe to North America. By 1900 the center of Western Civilization was no longer the Rhine, as it had been in the Middle Ages, but somewhere in the North Atlantic Ocean, its eastern flank still rooted in Europe but its western edge now anchored in North America.[263]

Canada. The westward shift of economic power from central Europe to the North Atlantic rimlands was accelerated by the fact that Canada, too, unified and industrialized in the nineteenth century. In 1867, led by the brilliant but alcoholic Scots-born Ontario lawyer Sir John A. Macdonald (1815-91) and his ally, the cool Quebecois Sir George-Etienne Cartier (1814-73) (Kahr-tee-YAY) – the pragmatic, middle-of-the-road co-founders of Canada's Conservative Party (originally called the Conservative Liberal Party) – Canada achieved both "home rule" (a kind of three-quarters independence that gave it its own Parliament, Prime Minister, and self-determination in domestic affairs, but obligated it to continue to follow Britain in matters of foreign policy) and confederation (unification of the formerly separate British colonies of Quebec, Ontario, Nova Scotia, and New Brunswick into one country). Within a decade, Canada had added two other former British colonies (Prince Edward Island and British Columbia), a brand new province (Manitoba), and a vast, resource-rich area known as the Northwest Territories from which it could carve further provinces in the future. Like the United States, Canada constructed a transcontinental railway (the Grand Trunk / Canadian Pacific tandem, it formed the longest continuous rail line in the West, stretching from rockbound Halifax on the Atlantic coast to tree-shrouded Vancouver on the Pacific) and enacted steep protective tariffs. By the time Macdonald died in 1891 (except for a brief five-year interregnum, he held the post of Prime Minister from confederation until his death), Canada had achieved home rule, confederation, and industrialization. Although it had only one-tenth the population of the United States, Canada nevertheless stood on the threshold of the Second Industrial Revolution, only a half-century behind Britain and three short decades behind the United States. And by 1914 it had nearly caught up.[264]

The Second Industrial Revolution and Its Consequences

In 1815 industrialization had been confined mostly to Britain, the northeastern United States, and the Netherlands, but by 1914 the First Industrial Revolution (defined as the use of water power to mass produce textiles) had spread to Belgium, France, Germany, Italy, Scandinavia, Canada, the rest of the United States, Spain, Portugal, much of Latin America, Australia, New Zealand, and South Africa. Indeed, it spread even beyond the West, to Japan, Russia, and China. Moreover, in 1856, with the invention of the Bessemer process by the English engineer Henry Bessemer (1813-98), Britain entered the second stage of industrialization, the so-called Second Industrial Revolution, defined as the use of fossil fuels (principally coal) to manufacture inexpensive steel. Like the First Industrial Revolution, the Second Industrial Revolution also spread to other parts of the world, and by 1914 the Netherlands, Belgium, Germany, Scandinavia, Italy, France, the United States, Canada, and Japan had also entered this second stage of industrialization.

Steel. Steel production in the West surged. An alloy of iron and small amounts of carbon, silicon, and manganese, steel is harder than wrought iron and less brittle than cast iron. It had been around for centuries, but had always been difficult to manufacture and therefore was very expensive. But the Bessemer process made inexpensive steel available for the first time. Cheap steel meant that it would be possible to manufacture steel rails that could support the weight of large trains, steel girders to hold up multistory buildings, steel cables from which to hang long suspension bridges, and steel cans to hold packaged food. In 1875 Britain had produced only 900,000 metric tons of steel, but four decades later in 1913 it produced 6,930,000 metric tons, a sevenfold increase. France produced 260,000 metric tons in 1875, but 4,090,000 metric tons in 1913, an eightfold increase. Upstart Germany surged ahead of both, producing 990,000 metric tons in 1880 but 16,240,000 metric tons in 1913, a staggering sixteen fold increase. But this was nothing compared to what occurred in the United States, which in 1870 produced only 77,000 tons of steel but by 1914 was producing twice as much as Germany

---

[263] George Brown Tindall and David Shi, *America: A Narrative History* (2004), 761-921.
[264] J. M. Bumsted, *A History of the Canadian Peoples* (1998), 145-302.

and nearly half of the world's supply. Just as Manchester in Britain, Lowell in the United States, Brussels in Belgium, and Amiens in France had been the textile centers during the First Industrial Revolution, so Pittsburgh in the United States, Essen in Germany, and Birmingham in Britain became the great smoky steel cities of the Second Industrial Revolution. The clang of the hammer and the roar of the blast furnace were now heard across the land.[265]

Spin-off Industries. The ready availability of cheap steel led to a corresponding growth in so-called "spin-off" industries, such as coal mining, food packaging, railroad building, and urban construction. The production of coal, the chief fuel needed to smelt steel, skyrocketed. In 1867 the United States mined just 14 million tons of coal, but in 1914 it produced 423 million tons. By 1890 almost 200,000 Americans worked as coal miners, and by 1914 there were nearly 600,000.[266] Steel girders permitted engineers to erect skyscrapers – buildings more than seven stories tall – which in turn stimulated the construction industry. Steel girders and cables made it possible to erect massive suspension bridges like the Golden Gate Bridge in San Francisco and the Brooklyn Bridge in New York, or the steel truss Victoria Bridge in Montreal, the longest truss bridge in the world. Steel cans permitted the development of a flourishing canned food industry. Steel was used for trains, bicycles, refrigerators, and automobiles. And the popularity of bicycles and automobiles generated a corresponding demand for rubber for their tires and, in the case of autos, gasoline for fuel.

An Increase in Wealth. As a consequence of the vast growth in steel production and all the new spin-off industries, wealth in the West increased dramatically. In the United States the Gross National Product (GNP) calculated in constant dollars quintupled from 1869 to 1914. Per capita GNP tripled.[267] A wide range of consumer items now became available for the ever-expanding middle class.

A New Class System. Industrialization also fundamentally altered the class structure of Western Civilization. The old system of trifunctionalism now almost vanished. To be sure, a few clergy, lords, and peasants still existed, but their numbers diminished each year. In their place rose a new class system composed of an upper class (a *haute bourgeoisie* of factory owners and other so-called "captains of industry"), a middle class (a *petite bourgeoisie* of managers and other so-called "professionals" – today sometimes called "white-collar" workers – who generally were paid annual salaries rather than wages), and a working class (a proletariat of factory workers, often called "blue-collar" workers, who generally were paid wages rather than annual salaries). The middle class and working class had starkly dissimilar lifestyles. According to the social historian Stuart Blumin, middle-class people typically had high-school educations, lived in the suburbs, owned their homes (complete with pianos, carpets, sofas, bookcases, and artwork), married in their mid-twenties, had family arrangements where their wives did not work outside of the home, had only two or three children, and kept their children in school until age eighteen. In contrast, write the social historians Louise Tilly and Joan Scott, most working-class people had only elementary-school educations, lived in inner-city apartments, rented rather than owned their homes (which rarely included pianos, carpets, sofas, bookcases, or artwork), married in their late 'teens or early twenties, had family arrangements where the wives worked outside the home for wages, had five or six children, and expected their children to join the workforce around the age of twelve.[268]

The late social historian Tamara Hareven used an innovative concept called "life course" to analyze the ways the working class organized their lives. According to Hareven, as they grow older, all people progress through a series of stages known as "life transitions." While some of these stages are universal (meaning that almost all people go through them) others are specific to gender, class, era, or ethnicity. Hareven outlined a typical life course for a white working-class woman in the nineteenth-century West:

> - *Age 0-6. Small child.* She is a young child at home with her mother. Her father is the only member of the family who is earning wages, so the family income is low. These are hard times.
> - *Age 6-12. Little mother.* She stays at home caring for her younger siblings, allowing her mother to go back to work. Family income increases, but times are still tough.
> - *Age 12-18. Young worker.* Now a teenager, she takes a job and earns wages. She contributes a portion of her wages to the family economy. Slowly, her siblings join her in the workplace. Family income peaks. She is allowed to keep part of her wages. Her personal expenses few, and she has money for clothes and dates. This is the best time of her life.

---

[265] Merriman, *History of Modern Europe*, 847; Richard E. Sullivan, Dennis Sherman, and John B. Harrison, *A Short History of Western Civilization* (1994), 575.
[266] *Historical Statistics of the United States: Colonial Times to 1970* (1975), 1: 589-590.
[267] Ibid, 1: 224.
[268] Stuart M. Blumin, *The Emergence of the Middle Class: Social Experience in the American City, 1760-1900* (1989), esp. 158-159, 187; Kenneth T. Jackson, *Crabgrass Frontier: The Suburbanization of the United States* (1987), passim; Tamara K. Hareven, *Family Time and Industrial Time: The Relationship Between the Family and Work in a New England Industrial Community* (1982), esp. 154-217; Sam Bass Warner, Jr., *Streetcar Suburbs: The Process of Growth in Boston, 1870-1900* (1978), 46-116; Louise A. Tilly and Joan W. Scott, *Women, Work, and Family* (1978, 1987), 61-146; Michael Anderson, *Family Structure in Nineteenth-Century Lancashire* (1971), passim.

> - *Age 18-20. Young wife.* The young woman marries. She and her husband move into their own apartment. She continues to work and earn wages. With only the two of them, expenses are pretty low, so the new family's income is fairly high. These are good times.
> - *Age 20-26. Young mother.* The mother stays home to care for the children, who are still very young. She no longer earns wages. Family expenses increase. These are hard times.
> - *Age 26-32. Middle-aged mother.* The oldest child is now old enough to care for the other children, and the mother goes back to work. With her wages added to her husband's, family income increases. But with all those mouths to feed, expenses are still high. These are still difficult times.
> - *Age 32-48. Matriarch.* As the children become older, they go to work, contributed their wages to the family economy. Family income increases. If enough of the children can find work, the mother stays home and manages the household. These are good times.
> - *Age 48-60. Older wife.* As the children marry, they leave the household and the family income drops. Of necessity, the mother goes back to work. Times start to become difficult again.
> - *Age 60+. Widow.* The husband dies and the children all move away. The widowed woman faces very hard times.

As Hareven shows, working-class people occasionally enjoyed good times. But they also knew that those times would not last long. Inevitably, hard times would come again.[269]

Overproduction and Declining Wages. During the early years of the First Industrial Revolution when there were only a few factories, profits boomed. But as industrialization continued, more and more factories opened, producing more and more cloth, steel, and other products. Supply soared. Demand dropped. Soon, the market was glutted with surplus products. Manufacturers found themselves with overstocked inventories and idle factories. They attempted to stimulate more demand by lowering prices. But in order to cut prices without also decreasing their profits, they ended up trying to squeeze more and more work out of fewer and fewer workers. The mechanism by which they accomplished this was something called the "speed-up."

Unlike today, when most workers are paid by the hour, the majority of nineteenth-century workers were paid piece-rate, which is to say that they were paid according the number (rate) of items (pieces) they produced per day. Under this system fast workers could (and did) earn higher wages than slow workers, although it was also fairly common for fast workers, once they had finished their "stints" (the basic number of pieces they planned to produce each day) to voluntarily put up their own work and help the slow workers (who frequently were relatives or close friends) finish their stints – a kind of mutuality that was especially common among women workers. Workers calculated how many pieces they had to finish in order to meet their own financial needs and planned accordingly, choosing their own pace. Within a few decades, the system had become so ingrained that all parties viewed it as eminently fair and reasonable.

But then the employers, beset by overproduction, lowered the amounts they paid per completed piece of work. The workers' incomes consequently declined. So they worked faster in order to catch back up again – hence the term "speed-up." Since speed-ups increased production without increasing total wages, they permitted manufacturers to reduce prices without cutting profits. The costs, however, were lower wages for the slow workers and greater stress for the fast workers. Because the fast workers now had more work to do, they lacked sufficient time to help the slow workers, as they once had done, and mutuality decreased. Moreover, even the fast workers became increasingly tired and careless, and industrial accidents increased. Workers were angry and sullen, resentful of the change.[270]

Pollution. Another negative consequence of industrialization was increased pollution. Water pollution increased as industrial contaminants combined with the vast growth in the total amount of human and animal wastes being discharged into rivers, streams, and harbors. Perhaps the worst water pollution was in the city of London, which had swelled to such a mammoth size that the Thames River was no longer capable of carrying away all of its waste. Consequently, the river became sluggish, clogged with contaminants. Sewage backed up the river and floated grotesquely outside of Parliament, where Britain's leaders could not help but notice it. At the same time clouds of the odiferous gas methane built up in the city's overburdened sewers. The entire city smelled like rotten eggs. The result was the "Great Stink" of 1858, when Parliament had to shut down. Engineers tried various schemes to eliminate the stench. The famous chemist Michael Faraday laid hundreds of pieces of blotter paper on the river's surface, hoping to soak up all the uric acid. It didn't work. Another engineer proposed drilling holes down into the sewers, placing hollow tubes in the holes, and lighting the escaping methane so as to create "natural gas" streetlights. He decided to experiment with this idea in the Parliament buildings, where it was noticed that substantial quantities of methane were wafting out of the sewers and rising up through a large stone tower. Leaning into the tower opening with a lighted torch, the engineer tried to light the methane, but the draft was so powerful that the torch kept blowing out. It was a good thing, too, because if the methane had caught fire, it probably would have exploded and blown up Parliament.

---

[269] Hareven, *Family Time and Industrial Time*, 1-8, 154-217.
[270] James L. Hurston, *Securing the Fruits of Labor: The American Concept of Wealth Distribution, 1765-1900* (1998), 84.

Eventually, the engineers "solved" the Great Stink by extending the sewers out under the river and into a large pipe that ran out to sea.[271] The British humor magazine *Punch* commented wryly:

> O Faraday, of Chemists,
>   The Thames we have to clear,
> The Thames, with which we slake our thirst
>   In water, or in beer.
> To take its foulness out to sea
>   Will cost the deuce knows what:
> Now in this strait can Chemistry
>   Afford us help or not? [272]

Air pollution, too, increased, the result of all the sooty bituminous coal that was being burned. And once again, London was one of the major victims. The famous London "fogs" weren't fogs at all, but were instead dense clouds of coal smoke. In 1857 Charles Dickens, Britain's greatest novelist, described a "debilitated old house" in London that:

> wrapped in its mantle of soot, and leaning heavily on the crutches that had partaken of its decay and worn out with I, never knew a healthy or cheerful interval.... You should alike find rain, hail, frost, and thaw lingering in that dismal enclosure, when they had vanished from other places; and as to snow, you should see it there for weeks, long after it had changed from yellow to black, slowly weeping away its grimy life. [273]

Or, as the environmental historians David Stradling and Peter Thorsheim write, "Coal smoke plagued [the West] for well over one hundred years. Cities that relied on soft coal for fuel, including London, Manchester, Glasgow, Chicago, Pittsburgh, St. Louis, and Cincinnati, all suffered through decades of dense air pollution before relief could be found." Respiratory diseases became more acute, especially tuberculosis, pneumonia, bronchitis, and asthma. By 1914, 248 tons of coal dust per square mile settled on London each year. In Pittsburgh the situation was even worse, with an astounding 1,031 tons of coal dust per square mile.[274]

New Sciences and Arts

Western science and art both changed profoundly during the Golden Age. New approaches, styles, and discoveries undermined the old certainties that had been in place since the Renaissance and Scientific Revolution. The modern idea that all the workings of the universe could be explained by a few simple, rational, and easily comprehended laws was now beginning to be called into question. The universe, it seemed, was more complicated than people had thought. The postmodern consciousness was struggling to be born.

The most important scientists of the Golden Age were the Englishman Charles Darwin (1809-82), the Austrian Sigmund Freud (1856-1939), and the German Albert Einstein (1879-1955). All three called into question firmly held assumptions from the era of the Scientific Revolution and the Enlightenment.

Darwin's theory of natural selection, based on observations he made while circumnavigating the globe aboard the British ship of exploration *Beagle*, stressed the importance of random mutations in the evolution of species. Furthermore, by positing that an organism's survival was in part determined by how well it adapted to its environment, it opened the way for the new, twentieth-century science of ecology. To the modern mind, with its emphasis on progress and its faith in human reason, Darwin's insistence that utterly random events played such a key role was disquieting. So, too, was his proposal that *Homo sapiens* had evolved gradually out of other species – that no sharp divide separated human reason from animal instinct.

Freud's science of psychoanalysis also undermined modern rationalism. He demonstrated that human behavior is not always rational, that we are governed as well by numerous, complex, and poorly understood irrational, subconscious, and instinctive drives.

Finally, Einstein's theory of relativity held that time, space, and motion are relative to each other and to the observer, and not absolutes as had hitherto been thought. This, too, made the modern mind uncomfortable. With its emphasis on mutability, and simply by supplanting older Newtonian physics, Einsteinian physics called into question people's faith in absolute scientific laws.

In art, too, rationalism was under siege. Renaissance art had emphasized realism, and for five centuries artists had strived to produce paintings and sculptures that mirrored reality as closely as possible. But in the late 1800s a revolution in art occurred, as realism gave way to impressionism. Until then, from the Renaissance through the Age of Revolution, art had functioned almost as a branch of science, and artists had studied anatomy, botany, geometry, and perspective, in order to achieve their goal of realism. Indeed, artists and scientists were often the same people – as the example of Leonardo da Vinci illustrates. But in the nineteenth century, artists

---

[271] Thomas F. Glick, "Science, Technology, and the Urban Environment: The Great Stink of 1858," in Lester J. Bilsky, ed., *Historical Ecology: Essays on Environment and Social Change* (1980), 122-139.
[272] *Punch*, 31 July 1858, 41.
[273] Charles Dickens, *Little Dorritt* (1857), 13.
[274] David Stradling and Peter Thorsheim, "The Smoke of Great Cities: British and American Efforts to Control Air Pollution, 1860-1914," *Environmental History* (1999), 4: 6-31.

moved away from realism. This may have been partly because of the invention of photography, which to some people made realistic painting seem no longer needed. But it was also tied to transcendentalism, romanticism, and other new, nineteenth-century philosophies that held that there were other ways of knowing things besides reason – that emotions, feelings, instincts, and impressions, too, were forms of knowledge. Impressionists did not attempt to create exact replicas of their subject, but rather to give an impression of their essence. Impressionism focused on the subject's color and connection to other things more than its exact shape. Painters like Frenchmen Eduoard Manet (1832-83), Claude Monet (1840-1926), Paul Gauguin (1848-1903), Auguste Renoir (1841-1919), Georges Seurat (1859-91), Paul Cezanne (1839-1906), and Vincent van Gogh (1853-90), and the American Mary Cassatt (1844-1926), peered beyond the mundane corporeality of their subjects and hunted the hidden truths within. Ultimately, impressionism said more about the feelings and attitudes of the artists themselves than it did about their subjects.[275]

Reform Movements

Numerous new social reform movements sprang up in the West during the Golden Age. The era's relative peace and stability, the galloping prosperity brought by the Second Industrial Revolution, the emphasis on equality that was the legacy of the not-yet-distant Age of Revolution, and the faith in progress that had been engendered by industrialization – these things combined to make people more open to change and reform. Among the most important of these new reforms were the movement to abolish slavery, the movement for women's rights generally and woman suffrage in particular, the movement to eliminate property qualifications for voting, the movement to improve workplace safety, the movement to abolish child labor, the union movement, conservation, temperance, dietary reform, the movement to create insane asylums and nursing hospitals, and the movement to prevent cruelty to animals. For most of the reformers, the first step was moral suasion – attempting to persuade other people that reform was both desirable and possible, and to undertake it voluntarily. But when reform proved slow in coming, many of the reformers turned to the government to right perceived wrongs.

The Abolition of slavery. Throughout the West, slavery came under ever-increasing attack. Many classical liberals – including Benjamin Franklin, Thomas Paine, and a young British Member of Parliament named William Wilberforce (1759-1833) – came to believe that slavery violated the slaves' basic human right to personal liberty, and thus should be abolished quickly by government fiat. The former American President Thomas Jefferson (1743-1826), himself a slave owner, endorsed a more gradual form of emancipation, in which the government freed the slaves slowly, compensated the masters for their loss, and resettled the freedmen in Africa. Convinced that "whites" and "blacks" could never live together in harmony, Jefferson (along with fellow former President James Madison, President James Monroe, Speaker of the House Henry Clay, Chief Justice John Marshall, and Senator Daniel Webster) helped found the American Colonization Society in 1817. In 1821 the Society purchased a parcel of land in West Africa from local chieftains (an action of dubious legality) and named it Liberia. The first clutch of colonists (they were free blacks, not slaves, for the U. S. government had not yet abolished slavery) arrived in Liberia in 1822 and founded the port town of Monrovia as the capital. In 1847 the Society turned over control of Liberia to the colonists, and it became a semi-autonomous American protectorate – which meant that legally Liberia was an independent republic, but everyone understood that it remained under American protection and economic control. Earlier, Britain had come up with a similar plan, founding the British crown colony of Sierra Leone, also in West Africa, with Freetown as its capital, as a home for British free blacks. There were, however, serious problems with colonization as a means to abolish slavery. First, it relied on voluntary emancipation, and few masters were willing to part with their slaves voluntarily. As a result, only a tiny fraction of American and British slaves made their way to Liberia and Sierra Leone. Most of the colonists were blacks who had already been free. Second, most African-Americans and Afro-Britishers didn't want to move to Africa. James Forten, an American free black and Revolutionary War veteran, a man who was born and lived in Philadelphia, spoke for the majority of Western blacks when he declared that the West, not Africa, was his real home. Third, from the very beginning the colonists in Liberia and Sierra Leone faced violent opposition from the native Africans, who regarded the land as theirs and the newcomers as just another type of Western invader. For generations to come the two groups – colonists and natives – would battle each other in long, draining wars. These struggles continue even today.[276]

---

[275] Sullivan, *Short History of Western Civilization*, 587-594, 600-602; Hendrik Willem van Loon, *The Arts* (1937), 551-560..

[276] M. B. Akpan, "Black Imperialism: Americo-Liberian Rule over the African Peoples of Liberia, 1841-1964," *Canadian Journal of African Studies* (1974), 7: 217-236; Frankie Hutton, "Economic Considerations in the American Colonization Society's Early Effort to Emigrate Free Blacks to Liberia, 1816-36," *Journal of Negro History* (1983), 68: 376-389; Donald Spivey, *The Politics of Miseducation: The Booker T. Washington Institute of Liberia, 1929-1984* (1986), passim; George Brown Tindall and David E. Shi, *America: A Narrative History* (1992), 580-581; George E. Brooks, Jr., "The Providence African Society's Sierra Leone Emigration Scheme, 1794-1795: Prologue to the African Colonization Movement," *International Journal of African Historical Studies* (1974), 7: 183-202.

Despite the arguments of anti-slavery advocates like Franklin and Wilberforce, most classical liberals actually opposed abolition, because like Jefferson, they believed that it would constitute an undue interference with the "property rights" of the masters. Thomas Paine had given the abolitionists a good rejoinder to this specious objection when he had observed in *The Rights of Man*, "Man has no property in man," but for most classical liberals the issue wasn't so simple. They found themselves torn between their beliefs in human rights on the one hand and their adherence to property rights on the other, and it wasn't always easy for them to decide which should take precedence. Ultimately, the deep stranglehold that racism had on Western culture prevented most classical liberals from viewing blacks as real people. Only whites, many reasoned, could truly be said to have rights. Many Westerners would doubtless have agreed with the Chief Justice of the United States Roger Taney when he wrote in 1857 in the case of *Dred Scott v. Sandford*, "the black man has for more than a century been regarded as...so far inferior, that he has no rights which the white man is bound to respect."[277]

For their part, early socialists like Karl Marx generally opposed slavery as an especially loathsome form of worker exploitation. Some early nationalists opposed it, too, because it infringed on the national rights of Africans. While the best-known abolitionists were white men like Franklin, Wilberforce, the American anti-slavery crusader William Lloyd Garrison (1805-70), or the American poet John Greenleaf Whittier (1807-92) – the majority were actually black men and black and white women, comparatively unsung heroes like Olaudah Equiano (c. 1745-97), Frederick Douglass (1818-95), Mary Prince (c. 1788 - c. 1835), Harriet Jacobs (1813-97), Sojourner Truth (1797-1883), Susanna Strickland Moodie (1803-85), Lydia Maria Child (1802-80), and Elizabeth Cady Stanton (1815-1902).

As we have seen, France was the first Western country to outlaw slavery, during the radical stage of the French Revolution. But, as we have also seen, the dictator Napoleon I restored it, which in turn prompted a massive slave revolt in the French colony of Haiti. As you already know, the revolt succeeded, Haiti became an independent country, and its new government outlawed slavery permanently, the first Western (or semi-Western) country to do so. Likewise, following the American Revolution the Northern province-states of the new United States of America also abolished slavery – Massachusetts, New Hampshire, and Vermont immediately in the 1780s, the others more gradually thereafter. However, slavery remained firmly in place in the Southern states. In 1807 Britain abolished the transatlantic slave trade for itself and its colonies. The United States quickly followed suit, but that was only because the Southern states already had all the slaves they needed. Some of the Latin American republics also abolished slavery, upon independence, including Mexico in 1821 – an action that eventually precipitated the Texas War of Independence.

But the biggest blow came when Britain, the West's military and economic superpower and – with its lucrative sugar colonies in the West Indies – one of the world's major slave-owning countries, abolished slavery in the 1830s. Abolitionist activity in Britain, begun by Wilberforce and others in the 1790s, had taken off in the 1820s. Between 1826 and 1832 British abolitionists flooded Parliament with more than 3,500 petitions demanding an end to slavery. Activists published thousands of abolitionist books and pamphlets, founded the Anti-Slavery Society, and even printed an abolitionist newspaper, the *Anti-Slavery Reporter*. In 1833-34 Parliament at last voted to outlaw slavery throughout the Empire. By 1838 the new law was in full effect. Moreover, the British, not wanting to have to compete at a disadvantage with slaveholding countries like Spain and Brazil, also attempted – with mixed results – to suppress the entire Atlantic slave trade.

Following abolition in Britain, the other Western countries somewhat reluctantly followed suit. The last to give up slavery were the United States in the 1860s and Brazil in the 1870s, and in both countries it took a war to do it. In most places slavery was quickly replaced either by contract labor or by sharecropping, where the former slaves became tenants of their former masters and paid a portion ("share") of their crops as rent. And although slavery had been abolished, racism continued, too deeply rooted into Western culture to be quickly overcome. Alas, almost nowhere in the West were blacks granted full equality with whites.[278]

Factory reform. Appalled by the long hours and dangerous working conditions in the factories, people like Charles Dickens called for reform. In particular, they advocated reducing the workday to ten hours, eliminating child labor; and redesigning machinery to provide for safer working conditions. But unlike abolitionism, few of these proposals were put into effect.

Women's Rights. The nineteenth century also witnessed the birth of a vocal women's rights movement. Feminists had several goals: equal pay for equal work, equal access to work, equal access to education, equal access to property, and fairer divorce laws. Women workers received on average only half the wages men received for the same or similar work, and the best jobs – doctor, lawyer, business executive – were closed to them. Most colleges would not accept them. Married women's wages and property, even what they had owned before marriage, legally belonged to their husbands. Divorce was only rarely granted, and even then the father normally received custody of the children. The feminists' key demand – and the most difficult to achieve – was the right to vote. But, with few exceptions, woman suffrage would not be achieved until after 1914.

Temperance. People today usually consider temperance the most baffling of the nineteenth-century reform movements. Yet in its heyday it had many thousands of ardent advocates. Temperance supporters (most of whom were white Protestant women) believed that the West suffered from acute alcoholism, and that "the

---

[277] Tindall, *America*, 617-618.
[278] Seymour Drescher, "Whose Abolition? Popular Pressure and the Ending of the British Slave Trade," *Past and Present* (1994), 143: 136-166; Audrey Smedley, *Race in North America: Origin and Evolution of a Worldview* (1999), 201-225.

demon rum" lay at the root of most social problems. They attempted to persuade tipplers (mostly men) to "sign the pledge," which meant to voluntarily stop drinking. Temperance was never very popular in Catholic countries, in part because wine was an integral part of the Catholic liturgy. But in Protestant countries like Great Britain, the United States, and most of Canada, it had many advocates.

The irony is that the rate of alcoholism was probably actually on the decline. Admittedly, it was still a serious problem, but not as much as in the gin-soaked 1700s. But it only *appeared* to be growing more widespread in the 1800s, because the rapid growth of cities had led to an increase in the number of visible saloons and bars. Moreover, city people needed alcohol. As industrialization intensified and the cities grew, the old Medieval sanitation systems – privies, chamber pots, open ditches in the middle of the streets – had quickly become inadequate. The profusion of privies contaminated the backyard wells that supplied most urban people with their drinking water. Bacterial diseases like cholera soon rampaged through urban areas, killing millions. With no refrigeration for milk or juice, beer and wine were often the safest beverages, especially for the new urban working class. By mid-century, most cities had at least one saloon on every block.

The worst drinkers were men, because social custom gave them easier access to alcohol. In most places women were not allowed to patronize the smoke-filled, profanity-laced saloons, which consequently functioned as all-male hangouts. The scene of a wife shivering outside in the family buckboard while her husband toed the bar inside, drinking his wages, became all too familiar. To encourage drinking, the saloons provided their customers with "free lunches," which were laced with thirst-inducing salt (hence the expression, "there's no such thing as a free lunch"), but which nevertheless attracted many poorly paid factory workers. The barkeeps also promulgated the custom that it would be impolite for their customers not to treat each other to rounds of drinks.[279]

Labor unions. To gain higher wages and better working conditions, workers not infrequently united to form trade unions, also known as labor unions. The object was to get all the workers in a particular shop or factory to join the union, which would then attempt to negotiate on their behalf with the employer, a process known as collective bargaining. Each side in such a negotiation had potential power – the employer could threaten to fire the workers or withhold their pay (known as a lockout), but the workers could threaten to withhold their labor (known as a strike), a real threat if the factory was under deadline to fill an order, or if there was a labor shortage. In order to succeed, however, the unions needed solidarity; in other words, the workers had to stick together, or the whole thing would fall apart. Workers who defied the union and worked during a strike were called scabs and were ostracized, and occasionally threatened with violence. In the Golden Age, unions faced three major obstacles that few of them could overcome: lack of solidarity, intimidation and threats by employers and professional strikebreakers such as the Pinkerton Detective Agency, and pro-employer laws that made strikes illegal in most Western countries. Like suffragists, unionists had little success before 1914.

The New Imperialism

In 1884 representatives from several powerful Western states met in Berlin, where they had been invited by Germany's "Iron Chancellor," Otto von Bismarck. Before the Berlin Conference adjourned, France, Britain, Germany, Belgium, Portugal, Italy, and Spain had agreed to divide Africa among them like a giant pizza pie. Thirty years later the European conquest of Africa was nearly complete and the plan put forth at the Berlin Conference was in place. France ended up with the biggest slice, measuring 4,086,950 square miles. But Britain took 3,701,411 square miles, Germany 910,150, Belgium 900,000, Portugal 787,500, Italy 600,000, and Spain 79,800. Only 393,000 square miles remained, and that was only because France had secretly provided Ethiopia with enough firepower to drive off an Italian invasion force, because France hoped someday to acquire Ethiopia for itself.

Earlier, in the Age of Revolution, the European colonial powers had lost most of their lucrative American colonies. France had lost Canada to Britain in 1763 in the French and Indian War, and then Haiti in 1801 in the Haitian Revolution, leaving it with only Guadeloupe, Martinique, and a few other small sugar islands, hardly a magnificent empire. Britain had lost its prized Thirteen Colonies in 1781 in the American Revolution, although it retained Canada (until 1867), Jamaica, Barbados, Antigua, Bermuda, and a few other small islands. In 1822 Portugal had lost Brazil, which became an independent monarchy. Spain, too, had lost the majority of its American colonies by 1822, including Mexico, Argentina, Peru, and Venezuela, retaining only Cuba and Puerto Rico. But now, in the nineteenth century, the West moved to replace its lost colonies with new ones in Africa, Asia, Australia, and the Pacific Islands, a monstrous land grab known as the New Imperialism.

One of the reasons that the New Imperialism was "new" was that it involved seizing new colonies in new places at a new time. But it was also "new" because, unlike the earlier conquest of the Americas, this "second expansion of the West" was closely linked to industrialization.

Industrialization explains why the new Western imperial powers – Britain, France, Portugal, Spain, the Netherlands, Belgium, Germany, Italy, Denmark, and the United States – wanted new colonies. There were two principal reasons. First, the new colonies would provide abundant supplies of industrial raw materials like

---

[279] Merriman, *History of Modern Europe*, 883-884; Pierre Berton, *My Country: The Remarkable Past* (1976, 2002), 242-256 (Berton is a Canadian).

cotton (a semi-tropical plant that would not grow in Europe), rubber (a tropical plant), sugar (another tropical plant), tea, coffee, cacao (factory owners preferred their workers to drink stimulants rather than depressants like alcohol), nickel, zinc, bauxite (for aluminum), and oil, all of which were in short supply in Europe. Thus the Netherlands seized the rest of the islands of the Dutch East Indies (today's Indonesia) not for the spices that grew there (the reason it had conquered Java in the 1700s), but because they sat atop a large pool of oil. To extract the oil, a well-financed consortium of Dutch and British entrepreneurs founded a mammoth new corporation, Royal Dutch Shell, which soon became one of the world's largest energy companies. Likewise, Britain conquered India not for spices, but so that the British East India Company would have a ready supply of cotton – and, as it turned out, opium (which grew in India) and tea (which the Company transplanted from China). Another colony, British East Africa (today's Kenya) supplied more cotton, tea, and coffee. Nigeria had oil. Malaya, yet another British colony, provided rubber, once British botanists figured out how to transplant rubber trees from Brazil. France, Belgium, Portugal, and Germany were able to extract large quantities of rubber, cotton, coffee, tea, and minerals from their colonies in Africa. The United States acquired sugar from Hawaii and rubber from Liberia.

The West also wanted colonies to serve as captive markets for its oversupply of industrial products. Overproduction had driven down prices, but finding new markets abroad could push them back up again. It was to force the Chinese to accept the British East India Company's surplus of opium that Britain fought the Opium War with China in the 1840s. To ensure that the teeming masses of its colony of India bought only British-made cotton products, the British government taxed the Indian cotton weavers out of business. Unable any longer to make their living as crafters, the weavers fled the cities and went out into the countryside looking for land to farm. But there were too many of them and too little land, and the countryside quickly became overpopulated. As a consequence, the overcrowded Indian farmers were forced to grow more and more crops on land and less land. Those who couldn't make the transition starved. The British royal governor Lord Bentinck, who opposed his country's policies, commented sadly in 1834, "The bones of the cotton-weavers are bleaching the plains of India." Something similar occurred in Ireland, another British colony, where wealthy, Protestant, Anglo-Irish planters owned the majority of the farmland and used it to grow wheat to sell in England. Only small drabs of farmland were left for the poor, Catholic, Irish farmers, who needed it to grow food, and had no choice but to plant every acre with potatoes, a New World "miracle crop" introduced to Europe during the Columbian Exchange that produced more calories per unit of land than wheat, oats, or barley. But in the 1840s potato blight (a fungus that attacks potato plants) struck the potato fields, killing most of the poor people's crops. Irish peasants starved by the thousands.

The phenomenon of crowding more and more people onto less and less farmland, and thus forcing them to cultivate their land ever more intensively while using only traditional farm tools, is known as involution. In many ways, involution is the opposite of industrialization. With industrialization, people react to overpopulation by inventing new and more efficient ways to produce more goods, and thus muddle through with minimal harm. But when people were not permitted to industrialize, they had little choice but to involute instead, for even if they had access to modern, industrial farm machinery (which they didn't), it would not have been cost-effective on a tiny farm of only a few acres. Ultimately, involution brought decline. Often, it brought famine as well. And it occurred in most of the new Western colonies in Africa and Asia.[280]

If a desire for raw materials and captive markets help explain why the West wanted to establish new colonies in the nineteenth century, new technologies explain how it was able to pull it off. Before the 1800s, the West had been unable to conquer vast territories in Asia and Africa; the people who lived there were too numerous, their states too mighty, and their technology too advanced. There few Western colonies that existed in Asia and Africa before 1750 were either small city-states like Malacca and Goa, or underpopulated regions like Cape Colony. The only reason the West had been able to conquer the Americas is because microscopic organisms – germs to which the Native Americans had no natural immunities – aided them. In the nineteenth century germs did facilitate the conquest of Australia and the Pacific Islands, as well, for like the Native Americans the peoples who lived in there lacked previous exposure to Europeans diseases. But Asians and Africans had long shared the same germ pool with the Europeans, and consequently had the same immunities. In fact, those Asians and Africans who lived in tropical areas had even *more* immunities than the Europeans, for they also had been exposed to malaria, yellow fever, and yaws. It was not disease that would aid the West this time. It was technology.

Industrialization had produced several new technologies that, for the time being, were available to the West but not to the Asians and Africans. According to the historian Daniel Headrick, the most important of these new "tools of empire" were quinine (a medicine that permitted Westerners to treat and control malaria), ironclad steamships (which permitted them to move troops, supplies, and goods in mass, and gave their navies a decided advantage over the Asians, who still used wooden sailing ships), steam shovels and bulldozers (which permitted them to construct the Suez Canal, Panama Canal, and numerous railroads), the railroad itself, the telegraph cable, and – most important of all – advanced weaponry in the form of rifles, breechloaders,

---

[280] Sullivan, *Short History of Western Civilization*, 627-637; Clifford Geertz, *Agricultural Involution: The Process of Ecological Change in Indonesia* (1963), passim; Jawaharlal Nehru, *The Discovery of India* (1941), passim; Henry Hobhouse, *Seeds of Change: Five Plants that Transformed Mankind* (1985), passim (the five plants are cinchona [from which quinine is made], sugarcane, tea, cotton, and the potato).

repeaters, and machine guns. It was a powerful arsenal, and Asia and Africa were not able to match it. Or, as one Westerner phrased it, "Whatever happens, we have got / The Maxim gun, and they have not."[281]

Western Colonies in 1914

British colonies: India, Burma, Ceylon, Afghanistan, Nepal, Malaya, Hong Kong, Australia, Samoa, Tonga, Fiji, Basutoland, Bechuanaland, Nyasaland, Rhodesia, British East Africa, Uganda, Zanzibar, British Somaliland, Nigeria, Gold Coast, Sierra Leone, Gambia, Egypt, Anglo-Egyptian Sudan, Jamaica, British Guiana, Ireland, numerous small islands.

British self-governing dominions: Canada, Newfoundland, Australia, New Zealand, South Africa.

British protectorates: Siam, Persia.

French colonies: Tunisia, Algeria, Morocco, French West Africa, French Congo, French Somaliland, Madagascar, Indochina, French Polynesia, numerous small islands.

German colonies: German East Africa, South-West Africa, Cameroon, Togoland, Papua New Guinea.

American colonies: Alaska, Puerto Rico, Cuba, American Virgin Islands, Canal Zone, American Samoa, Guam, Philippines, Hawaii, several small islands.

American protectorate: Liberia, Panama, Nicaragua, Haiti, Dominican Republic.

Belgian colony: Congo State.

Italian colonies: Eritrea, Italian Somaliland, Libya.

Dutch colonies: Dutch East Indies, several small islands.

Portuguese colonies: Portuguese Guinea, Portuguese West Africa, Portuguese East Africa, Portuguese Timor, Macao, Cape Verde Islands, several small islands.

Spanish colonies: Rio de Oro, Muni River Settlements, several small islands.

Danish colonies: Iceland, Greenland.

Migration

Elizabeth Vondy Hawbolt's careworn face stares intriguingly out of an old black-and-white photograph. The photo was taken sometime in the late 1800s, when Elizabeth was an older woman. She stands next to her seated sister, Sophia, holding a photograph in her right hand: perhaps it is of her deceased husband, perhaps not: it is impossible to tell. Typical of the times, Elizabeth wears modest, black-and-white widow's weeds that cover her from her feet to her high, buttoned collar. Her graying hair is parted severely in the middle and fastened tightly behind her head. Her only jewelry is a simple brooch at her throat and a watch chain at her waist. Her lined face has no make-up. She seems eminently practical and thoroughly Victorian, except that – quite unexpectedly – a slight, mischievous smile flits across her full lips, and a strange sparkle glints in her wide, watery eyes. That – and fact that she remains to this day an honest-to-gosh hero, still venerated more than a century later in her hometown of Chatham, New Brunswick, Canada – makes you want to know more about her. This is her story.[282]

The nineteenth century was an age of migration, and it was migration – the migration of other people, not of Elizabeth herself – that created the conditions under which this woman, who never spent a day of her life outside of her native New Brunswick, became a hero. Nineteenth-century industrialization had triggered one of the greatest mass migrations in Western History. The historian Kevin Reilly writes: "'Workers of the world, unite!' was the concluding call of the *Communist Manifesto*. [But] in fact, the call of capitalism might have been 'workers of the world, disperse,' [for] the great age of capitalist industrialization…witnessed one of the greatest

---

[281] Daniel R. Headrick, *The Tools of Empire: Technology and European Imperialism in the Nineteenth Century* (1981), passim.
[282] Caroline Daley and Anna Springer, *Middle Island: Before and After the Tragedy* (2002), 90.

mass population movements in world history."[283] According to the anthropologist Eric Wolf, not one but three principal waves of migration occurred in the West during the nineteenth century. The first wave took place during the beginning stages of industrialization and featured the movement of rural people into nearby cities to take the new factory jobs, as Harriet Hanson Robinson described in chapter six. The second wave was more dramatic: a mass migration of underemployed factory workers and displaced peasants from overpopulated Europe to less crowded places overseas, and which took place mostly between 1840 and 1914. Approximately fifty million people left Europe during this time, far exceeding the paltry two million who had emigrated in the three centuries between 1492 and 1800. About thirty-two million of the migrants went to the United States, but other important destinations included Argentina, Brazil, Australia, New Zealand, and – significantly – Elizabeth's own Canada. Most of the migrants were poor workers looking for jobs, either as factory hands or as farm laborers. They included thousands of men, women, and children from rural Ireland who in the 1840s and 1850s went to the United States and Canada. The third wave of migrants consisted of various subject peoples who had been born in the colonies, but who subsequently moved either to other colonies or, less frequently, to Europe or the United States. [284]

Many of the Irish who left Europe did so to escape the infamous Irish Potato Famine of the 1840s. Although the chief destination for most of the Irish was the United States, the very poorest among them often went to Canada instead, because transportation to Canada was cheaper. In those days, hundreds of timber ships sailed each year from Canada for Europe, laden with much-needed cargoes of boards, planks, and other lumber destined to be used to construct the new cities and factories of the Industrial Revolution. Cheap, simply made, uncomfortable, and frequently unseaworthy, these timber ships were crude and dangerous vessels and predictably had a tough time finding cargoes for the return voyage to Canada. So, frequently they took people instead of goods – dozens, sometimes hundreds of people – poor Irish, English, and Scots migrants who couldn't afford passage on one of the better ships, and so crowded into the tiny berths the owners had hastily constructed in the timber ships' otherwise empty holds. Because the timber ships were unsafe, the crews surly and ill paid, and the passengers frequently already suffering from infectious diseases, the death rates on these voyages were appalling. Canadians nicknamed them "the coffin ships."

On 17 April, 1847, the timber ship *Looshtauk* departed Liverpool, England, bound for Quebec, with a "cargo" of 462 poor Irish emigrants, most of whom had been living for several months in Liverpool's overcrowded, pestilential, portside shanties while awaiting passage. The ship's Canadian captain was a good man, rotund and genial, an experienced mariner with a thick beard and friendly eyes, named John Mount Thain. His first mate, George McAuley, was an idealistic, hardworking, young Briton who had only recently been married.

Only five days out to sea, two of the passengers on the *Looshtauk* became ill, probably with typhus. Thain quickly moved them out of the hold and onto the deck, where (he hoped) they would have the fresh air needed to recover and – more importantly – not infect the other passengers, who were still below deck. But two days later, eight more passengers took ill. Faced with a swiftly spreading epidemic, Thain ordered all the passengers out on deck and fumigated the hold with sulfur smoke, chloride, and lime, under the prevailing (but false) theory that disease was caused by miasmas, or bad-smelling air, and that removing the smells would halt the disease. It didn't work. The next day another passenger, a young woman, came down with what was probably scarlet fever. The two sicknesses – scarlet fever and typhus – spread rapidly, killing several of the children. After seventeen days at sea the entire crew except for Thain and McAuley were sick with either typhus or scarlet fever, and more passengers were taking ill each day. Fighting a turbulent Atlantic gale and enduring long, exhausting watches, the two men, Thain and McAuley, somehow got the *Looshtauk* across the Atlantic. But when they tried to enter the safe harbor of Sydney, Nova Scotia (the first port they came to), the harbor pilot, fearful of the disease, refused to board the ship and guide it into port. Grimly, the now-desperate Thain sailed on. Low on supplies, hungry for food and medical attention, too tired to sail on all the way to Quebec, he maneuvered the *Looshtauk* into New Brunswick's Miramichi River and its small port town of Chatham.

The authorities at Chatham were alarmed, as afraid of the disease as the pilot at Sydney had been. Thus, adhering to provincial law, they refused to permit the *Looshtauk's* passengers to disembark. Instead, they ordered Thain to moor the ship a few miles downriver, next to Middle Island, a small, isolated ait that the province sometimes used as a quarantine station for ships like the *Looshtauk* that had sickness. Up and down the North American seacoast, other municipal authorities had established similar quarantine stations, usually located on small, isolated islands like Middle Island. A Chatham businessman, Joseph Cunard, a shipbuilder and lumberman who would later would become world-famous as the founder of the Cunard steamship line, organized a drive to provide the passengers and crew with food. Cunard also dispatched some of his employees to hastily erect a few crude shelters on the island.

The sick passengers and crew needed more than food and shelter, however. They also needed a doctor. The town's two senior physicians refused to treat them, fearful that they, too, would contract disease. Finally, John Vondy, the town's youngest doctor, volunteered to go to Middle Island. The authorities told him flatly that they would not permit him to return until the quarantine was lifted, but Vondy was in his twenties, an idealistic young man with most of his life ahead of him, recently admitted to practice, and engaged to be married, and so

---

[283] Kevin Reilly, *Readings in World Civilizations* (1988), 2: 149.
[284] Eric R. Wolf, *Europe and the People Without History* (1982), excerpted in Reilly, *Readings in World Civilizations*, 149-160; Roger Daniels, *Coming to America: A History of Immigration and Ethnicity in American Life* (1990), 121-285.

he went anyway. In an old sepia-tone photograph Vondy appears serious and thin, with fluffy sideburns, a big bowtie, and a mammoth Canadian beaver-fur hat. He had his sister Elizabeth's wide, watery eyes, but not her mischievous smile.

Vondy, Thain, and McAuley carried the sick passengers and crew from the ship to the island. Some were housed in the hastily built shanties. Others were put in tents that they constructed from the ship's sails. Others slept only on planks laid on the ground. With no place to properly store the food that the locals had given them, it soon turned rancid, and those who ate it came down with dysentery on top of everything else. Moreover, two more ships also entered Chatham harbor, also carrying disease, further straining the situation at Middle Island, which was now a cauldron of several different diseases infecting everyone at once. The quarantine was extended. The idealistic young first mate McAuley took sick and died. Thain became feverish and incoherent, and almost died. Vondy, too, became sick, and eventually died. The situation was desperate.

When word reached Elizabeth Vondy in Chatham that her physician brother was dying, she went to Middle Island to care for him and the other victims. Although women were not, in those days, permitted to be doctors, Elizabeth came from an educated family and knew something of medicine; perhaps she had even assisted John in his practice, the historical record does not say. In any case, she arrived just in time to see her brother die. Trapped on the island (the authorities would not permit her to return until the quarantine was lifted), she now took over his duties and nursed the sick. Under her care, Thain recovered, as did most of the passengers and crew. Of the 462 men, women, and children who had boarded the *Looshtauk* in Liverpool, 146 died at sea and 96 perished on Middle Island, but 220 survived. Of the survivors, 53 eventually continued on to Quebec, but 167 decided to settle in New Brunswick, joining the province's already rapidly expanding community of Irish-Canadian immigrants. Too poor to buy farms or businesses of their own, most of the newcomers took jobs in the busy shipyards, sawmills, and lumber camps, swelling the ranks of Chatham's working class. Many of their descendants are still there, solid citizens and valued community members in Chatham and surrounding communities. Irish names are commonplace in the Chatham telephone book. Elizabeth Vondy, too, went on with her life, was married and then widowed. Like most of the survivors of the *Looshtauk*, she, too, spent the rest of her days in Chatham.[285]

Today Middle Island is a public park, connected to the mainland by a stone causeway. At the east end, in the middle of a wide grassy area often used by locals for picnics and concerts, the province of New Brunswick has thoughtfully erected a large, granite Celtic cross as a monument to the passengers who suffered there. A nearby plaque salutes John and Elizabeth Vondy for their heroism in caring for the sick. The Roman Catholic Church (most of the passengers had been Catholic) has consecrated the site as an official Catholic cemetery, and every now and again a piece of bone is washed out of some forgotten grave by the pounding north wind that blows off the cold Gulf of Saint Lawrence. Local historians have written down and published the story of the Vondys, Thain, McAuley, and the others, so that those who died and those who survived, those who behaved heroically and those who were more ordinary, might not be forgotten. Plain folk all, their story was just one of the many chapters in the larger saga of the coffin ships and the great migrations of the nineteenth century that spread the Western peoples across the globe.

-The Documents-

Abolition: Mary Prince and Susanna Strickland Moodie

As part of the anti-slavery activity in 1820s and 1830s Britain and the United States, several former slaves published "slave narratives" – autobiographical accounts of their lives under slavery. One of these narratives was that of Mary Prince (c. 1788 – c. 1835), who dictated her story to a young anti-slavery activist, Susanna Strickland (1803-85) (later Susanna Moodie), who subsequently moved to Canada and became a well-known writer.[286] Mary Prince was born c. 1788 in the British colony of Bermuda, the daughter of African-American slaves. While in her early teens her master sold her to Captain Ingham, the owner of a small merchant ship. She worked for Ingham for several years as a domestic servant before being sold again, to Mr. D------, who owned a salt works on Turks Island in the West Indies. There Mary worked as a laborer, shoveling salt in a large evaporation pond under a hot sun. Conditions in the salt works were brutal, and Mary suffered several debilitating injuries. In her early twenties she was sold yet again, to the Wood family who lived on Antigua, another island colony in the British West Indies. Mary worked for the Woods as a domestic servant. She married a free black carpenter and converted to Christianity. In 1727, when she was about 39 years old, the Woods took her with them on a trip to England, even though Parliament had recently outlawed slavery there. Realizing that she was now legally free, Mary left the Woods and moved in with the family of Thomas Pringle, a noted anti-slavery activist, for whom she worked as a domestic servant – for wages, this time. She hoped to earn enough money to allow her husband to join her in Britain. She had no children. Her narrative was

---

[285] Daley, *Middle Island*, 40-69.
[286] Charlotte Gray, *Sisters in the Wilderness: The Lives of Susanna Moodie and Catharine Parr Traill* (1999), 23-38.

published in 1831. Little is known of her life after that. It is generally believed that she died only a few years later, of complications from injuries she sustained while she was a slave.[287]

from THE HISTORY OF MARY PRINCE, A WEST INDIAN SLAVE,
RELATED BY HERSELF [288]

I was born at Brackish-Pond, in Bermuda, on a farm belonging to Mr. Charles Myners. My mother was a household slave; and my father, whose name was Prince, was a sawyer belonging to Mr. Trimmingham, a ship-builder at Crow Lane.

* * * *

[Mary learned that she was to be separated from her family and sold.]
The black morning at length came; it came too soon for my poor mother and us. Whilst she was putting on us the new [dresses] in which we were to be sold, she said in a sorrowful voice, (I shall never forget it!) "See, I am shrouding my poor children; what a task for a mother!" Our mother, weeping as she went, called me away with [my sisters], and we took the road to [Hamilton, the colonial capital], which we reached about four o'clock in the afternoon. We followed my mother to the market-place, where she placed us in a row against a large house, with our backs to the wall and our arms folded across our breasts. I, as the eldest, stood first, Hannah next to me, then Dinah; and our mother stood beside, crying over us. My heart throbbed with grief and terror so violently, that I pressed my hands quite tightly across my breast, but I could not keep it still, and it continued to leap as though it would burst out of my body. But who cared for that? Did one of the many bystanders, who were looking at us so carelessly, think of the pain that wrung the hearts of the Negro woman and her young ones? No, no! They were not all bad, I dare say, but slavery hardens white people's hearts towards the blacks; and many of them were not slow to make their remarks upon us aloud, without regard to our grief – though their light words fell like cayenne on the fresh wounds of our hearts. Oh those white people have small hearts who can only feel for themselves.

* * * *

My new master was a Captain Ingham, who lived at Spanish Point. After parting with my mother and sisters, I followed him to his store, and he gave me into the charge of his son, a lad about my own age, Master Benjy, who took me to my new home. When I went in, I stood crying in a corner. Mrs. Ingham came and took off my hat, and said in a rough voice, "You are not come here to stand up in corners and cry, you are come here to work." She then put a child into my arms, and, tired as I was, I was forced instantly to take up my occupation of a nurse. I could not bear to look at my mistress, her countenance was so stern. She was a stout tall woman with a very dark complexion, and her brows were always drawn together into a frown.

The person I took the most notice of that night was a French-speaking black woman called Hetty, whom my master took in privateering from a French ship, and made his slave. She was the most active woman I ever saw, and she was tasked to her utmost. A few minutes after my arrival she came in from milking the cows, and put the sweet potatoes on for supper. She then fetched home the sheep and penned them in the fold; drove home the cattle and staked them about the pond side; fed and rubbed down my master's horse and gave the hog and the fed cow their suppers; prepared the beds, undressed the children, and laid them to sleep. I liked to look at her and watch all her doings, for hers was the only friendly face I had yet seen, and I felt glad that she was there. She gave me my supper of potatoes and milk, and a blanket to sleep upon, which she spread for me in the passage before the door of Mrs. Ingham's chamber.

I got a sad fright that night. I was just going to sleep, when I heard a noise in my mistress's room; and she presently called out to inquire if some work was finished that she

---

[287] Moira Ferguson, "Introduction," in Mary Prince, *The History of Mary Prince, A West Indian Slave, Related by Herself*, ed. Moira Ferguson (1831, 1997), 1-51.
[288] Mary Prince, *The History of Mary Prince, A West Indian Slave, Related by Herself*, ed. Moira Ferguson (1831, 1997), 57, 61-67, 71-75.

ordered Hetty to do. "No, Ma'am, not yet," was Hetty's answer from below. On hearing this, my master started up from his bed, and just as he was, in his nightshirt, ran downstairs with a long cow-skin in his hand. I heard immediately after the cracking of the thong, and the house rang to the shrieks of poor Hetty, who kept crying out, "Oh, Massa! Massa! Me dead, Massa! Have mercy upon me – don't kill me outright." This was a sad beginning for me. I sat up upon my blanket, trembling with terror, like a frightened hound, and thinking that my turn would come next.

The next morning my mistress set about instructing me in my tasks. She taught me to do all sorts of household work: to wash and bake, pick cotton and wool, and wash floors, and cook. And she taught me to know the exact difference between the smart of the rope, the cart-whip, and the cow-skin, when applied to my naked body by her own cruel hand. And there was scarcely any punishment more dreadful than the blows I received on my face from her hard heavy fist. She was a fearful woman and a savage mistress to her slaves.

There were two little slave boys in the house, on whom she vented her bad temper in a special manner. One of the children was a mulatto, called Cyrus, who had been bought while an infant in his mother's arms; the other, Jack, was an African from the coast of Guinea, whom a sailor had given or sold to may master. Seldom a day passed without these boys receiving the most severe treatment, and often for no fault at all. Both my master and mistress seemed to think that they had a right to ill-use them at their pleasure; and very often accompanied their commands with blows, whether the children were behaving well or ill. I have seen their flesh ragged and raw with licks. Lick – lick – they were never secure one moment from a blow, and their lives were passing in continual fear. My mistress was not contented with using the whip, but often pinched their cheeks and arms in the most cruel manner.

My pity for these poor boys was soon transferred to myself; for I was licked, and flogged, and pinched by her pitiless fingers in the neck and arms, exactly as they were. To strip me naked – to hang me up by the wrists and lay my flesh open with the cow-skin, was ordinarily a punishment for even a slight offence. My mistress often robbed me, too, of the hours that belong to sleep. She used to sit up very late, frequently even until morning, and I had to stand at a bench and wash during the greater part of the night, or pick wool and cotton, and often I have dropped down overcome by sleep and fatigue, till roused from a state of stupor by the whip, and forced to start up my tasks.

Poor Hetty was very kind to me, and I used to call her my Aunt. But she led a most miserable life, and her death was hastened by the dreadful chastisement she received from my master during her pregnancy. It happened as follows. One of the cows had dragged the rope away from the stake to which Hetty had fastened it, and got loose. My master flew into a terrible passion, and ordered the poor creature to be stripped quite naked, notwithstanding her pregnancy, and to be tied up to a tree in the yard. He then flogged her as hard as he could lick, both with the whip and cow-skin, till she was all over streaming with blood. He rested, and then beat her again and again. Her shrieks were terrible. The consequence was that poor Hetty was brought to bed before her time, and was delivered after severe labor of a dead child. She appeared to recover after her confinement, so far that she was repeatedly flogged by both master and mistress afterwards. But her former strength never returned to her. Ere long her body and limbs swelled to a great size. She lay on a mat in the kitchen till the water burst out of her body and she died.

* * * *

[Several years later Mary was sold again.]

My new master was one of the owners of the salt ponds on Turks Island, and he received a small sum for every slave that worked upon his premises, whether they were young or old. This sum was allowed him out of the profits arising from the salt works. I was immediately sent to work in the salt water with the rest of the slaves. I was given a half barrel and a shovel, and had to stand up to my knees in the water from four o'clock in the morning till nine, when we were given some Indian corn boiled in water, which we were obliged to swallow as fast as we could for fear the rain should come and melt the salt. We were then called again to our tasks, and worked through the heat of the day, the sun flaming upon our heads like fire and raising salt blisters in those parts that were not completely covered. Our feet and legs, from standing in the salt water for so many hours, soon became full of dreadful sores, which ate down in some cases to the very bone, afflicting the sufferers with great torment. We came home at twelve, ate our corn soup called blawly as fast as we could, and went back to our employment till dark at night. We then shoveled up the salt in large heaps and went down to the sea, where we washed the salt from our limbs and cleaned the borrows and shovels from the salt. When we returned to the house, our master gave us each our allowance of raw Indian corn, which we pounded ourselves in a mortar and boiled in water for our suppers.

We slept in a long shed, divided into narrow slips, like the walls used for cattle. Boards fixed upon stakes driven into the ground, without mat or covering, were our only beds. On Sundays, after we had washed the salt bags and done other work required of us, we went into the bush and cut the long soft grass, of which we made trusses for our legs and feet to rest upon, for they were so full of sores that we could get no rest lying upon the bare boards.

Mr. D----- had a slave called Old Daniel, whom he used to treat in the most cruel manner. Poor Daniel was lame in the hip and could not keep up with the rest of the slaves. Our master would order him to be stripped and laid down on the ground and have him beaten with a rod of rough briar till his skin was quite red and raw. He would then call for a bucket of salt and fling it upon the raw flesh till the man writhed on the ground like a worm and screamed aloud with agony. This poor man's wounds were never healed, and I have often seen them full of maggots, which increased his torments to an intolerable degree. He was an object of pity and terror to the whole gang of slaves, and in his wretched case we saw, each of us, our own lot, if we should live to be as old.

There was a little old woman among the slaves called Sarah, who was nearly past work. Master Dickey [Mr. D-----'s son] being the overseer of the slaves just then, this poor creature, who was subject to several bodily infirmities and was not quite right in her head, did not wheel the barrow fast enough to please him. He threw her down on the ground, and after beating her severely, he took her up in his arms and flung her among the prickly pear bushes, which are all covered over with sharp venomous prickles. By this her naked flesh was so grievously wounded that her body swelled and festered all over, and she died a few days after.

Woman Suffrage: Elizabeth Cady Stanton

In the summer of 1848, five American abolitionists, Elizabeth Cady Stanton, Lucretia Mott, Martha Wright, Jane Hunt, and Mary Ann McClintock, frustrated that women as well as slaves did not enjoy equal rights in the supposedly democratic United States, organized a women's rights conference in Stanton's hometown of Seneca Falls, New York. And so one nineteenth-century reform movement gave birth to another. About 250 women and men attended the conference. They passed a Declaration of Sentiments, borrowing the format and language directly from the American Declaration of Independence – indicating that, as far as women were concerned, the promise of equality for all embedded in the older document still needed to be fulfilled.

Gerda Lerner points out that the Declaration of Sentiments was issued the same year that Karl Marx and Friedrich Engels published the *Communist Manifesto*. The coincidence, she writes, is fitting, for socialism and feminism were both powerful ideologies that profoundly challenged the old order. Yet unlike socialism, "the small spark figuratively ignited at Seneca Falls never produced revolutions, usurpation of power or wars." However, it did lead "to a transformation of consciousness and a movement of empowerment on behalf of half of the human race, which hardly has its equal in human history…. The women's rights demands first raised at Seneca Falls have in the United States [*today*] been generally achieved for middle-class white women and women of color, [*although*] progress has been very uneven…. Demands that seemed outrageous 150 years ago are now commonly accepted, such as a woman's right to equal guardianship of her children, to divorce, to jury duty, to acceptance in nontraditional occupations…. The acceptance of such ideas is still uneven and different in different places, but generally, the feminist program has been accepted by millions of people who refuse to identify themselves as 'feminists'." Yet, victory – if Lerner is right that feminism won – was slow in coming. It was not until 1920, seventy-two years after Seneca Falls, that woman suffrage – one of the key planks of the Declaration of Sentiments – was enacted throughout the United States. Only one of the women present at Seneca Falls lived long enough to cast a vote.

Still, as Lerner points out, the Seneca Falls conference was the beginning of something important, and as such has great historical meaning. "It shows," she writes, "that a small group of people, armed with a persuasive analysis of grievances and an argument based on generally held moral and religious beliefs" – in other words, making good use of moral suasion – "can, if they are willing to work hard at organizing, create a transformative mass movement. The women who launched a small movement in 1848 had to build, county by county, state by state, the largest grassroots movement of the nineteenth century and then build it again in the twentieth century to transform the right to vote into the right to equal representation." And they did it without "bloodshed, terror, and devastation." [289]

---

[289] Gerda Lerner, "The Meaning of Seneca Falls," *Dissent* (1998), 35-41.

from THE DECLARATION OF SENTIMENTS

When, in the course of human events, it becomes necessary for one portion of the family of man to assume among the people of the earth a position different from that which they have hitherto occupied, but one to which the laws of nature and of nature's God entitle them, a decent respect to the opinions of mankind requires that they should declare the causes that impel them to such a course.

We hold these truths to be self-evident: that all men and women are created equal; that they are endowed by their Creator with certain inalienable rights; that among these are life, liberty, and the pursuit of happiness; that to secure these rights governments are instituted, deriving their just powers from the consent of the governed. Whenever any form of government becomes destructive of these ends, it is the right of those who suffer from it to refuse allegiance to it, and to insist upon the institution of a new government, laying its foundation on such principles, and organizing its powers in such form, as to them shall seem most likely to effect their safety and happiness. Prudence, indeed, will dictate that governments long established should not be changed for light and transient causes; and accordingly all experience hath shown that mankind are more disposed to suffer, while evils are sufferable, than to right themselves by abolishing the forms to which they were accustomed. But when a long train of abuses and usurpations, pursuing invariably the same object evinces a design to reduce them under absolute despotism, it is their duty to throw off such government, and to provide new guards for their future security. Such has been the patient sufferance of the women under this government, and such is now the necessity which constrains them to demand the equal station to which they are entitled.

The history of mankind is a history of repeated injuries and usurpations on the part of man toward woman, having in direct object the establishment of an absolute tyranny over her. To prove this, let facts be submitted to a candid world.

[A long list of grievances followed.]

* * * * *

In entering upon the great work before us, we anticipate no small amount of misconception, misrepresentation, and ridicule; but we shall use every instrumentality within our power to effect our object. We shall employ agents, circulate tracts, petition the State and National legislatures, and endeavor to enlist the pulpit and the press in our behalf. We hope this Convention will be followed by a series of Conventions embracing every part of the country.

* * * * *

[The conference then passed several resolutions.]

Resolved, That all laws which prevent woman from occupying such a station in society as her conscience shall dictate, or which place her in a position inferior to that of man, are contrary to the great precept of nature, and therefore of no force or authority.

Resolved, That woman is man's equal – was intended to be so by the Creator, and the highest good of the race demands that she should be recognized as such.

Resolved, That the women in this country ought to be enlightened in regard to the laws under which they live, that they may no longer publish their degradation by declaring themselves satisfied with their present position, nor their ignorance by asserting that they have all the rights they want.

Resolved, that inasmuch as man, while claiming for himself intellectual superiority, does accord to woman moral superiority, it is preeminently his duty to encourage her to speak and teach, as she has an opportunity, in all religious assemblies.

* * * * *

Resolved, that the objection of indelicacy and impropriety, which is so often brought against woman when she addresses a public audience, comes with a very ill-grace from those who encourage, by their attendance, her presence on the stage, in the concert, or in feats of the circus.

* * * * *

Resolved, that it is the duty of the women of this country to secure to themselves their sacred right to the elective franchise.

Temperance: Frances Willard

Perhaps the best known of the temperance advocates was Frances Elizabeth Caroline Willard (1839-1898), a retired United States university professor. In fact, Willard was involved in many reform movements, but it was as President of the World Women's Christian Temperance Union that she became "the most famous woman in America." Born in rural New York, Willard never married. Instead, she was an example of the so-called "new woman" of the nineteenth century, a middle-class woman who chose a career instead of a family. (It was not until the mid-twentieth century that it was deemed acceptable for a middle-class woman to have both.) Upon graduating from the North-Western Female College in 1859, Willard became an English teacher, eventually rising to become a college professor (one of the first women to do so) and president of Evanston College for Ladies. In 1873 Evanston merged with the previously all-male Northwestern University. Willard was named Dean of Women and assigned to teach English classes to both women and men. Male students reacted badly to having a female put in a position of authority over them, however, and harassed Willard mercilessly. They deliberately squeaked their chairs, locked the doors to her classroom, scrawled graffiti on her blackboard, and even locked a yowling cat in her desk. Faced with such harassment and what was probably a mid-life crisis, Willard resigned, finding herself with no job and an ailing mother to support. Depressed, she joined some friends on a visit to Old Orchard Beach, Maine, for a temperance rally. She was soon hooked on the cause. She became recording secretary of the National Women's Temperance Union in 1874 and was elected president in 1879. In 1883 she organized the World WCTU. She also worked for women's rights and was active in the reform-minded Peoples Party (a farmer rights party) in the 1890s – all before women were permitted to vote in most of the United States. The following excerpt from her autobiography describes how Willard discovered temperance as her cause.

from *MY HAPPY HALF-CENTURY:*
THE AUTOBIOGRAPHY OF AN AMERICAN WOMAN [290]

In June of that year [1874] I resigned my position as Dean in the Woman's College and Professor of Aesthetics in the Northwestern University. Having resigned, my strongest impulses were towards the Crusade [the temperance movement], as is sufficiently proved by the fact that, going East immediately, I sought the leaders of the newly formed societies of temperance women, and these were the first persons who befriended and advised me in the unknown field of "Gospel temperance." With them I saw the great unwashed, unkempt, ungospelled, and sin-scarred multitude for the first time in my life, as they gathered in a dingy downtown square of New York City to hear Dr. Boole [a temperance advocate] preach on Sabbath afternoon.

With several of these new friends I went to Old Orchard Beach, Me., where Francis Murphy, a drinking man and saloon-keeper, recently reformed, had called to first "Gospel Temperance Camp Meeting" known to our annals. Here I met General Neal Dow, and heard the story of the Prohibitory Law [Dow, as mayor of Portland, Maine, had pushed through a city ordinance banning the sale of alcohol, and had then persuaded the Maine legislature to do the same thing state-wide, the first state to do so], and here in a Portland hotel, where I stayed and wondered "where the money was to come from," as I had none, I opened the Bible lying on a hotel table, and lighted on this memorable verse: "Trust in the Lord, and do good, and verily thou shalt be fed" (Psalm xxxvii, 3).

* * * *

The first saloon I ever entered was Sheffner's on Market Street, Pittsburgh, on my way home [to Illinois]. In fact, that was the only glimpse I ever personally had of the Crusade. I had lingered in this dun-colored city well-nigh a year, and when I visited my old friends at the Pittsburgh Female College I spoke with enthusiasm of the Crusade, and of the women who were, as I judged from a morning paper, still engaged in it here. They looked upon me with astonishment when I proposed to seek out those women and go with them to the saloons, for in the two years I had taught in Pittsburgh [several years earlier] these friends associated me with the recitation room, the Shakespeare club, the lecture room, the opera – indeed, all the haunts open to me that a literary-minded woman would care to enter. However, they were too polite to desire to disappoint me, and so they had me piloted by some of the factotums of the place to the headquarters of the Crusade, where I was warmly welcomed, and soon found myself walking down the street arm-in-arm with a young teacher from the public school, who said she had a habit of coming in to add one to the procession when her day's duties were over.

---

[290] Frances E. Willard, *My Happy Half-Century: The Autobiography of an American Woman* (London: 1895), 247-252.

We paused in front of the saloon that I have mentioned. The women ranged themselves along the curbstone, for they had been forbidden to anywise to incommode the passers-by, being dealt with much more strictly than a drunken man or a heap of dry-goods boxes would be. At a signal from our grey-haired leader, a sweet-voiced woman began to sing, "Jesus the water of life will give," all our voices soon blending in that sweet song. I think it was the most novel spectacle that I recall. There stood women of undoubted religious devotion and the highest character, most of them crowned with the glory of grey hairs. Along the stony pavement of that stoniest of cities rumbled a procession of heavy wagons, many of them carriers of beer; between us and the saloon in front of which we were drawn up in a line passed the motley throng, almost every man lifting his hat, and even the little newsboys doing the same. It was American manhood's tribute to Christianity and to womanhood, and it was significant and full of pathos. The leader had already asked the saloonkeeper if we might enter, and he had declined, else the prayer meeting would have occurred inside his door. A sorrowful old lady, whose only son had gone to ruin through that very death trap, knelt on the cold, moist pavement and offered a broken-hearted prayer, while our heads were bowed.

At a signal we moved on, and the next saloonkeeper permitted us to enter. I had no more idea of the inward appearance of a saloon than if there had been no such place on earth. I knew nothing of its high, heavily-corniced bar, its barrels with the ends all pointed towards the looker-on, each barrel being furnished with a faucet; its shelves glittering with decanters and cut glass, its floors strewn with sawdust, and here and there a round table with chairs – nor of its abundant fumes, sickening to healthful nostrils. The tall, stately lady who led us placed her Bible on the bar and read a poem, whether hortatory or imprecatory, I do not remember; but the spirit of these crusaders was so gentle, I think it must have been the former. Then we sang "Rock of Ages" as I thought I had never heard it sung before, with a tender confidence to the height of which one does not rise in the easy-going regulation prayer-meeting, and then one of the older women whispered to me softly that the leader wished to know if I would pray. It was strange, perhaps, but I felt not the least reluctance, and kneeling on that sawdust floor, with a group of earnest hearts around me, and behind them, filling every corner and extending out into the street, a crowd of unwashed, unkempt, hard-looking drinking men, I was conscious that perhaps never in my life, save beside my sister Mary's dying bed, had I prayed as truly as I did then. This was my Crusade baptism. Shortly after this I was made president of the Chicago [branch of the National] W. C. T. U.

Imperialism: Rudyard Kipling, Mark Twain, and Pauline Johnson

Sometimes referred to as the "poet laureate of imperialism," Rudyard Kipling (1865-1936) was born in India to British parents. Kipling was not a typical imperialist. To be sure, like most imperialists he truly believed that imperialism meant bringing the light of Western "civilization" to the "savage" peoples of the East. But unlike most imperialists, Kipling also had a deep regard for the native peoples he knew. His famous poem "Gungha Din" was not meant to denigrate Indians, but to honor the bravery and humanity of an Indian boy. The poem's refrain was, "You are a better man than I am, Gungha Din." When Zulu warriors in Africa stunned the West by defeating British troops in a famous battle, Kipling actually lauded the natives for having the military skill and martial valor to "break a British square." His *Jungle Book* and *Just So Stories* were intended to give European children a positive view of Asian and African culture. Yet, like most Westerners of his time, Kipling was also a racist, in the sense that he believed in the existence of races, believed that the "white" race was superior to other races, and used racism to justify imperialism. Kipling wrote his well-known poem "The White Man's Burden" in 1899 to celebrate the American victory in the recent Spanish-American War, which had resulted in Spain being forced to turn over to the United States four of its most valuable colonies – Cuba, Puerto Rico, the Philippines, and Guam. During that same decade the United States had also annexed Hawaii and American Samoa. Kipling's poem was meant to welcome the Americans to the ranks of the imperial powers, to tell them that they had finally "come of age" as an imperial power, and to instruct them in their new "duty" to "civilize" their "savage" subjects. It made no difference that the majority of the peoples who lived in the four formerly Spanish colonies were Roman Catholics, or that their leaders were literate and well educated; they were not "white," and therefore not viewed as being "civilized." Kipling's poem reminds us that one does not have to hate someone in order to be a racist. It also explains, in its way, why racism persisted so long after slavery was abolished – as an excuse for maintaining "blacks," "brows," "reds," and "yellows" as a submerged labor force and for conquering countries where nonwhite peoples lived.

Mark Twain (1835-1910), the greatest American writer of his generation (or any other generation, for that matter), was, unlike Kipling, a firm opponent of both imperialism and racism. His biting novels *The Adventures of Huckleberry Finn* and *Pudd'n'head Wilson* were intended as stern indictments of racism, and the latter (which dealt with the taboo subject of interracial sex) was consequently banned in the American South. With like-minded Americans, Twain organized the Anti-Imperial League to oppose the annexation of the Philippines and other colonies. He was repulsed by the bloody war American troops had fought against Filipino rebels in the first decade of the twentieth century. He also thundered against Belgian atrocities in the Congo. Twain was particularly irked by those Americans who argued that imperialism was God's will, His way of propagating the One True Religion. (A religious skeptic, Twain doubted that there was any such thing as the One True Religion anyway, but if there was, he was sure that the creed of conquest and greed was not it.) Using humor as his weapon, Twain wrote "The Battle Hymn of the Republic (Brought Down to Date)" as a rejoinder to Kipling's more famous pro-imperialist poem. It was a parody of the patriotic American battle anthem (thus anticipating Weird Al Yankovic by nearly a century); the original "Battle Hymn of the Republic" by Julia Ward Howe had proclaimed that the American Civil War was a great crusade against slavery, but Twain's pastiche, on the other hand, was intended to lampoon imperialism. The contrast between the two isms – noble abolitionism and greedy imperialism – was intentional. (When Twain wrote "Our God," by the way, he meant Greed, a perverse kind of "deity" that he believed lay behind both imperialism and racism.)

London was the cultural and literary as well as economic and political center of the West throughout the nineteenth century. So, like most colonial writers, London was where the thirty-three-year-old Canadian E. Pauline Johnson (1861-1913), Canada's first important woman writer, went in 1894 when she wanted to publish her poetry. Johnson had been born on a Native-American reservation in Ontario, when Canada was still a British colony. She was the daughter of an English mother and a Mohawk father, George Johnson, a linguist who worked for the government. When George Johnson died in 1884, the twenty-three-year-old Pauline turned to her pen to support herself and her mother. Her poems reflected the Native-American experience in North America – and by extension, of subject peoples throughout the British Empire – and she traveled throughout Canada, the United States, and Britain giving public readings in theaters. Her popularity with white audiences stemmed less from their appreciation of her considerable talent as a poet than it did from her novelty as a Native American. As she commented wryly, "They [wealthy British aristocrats] invite me into their houses as a 'great American Indian authoress, an astoundingly clever poet, a marvelous new interpreter of verse,' et cetera, and I go and am looked up to, and I amount to a little tin god, for the titled people pretend not to literature." Nevertheless, one recent critic comments that, ironically, poems like Johnson's "The Corn Husker" and the works of the East Indian poet Rabindranath Tagore actually "reversed the cultural flow of [the British E]mpire," bringing a new, non-Western viewpoint into Western literature. "The Corn Husker" is a haunting lament for a lost culture. Close contact with non-Western peoples meant that Western civilization inevitably changed, unconsciously absorbing some of the ideas and values of its supposedly "savage" subject peoples.

Kipling's "The White Man's Burden," Twain's "The Battle Hymn of the Republic (Brought Down to Date)," and Johnson's "The Corn Husker" are reprinted below.[291]

THE WHITE MAN'S BURDEN

Take up the White Man's burden—
Send forth the best ye breed—
Go bind your sons to exile
To serve your captive's need;
To wait in heavy harness,
On fluttered folk and wild—
Your new-caught, sullen peoples,
Half-devil and half-child.

Take up the White Man's burden—
In patience to abide,
To veil the threat of terror
And check the show of pride;
By open speech and simple,
An hundred times made plain
To seek another's profit,
And work another's gain.

Take the White Man's burden—
The savage wars of peace—
Fill full the mouth of Famine
And bid the sickness cease;
And when your goal in nearest

---

[291] Rudyard Kipling, "The White Man's Burden," in Rudyard Kipling, *Collected Verse* (1911), 215-217; Mark Twain, "The Battle Hymn of the Republic (Brought Down to Date)," in Mark Twain, *The Complete Works of Mark Twain* (1917), 20: 465; and E. Pauline Johnson, "The Corn Husker," originally published c. 1910, reprinted at *The E. Pauline Johnson Project*, http://www.humanities.mcmaster.ca /~pjohnson/husker.html.

The end for others sought,
Watch sloth and heathen Folly
Bring all your hopes to naught.

Take up the White Man's burden—
No tawdry rule of kings,
But toil of serf and sweeper—
The tale of common things,
The ports ye shall not enter,
The roads ye shall not tread,
Go make them with your living,
And mark them with your dead.

Take up the White Man's burden—
And reap his old reward:
The blame of those ye better,
The hate of those ye guard—
The cry of hosts ye humor
(Ah slowly!) toward the light:—
"Why brought he us from bondage,
Our loved Egyptian night?"

THE BATTLE HYMN OF THE REPUBLIC (BROUGHT DOWN TO DATE)

Mine eyes have seen the orgy of the launching of the Sword;
He is searching out the hoardings where the stranger's wealth is stored;
He hath loosed his fateful lightnings, and with woe and death has scored;
HIS LUST IS MARCHING ON.

I have seen him in the watch-fires of a hundred circling camps,
They have builded him an altar in the Eastern dews and damps;
I have read his doomful mission by the dim and flaring lamps—
HIS NIGHT IS MARCHING ON.

I have read his bandit gospel writ in burnished rows of steel:
"As ye deal with my pretensions, so with you my wrath shall deal;
Let the faithless son of Freedom crush the patriot with his heel;
LO, GREED IS MARCHING ON!"

In a sordid slime harmonious, Greed was born in yonder ditch,
With a longing in his bosom - and for others' goods an itch—
As Christ died to make men holy, let men die to make us rich—
OUR GOD IS MARCHING ON.

THE CORN HUSKER

Hard by the Indian lodges, where the bush
    Breaks in a clearing, through ill-fashioned fields,
She comes to labour, when the first still hush
    Of autumn follows large and recent yields.

Age in her fingers, hunger in her face,
    Her shoulders stooped with weight of work and years,
But rich in the tawny colouring of her race
    She comes a-field to strip the purple ears.

And all her thoughts are with the days gone by,
    Ere might's injustice banished from their lands
Her people, that to-day unheeded lie,
    Like the dead husks that rustle through her hands.

-CHAPTER IX-
THE SOUND OF THINGS BREAKING:
THE CRISIS OF THE WEST
1914-45

During the middle third of the twentieth century, the long Golden Age of the West came to an end, and Western Civilization found itself plunged into a deep crisis. Two deadly wars, World War I (1914-18) and World War II (1939-45) ravaged the land, killing and wounding millions of people, leaving millions more homeless and impoverished, and causing untold amounts of property damage. In between the wars, the Great Depression (1929-37) also struck, causing the economy to collapse. In this grim climate of war and depression dangerous new and radical political ideas – communism, fascism, and anti-Semitism – emerged and found numerous zealous and deadly adherents. Terrorists slew innocent people in the name of their false causes. Fear, hatred, misery, suspicion, and suffering lurked everywhere. Was Western Civilization falling apart? The Anglo-Canadian statesman and writer John Buchan thought that it might be. "Everywhere," he lamented in the 1930s, "can be heard the sound of things breaking."

-The Background-

The Causes of World War I

In 1914, after almost a century of relative peace and stability, the West once again went to war with itself – only this time the conflict was far worse than anything it had ever known before. The impact of this "Civil War of the West" was so staggering that the weary survivors could think of no other name for it than "the Great War." Today, we know it as World War I.

It began when Gavrilo Princip (1895-1918), an idealistic young college student and fanatical Serbian nationalist, assassinated the heir to the throne of the Empire of Austria. The Archduke Franz Ferdinand (1863-1914) and his wife Sophie had been easy targets, riding in an open convertible in Sarajevo, the storybook capital of the small Austrian province of Bosnia-Herzegovina, where they had gone on a good-will trip. They were smiling and waving to well-wishers when Princip leaped out of the crowd and shot them. He was immediately arrested (old photographs show him looking surprised as several grim, fez-wearing policemen grappled with him), put on trial, convicted, and imprisoned.

But that wasn't the end of it. Princip had not acted alone. He was a terrorist, someone who uses fear and death and destruction to get his way, an agent of the Black Hand, a sinister secret society of Serbian nationalists who had vowed to use any means necessary to accomplish their goal of independence and unification of all the Serb people. Consequently, it was not just Princip that Austria wanted, but the entire Black Hand, the organization that had sponsored his act of regicide. And that posed a problem, for Austria's leaders believed – correctly, as it turned out – that the Black Hand was secretly being run and protected by one or more shadowy, high-ranking officials in the government of Austria's neighbor to the south, the small but turbulent Eastern European nation of Serbia.[292]

The Black Hand existed at all because Austria was, at the beginning of the twentieth century, a decaying anachronism, a moldering, old-fashioned multinational empire still attempting to exist in a West where people increasingly were dividing themselves into modern nation-states. Dubbing Austria "that ramshackle realm," the historian Spencer Di Scala writes, "Consisting of territories collected by the Habsburg dynasty over the course of centuries, [Austria] opposed the constitutionalism and nationalism announced by the French Revolution of 1789 throughout the nineteenth century because [those ideals] envisioned a world of self-governing peoples under limited governments. These ideals threatened the Austrian Empire – a multinational construction held together by an absolutistic emperor [Franz Ferdinand's geriatric uncle, Franz Josef] and run by German-speaking Austrians who were an ethnic minority in their own realm – at the beginning of the twentieth century no less than [it had been] a hundred years before."[293]

In fact, not one but two dominant ethnic groups, the Germans and the Magyars (Hungarians), governed the sprawling Austrian Empire, with the Germans, admittedly, as the senior partners. But the principle was the same: the two groups together comprised well under half of the empire's population, for the majority of the inhabitants were peoples of other nationalities, a hodge-podge of Italians, Poles, Czechs, Slovaks, Slovenes, Byelorussians, Ukrainians, Gypsies, Croats, Romanians, and Serbs, none of whom had any real say in the way Austria was governed, and who resented it. The population also included substantial numbers of Jews and

---

[292] Samuel R. Williamson, Jr., and Russell Van Wyk, *July 1914: Soldiers, Statesmen, and the Coming of the Great War: A Brief Documentary History* (2003), 9-30; Robert O. Paxton, *Europe in the Twentieth Century* (1975), 51.
[293] Spencer M. Di Scala, *Twentieth-Century Europe: Politics, Society, Culture* (2004), 62-68.

Muslims, religious minorities that most people at that time viewed as ethnic groups, further contributing to the polyglot nature of the Austrian state. All of these groups had little in common with the ruling Germans and Magyars. Serbs like Princip spoke their own language, Serbo-Croatian, a Slavic tongue completely unrelated to either German or Magyar. They were Eastern Orthodox rather than Roman Catholic. They had historically been part of Eastern Civilization rather than the West. They even used a different alphabet.

Most of the residents of Austria's mountainous little province of Bosnia-Herzegovina were ethnic Serbs rather than Germans or Magyars, and the Black Hand's chief goal was to force Austria to renounce its rule and liberate the province so that it could unite with Serbia and form a new, larger, Serbian nation-state, called Greater Serbia. Indeed, the Black Hand's secret oath declared, "This organization is formed in order to achieve the ideal of unification of Serbdom; all Serbs, regardless of sex, religion, or place of birth, can become members, and anyone else who is prepared to serve this ideal faithfully." The Black Hand pledged to use "all means available, including violence," to "fight...those outside the frontiers [of Greater Serbia]" – by this they meant Germans and Magyars – "who are enemies of the ideal" of Serbian nationalism. The murder of Franz Ferdinand and Sophie had not been an isolated act. The Black Hand had struck before. Austria knew that it would strike again.[294]

Unknown to outsiders, not even to the Austrian police or the Prime Minister of Serbia, the Black Hand's secret leader was in fact none other than the head of Serbia's military intelligence, the ruthless, broad-necked, cold-eyed, thick-mustached Dragutin "the Bull" Dimitrijevic (1877-1917). In 1903, as a young army officer, Dimitrijevic had participated in the assassination of Serbia's old King Alexander, an ineffectual leader whose chief "crime" had been failing to support zealously enough the cause of Serbian nationalism. As a consequence of the Bull's suspected role in Alexander's murder, Serbia's new leaders feared him and took pains not to look too closely into his activities. Stanoje Stanojevic, one of the Bull's political opponents and a respected Serbian university professor, later (1923) described him as follows:

> Gifted and cultured, honorable, a convincing speaker, a sincere patriot, personally courageous, filled with ambition, energy, and the capacity for work.... He had the characteristics which cast a spell on men. His arguments were always striking and convincing.... He was in every respect a remarkable organizer. He kept all the threads in his own hand, and even his most intimate friends only knew what their own immediate concern was.... He was incapable of distinguishing what was possible from what was not and perceiving the limits of responsibility and power. He saw only his own aims and pursued them ruthlessly and without scruple.... He believed that his opinions and activities enjoyed the monopoly of patriotism. Hence anyone who did not agree with him could not in his eyes be either honorable or wise or a patriot.[295]

Following the assassination of Franz Ferdinand, Austria predictably issued Serbia an ultimatum: allow Austrian authorities to come to Serbia and have a free hand in ferreting out and destroying the Black Hand, or Austria would invade Serbia and implement its will by force. Under the terms of the ultimatum, Serbia was instructed not only to outlaw the Black Hand, but also to "suppress any publication which incites hatred and contempt of the [Austrian] monarchy and the general tendency of which is directed against its territorial integrity"; alter its school curriculum and content to make it more pro-Austrian; "remove from the [Serbian] military service and administration in general all officers and officials guilty of propaganda against [Austria] and of whom [Austria] reserves to itself the right to communicate the names and deeds"; and "accept the collaboration in Serbia of organs of the [Austrian] government in the suppression of the subversive movement directed against the territorial integrity of [Austria]." Militarily, Serbia was no match for Austria, but Prime Minister Nikola Pasic (in office 1906-18) was unwilling to passively turn his country over to Austrian rule. Offering to negotiate, he gave in to most of Austria's demands but balked at surrendering sovereignty to a foreign power, even one with a legitimate grievance. This response did not satisfy Austria, which prepared to invade.[296]

A second factor leading to World War I was something known as the European alliance system. In an attempt to create some form of collective security, during the late 1800s most of the countries of Europe had entered into defensive military alliances with some of their neighbors. The thought was that no state would be foolish enough to attack another if it knew that the country it was attacking had powerful allies. As a result, by 1914 Europe had become divided into two mighty alliance systems – two rival gangs, if you will – that faced each other with mounting suspicion, hostility, and wariness. One of these alliance systems was the Triple Alliance of Germany, Austria, and Italy, also known as the Central Powers. The other was the Triple Entente (ahn-TAHNT) of France, Britain, and Russia. There were also smaller, side alliances, including one between Russia and Serbia.

Thus it was that, following Austria's ultimatum to Serbia, the Serbian Prime Minister desperately contacted his only ally, the mighty Tsar Nicholas II (r. 1894-1917) of Russia, a reactionary and dim-witted autocrat who nevertheless viewed himself as the special protector of all Slavic peoples everywhere. (Like Serbo-Croatian, Russian belongs to the Slavic family of languages.) If Austria invaded Serbia, would Russia come to its defense? Nicholas hesitated. On the one hand, he abhorred the crime of regicide and was no friend of terrorism, nationalism, or revolution, especially seeing as he was actively combating all three in Russia. But on the other

---

[294] Williamson, *July 1914*, 43-46; Paxton, *Europe in the Twentieth Century*, 51-56.
[295] Qouted in Williamson, *July 1914*, 20.
[296] Williamson, *July 1914*, 36-41; Paxton, *Europe in the Twentieth Century*, 57-60.

hand, Serbia was his ally, and in a world of alliances one should support and protect one's allies. Moreover, Nicholas believed (correctly) that the West considered Russia backward, didn't take it seriously, and often pushed it around. He had recently given in to Austria on some other issue, and was feeling in no mood to do so again. He feared that if Russia backed down once more – if it failed to protect its ally against Austrian aggression, even if that aggression was warranted – it would forever lose the respect of the West. So he told the Serbians, "*Da*," Russia would fight for them – although he hoped that this time it would be Austria that would back down before things came to blows. The alliance system had been invoked.[297]

Meanwhile, Austria's leaders were becoming worried. They knew that Serbia and Russia were allies, and they feared the potential of Russia's massive though ill-equipped army, the largest in the world. So, to be on the safe side, they decided to contact *their* ally, Germany. Accordingly, the Austrian ambassador in Berlin quickly called on the impulsive, hotheaded German Kaiser Wilhelm II (r. 1888-1918). If Austria invaded Serbia and, as a consequence, Russia then attacked Austria, would Germany come to Austria's aid? Wilhelm shared Austria's anger at terrorism and regicide, as well as its desire to suppress the rising tide of ethnic nationalism – which threatened Germany's control of Polish-speaking Poland, French-speaking Alsace-Lorraine, and Danish-speaking Schleswig-Holstein as well as Austria's rule of Serbo-Croatian-speaking Bosnia-Herzegovina. "*Ja*," replied the Kaiser, Germany would fight – although, like Nicholas, he hoped that a show of force would get the other side to back down before it actually came to war. Austria was relieved. "Rest assured," the ambassador triumphantly telegraphed back to Vienna after his meeting with Wilhelm, "His Majesty will faithfully stand by Austria, as is required by the obligations of his alliance and of his ancient friendship." Historians refer to Wilhelm's promise of unconditional support for Austria as "the blank check." Now confident of German backing, Austria moved forward with its invasion of Serbia. In fact, there is some evidence that the mercurial Wilhelm may not have intended for Austria to take his pledge as a "blank check" after all. When he discovered that Serbia was willing to accede to most of Austria's demands, he quietly urged his ally to negotiate rather than fight. But Wilhelm changed his mind about such matters almost daily, so it is difficult to determine what he may have intended at any given moment.[298]

In Russia, the tsar was having second thoughts. He knew that Austria and Germany were allies, and while he believed that Russia could handle Austria, he worried that taking on both foes at once would be too much. So he contacted *his* ally, France. This was not difficult, for the French President, Raymond Poincare (in office 1913-20), was at that very moment in Russia on a state visit. The Franco-Russian alliance had been formed decades earlier, not because the two countries shared similar political ideologies (France was a liberal republic, while Russia was an ultraconservative absolute monarchy), but because both countries feared the consequences of German aggression. If Germany attacked Russia, would France honor its treaty and come to Russia's rescue? Poincare, whose family originally came from Alsace-Lorraine, the province that France had been forced to surrender to Germany after losing the 1870-72 Franco-Prussian War, still smoldered over old quarrels. Seeing an opportunity for *ravanche*, he said, "*Oui*," France would fight. (To be on the safe side, however, Nicholas also sent a series of telegrams to Wilhelm, who was his second cousin, addressed to "Dear Willy." Wilhelm replied with his own telegrams, addressed to "Dear Nicky." The so-called "Dear Willy, Dear Nicky" telegrams were a last-minute attempt to reach some sort of compromise, but events moved too quickly and no agreement could be worked out before the war began.)[299]

In France, Poincare was justifiably concerned about Germany's military might. The German army was better trained and better equipped than the French army. So he decided to contact *his* ally, the perpetually tired, vacillating British Prime Minister Herbert Henry Asquith (in office 1908-16) and his steely, tight-lipped, hawkish Foreign Secretary, Sir Edward Grey (in office 1905-16). If Germany attacked France, would Britain come to its aid? The British Cabinet met, considered the request, and found itself divided on the issue. For one thing, the *entente cordiale* ("friendly understanding") between Britain and France was not an official treaty, like the one between France and Russia, but instead a loose, unwritten, and informal understanding. Second, it didn't include Russia, which was France's ally, not theirs. Technically, the British were not actually obligated to help. However, the more hawkish of Britain's leaders, like Grey and his feisty First Lord of Admiralty, Winston Churchill (1874-1965), strongly resented Germany's growing military and economic power and saw this as an opportunity to knock it down a peg. Britain, Grey and Churchill insisted, was "honor-bound" to take France's side, treaty or no treaty. But other British leaders wanted no part of a costly continental war, and opposed getting involved. Moreover, at the time the Cabinet was focused on another crisis, a threatened revolt of British troops in Ireland (the soldiers were protesting the government's plan to grant Canada-style home rule to the Irish), and didn't want to be distracted by foreign policy problems. Ultimately, Britain's position, although never clearly stated (for Grey never clearly stated anything, if he could help it), seems to have been that it would fight the Germans only if Germany attacked France by marching through Belgium, a neutral country with which Britain *did* have a formal, written treaty. Unsurprisingly, the British were once again backing into something without carefully thinking the matter through.[300]

For its part, Germany – now fearful of being encircled by a strangling Russo-Franco-Anglo alliance – contacted the third member of the Triple Alliance, Italy. Would Italy fight with Germany and Austria against

---

[297] Williamson, *July 1914*, 110-133; Paxton, *Europe in the Twentieth Century*, 60-61.
[298] Williamson, *July 1914*, 73-98; Paxton, *Europe in the Twentieth Century*, 56-57.
[299] Williamson, *July 1914*, 138-143, 181-187; Paxton, *Europe in the Twentieth Century*, 61-62.
[300] Williamson, *July 1914*, 218-256; Paxton, *Europe in the Twentieth Century*, 62, 64-67.

Russia, France, and Britain? Showing remarkable (if temporary) intelligence and restraint, the Italians said, "No." For the moment, Italy would stay neutral. Needing another ally to take Italy's place, Germany persuaded the Ottoman Empire to join the fray on the Austro-German side. (The Turks had issues with the Russians.) Moreover, Bulgaria, an old enemy of Serbia, also joined the Central Powers. Thus two powerful alliance systems prepared for war. Neither side was wholly Western: Russia, Serbia, and Bulgaria were Eastern, after all, and the Ottoman Empire was Islamic. But most were. It was to be the Central Powers (Austria, Germany, the Ottoman Empire, and Bulgaria) versus the Allies (Britain, France, Russia, Serbia, and Belgium) in a fight to the finish.[301]

There were other, underlying, causes as well. There was Germany's not altogether unjustified belief that it was not being accorded what it viewed as its proper "place in the sun" – that it did not receive the kind of respect it thought it deserved, and that the other countries of Europe (especially its old enemy France and new rival Britain) were out to weaken it. There was Britain's fear that Germany was growing too big for its britches, too strong militarily and economically, and that it needed to be humbled before it became too much of a threat. There was France's desire for *ravanche* – revenge – for its humiliating defeat in the Franco-Prussian War. There was Russia's desire to be taken more seriously by the West. There was the belief of the German High Command that Germany was losing its arms race with Britain (the two countries had been expanding their arsenals at a near-frantic pace), and that if it didn't strike now, it would soon be too late. There was the misguided belief by the French High Command that the key to winning a war was not strategy, guns, or numbers of troops, but fighting spirit – *élan* – the one thing the French were sure that they had more of than anybody else. There was the mistaken belief by Kaiser Wilhelm II that little Belgium would never resist militarily an attempt by mighty Germany to send troops across its border to reach France, and that the "soft," bourgeois British would never go to war over "a scrap of paper" – their treaty with Belgium. There was the stubborn belief by the military leaders on both sides that they had to follow their prearranged battle plans unquestioningly, no matter what the consequences.[302]

The War Itself

Almost everybody expected that, once it began, the war would be brief. But it turned out to be a long, bloody, draining conflict that fundamentally altered the global balance of power. On July 29 Austria invaded Serbia. On July 30 Russia responded by mobilizing its army in preparation for war with Austria. On August 1 Germany declared war on Russia. Two days later, on August 3, Germany also declared war on France and attacked it by sending its army, as planned, through Belgium – a long-since worked-out strategy known as the Schlieffen Plan, based on the belief that the only way for Germany to avoid a protracted, two-front war was to invade and quickly defeat France in the west and then wheel to fight Russia in the east. Russia was too big for Germany to do it the other way around. Even if everything had gone right, it still would have taken weeks for German troops to drive all the way to the Russian capital St. Petersburg, which was hundreds of miles from the border. By that time France would have already attacked Germany on the west. On August 4 Britain came to Belgium's aid (and France's) and declared war on Germany. On August 6 Austria declared war on Russia.

Nothing went according to anyone's plans. Austria had expected Serbia to fall after only a few days of fighting, but instead it held out for months. Germany had expected Italy to enter the war and invade France from the south, drawing some of the French forces away from the north, where Germany planned to attack through Belgium, but Italy's neutrality meant that the Germans had to go it alone against France. Germany also expected that Belgium would simply stand aside and let its army march through, but it surprised everyone and decided to fight, slowing the German advance and bringing Britain into the war. France had expected the Germans to fight in Alsace-Lorraine, not Belgium. According to the historian Barbara Tuchman, the stubborn French generals refused to move their forces north to meet the German advance because they did not want to alter their own Battle Plan 17, which called for first retaking the "lost provinces" of 1870-72 and then counterattacking Germany in the center, along the Rhine. When the German troops finally did reach France, they consequently met little resistance, quickly driving to within a few miles of Paris. But then the two German wings moved out of sequence, a gap unexpectedly opened between them, and the Anglo-French forces counterattacked in the bloody Battle of the Marne. The German advance stalled, and the Germans ended up digging a long series of fortified trenches in northern France and Belgium, stretching all the way from the Alps to the North Sea. The Anglo-French responded by digging a parallel system of trenches of their own. The British High Command expected that they would be able to punch a hole in the German lines, get their cavalry through the gap, and defeat the Germans by attacking from the rear, but the German lines always held and the Anglo-French cavalry never got through. The German High Command expected that they could "bleed the enemy white" by forcing them into a series of protracted battles, but the French and British brought in reinforcements from their colonies – Canadians, Australians, New Zealanders, Indians, and black Africans – and it was the Germans who ran out of soldiers, not the Anglo-French.

---

[301] Williamson, *July 1914*, 149-177.
[302] Barbara Tuchman, *The Guns of August* (1962), passim; Di Scala, *Twentieth-Century Europe*, 128-135; Paxton, *Europe in the Twentieth Century*, 67-74.

Ultimately, both sides settled down for what proved to be a protracted war of attrition. Futilely, each side sent waves soldiers "over the top" and against the enemy's trenches, trying to break through, only to be met by sheets of machine-gun fire and cannonade, and deadly clouds of mustard gas. Casualties mounted rapidly, but neither side gained much ground. Northeastern France and coastal Belgium became wastelands of mud. Even the trees were casualties. Only the rats thrived, growing fat on the bloated corpses of men and horses.

In the east, Russia attacked immediately, hoping to catch Germany unprepared. But this plan, too, failed. It turned out that the Russian army was too poorly armed and trained to take on the Germans, and it fell before a fierce counterattack. German troops then drove deep into Russia, capturing and destroying thousands of square miles of prime farmland and besieging the capital at St. Petersburg. But Germany had been forced into the very two-front war that it had wanted to avoid, which slowly sapped its resources and manpower. With few overseas colonies to provide reinforcements and supplies, the Central Powers ran out of men and munitions, while the Anglo-French brought in not only fresh troops (the Canadians, Aussies, and Indian Sikhs turned out to be their best fighters, and the Canadian Arthur Curry their best general) but also substantial supplies of grain and meat from the Canadian Plains and Australian Outback and newly made weapons from the Canadian factories. Frantic to stop the never-ending waves of supply ships coming in from the colonies, Germany eventually unleashed its submarines (u-boats) in unrestricted submarine warfare.

To the south, British forces attacked the Ottoman Empire, but were repulsed in a furious battle at Gallipoli, near Istanbul – much to the surprise of the Westerners, who expected that the "backwards" Turks would be defeated easily. Italy at last came into the war, but on the side of the Allies rather than the Central Powers, and attacked Austria in the Alps. (Italy hoped to seize the Italian-speaking provinces of Tyrol and Trieste from Austria.) This attack, too, bogged down, slowed by heavy snow and rugged terrain. Everywhere, the war dragged on, month after month, year after year. Casualties continued to climb. The Central Powers grew increasingly desperate.

In 1917 and 1918 both sides finally began to totter from sheer exhaustion. In 1917, Russia, its ragtag army mauled by the better-trained German troops, its people suffering beyond endurance from famine and fuel shortages, collapsed in revolution. Tsar Nicholas II was overthrown, and first liberals, then social democrats, and finally communists came to power. The new government signed a separate truce with Germany and Austria and withdrew from the war. The United States, however, took its place, provoked by Germany's unrestricted submarine warfare. In the summer of 1918 the Austrian and Ottoman governments also collapsed, eviscerated by five years of total war. In autumn 1918, a similar collapse occurred in Germany. Reform-minded social democrats seized control of the German Reichstag, Kaiser Wilhelm II reluctantly abdicated, and the new leaders quickly negotiated a truce with the Allies. At 11:00 PM on November 11, 1918 – the eleventh hour of the eleventh day of the eleventh month – the West's Civil War finally stopped. Russia, Serbia, Romania, Germany, Austria, and the Ottoman Empire had been defeated. France, Britain, Canada and the other British dominions, Italy, and the United States had won.[303]

The Consequences of World War I

But at terrible cost. The consequences of World War I for the West were staggering. First, there were the enormous casualties. All told, approximately sixty-five million soldiers fought in the war, about two-thirds of them Western. Thirty-seven million – 58% – were either killed or wounded. The following chart breaks down the casualties:

Country	Population	Casualties (% of Population)
Russia	161 m	9 m (.055)
Germany	56 m	7 m (.125)
French Empire	80 m	6 m (.075)
Austria	49 m	7 m (.143)
British Empire	419 m	3 m (.007)
Italy	35 m	2 m (.057)
Ottoman Empire		1 m
Romania	6 m	536 k (.091)
United States	92 m	365 k (.004)
Serbia	2 m	330 k (.132)
Bulgaria	4 m	267 k (.067)
Canada	8 m	232 k (.029)
Belgium	7 m	93 k (.013)
Greece	3 m	27 k (.010)

---

[303] Pierre Burton, *Marching As to War: Canada's Turbulent Years, 1899-1953* (2001), 125-224; Tuchman, *Guns of August*, passim; Di Scala, *Twentieth-Century Europe*, 135-147, 154-158; Paxton, *Europe in the Twentieth Century*, 75-96.

One of the reasons that casualties were so high was because the weapons were so effective. Among the new weapons first used in a European war in World War I were machine guns, long-range cannons, poison gas, submarines, tanks, flamethrowers, and airplanes. So many people died in the war that the generation that came of age in the 1910s became known as the "lost" generation.

Second, the war fundamentally changed the balance of power, both in the West and in the Middle East. Before the war, the West had four great powers (Britain, Germany, France, and Austria) and two "middle powers" (the United States and Italy). But the great powers after the war were Britain, France, the United States, and Italy. Germany lost its colonies and some of its lands in Europe and (temporarily) became a middle power. Austria was stripped of most of its lands and was no longer a power at all. In the Middle East the Ottoman Empire (renamed Turkey) lost more than half of its territory, which was taken over by Britain and France. Britain now became the major power in the Middle East. Russia (renamed the Union of the Soviet Socialist Republics) lost a lot of territory as well. Serbia ceased to exist as a separate nation, and was incorporated into the new federation of Yugoslavia – which in fact was very close to being the Greater Serbia that the Black Hand terrorists had wanted all along. Out of the former Russian, German, Austrian, and Serbia territory were formed ten new states, none of them very large or powerful: six nation-states (Finland, Estonia, Latvia, Lithuania, Poland, and Hungary), two city-states (Danzig and Memel), and two multinational federations (Czechoslovakia and Yugoslavia).

Third, World War I was the first so-called "total war," a phrase coined by General Erich von Ludendorff, second in charge in the German High Command. "Total war" meant that the belligerents mobilized not just their soldiers, but their entire populations, converting factories and farms into mechanisms for producing war materiel. Soldiers – the bulk of whom were draftees – were sent off to fight at "the front," but civilians were expected to contribute to the war effort as well, on the "home front." And because factories, farms, and civilians were part of each country's war effort, they were fair game for attack, which was the logic behind Germany's unrestricted submarine warfare. War was not just for soldiers any more.

Fourth, the power of government increased tremendously. Waging total war meant that governments had to take control of their national economies for the duration of the conflict, creating what are known as "command economies." Although governments gave up many of their new powers when the war was over, they did not surrender all of them. They never do.

Fifth, World War I turned out to be a catalyst for woman suffrage. During the war middle-class women joined the workforce in unprecedented numbers, taking over jobs normally held by men, but who were now in the military. (Working-class women, it should be noted, already had jobs.) Women workers were essential in order to maintain sufficient production of war materiel on the home front. By 1918 women comprised 38% of the workforce at Germany's Krupp Steelworks. In Britain women workers moved into new jobs in banking and commerce. Having become more powerful economically, women insisted on a greater share of political power as well. Moreover, there were many people who believed that if women (who were thought to be naturally less aggressive and more nurturing than men) voted and held office, future wars would be less likely to occur; wives and mothers, such people reasoned, would likely use their newfound political clout to try to keep the peace. Other people believed that war widows and war mothers deserved the vote as a sort of just recompense for having sacrificed their loved ones. Too, many wartime politicians (the Canadian Prime Minister Sir Robert Laird Borden was one) slyly planned to receive the lion's share of the votes of the war widows and war mothers by playing on their patriotism, and so endorsed woman suffrage for purely political reasons. Before 1914 women could vote only in Norway (and then only since 1913), but by 1928 woman suffrage existed in Britain, Canada, the United States, Germany, the Soviet Union (the only non-Western country to permit women to vote), Poland, Czechoslovakia, Austria, Belgium, the Netherlands, Denmark, and Sweden as well. France, Italy, Switzerland, and Spain, however, remained male-dominated holdouts.

Sixth, to discourage strikes during wartime, labor union leaders were for the first time brought into the war cabinets of several countries. Finally, unions gained a seat at the table.

Seventh, World War I contributed to the rise of strong nationalist movements in both the West and the colonies – especially the British colonies. Britain had promised India that it would receive Canada-style home rule if its leaders agreed to support the war effort. They did, and many Indians joined the British army as soldiers and medics. But Britain went back on its promise. Betrayed, Indian leaders like Mohandas Gandhi (1869-1948) now vowed to work for complete independence. The decline of the British Empire had begun. In the Middle East, the British had likewise promised Arabs that if they revolted against the Ottoman Empire, they would receive independence as a reward. Arab rebels thus joined the war on the side of the Allies and performed valuable service, but when war was over the former Ottoman provinces of Iraq, Syria, Lebanon, and Palestine became British and French colonies. The Arabs had merely exchanged one alien overlord for another. Like the Indians, they smoldered with resentment and talked of revolution. Hoping to forestall a possible uprising, the British decided to endorse a plan to repatriate European Jews to Palestine – the idea was known as Zionism – figuring that the Jews who went there would be loyal British subjects and allies against Arab nationalism. The Zionists who migrated to Palestine saw themselves merely as exiles returning to their ancestral homeland, but the now-resentful Arabs saw them instead as agents of Western imperialism and resented them. Finally, the leaders of the British dominions that had already achieved home rule – Canada, Australia, New Zealand, and South Africa – rued the enormous casualties that their people had suffered "rescuing" the Empire from the consequences of its own bad judgment. As far as the Canadians were concerned "the New World had come to the rescue of the old," and it deserved to treated as an equal at the

Councils of Empire. The Canadian Prime Minister Sir Robert Laird Borden (in office 1911-20) informed his British counterpart David Lloyd George (in office 1916-22) that in the future, if Britain expected Canada to make such heavy sacrifices for the Empire, he wanted to be consulted about it *before* the shots were fired.

Finally, in return for American participation in the war, the United States President Thomas Woodrow Wilson (in office 1913-20) insisted on playing a major role in shaping the peace. And as a one-time university professor of history and political science, Wilson had plenty of ideas about what the new world order should be like.[304]

The Treaty of Versailles

In 1919 the leaders of the victorious countries – Britain, France, Italy, the United States, Belgium, and others – met in the old French royal palace at Versailles to hammer out a peace treaty. Historians frequently contrast the Treaty of Versailles to the earlier Congress of Vienna that ended the Napoleonic Wars. The earlier peace had been notable for it magnanimity. It had left France with most of its borders intact, had not required it to make any money payments to the winners, and had allowed it to maintain its army and navy – although the French were required to change their political system and restore the old monarchy. Versailles would be very different.

Wilson arrived at Versailles with an action agenda he called his "Fourteen Points." The most important of these points were (1) a magnanimous peace that did not punish Germany unduly, (2) the elimination of multinational empires in favor of nation-states, and, most important, (3) the establishment of a League of Nations to keep the peace through what Wilson called "collective security." However, Britain, France, and Italy had other ideas. They wanted (1) a harsh peace that punished Germany and Austria for their roles in the war, (2) reparations from Germany (money to pay for the cost of the war), (3) territory, (4) the dismemberment of the German, Austrian, and Ottoman Empires, and (5) disarmament, to keep Germany from rebuilding its military. In the end, Wilson got his League of Nations (although ironically the United States Congress refused to permit the USA to join it) and the creation of six new nation-states (Finland, Estonia, Latvia, Lithuania, Poland, and Hungary). But France, Britain, and Italy got their way on everything else. The treaty required Germany to make steep annual payments to the Allies (except for the Soviet Union, which had made a separate peace). It forced Germany to disarm. It required it to give up some of its territory. And it forced it to sign the infamous "war guilt clause," in which Germany acknowledged that it alone had been responsible for World War I and all of its misery. Versailles left Germany impoverished, weakened, and humiliated. In addition, the treaty also dismembered the old Austrian and Ottoman Empires. Austria was left with little besides the city of Vienna and a few ski lodges. The Turks lost all of their oil-rich Arabic-speaking provinces. These former Ottoman territories, along with Germany's ex-colonies in Africa and Asia, and parts of Austria, were turned over to Britain, France, and Italy. The winners exulted. The losers seethed. Some vowed revenge.[305]

Economic Problems

Although the Industrial Revolution had brought the West unprecedented prosperity, it had also given rise to a number of unexpected and serious economic problems. For one thing, by 1900 an ever-expanding income gap separated the affluent upper and middle classes from the struggling workers and peasants, as Western society became increasingly polarized between the "haves" and the "have-nots." For another, by 1900 the largest corporations had become so overgrown and had amassed so much wealth that they threatened to monopolize trade, set prices, buy off politicians, and otherwise dominate society. Further, a discouraging series of boom-to-bust economic cycles had set in around 1830, bringing alternating periods of robust growth followed by stagnation and uncertainty. At the same time, a long-term decline in prices had begun (caused mostly by advances in technology) – a boon to consumers but a bane to producers – and grew worse after 1880. Too, increased air, water, and soil pollution had brought unprecedented environmental degradation, especially harmful for the working class, peasants, and farmers, but also hurtful even for the middle class. And finally, by 1900 a particularly crass and tawdry materialism seemed to have come to pervade most aspects of Western culture, alarming traditionalists like the clergy and lords. In the 1930s the economy reached its nadir with the Great Depression of 1929-37.

The Income Gap

As we have seen, during the nineteenth century the rich had grown richer, the middle class had increased its size and affluence, but workers, farmers, and peasants had experienced only modest gains and found themselves working harder than ever. Even in the United States (which along with Canada probably had the

---

[304] Di Scala, *Twentieth-Century Europe*, 147-154, 160-183; Paxton, *Europe in the Twentieth Century*, 97-164.
[305] Di Scala, *Twentieth-Century Europe*, 185-204; Paxton, *Europe in the Twentieth Century*, 165-189.

most even distribution of wealth of any of the industrial nations), by 1920 the top two percent of the population earned fully 28% of the income, and the top one percent owned more than half of the wealth.[306]

It was not that the workers, farmers, and peasants were worse off than they had been before the Industrial Revolution. Far from it: between 1750 and 1900 industrialization had pushed up most people's income, at least a little, and declining prices had meant a rising standard of living for everyone. But workers' and peasants' incomes had not risen nearly as much as the middle and upper classes'. Nor had they gone up as much as many had hoped that they would. In Canada in 1900 the average low-skilled worker still made only about US $10 per week (approximately US $180 in today's money), or less than 25% of what a middle-class Canadian made. In the United States, the average factory worker brought home about $440 a year (approximately $8,000 in today's money), compared to a little more than $2,000 ($35,000 in today's money) for the average middle-class American. The situation was even worse in Europe, where workers typically spent half of their income on food – which was better than the 50% that they had spent *on bread alone* in 1789, but still nowhere near what they desired. And while it was true that workers in 1900 were better fed and clothed than their counterparts in 1800, the reason was more that the prices of food and clothing had declined, not that wages had surged. As the American social historians Nelson Lichtenstein, Susan Strasser, and Roy Rosenzweig write: "Rather than shrinking the gap between the rich and the poor, economic growth [actually] increased it. While corporate profits [in the United States] nearly doubled in the 1920s, factory workers' wages rose only modestly – less than 15 percent, by one estimate." [307]

And while there may have been more food on the table, the home the table was in had actually become more expensive, the result of rapid urban growth and rising real estate prices. By 1900 few Western workers were able to buy their homes, and the rate of homeownership declined each year, as more and more people became tenants. As the cities swelled and property values soared, rents surged upward. By 1900 more than 20% of a Canadian factory worker's income went for rent alone. To save money on rent, two or three families frequently crowded together in a single two- or three-room apartment. In 1890 more than 1.4 million people lived on Manhattan, and in some neighborhoods the population density exceeded 900 people per acre. In 1890 the New York journalist Jacob Riis described a typical Manhattan apartment building:

> Be a little careful, please! The hall is dark and you might stumble…. Here where the hall turns and dives into utter darkness is…a flight of stairs. You can feel your way, if you cannot see it. Close? Yes! What would you have? All the fresh air that enters these stairs comes from the hall-door that is forever slamming…. The sinks are in the hallway, that all the tenants may have access – and all be poisoned alike by their summer stenches…. Here is a door. Listen! That short, hacking cough, that tiny, helpless wail – what do they mean? … The child is dying of measles. With half a chance it might have lived; but it had none. That dark bedroom killed it. [308]

As cities grew, real estate values rose and even fetid downtown apartments like the one described by Riis became increasingly harder to find. Workers were forced to move further from their workplaces, yet could not afford the relatively low fares charged to ride the streetcars. Many walked to work, their shoes sometimes wearing out more quickly than they could replace them. Women garment workers in New York City occasionally walked to work barefoot, in order to save the wear on their shoes.[309]

The death rate for the West as a whole declined considerably between 1850 and 1914, the result of better nutrition and the widespread acceptance by doctors of the germ theory of disease. In the United States the death rate fell from 20.6 deaths per thousand in 1865, to 17.2 in 1900, to 13.3 in 1914, to 11.7 in 1925, a remarkable improvement. As a result, life expectancy increased – in the United States from 47 years in 1900 to 59 in 1925. But not all classes benefited equally. One in four working-class children born in Montreal in 1900 did not make it to their first birthday. In the United States, the rate of infant mortality for blacks and Indians was about twice what it was for whites. Diseases like cholera (a bacterium spread by drinking polluted water, and which reached epidemic proportions in large cities like London and New York), influenza, and tuberculosis spread rapidly in the overcrowded neighborhoods of the working class. Tens of thousands died. Increased air pollution exacerbated respiratory diseases like tuberculosis, pneumonia, and asthma. In the United States in 1900 the death rate for tuberculosis was nearly 200 deaths per 100,000; today it is less than three. The death rate for influenza and pneumonia was also about 200, while today is only about 30. [310]

Leisure time had increased for the middle class, but industrial workers still labored ten to twelve hours a day, six days a week. Low wages meant that most working-class families were unable to survive on only one income, so unlike middle-class women and teens, working-class women and teens joined their husbands and

---

[306] Nelson Lichtenstein, Susan Strasser, and Roy Rosenzweig, *Who Built America? Working People and the Nation's Economy, Politics, Culture, and Society* (2000), 2: A22.

[307] Ibid, 325; John Merriman, *A History of Modern Europe from the Renaissance to the Present* (1996), 687.

[308] Jacob Riis, *How the Other Half Lives* (1890), 17.

[309] David von Drehle, *Triangle: The Fire That Changed America* (2003), passim; J. M. Bumsted, *A History of the Canadian Peoples* (1998), 221-251; Mark C. Carnes and John A. Garraty, *American Destiny: Narrative of a Nation* (2003), 632-658; George Brown Tindall and David E. Shi, *America: A Narrative History* (2004), 802-840, 1059-1071.

[310] *Historical Statistics of the United States, Colonial Times to 1970* (1975), 55-63; Bumsted, *History of the Canadian Peoples*, 221-251.

fathers in the workplace. In Montreal, women comprised 20% of the labor force, and children five to ten percent. Overall, literacy had risen – but peasant and working-class children like Harriet Hanson still rarely had time for anything more than a grade-school education. And colleges and universities were reserved mostly for the children of the upper class and only the most talented offspring of the middle class.[311]

Falling Prices

Between 1880 and 1920 thousands of eager agriculturalists – armed with improved plows, harvesters, combines, barbed wire, and new, hardier strains of wheat – surged out of the old, tired, crowded champion lands and onto the vast, sweeping, but dry, windswept, thick-sodded, and formerly unfarmable grasslands that lay at the far margins of the West: the Great Plains in western North America (the Canadians called them "the last, best West"), the Pampas in southern South America, and the Outback in western Australia. Thanks to the invention of refrigerators, steamships, railroads, and other new technologies, giant food corporations like General Mills and the Chicago-based "Meat Trust" were able to transport vast quantities of cheap grain, meat, and milk from the new farmlands to the urban packing plants, and then re-transport the finished goods to the rapidly growing mass markets of Western Europe and eastern North America. Meat was no longer considered a luxury, as it had always been before. While in the 1870s the average German had consumed only 60 pounds of meat a year, in the 1910s he ate 105 pounds.

Falling food prices were good for consumers, but bad for farmers and peasants, many of whom had gone into debt to acquire their new lands, plows, and other farm implements. By 1920 more than half of a typical American sharecropper's income went for rent alone, with little money left over for luxuries. According to Lichtenstein, Strasser, and Rosenzweig, "Most [U.S.] black sharecropping women kept house with only a straw broom, a laundry tub, a cooking kettle, and a water pail." The result was a sort of speed-up for farmers, who found themselves working longer hours, putting more land into production, but making less money. Some gave up, abandoned their farms, and moved to the cities. Others resolutely put every scrap of land they had under the plow, trying to keep up with the falling prices. As a result, they degraded the land and created dust bowls. By 1920 farmers throughout the West were in serious trouble.[312]

In the Tentacles of the Octopi

Increasingly, giant corporations – industrial behemoths like the Standard Oil Company (today's Exxon Mobil), Royal Dutch Shell, United States Steel, Krupp Steelworks, Consolidated Tobacco, the American Sugar Refining Company, the "Meat Trust" (a loose combination of the U.S.-based Armour, Swift, Cudahy, Morris, and Wilson meat-packing companies), General Mills, Bayer, Michelin, Computing-Tabulating-Recording (today's IBM), the National Biscuit Company (Nabisco), and the United Fruit Company – came to dominate the Western economy. In the United States, in 1918 the wealthiest five percent of the corporations earned 80% of all corporate income. In a world of cutthroat competition, the giants grew bigger and stronger by absorbing and combining with smaller competitors to form mammoth trusts and cartels bent on monopolizing trade and production. By 1890 John D. Rockefeller's (1839-1937) Cleveland-based Standard Oil trust controlled 90% of all the oil production in the United States (as well the majority worldwide), by 1895 the Pittsburgh-centered United States Steel Corporation (which in turn was owned by J. P. Morgan's New York City-based House of Morgan banking and railroad empire) dominated American steel production, by 1905 James B. Duke's Durham-based Consolidated Tobacco Company dominated American tobacco production, and by 1910 the American Sugar Refining Company controlled 98% of all U. S. sugar production.[313]

Boom-to-Bust Economic Cycles

From the mid-1700s until the mid-1900s, the West's new industrial economy was characterized by wild, gyrating boom-to-bust economic cycles. Flush times occurred in the 1880s, 1900s, and 1920s, but inevitably gave way to deep recessions in the 1870s, 1890s, and 1930s. The worst recession was the Great Depression of 1929-37. In 1932, in the United States alone, 12 million people were out of work, or fully 25% of the labor force. In Canada 826,000 were unemployed, also 25%. During the recessions the competition for jobs was especially keen, and wages inevitably fell. For example, in 1932 the median income in the United States dropped to only

---

[311] Bumsted, *History of the Canadian Peoples*, 221-251.
[312] Lichtenstein, *Who Built America?* 52; Merriman, *History of Modern Europe*, 870-871; Donald Worster, *Dust Bowl* (2004), passim.
[313] Anthony Sampson, *The Seven Sisters: The Great Oil Companies and the World They Shaped* (1975), 21-69; Carnes, *American Destiny*, 600-617.

half of what it had been in 1928. In Canada it was 55%. Recessions resulted in widespread homelessness. In 1930, 200,000 people were evicted in New York City alone.

It is important to realize that, for all its misery, the Great Depression was not an anomaly. From the 1830s to the 1930s, depressions occurred regularly. They can be traced in the unemployment statistics. The United States began recording unemployment rates in 1890. For the period 1890-92 unemployment was low, hovering at around only four percent, indicating that a boom period was underway. However, in 1893-98 unemployment jumped to 12-19 percent, indicating that a six-year depression had set in. But then, in 1899-1905, unemployment dropped once again, to around five percent, reflecting the arrival of a new six-year boom. In 1906-07 it fell even further, to about two percent, a two-year "super boom." But the good times never lasted long. In 1908-17, unemployment rose again, to around seven percent, indicating the arrival of a ten-year sluggish period that was neither boom nor bust, but something in-between. Then in 1918-19 the United States entered World War I and unemployment plummeted to less than two percent, as a rip-roaring two-year "war boom" created thousands of new jobs. But this was followed in 1920-22 by a "postwar recession," when unemployment jumped to around 10 percent. Then came the six boom years of the so-called "Roaring Twenties" (1923-28), one of the greatest booms of the industrial era, when unemployment dropped to only about three percent. But then came the Great Depression of the "Dirty Thirties" (1929-37), the West's worst depression, with unemployment surging to a high of 25 percent and an average of around 20 percent. Obviously, for most people, economic stability simply did not exist. A depression always lurked just around the corner, threatening to wipe out any gains that had been made in the previous boom.[314]

Revolutions

One of the most frustrating things about the early twentieth century was that so many people had expected things to be so much better. The nineteenth century had seemed to promise the West so much – more jobs, higher pay, increased standards of living, labor-saving machines, modern education, unlimited progress, world-wide empires, democracy, home rule, and an end to major wars. But World War I and the Great Depression made a mockery of those expectations, and by 1917 change was in the air. Four political philosophies -- four roads that the West could take -- beckoned.

Laissez-Faire

Like the American entrepreneur Andrew Carnegie (1835-1919), many people in the West defended the new system of industrialization, rationalism, capitalism, and classical liberalism that had emerged out of the Age of Revolution. They did not deny that serious problems existed, but they believed that public-spirited businessmen could (and would) solve those problems by voluntarily investing their profits in charitable activities. But they were wary of what they considered "intrusive" government action in the "private sphere," no matter how well intentioned it may be, which they believed would threaten liberty and only make things worse. Their program of noblesse oblige, limited government, and resistance to reform is often referred to as *laissez-faire*, French for "leave it alone."

Like most political labels, laissez-faire is somewhat of a misnomer. Its advocates did not intend that government should do nothing at all. On the contrary, unlike the early-nineteenth-century French physiocrats who had coined the term, laissez-faire's twentieth-century supporters acknowledged frankly that government needed to play a major role in economic planning. But they believed that it should be limited to promoting business in a general way, such as by subsidizing the building of roads, railroads, lighthouses, canals, and port facilities; maintaining navies, police forces, and judicial systems; delivering the mails; establishing uniform systems of weights and measures; minting money; establishing systems of credit; chartering corporations; fixing standard time zones; subsidizing education and research; providing cheap access to raw materials such as farmland and mineral deposits; acquiring colonies and dispossessing the natives; and "protecting" employers from labor unions, consumer-protection groups, and other "radical" combinations.

They also believed that government should actively promote "morality," by which they meant religion, temperance, patriarchy, sexual abstinence, and law and order in general.

But they did not believe that government should establish minimum wages, health insurance, or old-age pensions; regulate safety conditions in the workplace; outlaw monopolies (which Carnegie and others saw as desirable and fair mechanisms for promoting business efficiency); restrict immigration; or enact protective tariffs, housing codes, or consumer protection laws. Such actions, they argued, would harm businesses, slow growth, and reduce profits and jobs.

Furthermore, they thought that it was better to leave charity in the hands of the rich than to trust it to government, for only the rich had the proven wisdom and virtue to manage it correctly.

---

[314] John Kenneth Galbraith, *The Great Crash: 1929* (1961, 1997), passim; *Historical Statistics of the United States*, 135; John A. Garraty, *The Great Depression* (1986), passim; William Sheridan Allen, *The Nazi Seizure of Power: The Experiences of a Single German Town, 1922-1945* (1984), 69-90.

Laissez-faire was syncretic. It combined the noblesse oblige, resistance to reform, emphasis on virtue, and belief in a "natural aristocracy" associated with the classical conservatism of Edmund Burke with the support for capitalism, faith in meritocracy (rule by those with the greatest abilities), and fear of big government embedded in the classical liberalism of Thomas Paine. In the long run, the ideas and values of the laissez-faire advocates would seem to have formed the ideological basis for today's neo-conservatism.

Social Democrats and Progressives

The second option was the middle path of moderate reform, one that rejected staying put like laissez-faire, but which also steered between the far left of the communists and the far right of the reactionaries. Like laissez-faire, this middle path was syncretic, combining elements from Thomas Paine's classical liberalism with ideas from early socialism, feminism, nationalism, and environmentalism. From classical liberalism came a strong belief in human rights, competitive capitalism, republicanism, democracy, and equality under the law; from early socialism came the belief that the government should play a major role not simply in promoting economic growth in general but also in ensuring that there would be economic justice; from early feminism came the belief that women were equal to men and thus should have similar rights and responsibilities; from early nationalism came the belief that societies were organic communities in which the "haves" had a duty to help the "have-nots," whether they wanted to or not; and from environmentalism came support for conservation and improving the environment.

The people who followed this middle path of moderate reform went by many names. In the United States and Canada they called themselves "progressives." In Britain they called themselves "Labourites," after the new Labour Party, or "Lib-Labs," after a temporary merger of the Liberal and Labour parties. On the European continent, they usually called themselves "social democrats," their most common name. In Europe they usually thought of themselves more as moderate socialists than as liberals, but in North America (where socialism was unpopular even with many in the working class) they viewed themselves mainly as reform-minded liberals. But however they saw themselves, they shared an abiding faith in the ability of democratic government to solve serious social and economic problems. They advocated government regulation (but not ownership) of the economy in order to make it work more fairly. They plumped for minimum-wage laws, child-labor laws, eight-hour workdays, consumer-protection laws, either the breakup or regulation of the large corporations, restrictions on the power of special-interest groups, and the extension of voting rights to women, poor men, and minorities. Reformers rather than revolutionaries, their goal was not to overturn liberal democracy and capitalism, but to reform them by making them fairer. In the long run, their ideas would seem to have formed the basis for today's neo-liberalism.

Communists

Communists (also known as Bolsheviks, a Russian term meaning "majority") rejected the moderate reforms of the Social Democrats and took instead the far-left path of extreme socialism. True revolutionaries, they advocated the overthrow of the existing system and its replacement with what they called a "dictatorship of the proletariat." Inspired by the nineteenth-century socialist thinker Karl Marx, they advocated a full-blown workers' revolution in which the proletariat would rise up and drive the bourgeoisie from power, just as the bourgeoisie had earlier toppled the aristocracy. The eventual result, they believed, would be a workers' utopia, a classless and egalitarian society where everyone would have a voice, a vote, and a job, and where a democratically constituted state would not simply regulate the economy, but actually own the means of production.

Among the leading communists of the twentieth century was the Russian revolutionary Vladimir Ilyich Ulyanov (1870-1924) who, in order to evade the tsar's ever-vigilant secret police, used the pen name Lenin. Although inspired by Marx, Lenin disagreed with him on several key issues. While Marx had believed that a proletarian revolt would most likely occur in the industrialized core of the West, Lenin thought that it would happen instead in semi-industrialized Russia, where both the tsar's government and the small bourgeoisie were weaker and thus could more easily be overthrown. And while Marx had left open the possibility of a gradual, peaceful revolution, Lenin believed that it must be quick and violent.

In fact, Lenin (who, like most revolutionaries, was actually from the middle class) thought that the idea of a spontaneous workers' uprising – especially one that relied on the ballot box rather than the Molotov cocktail – was naive. "The replacement of the bourgeois by the proletarian," he said flatly, "is impossible without a violent revolution." The bourgeoisie was, he believed, too powerful, too entrenched, too well organized, too thoroughly in command of the existing system, to be overthrown without a fierce fight. Thus he believed that only a "vanguard party" – a small, dedicated, tightly controlled, well-educated, mostly middle-class, and ideologically pure group of committed revolutionaries "consisting chiefly of persons engaged in revolutionary activities as a profession" – could pull off a successful revolution.[315] Such a party must, he was certain, resort to

---

[315] Vladimir Ilyich Ulyanov Lenin, "What Is to Be Done?" (1902), reprinted in Vladimir Ilyich Ulyanov

violence and terror, not just to overthrow the old order, but also to keep itself in power in the early days of the revolution until the last remnants of the bourgeoisie had been rooted out – otherwise the enemy would regroup, counterattack, and stop the revolution in its tracks. For this reason, even when the communists were firmly in power in Russia, they must work to promote similar uprisings in other states.

Lenin opposed democracy in the present, because he thought that it was too dangerous so long as the bourgeoisie was still active. "Democracy," he wrote, must never be allowed to be a "democracy for the rich folk," who would surely use their great wealth to manipulate the system to thwart reform. Instead, a "dictatorship of the proletariat" must temporarily be put in place – a tightly controlled, communist-led government that would, in the name of revolution, enact "a series of restrictions of liberty in the case of the oppressors, the exploiters, the capitalists." He explained, "We must crush them [*the bourgeoisie*] in order to free humanity from wage-slavery; their resistance must be broken by force; it is clear that where there is suppression there is also violence, there is no liberty, no democracy…. Only in [*the eventual*] communist society, when the resistance of the capitalists has been completely broken, when the capitalists have disappeared, when there are no classes…only then [*will it*] become possible to speak of freedom." [316]

Reactionaries

Then there were the reactionaries, the ultraconservative and ultranationalist revolutionaries of the far right like Adolf Hitler, Benito Mussolini, and Francisco Franco. They were not exactly alike in their beliefs and policies, any more than all of the communists or social democrats were the same. Neither Mussolini nor Franco was as murderous, insane, or hateful as Hitler. But in their shrill opposition to and unbridled hatred of not only classical liberalism, but also feminism, socialism, social democracy, and communism – in their love of militarism, appeal to super-patriotism, and willingness to use extreme violence – they were close enough. Thus we will examine Hitler as a typical revolutionary reactionary.

Born in Austria into a lower middle-class family of German Catholic background, raised in a small, quiet, German-speaking border town called Linz, even in youth Adolf Hitler (1889-1945) was a loner who didn't fit in. He quarreled with his father, who died when Hitler was in his early teens. In high school he made few friends, mostly other "misfits" like himself. He disliked most of the people he knew, was not active in any church or club, sneered at his teachers as too liberal, and was strongly attracted to racism, militarism, and anti-Semitism. Although moderately intelligent, he nevertheless earned poor grades because he failed to complete many of his assignments. He was intellectually incapable of seeing things from other people's points of view. It was important to him to be respected as somebody important, but he believed that status was something that one should acquire through birth, not effort. He was forever looking for something that made him feel like a big shot – being an ethnic German, being middle class, being artistic (which he thought he was), being smart (which he also thought he was) – but underneath it all he was always secretly afraid that he was inferior: because his father had been illegitimate, because his ancestors had been peasants, because his mother had been a servant, because he might have ancestors who were Jews. So he covered up his insecurities by being aloof, arrogant, and condescending. Although his family was plunged into poverty when his father died, Hitler – unlike his hard-working mother and sister – refused to take a part-time job, not because he was too lazy, but because he considered it beneath him to work in a factory.

An aspiring but only marginally talented artist, after high school Hitler went to Vienna – there was nothing to keep him in Linz – to enroll in art school. Twice, he applied; twice, he was rejected. Refusing either to return home (his mother had since died) or to take a factory job in Vienna, he barely eked out a living as a poorly paid commercial artist. He despised Vienna, a large, cosmopolitan city with many Jewish, Slavic, Gypsy, and other non-German residents. He hated his life. On some level, he probably even loathed himself. Miserable and lonely, he attended political rallies for the popular, anti-Semitic mayor of Vienna, Karl Lueger (1844-1910), the founder of the right-wing Christian Social Party. Standing unseen on the outskirts, Hitler admired Lueger, although he did not join his party or even vote for him. He remained aloof, the grim outsider, always watching but never participating. He listened to music by Richard Wagner (VAHG-nehr) (1813-83), the ultra-nationalistic and anti-Semitic German composer. He read hate-filled pamphlets and articles by several ultranationalist and ultraconservative Austrian political pundits. Among the reactionary writers that impressed young Hitler was Georg Ritter von Schonerer (SHUHN-ehr-ehr) (1842-1921), an ultranationalist who advocated pan-Germanism (uniting all ethnic Germans into one large nation-state) and who founded Austria's reactionary Nationalist Party on a platform of violent nationalism, anti-Semitism, anti-socialism, and union with Germany. Hitler also read polemics by Adolf Lanz (LAHNTS) (1874-1954), a fraudulent, anti-Semitic, misogynistic, racist, and reactionary monk who used the vague term "Aryan" to refer to Europe's Nordic whites, which he considered the "master race." Lanz viewed Jews and Aryans as separate races, and hypothesized that they were engaged in a titanic, pseudo-Darwinian struggle to determine which of them was the "fittest" – a struggle that only one would survive.

Lenin, *Lenin: Collected Works* (1961), 451-453.
[316] Vladimir Ilyich Ulyanov Lenin, *State and Revolution* (1917, 1932), 70-75, 78-85; Theodore H. von Laue, *Why Lenin? Why Stalin?: A Reappraisal of the Russian Revolution, 1900-1930* (1971), 70-99.

When World War I broke out in 1914, Hitler joined the German army. (The year before, he had moved to Germany, in order to escape the many Jews and other non-Aryans who lived in Vienna.) By most accounts a brave but fanatical soldier, he rose to the rank of corporal. He twice won the iron cross for valor under fire, once capturing an entire French platoon single-handed. But his fellow soldiers, put off by his frequent patriotic diatribes and insistence that, back home, their wives and girlfriends were consorting with Jews, did not like him. Badly wounded by poison gas, he lay recovering in a military hospital when word arrived that Germany had surrendered. Furious, Hitler blamed the defeat on the politicians, social democrats, liberals, and Jews – all of whom, he believed, had "stabbed Germany in the back."

After the war, Hitler drifted into the German city of Munich, where he encountered and joined a tiny ultranationalist, ultraconservative, fringe political party, the misnamed Nationalist Socialist German Workers Party, or Nazis. (The Nazi party was not socialist at all. Indeed, much of its literature was devoted to denouncing both social democracy and communism as Jewish plots to sap the strength of the German people. And its small membership was mostly from the lower middle class, not the factory workers.) In time, Hitler became the Nazis' leader, or *fuehrer*. In 1923, under Hitler's leadership, the Nazis attempted a violent but ill-planned *putsch* (coup d'etat) to overthrow the new German Republic, something that several other communist and reactionary groups had also tried. A miserable failure, the Nazi "revolution" was quickly suppressed, and Hitler was sentenced to prison. (In 1920s Germany, Communist revolutionaries were usually executed, while reactionaries like Hitler – protected by the sympathetic right-wing German military – received only short jail terms.) In prison, Hitler wrote *Mein Kampf* ("My Struggle"), a bitter, rambling, illogical diatribe of white supremacism. Released from prison in the late 1920s, Hitler returned to revolutionary activity and reorganized the Nazis into a small but vocal right-wing party that won a few seats in the German Reichstag, or parliament. He attracted new members by dressing his recruits in stylish brown uniforms, encouraging them to play out their fantasies of militarism by beating up Jews and social democrats. In a climate of increasing political violence and social disintegration, in a country where the army was limited by law to only a few thousand, several other German political groups besides the Nazis formed private militias. The Nazis had their *Sturmabteilung* ("Storm Troopers," also called "brown shirts"), but the Nationalists had their *Stahlhelm* ("Steel Helmet"), the conservatives their *Freikorps* ("Free Corps"), and even the moderate Social Democratic Party had its *Reichsbanner* ("Reich's Flag").

When the Great Depression struck in the 1930s, fringe groups like the Nazis and communists suddenly gained strength. Middle-class German voters, fearful of sinking into the despised working class, willing to blame the Social Democrats for the humiliation of Versailles and the dislocations and uncertainties of the Depression, terrified of a communist revolution, worried that modern life and classical liberalism had undermined and destroyed traditional values, unused to constitutional government, voted the Nazis into office. By 1932 they were the largest party in the Reichstag, the principal middle-class alternative to the working-class Social Democrats. In 1933 the aging German President Paul von Hindenburg (1847-1934) named Hitler Chancellor (Prime Minister). In 1934 Hindenburg died and Hitler took over Germany completely, abolishing the Republic, outlawing all opposition parties, purging the Storm Troopers to ensure the loyalty of those who remained, ghettoizing and arresting Jews, communists, liberals, and socialists, and otherwise establishing the dreaded Third Reich.[317]

It is easy today to dismiss Hitler as a madman (which, to a certain extent, he was), an isolated nut who somehow hypnotized the German people with his charismatic oratory. That is how many Germans today prefer to remember him. But if he was a madman, there were many madmen in the West in the early 1900s. Benito Mussolini (1883-1945) rose to power in Italy on similar ideas and similar tactics a decade *before* Hitler and the Nazis seized control of Germany. In 1922 Mussolini's Fascist Party replaced Italy's constitutional monarchy with a reactionary dictatorship, and although the Fascists did not establish concentration camps like those of the Nazis, they did murder their political foes and outlaw opposition parties. In Spain, the reactionary Dictator Francisco Franco's (1892-1975) Falangist Party also espoused a form of fascism, and came to power in the Spanish Civil War of 1936-39. In Argentina the reactionary soldier Juan Peron rode to power on a program of fascism. In Britain, King Edward VIII (1894-1972), who abdicated in 1936 to marry the American divorcee Wallis Simpson, was a closet fascist. There were fascists and reactionaries in the United States as well, right-wing revolutionaries like the popular but virulently anti-Semitic "radio priest" Father Charles Edward Coughlin (1891-1979), the Louisiana Senator Huey Long (1893-1935), and even President Franklin Roosevelt's (1882-1945) first Vice President, the thoroughly racist John Nance Garner (1868-1967).

These reactionaries (also known as fascists) were right-wing revolutionaries, usually violent, whose goal was to overthrow the West's liberal, republican, democratic, and capitalist regimes and replace them not with communism, which they despised, but a new yet ultraconservative, ultranationalist order based on what they considered to be traditional values. They opposed classical liberalism because of its emphasis on equality, republicanism, secularism, and democracy. They opposed socialism and communism because they saw them as unjustly elevating the working class to the level of the middle class. They opposed feminism as unmanly, untraditional, and unmilitaristic. They denounced both big business and labor unions as dominated by Jews. They advocated war because they believed that armed combat promoted courage, strength, patriotism, and

---

[317] William L. Shirer, *The Rise and Fall of the Third Reich: A History of Nazi Germany* (1950, 1960), 21-166; Allen, *Nazi Seizure of Power*, passim; R. G. L. Waite, "Adolf Hitler's Guilt Feelings: A Problem in History and Psychology," *Journal of Interdisciplinary History* (1971), 1: 229-249.

other traditional virtues. They trumpeted militarism, manliness, "blood and iron," imperialism, racism, anti-Semitism, and something that historians call totalitarianism, or the complete and total allegiance of the individual to the all-powerful, corporate state – a perspective that, ironically, they shared with their blood enemies, the despised communists. They claimed to believe in religion, in Franco's case sincerely, although in Hitler's only as a ploy to win the support of religious voters. They believed in the cult of the strong leader, the great man who knows all the answers and who will solve all problems.[318]

Things Fall Apart

From 1917 to 1939 reactionary revolutions rocked several of the Western nations, while social democratic reform parties were elected to office in others. Different countries had different results. Generally, in those countries with long histories of constitutional government (Britain, France, the United States, Canada, the Netherlands, Scandinavia), social democratic reformers challenged the neoconservatives and classical liberals in a series of elections, some of which they won. In Britain, the social democratic Labour Party first came to power in 1924, although it was a minority government that held office for less than a year before losing to the opposition Conservative Party. Labour came back to win again in 1929, but then lost again in 1931. In neither 1924 nor 1929 did Labour win an outright majority, but rather governed in coalition with the Liberals, Britain's third-largest party. Because the Labour-Liberal ("Lib-Lab") alliance was tenuous at best, neither of the Labour regimes lasted long. As a result, it was the laissez-faire Conservative Party that held power throughout most of the 1920s, 1930s, and 1940s. Unsurprisingly, reforms in Britain were few. In France a similar situation occurred, with the social democratic Socialist Party winning elections in 1924 and 1936, but losing in 1925 and 1937. Like the Labourites in Britain, the Socialists in France were forced to govern in coalition with other parties – usually the liberal Radicals – in fragile alliances that failed to last. Most of the time it was the parties of laissez-faire that held power in France, and as in Britain, reforms were few.

In the United States the situation was different. Although the laissez-faire Republican Party held office from 1920 to 1933, from 1933 on it was the progressive Democratic Party that was in power. Consequently, the Americans enacted deeper and more far-reaching reforms (the so-called New Deal of President Franklin Roosevelt) than either the British or the French. In Scandinavia social democratic parties came to power in the 1920s and 1930s and remained in office; here, too, real changes occurred.[319]

On the other hand, countries that did not have long histories of constitutional government (Germany, Hungary, Italy, Spain, Portugal, Poland, Russia, and Bulgaria) generally experienced tumultuous, full-bore revolutions, with results that were seldom good. Although social democratic regimes did briefly hold office in most of these countries, they eventually collapsed and gave way either to communists (in Russia) or reactionaries (everywhere else).

Thus, by the late 1930s the West was deeply divided. Laissez-faire still governed in Britain and France; social democracy seemed to have triumphed in Scandinavia, the United States, and Canada; communism ruled in Russia; and reactionary dictatorships governed Germany, Hungary, Spain, Portugal, Italy, Poland, Bulgaria, Greece, Yugoslavia, and much of Latin America. It was an unstable situation that could not last.

The following chart summarizes some of the revolutions and elections that brought advocates of change – either reform-minded social democrats (progressives) or revolutionary communists and reactionaries (fascists) – into power.

Some Revolutionary Regimes and Reform Governments, 1917-39		
years in power	country	group in power
1917	Russia	social democrats
1917-91	Russia	communists
1918-19	Hungary	social democrats
1918-39	Czechoslovakia	social democrats
1918	Germany	social democrats
1919	Hungary	communists

---

[318] Peter Fritzsche, *Germans into Nazis* (1998), passim; Richard S. Levy, *Antisemitism in the Modern World: An Anthology of Texts* (1991), 1-30; Elizabeth Wiskemann, *Europe of the Dictators, 1919-1945* (1966), passim; Wolfgang Sauer, "National Socialism: Totalitarianism or Fascism?" *American Historical Review* (1967), 73: 404-424; George L. Mosse, "The Genesis of Fascism," *Journal of Contemporary History* (1966), 1: 14-26; Hans Kohn, *Nationalism: Its Meaning and History* (1955), 73-81; Hugo Valetin, *Antisemitism Historically and Critically Examined* (1936), passim.

[319] Paxton, *Europe in the Twentieth Century*, 156-159, 240-253, 310-339; Jordan A. Schwartz, *The New Dealers* (1993), passim (USA); Robert Skidelsky, *Politicians and the Slump* (1967), passim (Britain); Joel Colton, *Leon Blum: Humanist in Politics* (1966), passim (France); William E. Leuchtenburg, *Franklin D. Roosevelt and the New Deal* (1963), passim (USA).

1919-44	Hungary	reactionaries
1922-44	Italy	reactionaries
1924	Britain	social democrats
1924-25	France	social democrats
1926-	Portugal	reactionaries
1929-	Denmark	social democrats
1929-31	Britain	social democrats
1930-39	Spain	social democrats
1933-	USA	social democrats
1933-	Sweden	social democrats
1933-45	Germany	reactionaries
1935-	Norway	social democrats
1936-37	France	social democrats
1939-	Spain	reactionaries

The Holocaust

Once in power, Hitler and the Nazis launched a program of unrestrained anti-Semitism and wholesale slaughter aimed at the subjugation and eventual extermination of the West's Jews and other non-Aryans that continued until the fall of the Nazi regime in 1945. "The Holocaust," says the United States Holocaust Memorial Museum "was the systematic, bureaucratic, state-sponsored persecution and murder of approximately six million Jews by the Nazi regime and its collaborators." As the entire Jewish population of Europe was only about nine million to begin with, two-thirds of European Jewry perished, making the Holocaust a true act of near genocide (killing an entire group of people). In addition to Jews, the Nazi regime executed approximately 10 million others, including political opponents (liberals, social democrats, labor union activists, and communists), Polish and other Slavic intellectuals (about three million Catholic Poles died, in addition to about three million Jewish Poles), Gypsies (40% of Europe's Gypsies were killed), homosexuals, Jehovah's Witnesses, handicapped persons, and approximately three million Russian prisoners of war, who died of mistreatment in German POW camps during World War II (1939-45). Greek in origin, the word "holocaust" means "sacrifice by fire" or "the burning."

Between 1933 and 1939 the Nazis established both ghettoes (restricted neighborhoods) and concentration camps in Germany, where they imprisoned Jews and others as slave laborers. When war broke out in 1939, Germany occupied Poland, Czechoslovakia, Austria, Hungary, and other countries with large Jewish populations. (Jews comprised only two percent of the population of pre-war Germany.) The Nazis erected new ghettoes and camps in these areas. At first the camps were slave labor camps, but after 1942 the Nazis began to build massive death camps like the infamous Auschwitz in Poland, designed for the wholesale slaughter of Jews and other "enemies" of their regime. And after invading the USSR in 1941, they established mobile killing units called *Einsatzgruppen* to murder Jews, Gypsies, and Soviet political leaders. In the last months of the war Nazi guards forced many of the surviving inmates onto grueling death marches, in order to prevent the advancing Soviet troops from liberating them.[320]

Causes of World War II

After coming to power in 1933, Hitler and the Nazis repudiated the Treaty of Versailles, rebuilt the German military, annexed a willing Austria, and organized the Axis, a powerful military alliance of Germany, Italy, and (as a junior partner) Japan (which was already at war with China). In 1938 Germany threatened to annex the Sudetenland, an ethnic German region in western Czechoslovakia. Hoping to prevent a major war, Britain and France warily agreed to meet with Germany and Italy in the German city of Munich to discuss the Sudetenland situation. To appease Hitler, the two democracies reluctantly agreed to permit Germany to take the territory. Czechoslovakia was too small and powerless to resist by itself. In return, Hitler promised that Germany would annex no further territory. But only a few months later, Hitler broke his word and Germany invaded and occupied the rest of Czechoslovakia. In 1939 Hitler went even further, ordering German troops into western Poland. At the same time the USSR advanced into eastern Poland. Britain and France decided to fight, and World War II began.

---

[320] United States Holocaust Memorial Museum, "The Holocaust," www.ushmm.org, retrieved 4/2/2003; Daniel Jonah Goldhagen, *Hitler's Willing Executioners: Ordinary Germans and the Holocaust* (1996), passim; Gerda Klein, *All But My Life: A Memoir* (1996), passim; Viktor Frankl, *Man's Search for Meaning* (2000), passim; Elie Wiesel, *Night* (1960), passim; Di Scala, *Twentieth-Century Europe*, 420-432; Paxton, *Europe in the Twentieth Century*, 448-453.

Why did the West go to war in 1939, only two decades after the carnage and devastation of World War I? Historians proffer two possible interpretations: blaming Hitler, and blaming Britain and France for misinterpreting Hitler.

Let's examine the second interpretation first. Known as the "revisionist interpretation" (because it revised the earlier interpretation of blaming Hitler), it was first elucidated in 1961 by the ornery British historian, A. J. P. Taylor. Taylor argued that, while Hitler was certainly a reactionary in his domestic politics, in his foreign policy he actually behaved more like a traditional German leader, attempting to acquire for his country the same sorts of things that previous leaders had sought: an end to the humiliating Treaty of Versailles, the right for Germany to rearm and defend itself, an empire commensurate with those of Britain and France, and the restoration of Germany's "historical borders" in the east, which meant German control of Austria, Czechoslovakia, Poland, the Baltic States, and those parts of Russia gained in the early days of World War I. Taylor's Hitler was a conniving opportunist more than a right-wing idealist, a cagy schemer whose warlike statements were merely Nazi rhetoric, designed mainly to appease the party faithful at home, and thus should not have been taken too seriously. According to Taylor, Hitler simply took advantage of the many openings the democracies gave him. In other words, as long as France and Britain allowed Germany to annex territories with impunity, Hitler would continue to do so – at least until it had reestablished its "historical boundaries." Taylor thus believed that when Britain and France caved in to Hitler at Munich, he had taken it as a signal that his blustering worked – that he could continue to threaten war and get what he wanted without ever actually have to fight, and was astonished when his invasion of Poland touched off World War II. Had the democracies stood up to him earlier, Taylor reasoned, Hitler would have backed down and World War II might never have occurred.[321]

Most historians, however, believe that Taylor's interpretation of Hitler is wrong. Alan Bullock, for example, argues that, while Hitler was indeed conniving and certainly an opportunist, he was also a reactionary ideologue thoroughly committed to racist and ultranationalist foreign policies and had in mind a specific (if not always clearly stated) program of expansion that went well beyond those of previous German leaders. According to Bullock, Hitler wanted *Lebensraum* (living room) for Germany, and thus had intended all along to conquer Czechoslovakia, Poland, Russia, and other Eastern European territories – partly to acquire territory to accommodate the expanding German middle class; partly to lay claim to important natural resources such as the Russian oil and gas fields around the Caspian Sea; partly to gain access to Eastern Europe's large Jewish population, which he intended to murder; partly to exploit the "inferior" Slavic peoples as submerged laborers; and partly because he believed that war in itself was glorious and necessary in order to strengthen and purify the German people for the coming struggle with the Jews and other non-Aryans. But at the same time Hitler knew that Germany could not hope to win a protracted war against Britain, France, and the USSR combined – World War I had already demonstrated that that plan wouldn't work. But he did believe that Germany could conquer its foes if it picked them off one-by-one in a series of quick, limited, individual surprise attacks – or, to use Hitler's term, by *Blitzkrieg* (lightning war).

According to Bullock, Hitler thus began to build up the German military for *Blitzkrieg* in the mid-1930s, before Munich. Official German government memos indicate that Hitler fully expected to fight Czechoslovakia, France, the USSR, and even Britain sometime in the 1940s, but that he wanted to face them one at a time, not all together. *Blitzkrieg* allowed Germany to defeat each country quickly, in only a few weeks, before they had a chance to fully prepare for war. He nearly pulled it off. *Blitzkrieg* beat Czechoslovakia, Poland, Denmark, Norway, the Low Countries, France, Greece, and Yugoslavia, and placed most of Europe in Hitler's hands. But in two instances, *Blitzkrieg* failed. Germany could not quickly defeat Britain (which was protected by its mighty navy) or the USSR (which was protected by its immense size and population). Thus the Axis eventually lost World War II.[322]

Timeline of World War II

Sep. 1931: Japan seizes the Chinese province of Manchuria.

Jan. 1933: Hitler becomes Chancellor of Germany.

Mar. 1935: Hitler announces a German air force, the *Luftwaffe*.

Mar. 1935: Hitler announces military conscription.

Oct. 1935: Italy invades and conquers Ethiopia.

Mar. 1936: Germany remilitarizes the Rhineland, the German territory along the border with France.

---

[321] A. J. P. Taylor, *The Origins of the Second World War* (1963), passim.
[322] Alan Bullock, "Hitler and the Origins of the Second World War," *Proceedings of the British Academy* (1967), 53: 259-287.

Oct. 1936: Germany and Italy form the Axis.

Nov. 1936: Germany and Japan sign Anti-COMINTERN Pact.

Mar. 1938: Merger of Germany and Austria.

Sep. 1938: The Munich Conference gives the Sudetenland to Germany.
Mar. 1939: Germany occupies the rest of Czechoslovakia.

Aug. 1939: Germany and USSR sign Nazi-Soviet Non-aggression Pact. (After Munich, the USSR no longer believes that Britain and France will stand up to Hitler, and the Russians know that they cannot defeat Germany on their own.)

Sep. 1939: Germany invades Poland from the west; USSR invades Poland from the east. (Although not part of the Axis, at this stage USSR is acting in concert with Germany.)

Sep. 1939: Britain & France declare war on Germany, but not USSR.

Sep. 1939: Poland is defeated.

Nov. 1939 to March 1940: USSR invades and conquers Finland.

Oct. 1939 to Apr. 1940: So-called "Phony War." No actual fighting occurs between France and Britain and the Axis.

Apr. 1940: Phony War ends when Germany invades and conquers Denmark and Norway. In each country reactionary collaborators are put in power. In each country a resistance of partisans (guerrilla fighters) develops.

May 1940. Germany invades and conquers Netherlands, Belgium, and Luxembourg. In each country reactionary collaborators are put in power. In each country a resistance of partisans develops.

May 1940: Germany invades France.

May 1940: Winston Churchill becomes Prime Minister of Britain and sets up War Cabinet of all three political parties.

June 1940: Paris falls. France surrenders. Marshall Philippe Petain and other French reactionaries set up the collaborationist Vichy government in southern France. The new regime is opposed by a resistance of partisans.

June 1940: Britain evacuates its troops at Dunkirk, but leaves massive amounts of materials behind.

Jul. 1940: Britain attacks and destroys the French fleet off the coast of North Africa, assuring continued British control of the Atlantic Ocean.

Jul. 1940 through May 1941: The year-long Battle of Britain occurs in the skies over England, with the Royal Air Force (RAF) and Royal Canadian Air Force (RCAF) fighting the German Luftwaffe. Massive bombing of Britain occurs (the Blitz). The RAF and RCAF win, preventing Germany from invading Britain either by sea or by air.

Jul. 1940 through Dec. 1944: The five-year Battle of the Atlantic occurs, as German submarines attack supply convoys from Canada to Britain. British and Canadian corvairs and destroyers defend the convoys. Massive casualties result.

Early 1941: Japan takes war beyond China, invading French Indochina (Vietnam) and British Malaya.

Mar. 1941: USA agrees to provide Britain with supplies on credit (Lend-Lease).

Mar.-Apr. 1941: Italy and Germany invade and conquer Greece and Yugoslavia. Reactionary collaborators are installed in power, as in France, Scandinavia, and the Low Countries. Greek and Serb partisans continue to resist. Reactionary Croats (Cetniks) side with the Axis and at Jasenovac, the "Auschwitz of the Balkans," exterminate Jews, Serbs, Gypsies, and Muslims.

Apr. 1941: German troops invade North Africa, drive British back into Egypt, and threaten to take Suez Canal.

Jun. 1941: Germany invades USSR in Operation Barbarossa. USSR now joins Britain and China in the war against the Axis.

1941-42: Germany advances to gates of Leningrad (St. Petersburg), Moscow, and Stalingrad. Leningrad besieged for 900 days. USSR moves its industry east into Ural Mountains, begins building tanks.

Dec. 1941: Japan attacks USA. USA now joins Britain, China, and USSR in the war against the Axis.

Jun. 1942: USA defeats Japan in Battle of Midway, turning the tide in the Pacific.

Oct.-Nov. 1942: Britain defeats Germany in Battle of El Alamein in Egypt, turning the tide in North Africa. By Apr. 1943 German forces were driven from North Africa.

Sep. 1942 to Jan. 1943: USSR defeats Germany and Romania in Battle of Stalingrad, turning the tide in Eastern Europe.

Jan. 1943: USSR breaks the German siege of Leningrad after 900 days.

Jul. 1943: American and British forces invade Italy. On 25 July Mussolini was overthrown in a *coup d'etat* by Italian army. German troops seize Rome and free Mussolini. As German forces fight the British and Americans, Italians battle each other in a civil war between Mussolini's supporters and his foes. Italy ceases to be an effective German ally.

Jun. 1944: American, British, and Canadian forces invade France on D-Day, turning the tide in Western Europe.

Dec. 1944: Battle of the Bulge. Britain, the USA, and Canada defeat Germany in the last major battle.

Apr. 1945: Hitler commits suicide.

May 1945: Germany surrenders.

Aug. 1945: USA drops atomic bombs on Japanese cities of Hiroshima and Nagasaki. Japan surrenders.

Consequences of World War II

World War II was even more brutal and devastating than World War I had been, with more than 40 million soldiers and civilians killed or wounded in combat, and another 20 million civilians perishing from disease, malnutrition, overwork, and outright genocide. Casualty totals are not exact, but the following chart provides a rough estimate:

Country	Battle Deaths and Wounded
USSR	20.5 m
Germany	10.5 m
China	3.0 m
Japan	1.5 m
Poland	1.2 m

World War II Casualties (Soldiers and Civilians)

British Empire	1.1 m
Britain (726 k)	
Australia (208 k)	
India (97 k)	
Canada (95 k)	
New Zealand (29 k)	
South Africa (2 k)	
USA	0.9 m
Yugoslavia	730 k
Austria	630 k
French Empire	600 k
Romania	520 k
Hungary	237 k
Italy	217 k
Finland	112 k
Belgium	64 k
Greece	64 k
Bulgaria	29 k
Czechoslovakia	15 k
Netherlands	9 k
Brazil	5 k
Denmark	4 k
Norway	2 k

World War II had other important consequences for the West. It brought an end to the New Imperialism. Except for the United States, the West was so devastated by war that most Western countries could no longer maintain their overseas colonies. In the four decades following the war the colonies gradually broke away and became independent states – a process that historians have dubbed decolonization.

The war also changed the balance within the West. Because at the end of the war North America (the United States and Canada) was less devastated and had suffered fewer casualties than Western Europe, the United States emerged from the maelstrom of the 1940s as the West's sole superpower. Paradoxically, in the East the war-torn USSR (and, too a lesser extent, China) also became superpowers, challenging the USA for global supremacy in the so-called Cold War (c. 1949-89), an ideological struggle that pitted Eastern and Asian communism against Western liberal capitalism.

Also, new technologies developed during the war sparked a Third Industrial Revolution based on computers, nuclear power, and micro-technology. Among the new inventions of the mid-1900s were the world's first electronic computers, ENIAC (Electronic Numerical Integrator And Computer), and its much more powerful successor, MANIAC (Mathematical Analyzer, Numerical Integrator And Computer), both of which had obvious military potential. Built during the war at Harvard University by International Business Machines (IBM) under a grant from the U. S. government, ENIAC had 500 miles of wire and 3,000,000 electrical connections, but used bulky vacuum tubes rather than microchips (which had not yet been invented) and had only enough memory to recall twenty-seven words. By comparison, the much larger MANIAC, although not ready until six years after the war ended, could retain and recall 40,000 bits of data and compute as many equations in one day as ENIAC could in three months. The Computer Age had begun.

Other new technologies that came out of World War II included atomic power (initially used to create bombs), jet engines, rockets, transistors, synthetic rubber, powerful new insecticides and defoliants (for waging war in the tropics), and SONAR. Clearly, the war had been a catalyst for change, speeding up the pace of industrialization and technological progress.

For obvious reasons, the Holocaust was also a catalyst for Zionism, as tens of thousands of Western Jews now fled Europe and migrated to the newly independent state of Israel.

Finally, while many people in the West emerged from the war with renewed faith in science, technology, and modern life, others wondered whether modernization and technology were really such good things. Scarred by the war, the Holocaust, and the enormous killing capacity of modern science, a new generation of writers and philosophers began to exalt emotion (especially love) over reason, tradition over progress, and community over technology. Sometimes called postmodernists, these thinkers included the Franco-Algerian Albert Camus (1913-60) (who concluded that God was dead, and that without Him the West had no future or hope except to develop its own moral code grounded in something other than religion or science), the French philosopher Jean-Paul Sartre (1905-80) (an existentialist who argued that people were only what they made of themselves), the Colombian novelist Gabriel Garcia Marquez (1928-   ) (who wrote about tradition and continuity in the peasant communities of his native South America.), and the Austrian psychologist Viktor Frankl (1905-97) (a Jewish Holocaust survivor who maintained that the true meaning of life lies in the choices we make and our connections to other people). Like many postmodernists, Frankl saw flaws in modern Western culture. "Since Auschwitz we know what man is capable of," he wrote. "And since Hiroshima we know what is at stake." But like Camus and Sartre, Frankl believed that people had the freedom to choose how they reacted to tragedy, and that within that choice lays the true meaning of life. Frankl argued that suffering could be turned into an achievement, that guilt could be harnessed as an incentive for self-improvement, and that the transitory nature of life was all the more reason to take responsible action. The true measure of humanity, the postmodernists insisted, was not the ability to reason logically, nor adherence to traditional belief, but caring for others.

-The Documents-

Laissez Faire: Andrew Carnegie

Like his arch-foe, the American labor leader Mary "Mother" Jones, Andrew Carnegie (1835-1919) was born in the 1830s in Europe (although in Scotland rather than Ireland), migrated to the United States as a child, and grew up in poverty. There, however, the similarity ends. While Jones became a union organizer, Carnegie worked his way up from poverty (this was unusual; almost all of the other entrepreneurs at least started from the middle class) to become a steel magnate and the wealthiest man in the world. As a businessman, Carnegie was ruthless. His chief engineer said of him, in admiration, "Andy was born with two sets of teeth and holes bored for more." Strongly anti-union, he used force to break strikes. Yet Carnegie was also the world's greatest philanthropist. By the time he died he had given away most of his money. The person who dies rich, Carnegie insisted, "dies disgraced." Despite his privilege and wealth – and his fundamental conservatism – Carnegie admitted that modern society had problems. One of those problems was poverty. Yet as a firm believer in laissez-faire economics, he did not think that the government should pass laws regulating the economy in an attempt to ameliorate poverty. Nor did he believe the poor should simply be given money. Rather, he saw himself and other tycoons as potential economic stewards. They would – or should – use their great wealth to build libraries, endow concert halls, support schools, and undertake other projects that would allow hard-working poor people to "pull themselves up by their own bootstraps." In an article called "Wealth," Carnegie outlined his laissez-faire approach to social problems.[323]

from "WEALTH"[324]

We accept and welcome...as conditions to which we must accommodate ourselves great inequality of environment, the concentration of business – industrial and commercial – in the hands of a few, and the law of competition between these as being not only beneficial but essential for the future progress of the race [by "race," Carnegie meant "the human race."] Having accepted these, it follows that there must be great scope for the exercise of special ability in the merchant and in the manufacturer who has to conduct affairs upon a great scale. That this talent for organization and management is rare among men is proved by the fact that it invariably secures for its possessor rewards, no matter where or under what laws or conditions. The experienced in affairs always rate the man whose services can be obtained as a partner as not only the first consideration but such as to render the question of his capital scarcely worth considering, for such men soon create capital; while, without the special talent required, capital soon takes wings.

Such men become interested or corporations using millions; and estimating only simple interest to be made upon the capital invested, it is inevitable that their income must exceed their expenditures and that they must accumulate wealth. Nor is there any middle ground which such men can occupy, because the great manufacturing or commercial concern which does not earn at least interest upon its capital soon becomes bankrupt. It must either go forward or fall behind: to stand still is impossible. It is a condition essential for its successful operation that it should be thus far profitable, and even that, in addition to interest on capital, it should make profit. It is a law, as certain as any of the others named, that men possessed of this peculiar talent for affairs, under the free play of economic forces, must, of necessity, soon be in receipt of more revenue than can be judiciously expended upon themselves; and this law is as beneficial for the race as the others.

Objections to the foundations upon which society is based are not in order because the condition of the race is better with these than it has been with any others which have been

---

[323] J. William T. Youngs, *American Realities: Historical Episodes* (2001), 2: 22-43.
[324] Andrew Carnegie, "Wealth," *North American Review* (1889), reprinted in William Benton, ed., *The Annals of America* (1968), 11: 222-226.

tried. Of the effect of any new substitutes proposed, we cannot be sure. The socialist or anarchist who seeks to overturn present conditions is to be regarded as attacking the foundation upon which civilization itself rests, for civilization took its start from the day that the capable, industrious workman said to his incompetent and lazy fellow, "If thou dost not sow, thou shalt not reap," and thus ended primitive Communism by separating the drones from the bees. One who studies this subject will soon be brought face to face with the conclusion that upon the sacredness of property civilization itself depends – the right of the laborer to his $100 in the savings bank, and equally the legal right of the millionaire to his millions.

* * * *

We start, then, with a condition of affairs under which the best interests of the race are promoted, but which inevitably gives wealth to the few. Thus far, accepting conditions as they exist, the situation can be surveyed and pronounced good. The question then arises – and, if the foregoing be correct, it is the only question with which we have to deal – What is the proper mode of administering wealth after the laws upon which civilization is founded have thrown it into the hands of the few? And it is of this great question that I believe I offer the true solution. It will be understood that fortunes are here being spoken of, not moderate sums saved by many years of effort, the returns from which are required for the comfortable maintenance and education of families....

There are but three modes in which surplus wealth can be disposed of. It can be left to the families of the decedents; or it can be bequeathed for public purposes; or, finally, it can be administered during their lives by its possessors....

The first is the most injudicious. In monarchical countries, the estates and the greatest portion of the wealth are left to the first son that the vanity of the parent may be gratified by the thought that his name and title are to descend to succeeding generations unimpaired. The condition of this class in Europe today teaches the futility of such hopes or ambitions. The successors have become impoverished through their follies or from the fall in the value of land.... Under republican institutions the division of property among the children is much fairer, but the question which forces itself upon thoughtful men in all lands is: Why should men leave great fortunes to their children? If this is done from affection, is it not misguided affection? Observation teaches that, generally speaking, it is not well for the children that they should be so burdened. Neither is it well for the state [i.e., for society]. Beyond providing for the wife and daughters moderate sources of income, and very moderate allowances indeed, if any, for the sons, men may well hesitate, for it is no longer questionable that great sums bequeathed oftener work more for the injury than the good of the recipients. Wise men will soon conclude that, for the best interests of the members of their families and of the state, such bequests are an improper use of their means.

* * * *

As to the second mode, that of leaving wealth at death for public uses, it may be said that this is only a means for the disposal of wealth, provided a man is content to wait until he is dead before it becomes of much good to the world.... The cases are not few in which the real object sought by the testator is not attained, nor are they few in which his real wishes are thwarted. In many cases the bequests are used as to become only monuments of his folly.

[At this point Carnegie went into a long argument in favor of inheritance taxes.]

There remains, then, only one mode of using great fortunes; but in this we have the true antidote for the temporary unequal distribution of wealth, the reconciliation of the rich and the poor – a reign of harmony – another ideal, differing, indeed from that of Communism in requiring only the further evolution of existing conditions, not the total overthrow of our civilization. It is founded on the present most intense individualism, and the race is prepared to put it in practice by degrees whenever it pleases. Under its sway we shall have an ideal state in which the surplus wealth of the few will become, in the best sense, the property of the many, because administered for the common good; and this wealth, passing through the hands of the few, can be made a much more potent force for the elevation of our race than if it had been distributed in small sums to the people themselves. Even the poorest can be made to see this and to agree that great sums gathered by some of their fellow citizens and spent for public purposes, from which the masses reap the principal benefit, are more valuable to them than if scattered among them through the course of many years of trifling amounts....

Poor and restricted are our opportunities in this life; narrow our horizon; our best work most imperfect; but rich men should be thankful for one estimable boon. They have it in their power during their lives to busy themselves in organizing benefactions from which the masses of their fellows will derive lasting advantage, and thus dignify their own lives. The highest life is probably to be reached, not by such imitation of the life of Christ as Count Tolstoy gives us [the Russian writer Tolstoy lived for a time in self-induced poverty on a collective farm] but, while animated by Christ's spirit, by recognizing the changed conditions of this age and adopting modes of expressing this spirit suitable to the changed conditions under which we live; still laboring for the good of our fellows, which was the essence of his life and teaching, but laboring in a different manner.

This, then, is held to be the duty of the man of wealth: first, to set an example of modest, unostentatious living, shunning display or extravagance; to provide moderately for the legitimate wants of those dependent upon him; and after doing so to consider all surplus revenues which come to him simply as trust funds which he is called upon to administer, and strictly bound as a matter of duty to administer in the manner which, in his judgment, is best calculated to produce the most beneficial results for the community – the man of wealth thus becoming the mere agent and trustee for his poorer brethren, bringing to their service his superior wisdom, experience, and ability to administer, doing for them better than they would or could do for themselves....

In bestowing charity, the main consideration should be to help those who will help themselves; to provide part of the means by which those who desire to improve may do so; to give those who desire to rise, the aids by which they may rise; to assist, but rarely or never to do all....

Social Democracy: Theodore Roosevelt

Theodore Roosevelt (1858-1919), an American progressive, was born into one of the wealthiest families in the United States. A small, sickly child, Roosevelt suffered from asthma and poor eyesight. When he was a boy, his parents sent him from their home near New York City to a summer camp in northern Maine, where it was hoped the fresh air would soothe his asthma. But on the stagecoach ride north, two older, bigger boys taunted Roosevelt. Enraged, he attacked his tormentors, only to have them easily fend him off. Humiliated, Roosevelt realized that the powerful could easily oppress the weak. Determined never to be powerless again, he began to lift weights to build his strength. As a teen, his parents sent him to a family-owned ranch in Montana, where he rode with cowboys. Roosevelt greatly admired the cowboys. Although they were neither wealthy nor educated, they were decent and resourceful men, more worthy of respect than many of his parents' snobbish society friends. Although he remained nearsighted and asthmatic, Roosevelt nevertheless gained strength on the ranch. Intelligent and a good writer, he went on to college, becoming first a lawyer and then a best-selling author of history books. He entered politics, where family connections guaranteed him success at the polls. He served as police commissioner of New York City, a member of the New York state legislature, and Assistant Secretary of the Navy in the administration of President William McKinley. As police commissioner, he frequently went on nighttime patrols in the poor, immigrant neighborhoods of New York City, often accompanied by the immigrant journalist Jacob Riis, also a progressive. When the Spanish-American War broke out in 1898, Roosevelt resigned as Assistant Secretary of the Navy (a boring desk job) and raised a company of volunteer soldiers he dubbed the "Rough Riders," after the cowboys he had known in Montana. Returning to the United States a war hero, the Republican Roosevelt was elected governor of New York State, and then Vice President of the United States. When President McKinley was assassinated in 1901, Roosevelt became President.

Big, active, and gregarious, Roosevelt liked people and people liked him. Americans referred to him as "Teddy" or "TR." But he was also a man of odd contradictions. Although himself rich, Roosevelt believed that the wealthy entrepreneurs and large corporations had too much power. Although he believed that most American workers were treated unfairly, he also disliked unions because he believed that they stifled individual initiative. An ardent imperialist and the driving force behind the creation of the American Empire, he also won the Nobel Peace Prize in 1906 for negotiating a truce in the Russo-Japanese War. An avid hunter, he was also a committed conservationist who as President had gone camping in Yosemite National Park (which he had been instrumental in creating) with the famed environmentalist John Muir. A racist who strongly disliked Native Americans (an attitude he acquired from his cowboy friends), he shocked white Americans by inviting Booker T. Washington, an African American, to dinner in the White House. A virulent opponent of socialism who would have been appalled if anyone had called him a social democrat, he nevertheless earned a reputation as a progressive. He broke up some of the largest corporations, championed consumer protection laws, established national parks, and promised workers and farmers alike a "square deal." On more than one occasion, he insisted that the government must regulate the economy in order to provide for the common good, and that if it did not, a revolution would likely break out that would destroy both capitalism and democracy. TR had tremendous faith in the ability of the government to do good, and viewed it as the people's greatest champion in the struggle against big business and special interest groups.

Roosevelt stepped down as President at the end of his second term in 1909 and set off to explore the Amazon River and hunt lions in Africa. He served as the first president of the American Historical Society. Bored with retirement, in 1910 TR decided to get back into politics. He ran for President again in 1912, but lost. His health, always precarious, soon began to deteriorate, and he died in 1919. As part of his return to politics in 1910, Roosevelt delivered a speech he called "The New Nationalism," but which in reality was a call for progressive reforms. Although he lost the 1912 election, the progressive ideas that TR put forth in this speech would reappear later, in the 1930s progressive program of his cousin, President Franklin Roosevelt – a program known as the "New Deal." The following is an excerpt from TR's speech.

from "THE NEW NATIONALISM"[325]

I stand for the square deal. But when I say that I am for the square deal, I mean not merely that I stand for fair play under the present rules of the game but that I stand for having those rules changed so as to work a more substantial equality of opportunity and of reward for equally good service....

Now, this means that our government, national and state, must be freed from the sinister influence or control of special interests.... [By "special interests," TR meant wealthy entrepreneurs and large corporations.] We must drive the special interests out of politics. That is one of our tasks today. Every special interest is entitled to justice – full, fair, and complete – and, now, mind you, if there were any attempt by mob violence to plunder and work harm to the special interest, whatever it may be, that I most dislike, and the wealthy man, whomever he may be, for whom I have the greatest contempt, I would fight for him, and you would if you were worth your salt. He should have justice. For every special interest is entitled to justice, but not one is entitled to a vote in Congress, to a vote on the bench, or to representation in any public office. The Constitution guarantees protection to property, and we must make that promise good. But it does not give the right of suffrage to any corporation.

The true friend of property, the true conservative [like most Americans of his day, Roosevelt used the word "conservative" to denote "classical," Thomas Paine-type liberalism], is he who insists that property shall be the servant and not the master of the commonwealth.... The citizens of the United States must effectively control the mighty commercial forces which they have themselves called into being. There can be no effective control of corporations while their political activity remains....

We must have complete and effective publicity of corporate affairs so that the people may know beyond peradventure whether the corporations obey the law and whether their management entitles them to the confidence of the public. It is necessary that laws should be passed to prohibit the use of corporate funds directly or indirectly for political purposes; it is still more necessary that such laws should be thoroughly enforced. Corporate expenditures for political purposes, and especially such expenditures by public service corporations [i.e., railroads], have supplied one of the principal sources of corruption in our political affairs.

It has become entirely clear that we must have government supervision of the capitalization, not only of public service corporations, including, particularly, railways, but of all corporations doing an interstate business [the American Constitution gives the federal or national government authority only over interstate commerce while state governments retain authority over strictly intrastate commerce]. I do not wish to see the nation forced into the ownership of the railways if it can possibly be avoided, and the only alternative is thorough going and effective regulation....

It is my personal belief that the same kind and degree of control and supervision which should be exercised over public service corporations should be extended also to combinations which control necessaries of life, such as meat, oil, and coal, or which deal in them on an important scale....

I believe that the officers, and especially, the directors, of corporations should be held personally responsible when any corporation breaks the law.

Combinations [i.e., monopolies] in industry are the result of an imperative economic law.... The way out lies ... in completely controlling them in the interest of the public welfare. For that purpose the Federal Bureau of Corporations is an agency of first importance. Its powers, and, therefore, its efficiency, as well as that of the Interstate Commerce Commission, should be largely increased....

The absence of effective state and, especially, national restraint upon unfair money getting has tended to create a small class of enormously wealthy and economically powerful men whose chief object is to hold and increase their power. The prime need is to

---

[325] Theodore Roosevelt, *The New Nationalism* (1910), 3-33.

change the conditions which enable these men to accumulate power... We grudge no man a fortune which represents his own power and sagacity when exercised with entire regard to the welfare of his fellows.... We should permit it to be gained only so long as the gaining represents benefit to the community. This, I know, implies a policy of a far more active governmental interference with social and economic conditions in this country than we have yet had, but I think we have got to face the fact that such an increase in governmental control is now necessary....

The right [of government] to regulate the use of wealth in the public interest is universally admitted. Let us admit also the right to regulate the terms and conditions of labor, which is the chief element of wealth, directly in the interest of the common good. The fundamental thing to do for every man is to give him a chance to reach a place in which he will make the greatest possible contribution to the public welfare....

No man can be a good citizen unless he has a wage more than sufficient to cover the bare cost of living and hours of labor short enough so that after his day's work is done he will have time and energy to bear his share in the management of the community, to help in carrying the general load. We keep countless men from being good citizens by the conditions of life with which we surround them. We need comprehensive workmen's compensation acts, both state and national laws to regulate child labor and work for women, and, especially, we need in our common schools not merely education in book learning but also practical training for daily life and work. We need to enforce better sanitary conditions for our workers and to extend the use of safety appliances for our workers in industry and commerce....

The object of government is the welfare of the people. The material progress and prosperity of a nation are desirable chiefly so far as they lead to the moral and material welfare of all good citizens. Just in proportion as the average man and woman are honest, capable of sound judgment and high ideals, active in public affairs – but, first of all, sound in their home life, and the father and mother of healthy children whom they bring up well – just so far, and no farther, we may count our civilization a success. We must have – I believe we have already – a genuine and permanent moral awakening, without which no wisdom of legislation or administration really means anything; and, on the other hand, we must try to secure the social and economic legislation without which any improvement due to purely moral agitation is necessarily evanescent.

The Forces of Reaction: Sergyei A. Nilus

The Protocols of the Learned Elders of Zion by the reactionary Russian polemicist Sergyei A. Nilus has rightly been dubbed "the greatest forgery of the [twentieth] century." Supposedly a detailed outline of a Jewish plot to conquer the world, it is in actuality a complete fake, a hoax, a fabrication. Yet reactionaries throughout the West believed every word of it.

It first was published in 1905, as a lengthy appendix to a new edition of Nilus's oft-printed reactionary pamphlet, *The Great in the Little, or Antichrist as an Imminent Possibility: The Confessions of an Orthodox Believer*. According to the Swedish scholar Hugo Valentin, the pamphlet was "of a mystical apocalyptic character, full of visions, omens, prophecies, especially those of the holy thaumaturge Seraphim of Sarov; mystical symbols, which are alleged to be due to the hosts of the Antichrist, are here interpreted. Orthodox Russia and...absolute autocracy are represented to be the last bulwark against Antichrist. In one chapter...it is asserted that the end of the world is at hand, that Antichrist will soon come to establish the dominion of the Devil over the whole earth, and that he, Antichrist, will be of the tribe of Dan and will be acknowledged by the Jews as the Messiah." Presumably, Nilus appended *The Protocols* to his pamphlet as "evidence" of the imminent coming of the Antichrist. It consisted of "a single statement [supposedly] laid before the assembled wise men of Zion by the leader of the secret Jewish world-government at twenty-four separate meetings with the object of initiating them, first into the methods adopted by this government in alliance with the Freemasons for inciting the Goyim (non-Jews) against one another and ruining them economically, politically and morally, and then the system of government it proposes to establish the future Jewish World-State." The central idea of *The Protocols* was that for centuries Jewish leaders had conspired with classical liberals, social democrats, feminists, atheists, and other people that reactionaries like Nilus despised in order to promote such "evils" as democracy, republicanism, constitutionalism, science, secularism, equality, pacifism, and sexual immorality. It portrayed Jews as sinister plotters lusting after world domination, and their liberal, socialist, atheist, and feminist allies as witless dupes.[326]

The entire work was a complete fabrication, of course. But, according to the American scholar Richard S. Levy, *The Protocols* was especially attractive to the early-twentieth-century reactionaries, who were psychologically disposed towards believing in the existence of such conspiracies. The idea of a Jewish

---

[326] Valentin, *Antisemitism*, 166-167.

conspiracy to dominate the world was so wildly and obviously far-fetched that only someone who was paranoid would accept it as true, but as it turned out, paranoia was commonplace among reactionaries. "*The Protocols*," writes Levy, "presupposes a secret Jewish government about to complete an age-old plan by means of stupendous feats of organization and an amazing system of communication. All sorts of front organizations and a variety of Christian dupes serve the purposes of the Elders. The ignorant masses, Freemasons, government officials, liberals, democrats, socialists, Bolsheviks – all are blind tools of the Jewish conspiracy. To keep the Jewish masses in line, the Elders periodically unleash anti-Semitism and 'allow' occasional pogroms, which spare the agents of the secret government." It was, Levy says, "a startling escalation into paranoia." But it "satisfied a deep emotional need in the postwar [i.e., post-World War I] world, providing a simple, all purpose explanation for a bewildering series of events," Levy writes. "The fall of dynasties, the decline of the aristocracy, bloody wars, national humiliation, the emergence of international communism, worthless currencies, the weakening hold of traditional religion, pornography, the 'new woman,' jazz, and a host of other unsettling trends were, each and every one, to be accounted for as parts of a well-thought-out Jewish plan.." *The Protocols* was so illogical on its face that even in the early twentieth century most scholars rejected it as an obvious fabrication. It made no more sense to a rational, unbiased reader than do today's endless and silly conspiracy theories about alien abductions, UFOs, mafia plots to assassinate JFK, or the secret machinations of the Trilateral Commission. But a certain type of people believed it, and for precisely the same reasons that people continue to believe such things.[327]

Nilus himself probably did not invent *The Protocols*, although he was not entirely honest about who had. He was, it seems, a bit of a fraud himself, a minor official of the Russian Orthodox Church stationed in Moscow who liked to call himself a professor, but who had never taught in any college or university, a man who had a difficult time distinguishing between fantasy and reality. He said that he had acquired the manuscript in 1901 (but why had he waited so long to publish it?) from Alexis Nikolajevich Souchotin, an official in the tsar's government, who in turn claimed to have gotten it from a mysterious "lady living abroad," whose name Nilus did not remember. Supposedly, this "lady" had unearthed the manuscript in France, for it was written in French and Nilus had had to translate it into Russian, a circumstance that, to certain readers, made it somehow seem more authentic. In actuality, much of it turns out to have been plagiarized from an obscure (and bad) 1864 French novel, *Dialogue aux Enfers entre Machiavel et Montesquieu ou la Politique de Machiavel au XIX Siecle, par un Contemporain*, written by the otherwise unknown writer Maurice Joly. Joly's novel was a thinly disguised attack on the French dictator Napoleon III (too thinly disguised, it turned out, for Joly did time in prison for having written it), in which "Machiavelli" (who represents Napoleon III) debates politics with the "Montesquieu" (who represents Joly), with "Montesquieu" defending constitutionalism and "Machiavelli" arguing for Napoleonic absolutism. Apparently, reactionaries within the Russian government stumbled upon the novel, rather liked "Machiavelli's" defense of absolutism, drafted the forgery, and gave it to the dim-witted Nilus to publish, hoping that it would attract the eye of the tsar, which it did. Their intent probably was not to stir up a pogrom against the Jews (such was happening anyway), but rather to impugn liberalism, democracy, republicanism, feminism, and other things they didn't like by associating them with Jews, who were widely despised by Russian Christians like the tsar. Many Western scholars were aware from almost the beginning that *The Protocols* was a forgery and several of them published books and articles that said so, but the reactionaries simply took this as evidence that the intellectuals were in on the conspiracy. As the scholars discovered, it is useless to argue with conspiracy theorists; they never listen.

When the Nazis came to power in Germany in the 1930s, Hitler ordered millions of copies of *The Protocols* printed and disseminated throughout the Third Reich. Even today, one occasionally runs into someone who believes it is an authentic document. It is easily found on the internet. As you read the following excerpt from *The Protocols*, ask yourself, what kind of people would have found such nonsense believable, and why? What kind of society did they desire? But please keep in mind: IT'S A FAKE![328]

---

[327] Levy, *Antisemitism in the Modern World*, 147-149.
[328] Valentin, *Antisemitism*, 172-180.

from *THE PROTOCOLS OF THE LEARNED ELDERS OF ZION* [329]

PROTOCOL NO. 1

What I am about to set forth, then, is our system from the two point[s] of view, that of ourselves and that of the goyim (i.e., non-Jews).

It must be noted that men with bad instincts are more in number than the good, and therefore the best results in governing them are attained by violence and terrorization, and not by academic discussions. Every man aims at power, everyone would like to become a dictator if only he could, and rare indeed are the men who would not be willing to sacrifice the welfare of all for the sake of securing their own welfare.

What has restrained the beasts of prey who are called men? What has served for their guidance hitherto?

In the beginnings of the structure of society they were subjected to brutal and blind force; afterwards – to Law, which is the same force, only disguised. I draw the conclusion that by the law of nature right lies in force.

Political freedom is an idea but not a fact. This idea one must know how to apply whenever it appears necessary with this bait of an idea to attract the masses of the people to one's party for the purpose of crushing another who is in authority. This task is rendered easier if the opponent has himself been infected with the idea of freedom, so-called liberalism, and, for the sake of an idea, is willing to yield some of his power. It is precisely here that the triumph of our theory appears: the slackened reins of government are immediately, by the law of life, caught up and gathered together by a new hand, because the blind might of the nation cannot for one single day exist without guidance, and the new authority merely fits into the place of the old already weakened by liberalism.

In our day the power which has replaced that of the rulers who were [just and fair] is the power of Gold. Time was when Faith ruled. The idea of freedom is impossible of realization because no one knows how to use it with moderation. It is enough to hand over a people to self-government for a certain length of time for that people to be turned into a disorganized mob. From that moment on we get internecine strife which soon develops into battles between classes, in the midst of which States burn down and their importance is reduced to that of a heap of ashes.

Whether a State exhausts itself in its own convulsions, whether its internal discord brings it under the power of external foes – in any case it can be accounted irretrievably lost: it is in our power. The despotism of Capital, which is entirely in our hands, reaches out to it a straw that the State, willy-nilly, must take hold of: if not – it goes to the bottom.

Should anyone of a liberal mind say that such reflections as the above are immoral[,] I would put the following questions: -- If every State has two foes and if in regard to the external foe it is allowed and not considered immoral to use every manner and art of conflict, as for example to keep the enemy in ignorance of plans of attack and defense, to attack him by night or in superior numbers, then in what way can the same means in regard to a worse foe, the destroyer of the structure of society and the commonweal, be called immoral and not permissible?

Is it possible for any sound logical mind to hope with any success to guide crowds by the aid of reasonable counsels and arguments, when any objection or contradiction, senseless though it may be, can be made and when such objection may find more favor with the people, whose powers of reasoning are superficial? Men in masses and the men of the masses, being guided solely by petty passions, paltry beliefs, customs, traditions and sentimental theorism, fall a prey to party dissension, which hinders any kind of agreement even on the basis of a perfectly reasonable argument. Every resolution of a crowd depends upon a chance or packed majority, which, in its ignorance of political secrets, put forth some ridiculous resolution that lays in the administration a seed of anarchy.

The political has nothing in common with the moral. The ruler who is governed by the moral is not a skilled politician, and is therefore unstable on his throne. He who wishes to rule must have recourse both to cunning and to make-believe. Great national qualities, like frankness and honesty, are vices in politics, for they bring down rulers from their thrones

---

[329] Sergyei A. Nilus, *World Conquest Through World Government: The Protocols of the Learned Elders of Zion*, trans. Victor E. Marsden (1920), reprinted at ftp.std.com/obi/Rants/Protocols/The_Protocols_of_ The_Learned_Elders_ of_ Zion, retrieved 6/30/2004.

more effectively and more certainly than the most powerful enemy. Such qualities must be the attributes of the kingdoms of the goyim, but we must in no wise be guided by them.

Our right lies in force. The word "right" is an abstract thought and proved by nothing. The word means no more than: – Give me what I want in order that thereby I may have a proof that I am stronger than you.

Where does right begin? Where does it end?

In any State in which there is a bad organization of authority, an impersonality of laws and of the rulers who have lost their personality amid the flood or rights ever multiplying out of liberalism, I find a new right – to attack by the right of the strong, and to scatter to the winds all existing forces of order and regulation, to reconstruct all institutions and to become the sovereign lord of those who have left to us the rights of their power by laying them down voluntarily in their liberalism.

Our power in the present tottering condition of all forms of power will be more invisible than any other, because it will remain invisible until the moment when it has gained such strength that no cunning can any longer undermine it.

Out of the temporary evil we are now compelled to commit will emerge the good of an unshakeable rule, which will restore the regular course of the machinery of the national life, brought to naught by liberalism. The result justifies the means. Let us, however, in our plans, direct our attention not so much to what is good and moral as to what is necessary and useful.

Before us is a plan in which is laid down strategically the line from which we cannot deviate without running the risk of seeing the labor of many centuries brought to naught.

In order to elaborate satisfactory forms of action it is necessary to have regard to the rascality, the slackness, the instability of the mob, its lack of capacity to understand and respect the conditions of its own life, or its own welfare. It must be understood that the might of a mob is blind, senseless, and unreasoning force ever at the mercy of a suggestion from any side. The blind cannot lead the blind without bringing them into the abyss; consequently, members of the mob, upstarts from the people even though they should be as a genius for wisdom, yet having no understanding of the political, cannot come forward as leaders of the mob without bringing the whole nation to ruin.

Only one trained from childhood for independent rule can have understanding of the words that can be made up of the political alphabet.

* * * *

It is only with a despotic ruler that plans can be elaborated extensively and clearly in such a way as to distribute the whole properly among the several parts of the machinery of the State: from this the conclusion is inevitable that a satisfactory form of government for any country is one that concentrates in the hands of one responsible person. Without an absolute despotism there can be no existence for civilization which is carried on not by the masses but by their guide, whosoever that person may be. The mob is a savage and displays its savagery at every opportunity. The moment the mob seizes freedom in its hands it quickly turns to anarchy, which in itself is the highest form of savagery.

Behold the alcoholized animals, bemused with drink, the right to an immoderate use of which comes along with freedom. It is not for us and ours to walk that road. The peoples of the goyim are bemused with alcoholic liquors; their youth has grown stupid on classicism from early immorality, into which it has been inducted by our special agents – by tutors, lackeys, governesses in the houses of the wealthy, by clerks and others, by our women in the places of dissipation frequented by the goyim. In the number of these last I count also the so-called "society ladies," voluntary followers of the others in corruption and luxury.

* * * *

Our State, marching along the path of peaceful conquest, has the right to replace the horrors of war by less noticeable and more satisfactory sentences of death, necessary to maintain the terror which tends to produce blind submission. Just but merciless severity is the greatest factor of strength in the State: not only for the sake of gain but also in the name of duty, for the sake of victory, we must keep to the program of violence and make-believe. The doctrine of squaring accounts is precisely as strong as the means of which it makes use. Therefore it is not so much by the means themselves as by the doctrine of severity that we shall triumph and bring all governments into subjection to our super-government. It is enough for them to know that we are merciless for all disobedience to cease.

Far back in ancient times we were the first to cry among the masses of the people the words "Liberty, Equality, Fraternity," words many times repeated since those days by stupid poll-parrots who from all sides round flew down upon these baits and with them carried away the well-being of the world, true freedom of the individual, formerly so well guarded against the pressure of the mob. The would-be wise men of the goyim, the intellectuals, could not make anything out of the uttered words in their abstractness; did not note the contradiction of their meaning and interrelation: did not see that in nature there is no equality, cannot be freedom; that Nature herself has established inequality of minds, of characters, and capacities, just as immutably as she has established subordination to her laws: never stopped to think that the mob is a blind thing, that upstarts elected from among it to bear rule are, in regard to the political, the same blind men as the mob itself, that the adept, though he be a fool, can yet rule, whereas the non-adept, even if he were a genius, understands nothing in the political – to all these things the goyim paid no regard; yet all the time it was based upon these things that dynastic rule rested: the father passed on to the son a knowledge of the course of political affairs in such wise that none should know it but members of the dynasty and none could betray it to the governed. As time went on the meaning of the dynastic transference of the true position of affairs in the political was lost, and this aided the success of our cause.

In all corners of the earth the words "Liberty, Equality, Fraternity" brought to our ranks, thanks to our blind agents, whole legions who bore our banners with enthusiasm. And all the time these words were canker-worms at work boring into the well-being of the goyim, putting an end everywhere to peace, quiet, solidarity and destroying all the foundations of the goya States. As you will see later, this helped us to our triumph; it gave us the possibility, among other things, of getting into our hands the master card – the destruction of the privileges, or in other words of the very existence of the aristocracy of the goyim, that class which was the only defense peoples and countries had against us. On the ruins of the natural and genealogical aristocracy of the goyim we have set up the aristocracy of our educated class headed by the aristocracy of money. The qualifications for this aristocracy we have established in wealth, which is dependent upon us, and in knowledge, for which our learned elders provide the motive force.

* * * *

The abstraction of freedom has enabled us to persuade the mob in all countries that their government is nothing but the steward of the people who are the owners of the country, and that the steward may be replaced like a worn-out glove.

It is this possibility of replacing the representatives of the people which has placed them at our disposal, and, as it were, gives us the power of appointment.

How the Reactionaries Came to Power

REICHSTAG ROLE-PLAYING EXERCISE

Dateline: Berlin, Germany, 1932. As a result of World War I, Germany has been made a republic. The Great Crash of 1929 has plunged the country into a fearsome depression. Germany's parliament, the Reichstag, is about to meet. Many different political parties ran candidates in the recent election. No single party won a majority of the seats.

Students will be divided into small groups of eleven players each. Each group will be a member of a political party, broken down as follows:

- Reactionaries (R)   3
- Communists (C)   3
- Social Democrats (S)   2
- Classical Liberals (Laissez-faire) (L)   1
- Monarchists (M)   1
- Nationalists (N)   1

TOTAL   11

Each party votes as a bloc, meaning that all members must vote the same way.

The object of the exercise is for each party to:

(1) Join with other parties to form a ruling coalition. The ruling coalition must have at least six (6) of the eleven (11) seats. The ruling coalition chooses the Chancellor (Prime Minister).

(2) Win passage of its legislative program.

A party gets two (2) points if it joins the ruling coalition. A party gets two (2) points if one of its members becomes Chancellor. A party loses one (1) point if it joins a ruling coalition that also includes an "unacceptable" party as another member (as "unacceptable" party is one whose goals are radically different from its own). A party gains one (1) point for each time the Reichstag votes its way on a piece of legislation. A party loses one (1) point for each time the Reichstag does not vote its way on a piece of legislation. The Reichstag may not vote on any legislation until after it has successfully chosen a Chancellor. Six (6) points are needed to win the game.

The instructor acts as Paul von Hindenburg, the elderly, doddering President of the German republic. Under the constitution, Hindenburg has few powers – the real leader of Germany is the Chancellor. However, Hindenburg does have the authority to disband the Reichstag and call for a new election if, in his judgment, no party can put together a ruling coalition or pass a legislative program. None of the parties knows how they will fare in a new election: some may gain seats, while others may lose seats. (The instructor knows, but is not telling.) If any party concludes that it cannot win the game, it may opt to block the other parties from winning (if it can) and gamble on the outcome of a new election.

The "unacceptable" coalition partners for each party are as follows:
- Reactionaries: C, S, L
- Communists: R, M, N, L
- Social Democrats: R, C
- Liberals: R, C
- Monarchists: C, S
- Nationalists: C, S

The Reichstag will vote on the following six (6) pieces of legislation:

(1) Install an economic system in which the government undertakes to regulate the economy, but leaves ownership largely in private hands; this will also include having the government take over ownership of the bankrupt transportation and communications systems.

(2) Restrict the civil liberties of various "alien" minorities, such as Jews, Gypsies, Slavs, homosexuals, labor union members, and the handicapped.

(3) Build up the military.

(4) Have the government assume ownership of the means of production.

(5) Create a series of public relief projects, in order to provide emergency jobs for the unemployed.

(6) Abolish the republic and establish an authoritarian system of government.

Each party's legislative program is as follows:
- Reactionaries: SUPPORT 1, 2, 3, 5, and 6; OPPOSE 4.
- Communists: SUPPORT 4, 5, 6; OPPOSE 1, 2, 3
- Social Democrats: SUPPORT 1, 5; OPPOSE 2, 3, 4, 6
- Liberals: SUPPORT none; OPPOSE all
- Monarchists: SUPPORT 3, 5, 6; OPPOSE 1, 2, 4
- Nationalists: SUPPORT 1, 2, 3, 5, 6; OPPOSE 2, 4,

EPILOGUE

World War II ended in 1945, which seems like a long time ago. But for historians, it might as well be yesterday. Most historians think of the period since the end of World War II as the Present, an era that has not yet quite slipped into History, something to be studied by political scientists, sociologists, economists, and philosophers rather than historians. That does not mean that historians are unaware of all the things that occurred since Hitler committed suicide and the Red Army rolled through Berlin. Far from it. There has been the Cold War between the United States and the USSR, the collapse of communism in Eastern Europe, the rise of the European Union, the creation of the United Nations, decolonization, powerful movements for minority rights and women's rights, the Green Movement, the New Left, the New Right, the attack on the World Trade Center, and countless other important events. Historians could easily assemble a detailed chronology of events that have transpired during the last sixty years. But that's all it would be: a chronology, a list of events – a long list, to be sure, but just a list. There would be no interpretation, at least not one that most historians could be sure of. This is so because historians cannot yet say what those events will mean, because the history of the present is still unfolding. Before it is possible for the Present to become History, it must cease to be the Present. Historians say that you cannot write history without historical perspective; what that means is that you cannot tell a story until it is over with – and has been over with long enough so that you can be sure about just how it ended. It is possible to write good histories of some of the events that have occurred in the last 60 years: the Cold War, the Vietnam War, the Sixties, and the Presidency of Charles de Gaulle, for example. But it is not yet possible to write a comprehensive history of the entire epoch because, as a historical period, it is not yet complete. (Or if it is, we cannot be sure that it is.) Someday – perhaps in about twenty years – historians will write good histories of the post-war period in the West. It might even be one of you that does it. But no one has done it yet.

How will historians characterize Our Times? What name will they give it? Will they call it the Cold War Era? They might, if they think the Cold War was the most important thing that occurred then. Maybe they will call it the Computer Age, or the Information Age. Maybe they'll call it the Age of Human Rights or the Age of Ecology. Or perhaps it will be the Post-Modern Age, or the Traditional Renaissance, or the Era of the New Modernism. It might be the American Age, or the Revival of Europe, or the Rise of Asia. Perhaps they will name it after a key world leader: the Age of de Gaulle, the Age of Reagan, the Age of Thatcher, the Age of Clinton, or the Age of Chirac. Well, maybe not. Maybe it will be named after a great calamity, like the Age of Global Warming. Or maybe they will conclude that Our Times was not a separate era after all, but simply a continuation of the previous period, the Crisis of the West, with World War I, the Great Depression, the Holocaust, and World War II followed by a fifth crisis, the Cold War, and maybe even a sixth, the Challenge of Asia, the Great Meltdown, or the Rise of Corporate Globalism.

What do you think?